GROWING UP IN KHAKI
LIFE AS A SERVICE BRAT

G. E. Allingham

RTP
RESEARCH TRIANGLE PUBLISHING, INC.

Published by
Research Triangle Publishing, Inc.
PO Box 1130
Fuquay-Varina, NC 27526

ISBN 1-884570-83-6

Cover Design by Kim Barefoot

Library of Congress Catalog Card Number: 97-76160

Printed in the United States of America
10 9 8 7 6 5 4 3 2 1

To all of those who appeared in this book in the hope that they, and their lawyers, will forgive. . .and forget.

CAPTAIN VUMPH AND THE MILITARY SALAD

SOMETHING IS SERIOUSLY WRONG. I can no longer remember anything before I turned six years old. A full half of my Wonder Bread years are gone. I've always assumed people who say they have memories of the womb are either lying, or they're evangelists, Shirley MacLaine, or believe they've been kidnapped by aliens (I'm especially fond of the group that believes they've had sex with aliens), but having no memories before the age of six is absurd. It's a good thing my parents don't know this, I can hear my mother now. . .

"All that money and he doesn't remember a damn thing!"

My father's perspective is somewhat different. . .

"Another martini my dear? . . ."

My earliest recollections are from Fort Myer, in Virginia. I was born just down the road from the post, in Washington, D.C., at the Columbia Hospital for Women. This was a source of embarrassment for me, since anytime it was mentioned, my friends all laughed. They were convinced that I had made some sort of colossal mistake. For the longest time, I thought I had. I was a middle child, born in October of 1946, and to make matters worse, my sister came along right behind me, just nine days short of a year. I was soon completely ignored. If the doctor had known, he would have probably stuffed me back in.

"A middle child? A Libra? He's doomed. He'll be forever wandering, looking for balance and fairness in the world. . .and he won't remember a damn thing before the age of six."

"Can't something be done, doctor?"

"I'm afraid not. . .the bread years are doomed."

"This isn't some sort of joke, is it?"

"No, good womb jokes are hard to find."

My mom immediately named me George, which I believe was in return for being forced to have a discussion with the doctor during childbirth. It's the only reason I can come up with for anyone being given the name George. So, I started off with three strikes and two balls; I was born in the Columbia Hospital for Women, I was a middle Libra child with a baby sister less than a year younger, and I was named George. No wonder I can't remember anything before the age of six.

The earliest thing I can remember is sitting around on a hot summer day, outside our small house on Fort Myer, and my brother Dave had just given me the standard Older Brother Summer Greeting.

"Get lost!"

He was really anxious to get rid of me because he offered me a whole nickel, which now sounds ludicrous. Today a nickel buys. . .nothing. The current going price for getting lost in the *Oxford Sibling Handbook* is. . .let's see. . .Eight-Year-Old Get Lost Fee. . .Seven-Year-Old. . .ah, here it is. . .Six-Year-Old Get Lost Fee. . .one dollar, but you may be able to get it cheaper using Japanese yen or German marks.

My brother wanted me to get lost because he was with a girl. I was too young to know much about girls, but I was starting to have some suspicions that there was more to all this than just running them over with your bike. Besides, if he were alone he would have wanted me to get lost anyway. But at that particular moment, I was having trouble understanding why I couldn't stay there.

"Why can't I stay here? I live here."

"Because you want this nickel, and the only way to get it is to get lost," he said.

Well, you just can't beat that kind of logic. Money changes everything.

"All right," I said.

"And don't come back here for the rest of the day."

"Give me the nickel."

"Tonight."

"No. Now, or I won't leave."

I wasn't a complete fool. . .no matter what the *Oxford Sibling Handbook* said.

He looked at me with distrust in his eyes. Then he handed me the nickel.

"If you come back, I'll pound you and take the nickel."

An Older Brother Pounding was reason enough not to come back.

"I won't come back."

"You better not."

"I won't."

"Well, you just better not."

Between kids it's always a good idea to state the terms five or six times.

"I said I wouldn't."

"Just make sure you don't."

Make that six or seven times.

I grabbed the nickel from his outstretched hand and I got lost. After traversing several water culverts and crossing a highway, I ended up at the Pentagon surrounded by some unsympathetic men in white caps and shinny boots. From the looks on their collective faces, I don't think I was expected.

"I'm here to see Eisenhower."

This didn't change anything. Apparently, you needed an appointment to see Eisenhower. I was held in custody while they called my mother and told her it was too hot for this sort of thing, and to come and get me. As soon as she came in the door I explained everything.

"It's all Dave's fault."

"Come on, let's go home and talk to your brother about all this. It's too hot for this kind of thing."

Everyone was agreed about the weather. I guess it would have been all right if it were only cooler, but summers in Virginia can be hot, so hot you don't even need a magnifying glass to set the ants on fire, they just walk across the sidewalk and obligingly burst into flames all on their own. Getting your kid brother lost is just one of the ways to cool down on a hot summer day. My brother had several others.

"Okay," he said. "Let's attack the gnat swarms with our squirt guns."

Squirt guns were standard equipment for all boys our age, and even if they were confiscated at school, which happened frequently, we had plenty to spare. My brother and I had invested our meager life savings, and both of us owned large machine-gun versions. My father nodded approvingly when he saw that they were authentic copies of the U. S. Army's Thompson submachine gun.

"Excellent choice."

Blasting gnat swarms is about the only useful thing you can do with them, and we ran around the yard attacking every swarm we could find.

"Always take the high ground, always advance, never dig in!" encouraged my father.

"Yes, sir!"

We had caught them by surprise and soon had vanquished them all.

"Good work," said my mother. She was very supportive of attacking gnats. It cleared our yard of the little buggers and chased them across to our neighbors, who were not as supportive.

"Mabel, get the squirt guns. Those damn kids next door chased the gnats over here again."

Well, once the yard was clear there was only one thing left to do, at least as far as my brother was concerned.

"Get the bikes," he said.

Now, being almost four years older and twice my size meant that I not only did everything he said, but I also fetched things. I ran around the back of the house, the flapping pant legs of my overalls rubbing against each other. Vumph. . .vumph. . .vumph.

"Yeah, this is a good day for a game," he said as he let his gaze fall across the expansive backyard. . .all twenty square feet of it.

Vumph. . .vumph. . .vumph.

"Here's your bike."

Vumph. . .vumph. . .vumph.

"Here's my bike."

I liked to announce things as I fetched, made me feel like I was accomplishing something.

"Don't forget the sticks."

Vumph. . .vumph. . .vumph.

"Here are the sticks."

"And the ball," he said.

Vumph. . .vumph. . .vumph.

"Here's the ball."

"Let the game begin," he said.

We mounted our bikes and faced off with the ball between us and a nasty-looking homemade hockey stick in each of our hands.

"Go!" he yelled.

And another game of bicycle hockey began. Only a kid can think a game like bicycle hockey is a good idea.

Whack!

My brother smacked the ball. I stood on my pedals and shot after it, a dirt rooster tail flying off my back wheel. The ball ricocheted off the house and came to rest near the drain-pipe. I hit my brakes and swung my back tire into a skid around the ball. With a tremendous blow, I fired the ball at his goal. The force knocked my stick out of my hand.

"Damn!"

I scrambled after it, but before I could get to it and get back on my bike, my brother had retrieved my shot and put the ball into my goal.

"One to squat."

"Damn!"

We faced off again.

"Go!"

We both hit the ball simultaneously.

Splat! The ball didn't move. While I was staring down at it, my brother quickly hit it again.

"Two to squat."

"Damn!"

Another face-off. This time I let him hit the ball, and as he began to pedal away, my stick slid from my hand and somehow ended up in the spokes of his back wheel.

"Aiiieeeeee! . . ."

He separated from his bike, doing a rather nice swan dive over his handlebars. I grabbed my stick and recovered the ball.

"Two to one."

"Damn!" he yelled.

He was snorting and spitting mad as we again faced off against each other. The dirt was smeared across his face and down the front of his shirt. His angry snorts had turned the dirt under his nose into a darkened wet streak.

"Go!" he yelled, and then he rammed his bike into mine. The force knocked me over. He stared down at me for a moment with cold dark eyes, and snorted with satisfaction. Then he started to push his bike away, but his pant leg had slipped over his pedal, and he lost his balance and came crashing down onto me.

"Ooowwwww! . . ."

The pain in my leg made me cry out. "Get off of me! You broke my leg!"

And he had.

"What's all the yelling for out here?" My mother opened the back screen door and swatted the air. "Damn gnats." They had retaken the high ground. "Why are you lying on the ground holding your leg?"

"It's all Dave's fault."

I was off to the hospital.

I spent the next few weeks recovering from bicycle hockey, waiting for my leg to heal. I sat in the backyard with the sun setting on a cast that started at my hip and went to my toes.

I healed. All kids heal fast, so fast that I don't really recall my cast being much of a bother, but my recollections have become very iffy. I'm suffering from Brain Cell Leakage. It's the only explanation I have for the small gray pile of dead brain cells left behind on the pillow each morning. I assume they just spill out of my ears during the night as part of some kind of biological housekeeping. There are always several important memories left lying in that pile. I just hope that they're nothing I really need. I've tried talking to my friends about this for some collective solace.

"I must be getting old. I'm having trouble remembering things. And that's not all. I don't seem to really feel anything anymore, everything has a grayness. . .a sameness to it. I wish I could feel something intensely again."

"And just who are you again? And why do you think this is a problem?"

"I could be having sex for God's sake, and I can't tell the difference between that and eating a stack of pancakes."

"I'd certainly have a lot more pancakes."

Collective solace is not a concept my friends are familiar with. Clearly, I need new friends.

I wasn't mad at my brother for breaking my leg, although in a later rematch I completely missed the ball and clubbed him across the head, requiring several stitches. I don't believe that it was revenge because I didn't even notice it until my brother fell to the ground howling. I think revenge requires some planning.

"Ooowwwww! . . ."

"What are you doing?"

"You hit me in the head!"

"Really?"

"What's all the yelling for out here?" Once again, my mother opened the back screen door and swatted the air. "Damn gnats. Why are you lying on the ground holding your head?"

Another trip to the hospital for my mother.

No matter how many times my brother and I clubbed each other over the head, we never broke the code. . .the code of silence. Never. This code, however, doesn't seem to exist in the world of kid sisters.

"Don't you know about the code of silence?"

"Give me money," she replied.

I went to the *Oxford Sibling Handbook*. The going price for keeping your mouth shut. Let's see. Seven-Year-Old Fee. . .Six-Year-Old. Ah, here it is. The Five-Year-Old Fee For Keeping Mouth Shut. . .male. . .ten cents. . .female. . .one dollar. . .military discounted rate. . .ninety-nine cents. What? Ninety-nine cents? I didn't have that kind of money.

"All I've got is a nickel."

"Too bad."

My sister broke the code of silence like she was born to the job. She was at the age where she truly enjoyed ratting on my brother and me. This stage lasted until she turned twenty-three. It was advisable to be on the lookout and never let her see anything we did, no matter how innocent we thought it might be. I have been hammered many a time for what I thought was innocent. Innocence, as it turns out, is strictly a matter of judgment, and kids are never allowed to be the judges.

I carefully avoided her gaze during dinner, so she wouldn't catch on to my new system for getting rid of my salad. This was a military salad, lettuce and Russian dressing that my father whipped up in the kitchen between martinis. Its quality was variable, depending on whether it was the Three-Martini Dressing or the Four-Martini Dressing.

I had to get past the three of them, my dad, my mom, and my kid sister. My brother was wise to me and just watched in total fascination as I made my salad disappear. It was quite a challenge, a nightly gauntlet of misdirection and slight of hand worthy of Houdini, and my brother enjoyed a good magic show as much as the next guy.

Military salad was always the toughest thing for me to eat during dinner. I could manage to choke down almost any vegetable, but salad was different. It would catch halfway down my throat and make me gag. My parents were convinced I was faking this, so they forbade my choking at the dinner table. I could choke anywhere else in the house, but not at dinner. They were satisfied with themselves over this decree. One night as I struggled to down a mouthful of salad by drowning it with my milk, the solution came to me while I thrashed about making obscene faces without choking. . .socks.

As I struggled with my salad with the Four-Martini Dressing, my hand thrashed around below the table, and came upon those wonderful, naturally stretchable, elastic-topped socks. Socks that could hold whatever might be pushed into them. . .like a military salad.

I scanned the table casually, waiting for an opening, making idle and innocent conversation. When the coast was clear, I removed a small amount of salad from the bowl and pushed it into my sock. My brother almost broke into applause as my plate seemed to clean itself before his eyes. Finally, there was only one small piece of lettuce remaining, which I dramatically ate after getting everyone's attention, and dramatically choking.

"What'd we say about choking at the dinner table?"

"Sorry. May I be excused, I've finished all my salad. . .see?"

My father inspected my bowl like it was a field-stripped M1 rifle.

"Now, wasn't that easy?" he said, with the air of parental righteous satisfaction, and like someone who didn't have to eat anything he didn't want to. Easy? Let's see him spirit away a whole bowl of military salad.

"Go on, you're excused."

I went into the bathroom and flushed the lettuce down the toilet. This was great! Each night I managed to remove all the lettuce, except for a small final piece, and put it in my socks. Soon, anything I didn't like was ending up there. My days of eating ghastly foods were over. The capacity of those socks seemed limitless. I was thinking of even buying my own, and getting the bigger kinds, knee socks and the like. That would have surprised them.

You want to buy socks?

"Why are your socks bulging like that?" asked my mother.

"What? . . ."

"Your socks. Why are they bulging like that?"

Run. Fake a death scene. Do something.

"I don't know."

"Come here."

Have a seizure. Fall down and thrash about.

Instead I froze. My brother excused himself and dashed out. He knew when to leave a room.

"Come over here. What have you got in your socks?"

"What socks?"

The Vinnie Barbarino Defense. I have found myself down to this pitiful plea all too often, with equally bad results.

I had been undone by a pair of kid's high-water pants. After that, I was required to eat dinner barefoot, although I soon found the virtue in the elastic waistband of my underwear.

Within a few weeks I was the first naked diner in my family's history.

WORLD WAR III DAY

Ordinarily, names don't mean much when you're a kid. I could have been a Bob or a Fred or a John or almost anything, but I wasn't anything, I was a George. In a kid's world George is the same as Fred or Bob or John, and it pretty much stays that way until you're old enough to get curious and look it up in the dictionary. Then you find out it means farmer. It's all downhill from there. Later came Georgy Porgy and George of the Jungle. I can only assume the world is out to get all the Georges it can find.

Once they heard about "kissed the girls and made them cry," no one looked at a George in quite the same way again. And what's with the running away when the boys come out to play? There's something suspicious about Georgy Porgy. Today he would be arrested on sight.

GEORGY PORGY CAUGHT! would scream the headlines. *BOYS HAVE COME BACK TO PLAY. . .GIRLS RESUME KISSING. . .NATION CELEBRATES.*

He sure didn't make it easy on the rest of us Georges.

My brother didn't care what my name was just as long as he got to be boss. . .any name would do.

"Hey, Jackass!" The short form of Georgy Porgy.

Brother Dave was big, just like my father. I hate to say it, but it's not like nobody noticed. Dave was husky. Husky is a polite word for overweight, which is a polite word for fat. If I called him any of those, I would receive the Royal Older Brother Pounding. But I was allowed to call him husky, because that's what my parents called him, and it was written on the department store sign hanging over the aisle where they bought his clothes. There was never much in this section, usually a pair of overalls and a faithful copy of Captain Kangaroo's suit, so my mom used to make his clothes. My parents tried to tell me he was "big boned."

"What are these. . .like dinosaur bones?"

We shopped in the beanpole section for me, and when together my brother and I looked like a Spanky and Our Gang version of Laurel and Big Boned Hardy.

Once in a while, when the time was just right and there were enough plastic models, my husky brother would schedule a World War III Day. You need a good supply of plastic models for a World War III Day.

We selected a few of our least favorite, for they would not return, and we placed them in the sandpit. We didn't have a sandbox, just a pit. Then we dug roads and fortified bunkers for each one. We spent a good deal of time doing this, for the more realistic the final scene, the sweeter the final act.

When everything looked right, we finished by squeezing out plastic model glue all over them, and then retired to our positions a few feet away. We both had a box of kitchen matches. His army against mine. Each of us laid out a row of matches, then took the first one from the long line, and stood it on end against the striking surface of the box, held there tightly by an index finger. Our other hand was positioned right behind the match, the index finger curled and tensioned against the thumb.

"Always take the high ground, always advance, never dig in!" my brother yelled.

And our index fingers flicked the match off the box, igniting it and sending it flying through the air toward the fortified bunkers. Many shots were wide of their mark, and some errant matches hurtled straight at my brother, but when one found its target the flammable glue made sure the models immediately burst into flames, sending off twisting black smoke. Within minutes the battlefield was a mass of destruction, models burned furiously and melted into gooey liquid as the flames spread. It was glorious! And over too soon.

"Ahhhhh. . .," I sighed with satisfaction.

A seven-year-old's orgasm.

"Clean up out there, it's time to get ready to go," yelled my mom out the back door. Dave had declared today World War III Day because it was a special day. . .and we also had enough models. The army had declared it World War III Day as well. We were waiting for my father to get home and pick us up for a family day on the post.

My father, The Colonel, although back then he would have been The Captain, and actually he was Dad to all of us most of the time anyway, was a life-size version of my brother. Although no one dared to call him Husky or Big Bones. He was over six feet tall and big. He didn't look fat, even later in life when he put on a lot more weight, he still appeared to be just big. To a little boy he looked like a mountain.

I liked being around my father whenever there was a family day on the post. He would be standing there with his Ray-Ban sunglasses on, all decked out in his uniform with his combat ribbons, and those braided coils attached to his shoulder that ended with gold nozzles hanging down on his chest. I had no idea what my father had done for the army to get to wear a hose, but they sure looked cool, and when he wasn't home I would often play fireman with them. I was sure when he was alone in his office at work, he did the same thing. I was sure they all did. And if you walked down the corridors you'd hear "shhuuuusssss" coming out of each one of their offices as they sprayed down the roaring inferno they imagined was coming out of their Kleenex box. Some of them also had model tanks and artillery on their desks, and you would've heard tank "rruuummmbbllee" and cannon fire "blamo." Down the corridor would come a cacophony of action noises from these men of action.

"Shhuuusssss."

"Rruummmbbbllee."

"Eeeeeiiii. . .blamo."

Unless, they heard someone coming down the corridor. Then it suddenly was. . .

"Huummphh. . .memo to General Eisenhower, things are moving along well here, need more of these braided coil hose things and battlefield simulation models. . .huummphh."

I was glad that my dad was in the army during family days on the post. The soldiers all saluted him, called him sir, and were real nice to me, making me feel important.

"Is this your son, sir?"

"Yes."

"Looks just like you."

Either there was a skinny beanpole kid hiding inside my father that all these guys were seeing, or somebody was fooling somebody. I was as thin as a rail and four feet high and would never have been mistaken for the mountain that was my father if I hadn't been standing next to him on family day.

The post commander walked around giving little hand salutes of recognition to everyone, looking like a royal procession. Wherever he went, the crowds parted like the seas before

Moses, nakedly exposing him and forcing him to continue with the royal hand wave. He called my father by his first name. "Fine-looking boy, Dave."

I was old enough to know that fine-looking boy really meant "I have no idea what to say about your little beanpole kid, but I am the chief and I do have to say something."

"Thank you, sir," said my father, which really meant "thanks for calling me by my first name."

The army had several family days during the year, most of these were holiday dinners where you got to eat in the mess hall with the troops, which was kind of neat. . .except for the military salad.

"No choking," said my father.

The salad dressing was better, since it wasn't my father's four-martini version, but nothing else much happened. But, once a year, in the summer, the army did something special. And today was the day. . .it was a Firepower Demonstration Day.

Big field tents were set up on the parade grounds with all sorts of amazements. We ran from one tent to another all day long, and saw something different every time. One had someone dipping a rubber ball in liquid oxygen and throwing it on the ground where it shattered like a Christmas tree ornament hitting the pavement. What this had to do with the army is anybody's guess, unless they intended to dip the enemy in liquid oxygen. Other tents had gun displays, and one had a field hospital with medical oddities in glass jars. I offered them my brother to complement their collection, but they declined.

"He's right over there and really deserves to be in one of these jars.". . .labeled Husky Kid.

"That's okay, son. We don't have a jar that big."

From one tent to another we ran, hardly being able to take in what we were seeing before running off to the next. There were paratroopers who strapped us into a real parachute and hoisted us up in a jump simulator, and rangers with blackened faces were doing camouflage makeovers on kids like me. There was a firing range with instructors and BB rifles, and targets we got to keep. A huge supply tent was erected right in the middle, and we could buy canteens and web belts and holsters and helmets and Sherman tanks. There were howitzer cannons where we could work the breech and load in empty shell casings, and all kinds of other things that today's America would have immediately banned as way too much fun.

Jeeps, trucks, tanks, and helicopters were parked around the field for us to climb all over, but what we really wanted. . .what we waited for all day long, was the firepower demonstration. My brother and I, and all our friends, dearly loved them. All day long we felt the excitement. It was like being at a Christmas show, and knowing that there were still presents waiting at home. Firepower demonstrations were better than any Fourth of July fireworks you've ever seen, and it was louder.

Grandstands were set up facing a large field, and the post commander gave his welcoming speech.

"Huuummpphh. . .memo to General Eisen. . .no. . .no. Let's see. . .ah. . .yes. I would like to welcome all of the families to. . .blah. . .blah. . .and that concludes my remarks. Huummpphhh."

Once that was finally over, another officer would take the podium to explain what was taking place, but he was totally superfluous and justifiably ignored.

Out in the distance was a small building (there was always a small building in the distance), and we could see the soldiers in their combat gear moving slowly across the field toward it. I squirmed with anticipation, ready to cover my ears.

Then the air crackled with the sound of small explosions, and the troops all hit the ground and started firing at the building. Soon bigger guns started firing as tanks moved up, then helicopters began firing rockets, and finally jets came screaming low over the field, dropping bombs, firing rockets, and letting loose blazing napalm explosions that streamed across the field. It was glorious!

The troops kept advancing, and flame-throwing tanks sprayed fiery streams, engulfing what was left of the building. The troops surrounded the burned-out hulk in victory. Little buildings stood little chance during firepower demonstrations. It was my second orgasm of the day, something of a record that stands even today. When it was all over, my mother stood up and said. . .

"That was so noisy."

Women have no appreciation of the finer things in life. I must say that I have never heard her voice much of anything against the carnage and bedlam of the Macy's basement sale. From what I've seen, this could qualify as a firepower demonstration all its own.

I went home, snuck into my father's closet and played fireman with his hose things.

"Shhhuuussss."

ROLLO AND THE BIG LEAP

SHORTLY AFTER WATCHING THE American army pulverize an undefended hut, my father came home and sat us all down.

"We're going to Germany."

"Right now?" I asked.

"No, but very soon."

"Are we still in the army?"

"Yes."

"The American army?"

"Yes."

"Stupid," said my brother.

"Fat. . .er. . .husky."

We left from New York in January on a military transport ship. It was like a floating barracks, and no fun at all, unless you consider knocking icicles off the railings some sort of shipboard amusement. I have blotted out most of the Atlantic crossing and only remember my mother mummified in dozens of blankets, lying on a deck chair, green with seasickness, and the ship's doctor constantly at her side. Hopefully, she has blotted out the crossing from her memory as well.

We took a train from a North Sea port to southern Germany, and ended up outside Nuremberg. We temporarily moved into a small cottage. Without a moment's hesitation, or checking with my mother at all, my father brought home three German Shepherd puppies all at once. Being in the military, I believe his rationale was you never went anywhere without an army. All of us were really excited, except my mother, who had to be revived. So, I was surrounded by three genuine German Shepherd puppies, who were just about as grown up as I, so we immediately bonded, and my father named them Rollo, Bollo, and Bello. Names were not his strong suit.

We lived at the foot of the Black Forest in the small cottage, which apparently, from the look of it, had belonged to Hansel and Gretel, and in like fashion, my sister and I promptly got lost. Getting lost was one of my strong suits. We were found near a hunting lodge deep in the forest, which I seem to remember was inhabited by Vikings. There were deer carcasses strewn about and barrel-chested men with red cheeks, dressed in forest garb, who greeted each other with Teutonic grunts as they carried sides of meat over their shoulder. I expected at any moment to see the king's cavalry come riding in, with their swords drawn, instead my dad drove up in an army staff car.

Our temporary housing became semipermanent, as it was hard to find a house in Germany in the early fifties that still had a roof, and if you did, it was usually missing some walls. Most of the cities were still in ruins, so we stayed in this country house on the outskirts of the town far longer than we expected. In the summer evenings I would take my glass of grape juice out onto the front steps and watch the handyman, who seemed to have come with the cottage. He cut slices of black bread and drank his beer from a dark brown bottle with a massive ceramic contraption that he claimed was a cork. My mother swears we spoke German to one another. I'll have to take her word for it, since the only German I know today are beer company names. Across the road was a large farm, which always had a horse-drawn wagon roaming the fields.

"That's a honey wagon," said my father.

"A what!?"

Don't buy your honey from Germany. Or, at least, don't send my dad to get it.

I lived in fear of falling into the cottage's cesspool out in the backyard. Once I saw what was in there, I was careful to avoid even walking over its huge wooden cover, and, for my money, the whole thing should have been located someplace very far away. If that was a honey wagon, then this must have been the honey pot.

I never knew exactly what my dad's job was in Germany. The only time I saw him at work was on a family visiting day where he was in a field surrounded by tents, tanks, and mud. He was standing there, talking with the other soldiers, dressed in his combat gear, so I was expecting him to attack an undefended hut at any minute, but it never happened. I assumed this was all a joke of some kind, dreamed up to discourage family visiting days. We sat down in a field mess tent, and were served a big military salad.

We finally left the country house by the Black Forest and moved into the city of Nuremberg. It was a city house with a garage and fenced-in backyard and no cesspool. I was able to sleep better at night, no longer dreaming that I had fallen in.

"*Help! Help!*"

"*Was ist los! Ach der Lieber!*"

"*Help!*"

"*Nicht verstehen.*"

What's there to understand? I was going to drown in a cesspool because the handyman couldn't speak English, and didn't understand that I wasn't out there for a midnight dip. Luckily, your sense of smell isn't functioning while dreaming.

The dogs came with us, but we were soon down to just one. . .Rollo. Bello contracted some disease and never came back from the vet. Bollo attacked a motorcyclist, and he was executed for this crime. That left Rollo. . .my dog. Rollo and I played together constantly, and he followed me wherever I went. After school he always met me at the bus stop, and we played circus in the garage. It was empty since we had no car. I was the ringmaster and Rollo was all my animal acts, and he tried hard to be everything I wanted. . .elephants, lions, tigers, horses, gorillas, dinosaurs, outer space monsters. . .for mine was a very special circus. He always put his big head in my lap in the evening, which was a problem because I couldn't move it, and when I tried, he would roll over and arch his back to hold me down so I couldn't get up.

"Help! . . ."

"What are you doing to the dog?"

"To the dog? He won't let me up."

"Rollo!" my father would roar, and Rollo would stop. He may have been my dog, but he knew the leader of the pack when he heard him. I believe Rollo thought I was his brother, equals, so he must have thought we were twins. If the truth be known, he was probably the better-looking twin, because everybody would come up to him first, and say how beautiful he was. I waited, but no one was offering me the same assessment. We were fraternal twins.

We had a large porch on the back of the house, our first. It was high, a good ten feet off the ground, where we could imagine it to be a lookout tower or a castle fortress. And what do you do in a castle? Well, I don't know about medieval kids, but we played tag. Several of the neighborhood kids would join in for team tag, the professional version, and it would spread to other houses. Everyone knew to stay out of my mother's way, so our house was off limits. Not so with the others, and we ran amuck through the neighborhood.

I trapped myself on our porch, nowhere to go except. . .over the porch railing. I dove off aiming for the grass, but good fortune was not with me, and I landed on the concrete sidewalk. I only had time to cover my face with my arm after I realized, midair, that I was in trouble.

Crack!

It was my arm, actually my elbow, since I had it bent in front of my face, making me resemble an arrowhead as I plummeted to the ground. If I had actually hit the lawn, I imagine I would have stuck in the ground like a dart. The pain was immediate and I screamed out. Rollo came running over, and licked my face as I howled in pain. I grabbed my elbow and protected it. He seemed to realize that I wasn't playing any longer, and lay down next to me. He kept trying to push his head in between my arms, which would make me howl all the more, and this caused Rollo to try even harder.

My mother came out onto the porch and saw me lying on the ground.

"Why are you screaming!?"

"My arm!"

"He dove off the porch!" my friends said.

"Yeah, and landed on his head!"

She didn't ask why I dove off the porch, she just came down and told me to move my hand out of the way so she could see my arm.

"Didn't bicycle hockey teach you anything?" she asked.

"Yes, don't let Dave fall on you."

All my friends nodded in agreement.

"Well, yes, but you should have learned don't do anything stupid. . .and stay off the good furniture."

My elbow began to swell to the size of a lemon, then kept right on growing, right up to an orange. When my mother saw this she pulled Rollo off me.

"Don't move."

I believe she was talking to both of us. She let Rollo stay nearby, where he lay down and quietly waited, and she went back into the house. In a little while an ambulance came and took me to the hospital. They took x-rays and held a conference with my parents.

"He has a very bad break. His elbow has multiple fractures, it has been shattered," said the first doctor.

"He's going to have to stay with us in the hospital for a while. We won't be able to place his arm in a cast until these fractures begin to heal. We have to be sure the elbow is knitting together," continued his colleague.

"We're going to apply some heat to the elbow, and monitor the progress. I don't want to alarm you, but there's a danger with a break this severe. If the elbow doesn't respond and start to heal over the next week or two, we may be forced to amputate the arm."

"What should we tell him?" asked my mother.

"He's young and chances are good that the arm will respond to treatment, so I wouldn't tell him everything. Just say that he has to stay here because we need to watch his arm."

Over the next week they applied hot pads, soaked my arm in warm water and hot water, and placed it in different wraps— it didn't respond. Things were looking bleak, and in the second week they began to prepare me for the shock.

"Your arm isn't healing, George."

"Why?"

"We don't know. Time's getting short, and we may have to do something we really don't want to do."

"What?"

"We may have to amputate your arm."

I wasn't sure what this really meant.

"Did my parents say it was okay?"

"Your parents know."

"Okay."

Near the end of the second week with still no change, one of the doctors decided to stop the heat treatments altogether, and in desperation, reversed it. My arm was soaked in cold water. Miraculously, the arm began to respond.

"Your elbow's starting to heal. In a day or so, we'll be able to put your arm in a cast. You'll be in a cast for a long time."

My parents were standing beside my bed. "How long?" asked my father.

"Two months in this cast, then we'll place his arm in a removable one for another two months. Every week he'll have to come in for an hour of physical therapy. We'll remove the cast and work the elbow. Without this, the arm would soon freeze in one position from being immobilized for so long.

"George, your arm is going to get very thin, but don't worry, that's normal, and it'll soon get big again."

I had the first cast on for two months, just like they said, and it was from the wrist to the shoulder. When I first came home, Rollo must have smelled it for two days. Then he ignored it and went back to lying on me.

"Help! . . ."

We resumed our garage circus with the addition of the new Plasterman attraction, and The Man Who Always Points to the Right. Rollo was dejected when he found out that there were no new roles for him, so we came up with Dog of Man Who Always Points to the Right. He was happy—not only did he have a new role, but also it was the first time he was actually able to be a dog in the garage circus.

I returned to the hospital two months later and my arm was just as they said it would be, the size of a mop handle, and the grillwork pattern of the gauze was impressed into it. I had seen better-looking arms on Saturday-matinee space monsters. They put my arm into a large steel tub, filled with hot water. At the press of a button, a jet stream of water whirled around the tub. I was in there so long that the gauze pattern was replaced by a waterlogged prune pattern.

"You're done."

A nurse gently lifted my arm out of the water and placed it in her lap.

"I'm going to slowly bend your arm, let me know if you feel any pain."

She placed one hand near my elbow, and with the other she pushed at my wrist, slowly bending my arm. I was braced for pain.

Instead, it was like bending a leg you've been sitting on for an hour, except magnified a thousandfold. My arm was crying out to be bent, and instead of an exclamation of pain, the nurse received the sigh of orgasmic delight. I don't think she was prepared for it, because she stopped bending my arm and gave me a strange look.

"No, don't stop, right there, that's it, keep doing it, aaaahhhhh."

Afterward, my arm was placed in a removable cast, and I came to the hospital every week for more physical therapy.

"No, don't stop, right there, that's it, keep doing it, aaaahhhhh."

A new removable cast was fashioned each time, it was made partly from plaster, and wrapped with an elastic bandage. Each time Rollo would smell it for two days, then lay on me.

"Help! . . ."

Eventually, my arm grew from the spindly mop handle back into my normal spindly shovel handle, and worked just fine.

I never appreciated how close I had come to losing my arm, even after my parents had explained it carefully to me, until the day I saw a girl about my age in a restaurant. Her arm had been amputated just above the elbow, and I found the sight both shocking and disturbing. That was the first time that it sank in. . .that it had almost happened to me.

WE BEGAN PACKING one winter to leave this house and return to the States. It was all very interesting to Rollo, he unpacked about as many boxes as I packed.

"George, keep Rollo away from the boxes. Go play circus or something. . .but no tag."

"Mom!? . . . Do you think I would jump off the porch again?"

"Yes."

Our final day arrived, and we sat on some of the boxes in the hall downstairs, waiting for my father. An army staff car pulled up in front, and a soldier got out and walked up to our front door.

"Hello?"

My mother went to the door. "Hello?"

They talked for a while, and then my mother called for my sister and me to come out front.

"Dad is going to be a little late, so he sent a car to take you for a ride."

"Great!"

I was really excited. My father had never sent a car for us before. We jumped into the backseat and were driven away. We rode around the city and I waved at all my friends.

"Hey guys, look at me!"

"Hey! There goes the man who always points to the right!"

When we returned, we found out why my father had sent a car.

Rollo was gone.

"I don't understand," I cried through my tears.

"We couldn't take him, son. Taking a dog to another country is very difficult. He has a good home here, and we'll get another dog when we get to our new post."

I had dreams about Rollo for years after that. And they were always that he had found me.

★   ★   ★

WE RETURNED FROM Germany and moved to upstate New York, where my father became the ROTC commandant at Niagara University. As a family we were suffering from the indignity of arriving during a Niagara winter, and I was still under heavy sedation from losing Rollo. Through a mystery only known to parents, mine decided that it would be good solace for me to learn how to ice-skate. Little did they know that one of my garage circus acts was the famous skating lion, played of course by Rollo. So this whole episode only deepened my depression, especially when it was painfully obvious that Rollo was a much better skater than I ever hoped to be.

On one of the campus ponds, where the cold went right through our long underwear and down to the bone, we assembled the tools of the trade. . .skates, arctic outerwear, and kitchen chairs. The most important stuff was the arctic outerwear, for in Niagara everyone considered Buffalo to be tropical.

"Grab the back of the chair, and skate along behind it," said my mother.

"I don't know how to skate."

"Well, just push along behind it."

"Why do I have to push a chair around?"

"In case you start to fall."

"In case I fall?" Am I supposed to be able to sit in it instead of crashing to the ice. . .some kind of a midair pirouette into a sitting position?

"It will keep you from falling."

Well, of course it didn't. Instead of lying in a crashed prone position, I ended up lying in a crashed prone position holding onto a kitchen chair.

There we were, with our ankles pointing north and south, stumbling around the frozen pond, the only family to ever have brought along the kitchen furniture while ice-skating. The campus newspaper reported that bizarre creatures had taken up residence on the pond. When we returned for our next family lesson, there was a small crowd of curious students waiting. It didn't bother me, I liked a good circus crowd, and I stumbled around waving to the audience. They cheered and I waved, they cheered and I fell, they cheered and I tumbled. Soon we were joined by students with their own chairs. Before long there wasn't a dinning room chair to be found in any of the cafeteria halls. It got so crowded that we were pushed off the ice entirely, and could only watch as the Niagara students evolved it into a winter gymnastic event. This all ended with a massive chair pileup when signals got crossed on who had the right of way. So, what became known as the Niagara Ice Chair Ballet, also known as The Great Winter Chair Riot, was started by my mother in 1953. . .and ended in 1953. And I never did learn how to skate.

★ ★ ★

AS THE WINTER passed into spring, I joined in with our neighborhood gang and explored the area. My brother and I were instantly popular because we had real army stuff with which to play war. These were civilian kids, and before we came along, they were using their moms' kitchens as quartermaster, making do with pots and pans. Now we had real helmets, web belts, canteens, holsters, and even fatigues. We were the best-dressed Kid Army around.

The neighborhood was one long street, straight as a die, right off a state highway, across from a high school. Houses lined both sides, and the street dead-ended near a huge lime pit. On our side of the street, a creek ran parallel to the road, and widened at the end as it meandered out of the neighborhood and through the lime pits. Right behind our house was the crash site of an air force jet. The ground was still blackened and cratered. Fused metal and small glassy bits were lying all around, twinkling in the sun, but the big pieces had been hauled away long ago.

"Did the pilot die?"

"I don't know."

We stood around the site, dressed in our army gear, feeling proud of our plane crater. We had real gear and a real crash crater.

We built a raft, a solid and big raft, one that could take us all for a ride down the creek. We floated out of the neighborhood and into the alien landscape of the lime pits. No one dared put their hands or feet in the water, for we knew that the lime could eat flesh to the bone faster than a piranha.

"Freddy went in there, and never came out."

The mounds of whitish lime powder were piled higher than the hills surrounding Niagara. Actually, there were no hills surrounding Niagara, and Freddy's family left with him fully intact a month earlier, but I was taking no chances as we drifted along and kept myself centered on the raft. A joker named Ralph, they're always named Ralph, started rocking the boat.

"Hey! We're in a storm!"

Jimmy, the oldest and strongest outside of my brother, didn't even turn around to look at him.

"Ralph, you looking to go for a swim?"

The raft stopped rocking.

"Look! There's a body lying by that pile!"

I had to admit it looked like a leg sticking out, but by its size it would have to have been Paul Bunyon's leg.

"It's just the way the lime slid down. Besides, you can't get in there, the bank's too steep and the fence is too high."

"Freddy got in there."

"No he didn't. He's in Buffalo with his parents."

Enjoying the tropical climate.

"I saw him."

"Ralph, you're lying."

"I did. He went in there on the day that George tried to kill Sally with his bike."

"He was already gone when George tried to kill Sally."

"Hey! I didn't try to kill anybody. . .Sally tried to kill me!"

"What are you taking about, you ran right into her."

"No I didn't. I didn't do anything, I was riding between you and my brother. She came down the street, right through the middle of us, and rammed into me. She could just as easily have hit one of you. I still don't know why she didn't move to the other side of the road when she saw us coming."

It was my first encounter with a woman driver.

"I don't think she saw us. Still, you could have yelled something."

"Didn't see us!? How can you miss my brother. . ."

"Hey! Watch it!" protested Dave.

". . .or all of us, on bikes, coming right at you? Wouldn't you move?"

"I don't know. Maybe she froze."

"She bent my wheel too. Hit me straight on."

"You practically killed her."

We came out of the lime pits and drifted to the bank where a tire had been hung from a tree. It would be a brave man who would take a ride on that tire and risk falling into Lime Creek.

"To mark this adventure, we all have to swing out over the creek in the tire," said Jimmy.

"Why?" I asked, the lone voice of reason.

"To mark this adventure. . .," Jimmy said again.

"Can't we just pee on the tree?"

"There's no daring in doing that. . .watch." Jimmy walked over and peed on the trunk. "See?"

I had to admit it sure didn't look daring. The tire was calmly hanging from one of the high branches, right over the middle of the creek.

"Who's going to get the tire over to the bank?"

"I will," said Paul, and he stepped forward. Paul was a slightly built kid who rarely said anything, so it was pretty shocking that he not only spoke up, but that he was going to get the tire. "I'm good at climbing trees." And with that he was off, like a human fly, scooting up the trunk where there were no lower branches to grab onto.

"How can he do that? What's he holding onto?"

"I guess the bark."

"You can't climb a tree by holding onto the bark."

"Well, he just did."

Paul climbed the bark up to the branch and shimmied along its length until he came to the rope. He grabbed hold of it, and began crawling backwards while holding on. The tire started coming toward us, but it was rising at the same time until it was out of the reach of everyone but Jimmy.

"I'll go first," he said as he took hold of the tire.

He put both hands on the rope, jumped up, and thrust his feet though the center. Out he swung over Lime Creek, and back to the bank. He didn't stop, but went out again.

"This is to show you that this creek don't scare me."

This time he pulled his feet free and came to a stop, standing on the bank.

"Who's next?"

Ralph, never one to be outdone, stepped forward.

"Me."

"Okay, Ralph. I'll hold it while you get in."

"I'm going to stand."

Several of us inhaled with surprise.

"Stand? Are you crazy?"

"You guys are chicken. I'll show you how to do this."

Jimmy held the tire while Ralph climbed on and stood with his feet on the inside rim of the tire and his hands holding the rope.

"Okay," he said.

Jimmy let go and Ralph went swinging out over the creek.
"Now—one hand!" he yelled and let go of the rope with
his top hand.

We were mesmerized by this. . .this was true daring.

"One foot!" He was swinging out there with one hand on
the rope and only one foot on the tire. The tire began to push
away from his body, and he was suspended for a moment, spread
eagle as he swung. The tire continued to push away until he
could no longer keep his foot on the rim. It came out, and
Ralph tried to grab the rope with his free hand, but it was way
too late.

"Aaaiiiieeeeee! . . ."

Ralph hit the water with a monstrous splash. We all stood
up expecting the worst, but there was no human Fizzie, no bub-
bling or boiling or frothing water, and no clean-to-the-white-
bone skeleton washing onto the bank.

"Hey, there's nothing wrong with this creek, it feels just
like my Saturday-night bath!"

Now we were all ready for this daring adventure, and
quickly stripped down to our shorts. One after the other we
dove into the water.

"Maybe they just don't want anyone finding out about this
place, so they just started a rumor to keep us out."

"Yeah, I bet that's it."

"Could've been some other kids just trying to keep this
place for themselves."

"Well, now we know."

"Yeah, now it's our swimming hole."

That night every one of us developed a rash all over our
bodies. I heard my mother on the phone.

"That's right, Doctor. It looks sort of like measles, but he's
had those, and it doesn't itch him. He says it stings when you
touch it. Yes, hold on a moment." I heard footsteps coming to
my room. "The doctor wants you in a tub of water right now.
This is the third call he's had tonight about the same thing.
Where were you this afternoon?"

"Out playing."

"Out playing where?"

"Down the street."

"Did you get into anything?"

"We were just playing army in the woods."

"Hmmm. . .well, get into a warm tub. . .now."

"Mom!" my brother called out.

"What!"

"I've caught that rash. . .from George."

"What!?" I cried out.

"Everybody in the tub!" screamed my mother.

None of us told that we all had gone in Lime Creek. In about a week, the rash cleared up and I went back to head-on collisions with Sally.

THE DEEP FIELDER

WE LEFT NIAGARA AFTER, I'd say, about six more Sally crashes, and we returned to Military Mecca. . .Washington. There are about four thousand military installations surrounding D.C. My father had received orders for Vietnam, and we were to stay in D.C. while he was away. I really didn't understand that I wouldn't see him for the entire year. I didn't know anything about Vietnam, so I naturally thought we would all be going along, we had always gone before, so why not now?

"Because there's a war going on there," he said.

Huts that shoot back. Say no more.

He went down the line giving us his final parting words.

"Don't pick on your brother."

"Stay out of the Pentagon."

He seemed stumped for a moment with my sister, then. . .

"You're perfect."

Why was I not surprised?

We waved good-bye at McQuire Air Force Base as he boarded his plane. After a while, I got used to him being gone, then I started to worry that I wouldn't like it when he came back. First, I didn't want him to go, and then I didn't want him to come back. What gave?

We moved to Virginia and settled into a townhouse apartment in Alexandria. The complex surrounded a solitary hold-out farmer living in a dilapidated house, who had walled himself in with an elegant eight-foot-high cinder block version of the Great Wall of China. We still climbed to the top of it, even though everyone said he had a shot gun filled with rock salt just for kids like us. It didn't bother me since I had no idea what rock salt had to do with a gun, and I was more worried about the black widow spiders that lived in the wall than I was about him anyway. I think he cultivated the spiders himself.

The complex was full of kids, and we went on many BB gun hunts through the woods on his property, down to the electric relay station near Main Street. The real object of the hunt was buying snow cones from the drug store.

At the end of our street was a baseball field, "field" in the *Farmer's Almanac* sense of the word. The only reason it was there at all was because the land sloped away so steeply that it wasn't economically feasible to build any more apartments. So, they magnanimously made it into a baseball field, a field where only those playing a very shallow outfield could still be seen, even if it was only their heads. Deep Fielders were there only to keep the ball from rolling completely down the hill and becoming a runaway killer missile as it approached the speed of sound, and finally stopping somewhere in Maryland. In fact, we penalized anyone who hit a ball past a Deep Fielder. This was abused a lot, since no one could actually see what was going on down there, but everyone took the word of a Deep Fielder. No one else wanted to play way down there in the next county, and didn't want to antagonize anyone who did into quitting.

"Oh yeah, well you come down here and play Deep Fielder if you don't believe me!"

"Ahhh. . .that's okay, we believe you."

The threat of quitting Deep Fielder was good for more than just getting your way on the field.

"I want to sit in the front seat of the car all week, or I won't play Deep Fielder."

"Okay."

"Hey," said my sister. "No fair."

"I want to trade Dusty Rhodes (a Dusty Rhodes came in every pack of baseball cards) for the Dodger's team card, or I won't play Deep Fielder."

"Okay."

The weak, the young, the infirm were given the Deep Fielder position, so I was out there a lot, and didn't see much of the games. I was also given the other choice position. . .playing catcher, which would have been called retriever if a breed of dog didn't already have the rights to the name. I tried it only once.

Crack!

Boink!

Foul ball right off the noggin. Protective equipment was unheard of in sandlot baseball.

"Aaaaiiiiieeeeeeeee. . .," I screamed all the way to my house.

"Why does the bump on your head have these little cross-stitch patterns if you fell off the farmer's wall as you say?" asked my mother as she held an ice pack to my forehead.

"It's all Dave's fault."

"Yes, I imagine it is."

I went back to Deep Fielder and waited for my hat to fit back over my catcher's forehead.

All of the permanent members of the Deep Fielder group were excluded from team captaincy, a position that came with choosing rights, and the associated "fisties" on the bat. Both captains went hand over hand up the bat handle until there was only room for one last grip, by the winning captain. The victory didn't go unchallenged by the losing side. First it was just a whack of the bat to make sure the last grip was a fair one, one that could still hold onto the bat when it was given a solid thump. Every captain managed to hold onto the bat for this, even if they were only clinging to the knob with fingertips. So, this was immediately escalated to a leg kick, which became a two-block running karate kick practically overnight. This practice was abandoned after a few black and blue knots the sizes of a "catcher's foot" were endured. It was decided to smack the dangling bat with another, which was fine until kid's started showing up with "loaded" bats just for this purpose. Then someone brought a sledgehammer—finally a kid brought his father's impact hammer complete with portable air compressor. This ritual started to take almost as long as the game.

I suspected Deep Fielders were sometimes not even called in when it was our turn to bat. We could hear the snickering coming from up on the field.

"What are they doing up there?"

"I don't know."

"Crawl up and take a look."

"Not me."

We didn't dare peek. No one wanted to risk a Pounding Frenzy by the Older Guys. All I know is that some of them had bat blisters and we never even came close to getting one. Well, that's not all I know, it's just one of the things I know. It wouldn't be good to get this far and only know one thing, and for it to be about bat blisters to boot.

On the spud field we were all equals, and it was coed. We held gigantic spud games that lasted into the night, illuminated by the streetlights, and only ending when our parents finally wanted to know what had happened to their kids. This was before there was a risk of our picture ending up on a milk carton holding an official size and weight spud ball. The only picture on a milk carton back then was Borden's Elsie, the contented cow, and if she went missing it was because she had finally made a run for it.

"Moooohhheeellllppp. . .they make me wear dresses!"

We were enrolled in a Catholic school—St. Rita's. It was one of my main fears as a kid, and I hoped against hope there wouldn't be a Catholic school nearby, but there always was. What's the story here, shouldn't these people be off in the jungles, doing missionary work or something? For my brother, the news was worse. He was entering high school, and they not only found a Catholic high school for him, but a Jesuit Catholic high school—Gonzaga. This was the pinnacle of Catholic School Phobia for a kid. While we were playing spud, he was studying Greek, which I believe will come in handy when he has to speak with Zeus. I decided after watching him go through this torture that I would have to run away and become a hobo if I were ever faced with a Jesuit high school.

"Why do you have to study Greek?"

"So, I don't have to study Latin."

Which will come in mighty handy when he's called to defend Sparticus in the Roman Senate.

These were the early years of the Catholic Church's war on rock-'n'-roll, and although they were losing badly, it affected us daily. Elvis banners were flying on Main Street promoting his first movie, and we were required to avert our eyes when we passed, walking with our heads bowed like some Kurdistan Buddhist monks who walk through the world with their eyes closed so they don't see any evil. I admit I peeked, and I wasn't struck blind like my mother said I would be. But she did smack me on top of the head, which was close enough in my book. The Pope had placed the movie on the church's condemned list, which required my mother to obey. She followed every precept without question, and did so to her dying day. If they had said the new mass required everyone to attend naked, she would have strolled bare-assed up to the communion railing. Right to the end she was faithful, she even kept the belief in Limbo, a place even the church gave up on and eventually gave all the rights to Chubby Checker.

My brother and I were forced into the rock-'n'-roll underground for almost two years, until the peace accords of '58 were signed and rock-'n'-roll was let into Catholic schools. But it had brought us all together as kids, and going to the record store with my allowance in my hand was a weekly ritual. It was also responsible for my first encounter with a girl, other than to run her down with my bike.

She lived next door, and she was my first girlfriend, of sorts, since I was only ten. She was an older woman. . .eleven. Her name was Jean. We played the records we bought on a record player my mother had won at church bingo. I argued, unsuccessfully, that if the church had really been serious about their war, then they would have excluded a record player as a bingo prize. I quickly learned that bingo is only rivaled by the Pope in power and autonomy within the church. We would listen to the records down in the basement at low volume, so as not to antagonize my mother.

A feeling started to develop in my ten-year-old body, something entirely new. For the first time, I wanted to be around a girl. I even turned down a BB gun hunt to be near her. Clearly something was wrong. After spud games, I would talk to her through our adjoining screen doors. Then one day she asked me the unthinkable.

"Do you like me?"

I froze. The electrical impulses in my brain overloaded, smoke came out my ears. With supreme courage and superhuman effort, I fought back the natural fears and answered her.

"Yes."

It about killed me. A warm, embarrassed glow came over me after I said it. It was my first experience with the instinctive male fear to never say anything remotely like this to a girl. I vowed to never do it again.

That summer my mother took us to the pool at Fort Myer for swimming lessons, my brother, my sister, and me. At first, I didn't really care for the lessons, but I liked the pool and I liked our instructor even more. She was beautiful. What was happening to me? I hadn't even recovered from the brain hemorrhage of admitting I liked Jean, and I was already lusting after another? Washington was having a bad influence on me, I was turning into a congressman.

Our swimming instructor was the first girl who caused me to do stupid things. . .she hasn't been the last. This in itself was disturbing. I thought the "do you like me" incident was as bad as it could get, and I wasn't aware there was more that could go wrong. Up to then, all my stupid acts were my own. I thought them all up and I did them just for my own amusement. Now, a girl had changed all this, I was losing control, what was happening to me?

"Dave, why is this happening?"

"Get lost."

After our swimming lesson I would try to show off and catch her attention.

"Hey, look at me." The kid with the idiotic look, and spastic body. He's doing the one-foot telephone booth Superman launch, with flying, midair, dead-eye shot to the chest from the OK Corral, with a finishing Dead Man Swoon and final tumble with a full twist into the deep end of the pool. After all that, she must have surely realized we were destined to be together.

I surfaced and she was polite enough to smile at the goofy kid doing these stupid things and yelling out her name, but that was all. Hmmmmm. . .maybe the cannonball entry with leg extension, she surely wouldn't be able to resist me then. . .

. . .a backward swan dive with gagging facial contortions while calling out her name. . .

. . .continual motions "running through the air" arc off the diving board, complete with Jerry Lewis choreography. . .

. . .a Charlie Chaplin "I didn't see the pool" pratfall with a sorrowful, unrequited-love facial expression, held until completely disappearing from view just like a Deep Fielder taking his position. . .

Through it all she smiled politely, which I hoped meant she liked me, but then she smiled politely at everyone, including my sister. I redoubled my efforts, managing to splash more water onto the pool's concrete runway than Sea World's Shamoo. That should have, at least, counted for something.

"What do I have to do to get her to notice me?"

"She notices you, all right," said Dave. "You can't miss a beanpole jackass floundering around in a pool."

"You really think so?" I was encouraged.

Everyone shares the blame for a lot of this, because if this had been nipped in the bud instead of reinforced with polite smiles and my brother's encouragement, I would have stopped doing stupid things while calling out girl's names long before I got into my twenties.

The effort was exhausting, and I took occasional breaks sitting at one of the umbrella tables that surrounded the pool. I sat back and ordered lunch. My mother seemed totally unaware of everything, she was wrapped head to foot in terry cloth coverings, completely avoiding the sun like some subterranean creature that would melt if a ray of sun actually landed on any exposed flesh. If she discovered a ray landing upon her she would instantly become erect and scream. . .

"Arrggghhhh. . .I'm being fried alive!"

I loved getting French fries and listening to the jukebox. French fries had to be a money-losing proposition for the snack shack, for I had a small pile of fries, with a quart of ketchup.

"Would you like a pine float with that?" asked my brother.

"Sure."

He gave me a glass of water with a toothpick floating in it.

"Thanks."

This was a joke to other kids, but I really liked pine floats. The only thing better was to discover they had mint flavored toothpicks. I didn't have any money, so I had a lot of pine floats, and I was at the mercy of whatever music anyone decided to play on the jukebox. My mother refused to lend me my allowance so I could play a song.

"You might as well walk right over there and throw your allowance in the gutter."

Sometimes, in between Guy Lombardo and Tony Bennett, someone would play Elvis or Fats Domino, and I loved to eat my French fries and listen to my mother say how awful this music was. The church might have given up, but my mother hadn't. I liked the awful music. The fact that she didn't made it all the more enticing. I was glad someone had decided to throw money away in the jukebox and not the gutter.

"You can't go back in the water for an hour after you finish your lunch."

An hour! For some French fries? It didn't seem right.

"Why?"

"So you don't get a cramp."

"How much of a cramp do I get from French fries?"

"Don't get smart with me."

I wasn't getting smart, I really wanted to know. Maybe French fries were only worth a half-hour, or something. Everything can't be the same.

"You mean if I ate a horse, it's still an hour?"

"Be quiet," explained my mother.

"He just wants to show off for the swimming teacher."

Little sisters like to torment you in the middle of your pine float, taking the zest right out of it.

"I do not."

"Yes you do."

To save time, we both immediately escalated into the very fashionable machine gun "not. . .not. . .not. . .do. . .do. . .do" We both looked and sounded like we were doing Muslim yodeling. It was also plainly evident why Muslim women wear veils while doing this.

"Stop it, the both of you."

Mom cut off our debate to the visible relief of everyone sitting around us who had been hoping to actually hear the music they had just paid for. We both withdrew into sullen silence. I wasn't allowed to administer an Older Brother Pounding to her in public.

"Don't ever come into the Deep Outfield."

"What?"

"You heard me."

I still think about the pool girl whenever I eat French fries.

FORT LEWIS

My FATHER ARRIVED HOME from Vietnam late in the day. The afternoon sun was low on the horizon, right at the dinnertime angle. As a kid, I knew lunchtime and dinnertime by the look of the sun. When it was cloudy, all of us, including my brother, were like the mole people caught outside during the day, except we didn't fuse into a pile of ashes. . .we wandered aimlessly. Like one of those old electric vibrating football games, we bumped around going in all the wrong directions. My brother had one of those games and he always forced me to play with him because it took hours to set up. By Older Brother Decree, I was the set-up specialist. As soon as you hit the switch every piece immediately went everywhere except in the direction you wanted them to go. You were lucky if you found one man in the whole set that went in a straight line. And, laughably, a kicker was included. Someone had a little too much schnapps at Electrorama. It was a huge piece, with a spring-loaded contraption for shooting a tiny felt football at the goal posts. Apparently, by design, it was supposed to either launch the ball out of existence, or keep it stuck in the holder. Either was equally possible.

The sun was out the day my father came home, right at the dinnertime angle. But instead of going in for my dinner, I was hiding in the bushes, waiting for him, and unsure of how I was feeling about it. An army staff car drove up and suddenly there he was, dressed in his uniform. He stepped out and right behind him came three collie puppies. My mother immediately fainted dead away, and I came running out of the bushes.

"What are their names!?"

"Laddie, Lassie, and Lady."

My father should never name dogs. I wanted to ask him why they always had to rhyme, but couldn't bring myself to be so bold. Besides, I was too happy about it, and rolled around the ground with them while my mother was revived. They were happy too, and we all rolled around together, and we peed everywhere. My mother was revived just in time to see this, and fainted dead away again. My father also brought back a tape recorder, the first I had ever seen. Later, at the dinner table, he showed us how it worked and asked each of us to say something. After giving this much careful thought I took the mike and pronounced.

"There's a rat in the refrigerator."

Careful thought was not my strong suit.

My mother looked stunned.

My father checked the refrigerator.

Everything was now just like it had been before he left.

"Everyone. . .there's one more thing. I have new orders. We're going to Washington."

"We're in Washington," I said.

"Washington State, we're going to Fort Lewis."

"Stupid."

"Husky."

"When?" asked my mom.

"December."

"They're being taken out of school in midyear again?"

"I know. . .nothing we can do about it."

"Just once, I would like to do things normally. That barely gives us enough time to find out if there's a Jesuit high school out there."

I looked at my brother and gave him my special diabolical grin to compound the misery he was now feeling. I had been working on my diabolical grin for the past month, just waiting for the right occasion to unveil it.

"Come on," said my father to my mother. "Let's take a walk, just the two of us, without these kids."

My mother seemed reluctant to leave us alone without all the good china safely put away, but relented and they left. My brother unveiled his own diabolical grin to compound the misery he was about to inflict.

"Oh, stupid. . ."

"What do you want. . .Fat Boy?"

I jumped off the chair and ran out the front, the screen door banged against the side of the house as I crashed through it. I leapt off the front stoop with him hot on my tail. I know it's the role of a little brother to be tormented. I was busy tormenting my younger sister, and my big brother was busy tormenting me. This is a proper and balanced kid's world.

He had the upper hand until he pushed me into the bushes, and I tumbled out the other side to come face to face with Jean. This made me angry and embarrassed, and I no longer cared to run away.

"I'll kill you!" I screamed.

"Hah! You little pipsqueak, you couldn't kill anyone, especially me."

My brother grabbed one of my favorite trucks off the lawn and flung it across the yard.

"Now, what are you going to do?"

I stood there dumfounded at this complete breach of chase etiquette. No one fooled with your toys! He ran over and picked it up and threw it again! It was too much for me.

"I. . .I. . .I'll kill you!" I was flushed with rage, and desperately wanted to say something much more vicious, but how can you top "I'll kill you?" "I'll kill you. . .er. . .more?" I settled for running right at him, screaming like a banshee.

"Iiiiiieeeeeeeeee!"

"Do you hear that?" asked my mother as she walked along with my father, long out of sight from the apartment.

"Hear what?" replied my father.

"Sounded like a banshee."

"There are lots of other banshees in the neighborhood, it doesn't mean that it's one of ours."

"Still, maybe we should head back."

My brother looked startled at my sudden transformation. He took off for the house and laughed as he ran, enraging me even more. Around and around the house we flew, each of us alternately tripping and sprawling in the dirt, but I was never able to close the distance. He taunted me and threw dirt clods whenever I got close. Then he made his fatal mistake, he went into the house. I threw open the screen door and followed him. He ran into our bedroom.

Hah! He was cornered. I needed a weapon! I ran into the room right behind him and grabbed my toy rifle. Toys were much more solid back then, made to last and take a beating, huge metal and wood things that could absorb all the punishment dished out to them. My toy rifle would make a good club. He was going back to the hospital for more stitches!

As I rounded the bed he jumped over it and went back out the bedroom door. My mother was coming up the sidewalk.

My brother saw her and stopped in his tracks. Desperately he looked around for a place to hide, then ran into the bathroom and locked the door. I could hear him laughing in there. I was furious.

I held my rifle tightly, and quivered with anger.

"Aaarrrgggghhhh!"

I charged the door and rammed it with my rifle. The steel barrel went completely through it. The same people who built the baseball field had built the bathroom door.

My anger melted away when the front door opened and my mother walked in. I was standing there holding the gun with three collie puppies at my feet, peeing everywhere. I was in trouble, but there was no one laughing behind that door now.

My mother stared at the barrel imbedded in the bathroom door, then at all the pee on the floor.

"It's all Dave's fault," I said.

My father came in behind her. "We're gone ten minutes..."

"I think you were saying something about someone else's banshees, and, by the way, I'm the one who's been gone ten minutes. You've been gone for a year."

★ ★ ★

THAT DECEMBER WE left for Washington State. My mother was happy, she had found Belermine, another Jesuit high school. My sister and I were happy, there were no Catholic schools available for us. Apparently, in Washington State, there was a lot more missionary work than in Alexandria. My brother was not happy.

Halfway across the country, in Oklahoma, the car began to make strange noises. It started to sound like our wringer washing machine the day my sister and I tried to use it to flatten Play-Doh, and its gears started to grind away as the dough oozed everywhere.

"Is the car supposed to sound like our old washing machine?"

"Ummmmuuugghhh...," said my father, which I interpreted as no, a '54 Buick should never sound like a Play-Doh-encrusted wringer washing machine.

We made it to Fort Sill, where my father knew people. My father always knew people, it didn't matter what kind of base, army, navy or air force, there were Four-Martini Salads at them all. The post motor pool mechanic looked over the car and said the engine needed an overhaul.

"It'll take a few days."

We stayed with some old friends of my parents at their house off the post. The backyards were all fenced in, something that you never saw on a military base. There's only one fence on an army post, and it surrounds the whole place. The Oklahoma countryside was flat as a pancake, and you could see backyard fences stretching to the horizon.

I went outside by myself, and did the only thing you can do with a fence. I climbed it. As I straddled the top, my foot slipped, and I came crashing down on the top chain links of the crossbar. . .right in the crouch.

Those top links had impaled me, at least that's what it felt like, and I tumbled to the ground. . .wounded.

"Ooooowwwww. . ."

I got up, and pulled down my pants to see what awful injury I had done to myself. This, of course, is when every family in the neighborhood decided it was time for their backyard barbecue.

"What are you doing!?" screamed my mother, mortified at the sight.

It's hard to satisfactorily explain yourself while standing around with your pants down at your ankles. It tends to detract from any plausible explanation you might have. I imagine this applies equally in the adult world.

"I. . .I. . .the fence. . .I fell."

"And this caused your pants to fall down?" inquired my father.

"I thought I was hurt."

"Well, get 'em up and come inside and we'll have a look. You know, you may have a future in Congress."

The barbecues were delayed while I pulled up my pants and went inside. In a repeating scene of backyard barbecues that went out to infinity, they were all watching me. It stretched as far as the eye could see. They probably thought they were having a vision. It was, after all, Oklahoma.

★ ★ ★

EVERYONE TOLD US to be prepared for a lot of rain in Washington State, although I don't exactly know what they expected us to do. So we bought more umbrellas and rain hats, and hoped for the best. We arrived in the small town of Dupont, during the Great Drought of '58. We moved into a section of Fort Lewis known as Splinterville. These were old war-era wooden buildings used to temporarily house newcomers. The first night of our arrival I caught my mother, tired from the journey, in a weak moment, and talked her into buying me a Buddy Holly record. She only did this after I convinced her that he was an orchestra leader. It said so right on the label ". . .with orchestral accompaniment." She gave me a suspicious look, but was too tired to deal with my nagging her. . .something of a role reversal. I showed my prize to my brother.

"How'd you do that?"

"It's because he's an orchestra leader. . ."

"You know, Mom, Buddy Holly isn't a. . .," started my brother. Then he looked over at me and for some reason stopped. I was puzzled. . .it wasn't like him. Then he returned with a record of his own.

"Mom, they have a record here by the Chuck Berry Orchestra. . ."

My brother and I were both avid record collectors, and we prided ourselves on our collections and our knowledge. My sister even bragged to some kids at the school bus stop that her brother knew everything about rock-'n'-roll records.

"Oh yeah?!" They turned to me. I prepared myself for the challenge. ". . .who did. . ."

"Oh, not this brother, my other brother."

I was left deflated at the curbside, it was the first of many flat tires to come in my life. Eventually, we moved into real housing. My brother entered another Jesuit high school, and I entered the local junior high school in town.

Fort Lewis was the site of my first general life lesson. After badgering my father for what seemed liked months, he relented and let me buy a life-size tank advertised on the back of a comic book. He had a soft spot for tanks. It was part of the same advertisement that also sold an entire battlefield scene, complete with two armies, artillery, tanks, trucks, half-tracks, jeeps. . .and all for $1.98. The tank was $5.00, an astronomical sum in those days for anything on the back of a comic book. When the tank arrived, I hurriedly assembled it in my room. When I was finished, I sat back to admire it. It was significantly different from its illustration. I looked at the drawing on the back of the comic book, then at my tank on the floor. Theirs was a modern-looking tank, huge in comparison to the kid standing next to it. Mine was much smaller, it looked more like a World War I version, and had a square cannon barrel protruding out of the front. It didn't have a turret, just a narrowing of the box and a printed illustration on the outside of the cardboard to suggest a turret might be there. To get in, you lifted the tank off the ground, and let it settle back over you through the square opening in the bottom. It was very cramped inside, too small to move around. If you turned your shoulders, the whole tank turned with you. I sat on the floor wearing my tank, and had a revelation.

"I've bought a $5.00 cardboard box."

My father gave me the general life lesson.

"Never buy anything from the back of a comic book."

Later, I would fall for a related trick, selling boxes of Christmas cards for prizes. I believe it was from the same people. Selling ten boxes got you "engraved" pencils, a bicycle went for selling fourteen thousand boxes.

I've bought a lot of little cardboard boxes.

★   ★   ★

OUR MOVING INTO a brick house in a newly built housing area coincided with my brother issuing his first official Older Brother Decree, something he had just discovered he could do. From his throne atop Older Brother Mount he pronounced. . .

"From this moment forward, you and I will not buy the same records, in fact, we will confine ourselves to totally separate artists. If there are any disputes, I will be the court of last resort. . .as well as first resort."

"Yes, your loathsomeness."

"You may have Buddy Holly."

"Yes, your slothfulness."

"I will have Chuck Berry and Little Richard."

"But that's two to my one, your gluttonness."

"Your point?"

"Your rationale?"

"I'm older, bigger and can pound you into dust. . ."

"A wise, and just decision, your pudgefulness."

"Do I detect dissatisfaction?"

"Not from any of us down here in the salt mines."

I saw the logic of his argument, for I had been pounded into dust on many previous occasions.

"We will share Elvis, for I am not totally without compassion."

"Thank you, your repugnantness."

"You know, I'm enjoying this Older Brother Decree business. You should prepare yourself for many more to come."

"That would be joy in my life."

"You should also prepare yourself for Friends of Older Brother Decrees."

"It seems only natural."

"Yes, it does."

I tried this same ploy with my younger sister, after which she just looked at me for a moment, then screamed. . .

"Mom!"

Clearly, I had a lot to learn about these Older Brother Decrees. Obviously there was a trick to this that I didn't know. Thanks to her, I was now faced with a Mother Decree, a Father Decree, and a Parental Decree.

I sat in my tank licking my wounds.

In spite, I went out and bought a Chuck Berry record, secretly, of course.

★   ★   ★

MY BROTHER ENTERED the high school, and in blatant violation of both an Older Brother Decree and Friends of Older Brother Decree, I spied on him and his friends as they studied in the living room. Occasionally, on some unspoken sign, two of them would get up and go upstairs for a while. It was always just two, and always a boy and a girl. I hid in a closet to find out what was going on, but was caught and put on trial.

"Read the charges."

"Violation of Older Brother Decree, violation of Friends of Older Brother Decree, violation of Girlfriend of Older Brother Decree, several counts of violation of Girlfriends of Friends of Older Brother decree."

"Verdict?"

"Guilty."

"Guilty."

"Guilty."

"Sentence?"

"Pounding."

"Pounding."

"Pounding."

I tried to convince them to show me what was happening upstairs.

"What can you be doing that you want to hide so much?"

They quickly reconvened. . .*this kid just might say something to the wrong people.* So they shoved a cigarette in my mouth and showed me how to smoke instead. I sat in the living room chair, dizzy and nauseous.

"I'm sick."

Whenever any two of them left for the upstairs, the rest would find me and shove another cigarette in my mouth. Finally, whenever anyone left for upstairs, I took out a cigarette from my own pack, single-handedly flipped open my own Zippo lighter, snapped my finger over the flint wheel, and lit up. Soon, I would light up of my own accord, and then everyone would head upstairs in response. Thanks to my brother and his friends, I was smoking a pack a day, and they were spending a lot more time on the second floor.

★　★　★

FORT LEWIS IS set in the pine-forested hills below Mount Rainier, a huge military reservation. The post included several lakes, the largest of which was used for swimming and boating. In true military fashion, there were separate areas for officers and NCOs. The NCO area had a giant slide, several floating platforms of various sizes all linked together, racing lanes laid out, volleyball courts both on the beach and in the water and a huge snack bar with jukebox and dance floor. I was forced to make due with the officer's area, which had a lone, small, floating platform. The officers lavished their funds on the bar and the beachfront club, forget any of this swimming nonsense. They did have a boat dock, and I did try water-skiing. However, I don't think that being pulled through the water with your head looking through two water-ski spires while the rest of you is being dragged below the surface is the intended result.

My father said I looked like a beachball tied to a rock. However, I didn't see him out there giving it a try, not even a three-martini version of a try. Hooking up the hydroplane Gold Cup winner only towed me through the water at a faster pace, and blew off my swim trunks.

I sat in my tank, with shredded trunks, licking my wounds.

It was possible to swim under the float and come up between the fifty-gallon metal drums the platform rested on. It was here that I met more adventurous girls, brave enough to swim under the platform, and interested in more than just bobbing like apples between the drums. So, even though the plum of the summer was an invite to the NCO area, there was still a powerful attraction waiting under the float at the officer's area.

Just before the Fourth of July my brother issued another decree.

"This will be Older Brother Decree number...let's see...number..."

"147," I said.

"147...thank you. You cannot have any M80s, those are reserved for me...and my friends."

"What can I have, your pismireship?"

"You may have these...Texas Busters."

He, along with his friends, was able to detonate the loudest explosions in the neighborhood. My Texas Busters sounded like LadyFingers in comparison. Then I discovered the clothesline poles in the backyard. The poles were four-inch iron pipes, with a cross-T. I threw a Texas Buster into one open end of the cross-T pipe.

KABLOOM!

Fire and smoke shot out both ends. The explosion was the new record holder.

"Whoa!" yelled my brother from our upstairs bedroom. He stuck his head out the window.

"How'd you do that? Did you take one of my M80s?"

"No way!"

"Then, how'd you do it?"

"I'll tell you if you give me one of your M80s."

He suspiciously narrowed his eyes.

"This better be worth it."

From the window he tossed down one of the precious minibombs.

"Watch this." I lit the fuse and pitched the M80 into the cross-T.

KKAABBBLLOOOMMMM!!

Smoke and fire shot past me, billowing out into the yard. The pipe split and one end of the cross-T fanned out like metal spider legs. The clotheslines fell to the ground.

"Nice job," said my brother. "I wonder what Mom will think of it?"

"This will be Mother Decree number...let's see...number..."

"152," I said.

"152...thank you," said my mother.

I sat in my tank, with blackened face and hands, licking my wounds.

★   ★   ★

I BECAME A teenager at Fort Lewis, and entered that most secret
of worlds. . .the Post Teen Club. The route to the teen club
took you right past the military police station house. I was able
to start walking this well-trodden path when I got within six
months of my thirteenth birthday. Those were the rules, when
you were six months from being a teenager, you could join.
This junior member status was loathed by my brother and his
friends, although if the truth be known, they loathed everyone
younger than they, for that's the natural order of things, and
well understood and accepted by all of us. So I didn't dare get
in their way as they trod the same path. I hung back, well out
of sight, and watched them as they performed their rituals of
slapping, punching, whooping, laughing, and weaving around
each other, all the while moving steadily along. They would
look around occasionally, making sure no one was following
them. I would stay off the path, and use the trees to obscure
their sight. Older Brother Decree 148 called for severe
poundings if I was caught following. This time they were more
subdued than usual, and frequently checked the path behind
them. Something was up.

Just before they got to the MP station, they left the path
and disappeared into the woods. I thought I had been spotted,
and they were now surrounding me for the kill. Nervously, I
ran for the station house.

"George!"

My brother suddenly appeared out of the woods like some
kind of tree man from a Buck Rogers serial.

"What? . . ."

"Get out of here!"

My brother waved for me to leave. I ran ahead a short way,
and lay on the ground under a big pine tree with a good view
of them. One of his friends lit a cigarette, and I could see my
brother holding the jewel of his July Fourth fireworks stash,
the mammoth aerial bomb.

So, this was why he was saving that one.

The flame was quickly extinguished, and I could see the
red ember of the cigarette waving around, then coming to a
rest about where my brother was holding his bomb.

What were they doing?

They all scattered except for a solitary figure, which
crouched low and approached the station. The red ember of

the cigarette seemed to dangle at his waist as he silently closed in on the front door. When he was very close, he reached out, the red cigarette ember reached out with him. He looked like he was putting the cigarette on the station steps. As the light from the doorway illuminated his arm, I could see the aerial bomb, with the cigarette dangling from the fuse, being pushed onto the steps. Then he was up and running like a deer, back into the trees along the path.

Everything was quiet. They didn't move, so I didn't move. The pine needles I was lying on were beginning to itch me. I quietly ran my hand down to scratch. . .

BOOOOOMMMMMMM!

Almost immediately the station doors burst open and several MPs came charging out on a dead run.

"Freeze!"

There was no one there to freeze.

KABOOOMMM!

The second explosion went off overhead.

"Aarrggghhh! . . ." They yelled in frustration, and began to run in all directions, just like the pieces of my brother's vibrating football game, screaming at every tree and bush as they scurried around.

"Freeze!"

"Freeze!"

"Freeze!"

"Wow, this is really cool."

They began cursing as they darted around.

"Goddamned little dependent assholes!"

How'd they know it was goddamned little dependent assholes?

As chance would have it, when you scurry around long enough, you're bound to get lucky. One of the MPs ran into the trees and smack into one of my brother's friends.

"Got 'em!"

The rest of the MPs, although slightly dizzy from all the circles they had run, converged and extracted everyone.

I waited until it was clear, then went on to the teen club.

"Where's your brother?"

"I don't know." Which was true, I didn't know to which cell he had been taken.

When I got home, my father was intently talking with my mother at the kitchen table. I quietly went on up to my room.

My brother was sitting in my tank, licking his wounds.

"What happened to you? Everyone was asking at the teen club."

"Parental decree 12."

"Twelve? I'm up to 104. And that was all? Nothing else?"

"I got a Military Police Decree, I don't know what the number was, and a Father Decree. . .number 14."

"Fourteen? I'm up to 122."

★ ★ ★

SEVERAL WEEKS LATER, my friend Chavas and I were talking as we walked up the dirt road that lead to the top of the bluff, and continued on, into the military preserve section of the post.

"What? They're only in for two or three years?"

"That's right," said Chavas

"How do you know?"

"My father told me. That's what those REUP signs mean. They have to ask to stay in."

"No! . . ."

"He said it's called re-enlistment."

"I'll be damned."

I thought the army was so much fun that when soldiers joined, they joined for life, like my father. This news was as astounding as when I found out that war lasted more than one day.

"But you get to stay in, right? There's no chance they wouldn't let you stay?"

"Yeah, I guess."

"Whew." What a relief. We knew they all wanted to stay so they could chase and curse "the goddamned little dependent assholes."

We often went up on the bluff and followed the road to the obstacle course or deep into the forest where the Boy Scouts had built a cabin. We took one of the collies. . .Laddie. He loved it, running after the deer, running away from the bears. . .we all ran away from the bears. The old forest adage is, you don't have to be faster than the bear, just faster than the guy you're running with, and I always went with Chavas, for he was very slow.

We ran the obstacle course, ducking under the barriers, climbing the ropes, leaping off the platforms, crawling under the barbed wire.

"Look at this!"

Chavas held a grayish cylinder, about six inches long and four inches in diameter. There was writing on the outside in the block letter military fashion. INCENDIARY SMOKE DEVICE MIL-40-1095-645 DANGER EXPLOSIVES.

"Wow! You found a smoke grenade."

"What should we do with it?"

"I'll bet they'll want it back."

"No way. This is mine."

We called the dog and ran back home. Chavas kept it tucked under his shirt so no one would see it. In the large common parking garage that was behind our housing area, we climbed into the rafters and opened up one end of the cylinder. There was a gray powder inside and we poured it out into a big pile between us.

"I'll get some matches," said Chavas, and he climbed down and ran into his house. A minute later he was back and we sat cross-legged, staring at the pile of powder that lay between us.

"Watch out!" said Chavas, and he lit a match and tossed it onto the mound.

We ducked away, being used to the instant reaction when a match hits gunpowder. Nothing happened. Chavas lit another and threw it on the little powder mountain. We ducked again. Nothing happened.

"What's wrong?"

"Maybe it's wet."

Chavas stuck his finger into the powder.

"No, it's dry."

He lit another match and tossed it onto the pile.

Nothing.

"Maybe it's not gunpowder."

"It said 'Explosives.'"

"Hmmm. . ."

We both began lighting matches and throwing them onto the pile. Nothing happened. We got closer, right up next to it. Matches were lying all over it, some burning, some smoldering, others dead and cold.

"I don't think this is ever going to burn."

"What's wrong with. . ."

Then it went off.

The world turned orange for a moment. It wasn't an orange ball of fire, but shooting bolts going out in different directions. One caught my hand and knee, burning a hole right through my jeans. Another bolt knocked Chavas right out of the rafters.

"Aaaiiiieeeee! . . ."

He went screaming across the lot toward his house, smoke trailing behind him. The smoke was everywhere, very thick and white, and billowed out of the garage, filling the neighborhood.

I looked at my hand and then at my knee. They both were blackened and blistered. I didn't feel anything, no pain, but I was lightheaded, like coming out of the matinee movie and into the afternoon sun. I don't know how long I sat there, but when I heard sirens I climbed down and headed for my house. The first of the fire engines pulled into the garages as I went in my back door.

The knee of my jeans was still smoldering. My knee wasn't too bad, the pants had taken most of the beating, but my hand was a lot worse. The only thing I could think of doing was to hide it. I figured in a couple of days it would pretty much heal by itself. And I'll tell you something else, parents tend to notice when you start walking around with your arm tucked behind your back, and your pants smoldering. So don't even bother to try it.

"Why are you walking around with your arm behind your back?"

"Who?"

"Who do you think?"

"What arm?"

"The one behind your back."

"What back?"

"Why are you pants smoking!?"

"What pants?"

A classic, and failed, use of the Vinnie Barbarino defense. I eventually had to bring out my blackened hand. My mother skipped right over issuing a Mother Decree and went out to the fire engines. She managed to get an ambulance sent over.

I sat in my tank. . .but not licking these wounds.

The corpsman extracted me, and I was whisked away to the hospital.

I recuperated in my bedroom, and my parents worked on several new Parental Decrees. . .numbers 105 to 125. After a week, my hand felt pretty good, and I was restless from being trapped in the house with nothing to do. It was the weekend and I wanted to get out and go to the teen club.

"No," said my mother. "You're being punished."

"Can I go to the food store with you?" I was desperate.

"No. Stay in your room and rest." And she left the house to go food shopping by herself.

I wandered around the house, looking for amusement, when I spotted my brother and his girlfriend crossing the court-yard, heading for our front door.

Instantly, a whole scenario flashed in my mind. It was a completely formed scenario, and enough to make you believe there is a devil passing these things along. It took no effort, and I was powerless to stop it. As they crossed the street and came up the front walk, a Texas Buster fell from my hand as if in a dream, and landed in a basement window well.

KABOOOOM!

First they jumped straight up, and then they jumped into each other's arms. He should have thanked me for coming up with a way to get her to jump in his arms. However, he didn't see it that way.

I would've sat in my tank, licking these wounds. Instead, I wore its remnants as a necklace, courtesy of Older Brother Decree 149. Fort Lewis was a pretty explosive place.

★   ★   ★

IN '59, WE all bought red-lensed army goggles at the post surplus store. No one knew a good reason why we did it. Something told all of us that there would be a time when we would need them. On a hot summer day, as I was sitting on the curb with my fellow Red Goggle Club members, an army truck appeared in the neighborhood quite out of nowhere. We were eating the lunches our mothers had packed for us to take on our daily summer expeditions. They were very supportive of long expeditions away from the house.

"Smell this, does it smell funny?" My friend stuck his tuna fish sandwich in my nose.

I recoiled. "First of all, there's no humor involved here, especially with tuna fish."

The army truck turned into our housing area and thick, billowing clouds of insecticide began pouring from the back of the truck, obscuring everything in a dense white fog. Without so much as a word, we all knew exactly what to do.

Quickly, we scattered for home and shocked our mothers by our early arrival, for some belonged to the Naked Housewives Club. Mine belonged to the Keep Off the Couch Mothers Club.

"We didn't make sandwiches for you just so you would come home before dark!" they all said. They all belonged to the Keep the Kids Out of the House Club.

We reconvened mounted on our bikes and wearing the full regalia of the Red Goggle Club. Then we all sped off, riding behind the DDT truck, lost in the thick clouds of insecticide, flying our bikes in fantasy aerial combat.

We darted in and out of the cloud, following the truck around the post. We couldn't see a damn thing, and ran into just about every obstacle along the way. In the cloud, the only sense still functioning was hearing.

"Oouch!"

Clank!

"Oooof!"

Crunch!

"Owww!"

The hardest part was trying to hold your breath and miss running into another bike slashing across your path as they suddenly appeared out of the chemical fog. We were joyfully lost in the grand illusion of our lollipop red fighter pilot world, and sucking far too much DDT into our lungs. We were kids, so we were indestructible.

The red goggles had proved to be a smart investment in spite of my mother's assessment.

"What can you possibly want with those?"

I don't know if the DDT hurt me or not. Later I grew a mole that looked like a frog. I also found some surface arteries on my leg that formed a perfect "Z" for Zorro. I was proud of that, but never about my frog mole.

That night I went to the Dupont Summer Carnival at the junior high school just to see our teachers suspended over water tanks on the baseball toss platforms, or with their heads exposed for the shaving cream pie toss. There was a jail where for twenty-five cents you could have a warrant served on anybody, and they couldn't get out until someone put up bail. . .another twenty-five cents.

I took a town girl, from Dupont, a town of fourteen people. She was tall and appeared to be about twenty-five. She had a mouth that would have made Martha Rayes' look petite. She spotted some friends of hers and yelled out to them. . .

"Hey! Hey! HHHEEEYYYYYY!"

She looked like Joe E. Brown, and I couldn't help thinking my father could probably park his washing machine Buick in there. That's when I went up and paid to have myself thrown into carnival jail for the night.

She spotted some of my friends wearing their red-lensed goggles. Any insect that came near them immediately keeled over and spiraled to the ground.

"Hey! Hey! HHEEEYYYYYY! Will you guys quit having him put into jail!"

"We're not putting him in jail."

"Well, somebody is, every time I get him out, someone has him thrown back in again!"

It was starting to feel like I was with Daisy Mae at the Dogpatch Summer Carnival.

An aerial bomb went off outside, and everybody ran to look.

"Dave," I said.

Later, I sat in my tank remnants, wearing my goggles, and felt good about owning them both. Keeping myself in jail had cost me $4.50.

SS *AMERICA*

THE BUICK WAS NEVER the same after letting the Fort Sill motor pool mechanics have a go at it, probably due to improvising tank parts to get it running again, so my dad bought a '58 Mercury while we were stationed at Fort Lewis. It took a while for us to warm up to the car. Up until then, we had always been a Buick family. It was rather shocking to see a car parked in our driveway without the customary blinding chrome grill of a Buick. But since she was just as big as a Buick, scared the crap out of the birds and little children whenever my father drove it into the neighborhood and floated down the road just like a Buick, we all soon decided she was a Buick. . .without the extra chrome option.

I had an evening paper route that I delivered right after school using my American-style fat tire bike that they now sell for small fortunes as mountain bikes. Back then it was just a bike with fat tires and newspaper saddlebags hanging over the back fender. The saddlebags were cool, the newspaper was the *Tacoma News Tribune,* and the saddlebags had big, black outlined, orange letters. . .TNT. How could a kid not like that?

The newspapers were dropped off by truck in bundles. All of the paperboys sat on the curb rolling papers up and stacking them on end in the saddlebags. Then we could just ride along without stopping, reach back and pull out a tight paper cylinder and launch it in the general direction of the front door. Front doors have a wide definition for paperboys.

Every Sunday, the *Tacoma News Tribune* became a morning paper. The trucks dropped off the bundles early. . .five A.M. No one was up—the neighborhood was deathly quiet. The morning fog wove through the trees and the chill cut through our jackets. The birds stared at us like we were deranged, and we could tell from their looks that if they had a bed around, they'd be lying out in it like nobody's business at five A.M. on a Sunday morning.

It was impossible to roll up Sunday papers, or fit them all in the saddlebags. It required a little logistical planning and good balance, for whatever didn't fit in the saddlebags was suspended between our legs on top of the bike's crossbar.

After a few Sundays of dealing with this, my mother volunteered to drive the route with me. I eagerly accepted. There were some drawbacks to this arrangement.

"Are you going to wear *that* delivering the papers?"

"What?"

"Comb you hair before we leave the house."

"What?"

"Don't put the papers in the backseat like that, stack them neatly."

"What?"

"Zip up your jacket when you get out of the car."

"What?"

I endured all of this because it was cold out there, and I had been able to talk my mom into letting me drive the car a little. Yes, she let me drive the car a little. That alone was worth. . .

"Go back and put the paper closer to the door."

"What?"

So every Sunday, as we rounded the traffic circle at the farthest reaches of my paper route, my mother let me take the wheel. I eagerly anticipated this, and we happily conversed as I took the wheel.

"Slow down."

"What?"

"Slow down!"

"What?"

"You're accelerating too fast."

"What?"

"Watch out for the curb."

"What?"

"Don't jerk the wheel like that."

"What?"

"Stop."

"What?"

"Stop!!"

"What?"

The weeks passed without incident. Every Sunday I drove a little, and every Sunday my mother was able to say to me all the things she wanted to say to my father when he drove, but didn't dare. As I got better, I determined that the speed my mother was comfortable with was the same as that of the turtle family on our block, and I began to sneak the speed upwards.

"Slow down."

"What?"

"Watch out for the turn, you're going too fast!"

"What?"

She reached over and slammed her foot down on the brake pedal. Unfortunately for everyone, my foot was on the brake pedal, and I didn't feel another foot on top of mine. This was because her foot really landed on the accelerator, smashing it flat to the floor. The Mercury shot forward, all eight cylinders roaring like a bull elephant.

"Aaiiiieeeee! . . ." we shouted together.

The car did a 180-degree spin, jumped the curb, shot across the lawn, and headed straight for a house.

"Mom, you're on the accelerator!"

"What?"

"Get your foot off the accelerator!"

"What?"

The house was coming up fast.

"Mom! . . ."

"What?"

I pushed down the brake pedal with both feet and spun the steering wheel around. The Mercury turned sideways on the lawn, throwing open the back door, and delivering a hundred Sunday newspapers to the front stoop of the house.

Whooosssshhhh. . .

The sound of the papers sliding out of the backseat was followed by the frumping sound of them sliding up and burying the front door. The Mercury had come to a halt in the tire grooves we had dug into the lawn. The engine stalled, the dashboard warning lights came on, and we sat there in the quiet morning, surrounded by the fog and the birds who knew a couple of idiots when they saw them. The only sound was the front door of the house opening. A combat-helmeted subscriber peeked out.

"Hello? . . ."

★   ★   ★

SHORTLY AFTER THAT, my father told us at the dinner table that it was time for new orders.

"Since, we're already on the West Coast, then we're probably going to get orders for the Far East. . .maybe Japan."

Of course, when the orders came, they were for Germany. Never try to second-guess the army.

"It's because you mentioned Japan at dinner," said my mom. "If you hadn't, we'd be on our way right now."

"You wanted to go to Japan?"

"It would certainly be something different, we've already been to Germany, and we have to drive across the whole country again." She waggled a finger at me. "And this time, young man, keep your pants on in Oklahoma." Then she looked over at my father. "And there will be no more dogs."

"I think we've had enough dogs for a while," said my father. "I'm going to take a month's leave, so let's get everyone involved in planning a cross-country trip."

My mom brightened considerably. "We'll stop in Disneyland. . . .and Las Vegas. . .the Grand Canyon. . .and visit my family!"

Oh, Lord help us.

We mapped out our cross-country tour, going down the Pacific coast to Disneyland, across to Las Vegas, continuing on to Texas, up to Indiana, and due East to Connecticut.

We began early one morning, driving down the coast highway, dangerously close to the rocky edge. We three kids rotated the dreaded middle of the backseat. Dave read most of the time. However, he took breaks to continue perfecting his craft. . .the cauliflower fart. They were extremely pungent, close to a rotten head of cauliflower. He wouldn't let on as to how he was able to produce such a smell, but I suspected it must have something to do with his big bones. He was definitely proud of those farts, especially if he made my father open his driver's window to both air out the car and to check if the fumes had caused any of the paint to peel. My mother being such a straight-laced woman, wouldn't even acknowledge something was wrong, and tried to pretend we were passing through farm country, even through we were on the Pacific Coast Highway.

"Ah, good country air," she would say.

Good country air turned out to be something from a German honey wagon.

We stopped for a few days outside of Los Angeles, visiting Knott's Berry Farm, then Disneyland. I have a foggy memory of sitting in a fifties-style city diner somewhere in LA—a memory triggered whenever I hear Frank Sinatra songs from this period. This is the only thing I have ever found Frank Sinatra songs good for. Knott's Berry Farm was a bust, all that's left to memory is the name. I don't even remember the berries.

In Disneyland, my brother and I quickly ran to the motor speedway ride with visions of LeMans in our heads. It wasn't quite what we expected. The track was really a single lane with cars sitting over a guide rail, no racing. . .we were touring. I was in the car in front of him and decided to put as much distance between us as possible. I would have a symbolic victory of having the faster car.

"Catch me if you can, Dave!"

Unfortunately for Dave, his car was defectively slow. He couldn't go much faster than a crawl. I left him in the dust as he began an unwelcome metamorphous into the little old lady of the Disneyland motor speedway. Cars were packed bumper to bumper behind him. I laughed uproariously whenever I caught a glimpse of him as I crossed the overpasses and came out of the underpasses. He was the figure of abject despair, slumped in his seat with everyone behind him yelling and beeping. This had to be retribution for those cauliflower farts. Of course, if they had known he was capable of unleashing one of those babies, they would have kept a more respectful distance.

My father gave Dave the job of keeping track of the car mileage and fuel, computing the day's miles per gallon. I figured this was just a trick, an unsuccessful attempt to divert his attention as a preemptive strike against any cauliflower bombs. I can't tell you how many times good country air came our way, and it gave new meaning to "see the USA in your Chevrolet," even if we were in a Mercury.

We arrived at Las Vegas and feasted. I had never seen so many long tables full of food, and it was free. . .really free, and it was everywhere you went, as long as the place had "nugget" in its name.

That night, I privately went out to the motel's playground, not wanting anyone to see me, or to know that I still liked playing on playgrounds. I became a little overzealous on the spring suspended rocking horse, and the steel ear came up and conked me in the forehead. I fell to the ground. . .and fell unconscious. I awoke covered with blood and staggered back to the motel room.

"Oh Lord! What have you done to yourself now!?" screamed my mother.

"I tripped in the dark and something hit me. I wasn't playing on the rocking horse, honest."

"Didn't you see Dave out there? He went to play in the playground."

"What? . . ."

"You're going to need to go to the hospital and get a stitch."

Old war-horse dad wouldn't hear of it. "Just put a Band-Aid on it and get back to the front," he said.

I still have the scar that didn't need a stitch right over my left eye.

★　★　★

WE MADE IT to Connecticut after leveling half of the Midwest with cauliflower bombs, and just in time to participate in one of the unique rituals of a service family's life. . .Name That Relative!

Aunts. . .uncles. . .cousins. . .they all can play!

We assembled for the game at my Uncle Fred's house, since his was the largest.

"George. . .you were only this high the last time I saw you. Do you know who I am?"

"My father's parole officer?"

"What? . . ."

My mother grabbed my arm. "Stop it, before I get mad."

That would certainly be a good time to stop.

"See if you can recognize anyone," said an uncle. This is a variation of the same game. Instead of asking me who they are, I get to pick someone out and go for it.

"Uncle Joe?"

"No, that's the mailman."

I looked around and pointed again.

"Uncle Joe?"

"No, he's here to work on the sewer lines."

"Try someone who's actually in the house." A game hint from. . .

"Uncle Joe?"

"No. . .I'm Aunt Jenny."

My brother hooked up with a cousin about his age and they made a break for it, escaping into the night. After misidentifying everything and everybody I held up my hands and announced. . .

"Listen everybody, I'm willing to admit that I don't have the faintest idea who any of you are, so. . ." Before the sentence was half out of my mouth, my mother grabbed me and whisked me off to the side.

"What are you saying? This is your family."

"I thought *you* were my family."

"We are. . .and so are they, these are my brothers and sisters, and their families, so behave."

"Don't any of them belong to Dad?"

"His whole family martini'd themselves to death years ago."

"Gee, I bet they never had a decent salad dressing. . ."

"What?"

"Do I have to keep guessing who everybody is?"

"Yes. They look forward to it. They've waited three years for our return."

"I don't think they were really waiting for our return." Especially since there wasn't going to be a bottle of booze left within a ten-block area once my father got through with the place.

"Shut up. . .and be nice. Now go out there and be with your family."

I returned to the main room as my sister was trying to guess who was pinching her cheeks. . .all of them.

"Uncle John?"

"He's in Indiana. That's three down and four to go."

"Uncle Bill?"

"I'm going to turn all the cards over, little lady, because you've been such a good contestant on Name That Relative. I'm Uncle Adam!"

When the ordeal was finally over, I still didn't know who anybody was, but I figured it was more important that they knew who they were. Since they all seemed fairly confident about that, I comfortably forgot everyone again, thereby setting up the next Name That Relative game three years hence. We were split up and I was shuffled off to bunk at Aunt Jenny's house. My sister got to stay with Aunt Sophie, which was considered the plum assignment. Dave went off to cousin Obbie's house. I wanted to hang out with my brother and our cousin, but they wanted no part of me.

"Why is he called Obbie?" I asked my aunt.

"Because your brother called him that when he was very little, before you were even born, and he's had the name ever since."

I bet Obbie can tell you a drawback or two of playing Name That Relative!

On the morning we were to leave for New York to catch our ship to Germany, we assembled for a farewell breakfast. At the kitchen table, I sat between my brother and my cousin Obbie. I had been eavesdropping on their conversations ever since we had arrived. . .sneaking around and listening to them when they thought they were alone. Now, sitting at the kitchen table surrounded by the entire extended family, I decided to impress everyone with a word I had heard the two of them use. I can tell you now that you should never call your aunt a douchebag. . .not even Aunt Douchebag. And this after having called her Uncle Joe.

"I think we can assume that you're out of Jenny's will," said my mom. "And by the way, you don't have an Uncle Joe."

I left Bristol, disinherited, and we were off to New York in another fog of good country air. This was pretty typical of all our family visits to our hometown. I did manage to accidentally shoot my cousin Judy in the back with a BB gun on one return trip. My mother just looked at me with a tired expression in her eyes.

"Couldn't you just have called her douchebag? . . ."

★   ★   ★

THE FIFTIES WERE winding down as we set sail from New York on the SS *America*. She was a large and graceful ocean liner. We left the States over the 1959 Christmas holidays for a winter crossing of the Atlantic. This tells you all you need to know about how things generally go in my life. I'm forever going to Texas in July or Chicago in January. Two days out to sea and we ran into a winter Atlantic storm. Red felt ropes were strung across all the open hallways and stairwells so you could make a last frantic stab at grabbing hold as you were tossed around by the ship's pitching and rolling. The outside decks were placed off limits, but that didn't stop my brother and me from sneaking out there and leaning into the gale. I've never heard wind sound like that—it had gone past a howl and was now a deafening scream as we stepped onto the deck. We were able to spread out our arms and lean forward and not fall on our faces—our full weight was completely supported by its force. I knew we had no choice about when we went to Europe, we were at the army's mercy and this was their little joke at our expense, but I wondered what all the other people were doing out there with their arms spread in the wind.

There were three separate classes onboard ship, which meant three separate bars to my father, for that was his main hobby. He had cleaned out the town of Bristol of their booze, and now he would drain the SS *America*. My brother and I wandered the ship at will, and crossed between the different travel classes pretty effortlessly. Only a flimsy wooden gate marked the boundaries, and you could easily slide under it. We checked out the different swimming pools, game rooms, and lounges. We were never stopped or questioned by anyone, except when we returned to our own staterooms in the first-class section.

"Hey, what are you two doing in first class?"

"This is our room, honest."

"Who do you think the two of you are fooling? Get back in steerage before I tell the captain and have the both of you put off the ship in the Azores."

The Azores? Later in life I found out the Azores were one of many places known to the service as Bumfuck, Egypt.

Our waiter was a foreign guy who constantly smiled and mispronounced everything. He was great. It was like playing *I've Got A Secret* at every meal. You never knew what you were

going to get. I ordered peaches and got pigeon. Dave ordered
ginger ale and got ginger wafers. . .small shriveled orange disks.

"Bllaaaagghh. . .here try one."

"Do I look that stupid?"

"Yes."

Hmmmm. . .he could be trying to fool me with the old
"just don't throw me in the briar patch" scam. Would they put
something on the menu that was bllaaaagghh? So. . .he just
wants all of these for himself. . .

"Bllaaaagghh."

I am that stupid.

I spit it out into my napkin. He laughed uproariously. "What
an idiot."

"These taste like soap."

"I don't think they're as good as soap, certainly Ivory tastes
better. . .these are more like Tide. . .Tide Wafers. . .yep, these
should be on the menu as Tide Wafers." Dave took a handful
and put them into his pocket.

"What are you doing?"

"These may come in handy."

If you knew Dave, then you knew what he meant by
handy. . . *"Hey kid, want some candy?"*

Through it all our waiter smiled like he was doing a great
job of serving us, like we were the royal family of Siam. We
figured that was where he was from.

Every meal it was the same—we ordered—he brought out
his own interpretation—we ate.

"Bllaaaagghh."

"Bllaaaagghh."

"Bllaaaagghh."

"Bllaaaagghh."

"Bllaaaagghh."

We finally just pointed, but that really took the fun out of
it, however the quality of the meals improved immensely.

In mid-Atlantic the weather calmed and got downright
balmy. We were able to go out on deck and try out some shipboard games. There's a bizarre form of tennis played on passenger ships. It's called deck tennis. It consists of what looks
like a small volleyball court, with a high net and a rubber ring
about the size of a small pie plate. Once you get over the fact
that this game has absolutely nothing to do with the real game
of tennis, you can get down to the business of dealing out a
crushing defeat to someone. . .like your brother.

There were no rackets, you simply threw the ring over the
net where your opponent would catch it before it struck the
ground, and then return it back over the net.

Well, we started out with a few stray shots that landed on a passenger reading her book in a deck chair, and ringed a drink as it dangled invitingly from another's hand. Then we settled down into a nice little vicious game of kill your brother.

The shots and returns were coming fast and furious with pirouette catches and jai alai-style rocket launches into the back corner of the court. We had gathered a good little following of deck tennis groupies admiring our style when I sent a nasty bullet to the opposite corner for a sure winner. Out of the blue, a human streak made a last-second desperate grab at this missile, and to the disbelief and awe of the entire crowd, snatched the ring out of the air, and in one continuous motion, still talked about on the promenade decks of all the passenger ships on the Atlantic route, my brother made the first triple layout spinning return move with a full twist ever seen on the outdoor circuit. The ring shot back with a mind-boggling velocity that drew gasps from the audience. What a grab! What a shot! It would have made deck tennis history if he had actually been facing my side of the court when he fired off his return.

Unfortunately, he was facing the Atlantic Ocean, and the ring hurtled off the side of the ship as if it had been shot from a cannon. We never actually saw it hit the water; the ocean waves had whipped up a frothing brew, and we lost sight of it shortly after it left the deck. I believe it was next picked up on a NASA tracking station.

We all stood in silent admiration, except for the ship's athletic director, who was noticeably dismayed as the ring settled into a low Earth orbit.

"Dave, I have to give you the point. That was just beautiful," I said to my brother. A shot worthy of bicycle hockey.

The crowd nodded in agreement and broke into spontaneous applause. Soon, several games of launch the deck tennis ring into the Atlantic Ocean started. None of them, however, ever developed into the combination of ballet grace and brute strength of our original.

The athletic director was going crazy, giving us murderous looks in between scrambling around trying to recover his deck tennis rings, but it was no use. Before the cruise was three days old there wasn't a deck tennis ring to be found on the entire ship.

There is a valuable life lesson here that ranks right up there with "never buy anything from the back of a comic book"—it's not whether you win or lose, it's how you look when you win or lose.

We moved on to shipboard basketball, and left a trail of floating balls in the ship's wake. This was not our fault either.

The ship's sports director banished the both of us, and we were reduced to attempting to play Ping-Pong on the rolling promenade deck. The ball would violently jump at odd angles as the deck pitched back and forth, and would invariably miss the table and end up under a passing shoe. Unfortunately, there was also someone in the shoe at the time, and the ball was crushed flat without even as much as a "howdy do" being exchanged. When we returned the package of flattened Ping-Pong balls that had been jealousy allotted to us, the director developed an instant tick in his left eye and mumbled some unflattering comments under his breath. We were finally banished from any area on the ship that had anything to do with sports-related projectiles.

After that, my days consisted mostly of ordering chicken sandwiches and Cokes from the upper deck pantry. When I found out that everything was free, I constantly called the pantry for chicken sandwiches and Cokes at the most ungodly hours. Then I set out to find a shipboard romance, which was in short supply for someone who just turned thirteen. At the request of the entire upper-deck kitchen galley crew, the ship's purser introduced me to a girl my age. Someone had tipped him off about the swimming instructor at Fort Myer, and I know who. To the general amusement of all, I soon became preoccupied with acting stupid around her for the rest of the voyage. By the time we docked in Germany, I had found no romance, but had consumed 114 chicken sandwiches and 323 Cokes.

No matter what time it was, or what passenger class we were in, we always seemed to run into The Colonel at different lounge bars. No matter how fast we ran, there he was, at their bar. He'd be in the second-class lounge, and we would scamper under the tourist-class barrier, and there he would be in the tourist-class lounge. We'd dash under the second-class barrier, and back across the first-class barrier, and there he'd be in the first-class lounge. I have no idea how he was able to do it, or how he managed to get under the gates. He was serious about his hobby. He had been left pretty much unsupervised himself, which was a separate problem all its own.

My mother had boarded the ship in New York and immediately set to work being seasick. Before the first blast of the ship's horn, she had become an invalid, and remained that way for the entire six-day voyage. They would bring her out of her cabin in the morning, and fetch her at night. She was placed in a lounge chair on deck, bundled in blankets, and immobilized for the day. The Colonel held court at all the lounges while she waited for a crew member to cart her back to the cabin in the evenings. The ship's doctor spent his days at her side. Two adjoining deck chairs were permanently assigned to them, complete with nametags. He tried every cure in the ship's store, but he had no idea with whom he was dealing, and my mother successfully fended off his every attempt. He has since become a well-known physician on the strength of publishing several medical papers, all thanks to my mom.

As the ship finally docked in Germany, we waited patiently by the gangplank for Mom to be carried out and for Dave to show up.

"Do you know where your brother is?" asked my dad.

"No, I haven't seen him for a while."

"Aaaiiiiiieeeee! . . ." A screaming kid came streaking by us, a Tide Wafer spit into his hand, and hell bent on finding the closest bathroom.

"I think Dave will be along shortly."

Sure enough, there he came, his pockets a few wafers lighter.

We were the last ones down the gangplank. We were delayed by the throngs of drinking buddies my father had acquired, and the need to have some of the crew carry my mother off the ship. They struggled down the narrow walkway, almost losing their grip on her deck chair. She had spent so much time in it that it had become permanently affixed to her. That would have been a sight, Mom dumped into the North Sea.

We followed along behind her with my father bringing up the rear. He stopped frequently to return the salutes and choruses of good wishes from the legions that lined the deck railing. They all seemed to know The Colonel. When my mom was finally placed on solid ground, she was up and fit as a fiddle immediately. This was short lived however, as soon as we got into a waiting auto, she instantly became carsick. The ship's doctor took notes furiously.

We went on to our new quarters, while The Colonel took care of the higher priorities. . .

"Where's the officer's club?"

NICK FURSTAYEN

JANUARY—1960. I STOOD dockside in Germany with my family. The fifties were over, and here I was. . .dressed like I thought I would always be dressed. I hadn't yet figured out that evolution also applied to me. I knew it meant that monkeys would eventually be making their own martinis, but they would be doing it dressed like me, with greased hair, wearing pegged pants with skinny little belts, and they'd have dresser drawers full of white socks in their split-level banana tree houses.

That was the world. It would not change. However, my parents said. . .

"You won't feel the same way or do the same things as you get older."

"Does this mean you'll stop drinking, Dad?"

"Well. . .er. . .that. . .er. . .go play outside."

"Gee, you're right. . .things do change. . .I no longer go play outside."

I went outside for a cigarette instead.

Evolution for humans, as it turns out, is called fashion, and we were greeted by everyone asking what was new in the States. It turned out we were supposed to have brought all the latest and greatest in evolution from back home. Why don't they tell you these things before you've gone ahead and sailed an entire ocean without bringing the necessary evolutionary facts and figures along with you? Everyone depended on the new arrivals to catch them up on what was going on in the USA. The responsibility was too much. I wasn't prepared. I was only thirteen. I only knew how to smoke. I needed my tank. Help.

Everyone depended on *my* family to find out what was new. What a hoot! Imagine anyone coming to us for styling tips. Can you imagine a whole town going around looking like my brother and me? We were Sears people, and if we went up-scale, it meant J.C. Penney.

"Everyone's wearing Mohawks now. . .and knickers," my brother told them.

"So how come you aren't?"

"We can't afford them. . .and these are now very popular, faithful copies of Captain Kangaroo's suit in big bone sizes. . .would you like some candy?"

Luckily for everyone, another family arrived within a week, taking the heat off of us.

"Why is everyone wearing Captain Kangaroo's wardrobe?" they asked.

Our new quarters were in a European-style apartment complex called Im Engamoor, which is German for European-style apartment complex. We were on the first floor, in a four-bedroom unit. The stairwell had an automated light switch on each floor, the kind you pushed. The lights came on for exactly one minute, which was just enough time to fumble around for a key and then be plunged back into total darkness at just about the same time you started looking for the keyhole. There were maid's quarters on the top floor, one small room for each apartment. Adjoining these chambers was a large communal playroom, completely empty.

"Get back down here and help unpack," yelled my mom up the stairwell.

"Okay, Okay."

To preempt any arguments over who got what bedroom, my father had already assigned us quarters by the time we got back downstairs.

"There are rooms on the top floor," I told my mother.

"I know."

"Can I live there?"

"No."

"How about me?" asked Dave.

"No."

"Maybe next year?" I asked.

"Maybe."

The maid's room remained empty for three years.

"Look, we have a phone!" yelled my sister. She raced over to the desk and picked up the receiver. She wanted to call somebody. . .anybody, but she didn't know somebody. . .anybody. She was so desperate she would have called me.

"Forget it," said Mom. "Every phone call over here costs money, even the local ones, so there will be no using the phone."

"Ever?"

"Ever, unless it's an emergency. . .or you care to pay for the call out of your allowance."

The phone became a paperweight.

We all began to unpack. My room faced the front of the building, which was on a large circular roadway that went through the complex. There were eight large apartment buildings that ringed the road. Periodically an army bus came through and stopped near our building. I could just about see the bus stop if I stuck my head out the window, which is what I was doing when I saw this kid strolling down the sidewalk, walking his dog. He wasn't much bigger than the dog, and he was wearing a red satin jacket with a map of Germany embroidered on the back with a "You are here" label sewn next to the city of Bremerhaven. He came into our building, walked up to our front door, and introduced himself. This was a ballsy move in my book. I met everyone I knew at school, and would never go to their house and introduce myself. Only Eddie Haskell would do that. . .and why did Wally hang out with that jerk anyway?

My mother got nervous when she saw the dog.

"This isn't a delivery, is it?"

"Delivery?"

"My husband didn't order a dog, did he?"

"This is my dog."

I knew it wasn't a dog delivery. . .there weren't three of them.

He asked if I'd like to take a look around the neighborhood. There was something suspicious about all of this.

"Okay," I said. "But I'm telling you right now, I've got my eye on you."

"My name's Ted."

"Did you say Ed?"

"No. . .Ted."

"Mine's George."

"Sorry."

"Tell me about it."

We walked out of the neighborhood, and when we did we also left all that was American. I was now in the middle of Germany, my first real look since those early years of avoiding walking over the cesspool cover. Everyone had roofs again.

Ted's purposeful stride had a destination in mind, which was good because I was just wandering around behind him and staring at everything. Boy, this certainly looked different. . .the cars, the streets, the buildings, the clothes they wore, and especially the signs, all the signs. . .street signs, store signs, signs on the sides of the trucks. The roadway looked different, they even changed the curbs.

"What's with them? I think they have a different way of doing everything," I said to myself.

"Come on," said Ted. "Quit staring at the cobblestones."

I started feeling a little conspicuous. . .like I was some kind of foreigner. Ted moved along like a native. Next to the housing area was a train station. It wasn't the main train station for the city, just a satellite commuter stop on the line, but it was large enough to contain a German bar. . .a gasthaus. There were two sides to it, each with a separate entrance, and they were equivalent to upper class and lower class. Ted knew exactly where we belonged and marched straight into the lower-class side. I peeked into upper class and saw white tablecloths with candles on each table. Our side had solid wooden benches with huge oak tables, and the only tablecloth was tied around the bartender's waist.

Ted marched right up to the bar, got two beers, and we both sat down at a table in the corner. I was sure the police would be coming in at any moment.

Well, I had been in the country all of a few hours and there I was sitting at the table. . .swacked, with a beer in front of me, while Ted was playing a German version of a slot machine. He had a beer in one hand and a cigarette dangling from the other.

I would be dead in three years.

Ted returned me to where he had found me, and pulled the Eddie Haskell routine with my mother once again, diverting her attention from my slightly wobbly condition. My estimation of the real Eddie went up immensely, and I began to wonder just what he and Wally were up to while the rest of us were busy watching the Beaver.

Later, that same day, my brother grabbed me. Older brothers are allowed to grab you whenever they want something. This is not reciprocal—grabbing an older brother only ensures an Older Brother Pounding.

"Come on, let's explore the city. There's a route bus we can catch."

"Well, it's obvious you haven't found any friends yet if you're asking me to come along, but I've already seen it. Besides, I don't know if I can, I'm not feeling real steady."

"Come on, let's catch the bus, it runs every half hour."

So I wobbled out the door again. The American base in Bremerhaven was actually a series of small sites scattered throughout the city. The housing areas, PX, commissary, main base, and the high school were dispersed at the four corners. There were three separate housing complexes, one for officers, one for NCOs, and one for government employees. The main military complex was located outside of town, almost on the coast. The route bus connected everything.

"Hey, Dave, remember when I got lost at Fort Myer, after you gave me a nickel. . .and told me to get lost."

"Fondly."

"Well, this time you've done it to yourself. . .and for free."

We had left as explorers, navigating through the city. And now we were stuck on the bus, for once we got on, we didn't know where to get off.

"Where are we?" my brother asked the driver.

"Was?"

"Vaas?" my brother repeated.

"He said 'vaas,'" I repeated.

"I know what he said. . .it's like he's speaking some other language or something."

"Try Greek on him. . .heh. . .heh."

"Shut up."

"I think he's German."

"What's he doing driving a U.S. Army bus, if he's German? Answer me that."

"I think it's his job. I think the bus drivers are German."

"That's absurd. Hey! Are you German?"

"Ja, Ich bein ein Deutscher."

"Well, you may be right about this. Hey! Do you remember where we got on? Can you get us back there?" asked my brother.

"Nicht verstehen."

"Hmmm. . .," said my brother. "Sounds like we got on at some place called Furstayen."

"Maybe that's his name. . .Nick Furstayen."

"I don't think so. I didn't ask him his name."

"Will he tell us when we get back to Furstayen?"

"I don't know. Hey! Nick! Can you tell us when you get to Furstayen?"

"Was?"

"'Vaas,'. . .again with the 'vaas.'"

"Maybe that means yes."

"Could be. Hey!" My brother signaled him okay and yelled out. "Okay!"

The driver smiled back and yelled, "Okay!"

"We're all set," said my brother.

A half-hour later.

"You'd think we'd have gotten to Furstayen by now." At each stop my brother asked again, "Furstayen?"

"Okay!" yelled the driver.

"I'm starting to think there's something fishy about this whole Furstayen business."

We tried to recognize something. . .like where we lived. Finally, I saw the train station with the gasthaus where Ted had taken me.

"Here, Dave. We get off here."

"How do you know?"

"I was here today."

"You were here today?"

"Yeah. We live right down there."

"How could you have been here already? . . ."

"I went with Ted while you were unpacking."

"Who the hell is Ted? . . ."

The bus stopped next to the train station and we jumped off. My brother looked up and down the street and then said to the driver.

"See you later, Nick."

"Ja, Okay!"

Drunk and lost on the first day. I would be dead in two years.

★ ★ ★

OUR PHILCO TELEVISION sat in the corner for a few weeks after we had settled into the apartment, ignored and covered with a tablecloth. Then my father came home and said. . .

"We're going to have the TV converted."

"To what religion?" said Dave.

"To Catholic, of course," I said.

"Are you two through?"

Dave and I looked at each other, then nodded.

"All right then, I'm going to have the set converted to the European standard, so we can watch television."

We all thought this sounded like a good idea, and then we promptly forgot all about it, since conversion of televisions takes just about as long as conversions to the Catholic religion. Then one day. . .

"Someone come out here and help me bring in the set."

"You mean it's really here?" asked Mom.

"You bet, and it looks brand new," answered my father.

"Why does it look new?"

"I don't know, they cleaned everything up, and it looks just like the day we bought it at Sears."

We all helped bring it in, five people on the five corners. . .er. . .five people on the four corners. So. . .someone was definitely cheating on this deal.

We all sat right in front of the screen while my father finished attaching the antenna.

"Okay. . ."

The screen flickered to life and there was the Lone Ranger riding across the German countryside.

"Seems like the programs are a little old."

"Sssshhhhh. . ."

Tonto walked up to the Lone Ranger. . .

"Guten Tag, Kemosabe. Was ist los?"

We were stunned.

"'Vaas'. . .again with the 'vaas.'"

"I guess Tonto is speaking Indian," I said.

"I'm starting to think there's something fishy about this," said Dave.

"Wie gehtes, Tonto? . . ."

"The Lone Ranger is speaking Indian too."

"Stupid."

"Husky."

" . .*haben sie grunden Black Bart's Gang?"*

"Boy, I think Black Bart is in for a big surprise."

One by one we drifted out of the room. By the end of the week the set was back covered with a tablecloth, and a flower vase had been placed on top.

GERMANY SURRENDERS

As AUSPICIOUS AS THE start was, it slowed down immediately into a survivable pace. Dave got his first nickname, at least it's the only one I remember him ever having. . .Bear. My suggestion that we call him Big Bones was summarily dismissed without receiving due consideration, unless an Older Brother Pounding can be interpreted as due consideration. Bear was pretty accurate, he really did resemble a bear. He was big—six foot, five inches and roly-poly—but no one thought of him as fat, everyone now thought of him as Bear. Even when he went over three hundred pounds, you still didn't think of him as fat, you thought of him as just a larger bear. . .Big Bones the Bear.

My brother managed to get himself a girlfriend right away, and felt comfortable enough in his new peer group to begin completely ignoring me—and this after I stood by his side through the entire Nick Furstayen debacle. He resumed another hobby of his. . .derogatory names. Dave was capable of charming the birds out of the trees. He was also just as capable of poisoning them all as well. Me? I had to make do with just being extremely good looking.

Dave was quite good at coming up with derogatory names. He worked hard at it, because they had to have some basis in fact, and be memorable. I had a habit of licking my fingertips whenever they got dry, apparently I was unaware of hand lotion, and I don't think I would have used it anyway. Lotions were something my mother plastered on herself every evening until she could've slipped through our keyhole without the stairwell light even getting close to going out, and also qualify her as a member nation of OPEC. I'm sure if I had used lotion, I would have left myself open for far worse abuse. My brother took to calling me chocolate fingers, just to annoy me, and it worked.

But he did leave me alone most of the time, because I wasn't exactly defenseless when it came to retaliation, as Elephant Girth found out (a neat skirting of both the overweight and fat prohibitions), and to which he retorted. . .

"You sniveling little shit." This lacked his usual flair, but he made up for it by administering an Older Brother Pounding as only Elephant Girth could.

Still, it was fun to see what Dave would think up. Others endured far worse, as Sally Smelly Belly soon found out. One can only wonder what the Older Guys were doing to have made this discovery. I doubt Sally thought any of this was fun.

It was all kind of a marvel for me to watch him and his friends. I was in the teen club, but I really wanted to be in the high school. They just did things that made me long to be one of them, like taking a drag off a cigarette, kissing their girl-friend, and then she exhales the smoke. I know this sounds pretty gross now, but I thought it was sensuous, and it con-jured up all kinds of images in my fertile little mind of what else was going on in the high school. It made my jaw drop wide open in astonishment.

I had to suffer through the last part of eighth grade, where Easter egg hunts were still considered a big deal.

"We're going to high school. We're going to high school," we chanted as the school year ended. "We'll need lots of ciga-rettes."

It was summer, Germany now felt like my native country, my friends felt like my native brothers, the country was almost completely recovered from the war, and, with a few notable exceptions, there were roofs for everyone. The dollar was strong, and Americans were mostly a wonderment. Today it's hard to believe it was ever that way.

Just off the coast there was one of those roof exceptions, and a very powerful attraction. . .the North Sea bunkers. I don't know if these mammoth structures still exist, but back when roofs for the towns came first, the bunkers were just sealed off with barbed wire, and signs posted to warn off the curi-ous. . .meaning me, and any of my native brothers. If they thought a sign was going to keep us away then they didn't know we couldn't read German. Still, in hindsight, it was a terrifi-cally stupid idea, right up there with bicycle hockey. Stupid ideas happen to be one of my specialties.

One bright, sunny, summer day, we organized ourselves for an all-day expedition to the coast. We took the bus to the main base, and headed out across the salt marsh flats to the North Sea. Man, we were excited! The stories of what was in those bunkers had been making the rounds from the day I arrived, tales of basement levels full of Nazi treasure. . .helmets, uniforms, guns, and. . .skeletons. Not that I was looking for a skeleton myself, but almost everything connected with the Nazis was banned in Germany, including Nazi skeletons, which immediately increased their worth and desirability a thousandfold. I had grandiose visions of finding, with a little luck, a helmet, but I would settle for our expedition's Holy Grail. . .anything with the swastika insignia.

Finding a diamond would have been easier than finding a swastika. The Germans had been pretty thorough in erasing anything Nazi, and its mere mention caused the kind of public hysteria we reserve for sex in the United States. So naturally I wanted the real thing.

It seemed like we trekked across salt marshes for most of the day, but then the majestic skyline of the bunker suddenly appeared dead ahead, looking like some medieval fortress, a gray and black stone castle from Translyvania. We came upon a group of small support buildings on the shore and stopped to rest. One couldn't help but admire the bunker looming in the coastal waters. It was huge, a concrete island resting off the coast. No bridge, no road, and completely cutoff from the mainland.

Wait a minute. . .no road?

How do we get out there? We can't be swimming! I wasn't prepared for anything like that.

"How do we get out there? I'm not gonna swim."

"We don't have to swim. There's a tunnel that leads right from these buildings to the bunker. . .but it's flooded."

"I'm curious to see why you think that changes anything."

"You can see the top of the tunnel just barely sticking out of the water. We can walk over on the top."

"So, what you're really saying is. . .we're swimming."

The six of us stared out at the bunker, vainly looking for the top of the tunnel, and chattering away.

"How'd you find this out?"

"My older brother told me. . ."

"Oh, that's just great. . .I've had experience with what older brothers tell you."

"No, this is true, he's been out there."

"Hey, is that a fence out there in the water? . . ."

"What's that boat doing out there?"

"What boat? . . ."

"What fence? . . ."

"Who's got my canteen?"

"Is this low or high tide?"

"It better be high tide."

"That's a police boat!"

"That is a fence. . .and it's on the tunnel."

"I tried to tell you about older brothers, but nooooo. . .you didn't want to listen. They're probably watching us right now, just waiting to see us fall off that fence. . ."

"And get picked up by the police boat. . ."

"Come on, we're wasting time."

We deftly danced along the top of the tunnel, trying to keep our balance on the slippery bricks, and attempting to keep our feet out of the lapping water. About halfway out from shore, a chain-link fence topped with barbed wire blocked our path. A sign was posted.

ACHTUNG! VERBOTEN!

"Can anyone read this?"

"Yeah, this word means attention. The second one, I think, is something to do with those boats."

We looked at him incredulously.

"Where'd you learn your German?"

"I don't know German."

"No shit."

"What do we do now?"

"We climb around it."

"I knew I was going swimming."

"We have to go around."

"Let's just quit talking about it and do it."

So we did. . .six human flies climbing around the fence and back onto the tunnel on the other side. As I struggled to keep my feet from slipping, I saw myself trying to do this again on the way back. . .and I also saw myself going for a swim.

The bunker had gotten a lot bigger now that we were getting close, bicycle hockey was small potatoes compared to this stupid idea. You could feel the danger. It was making me nervous, and the closer we got the more I thought this was a <u>really</u> bad idea, the next level up. I'm sure this thought was crossing everyone's mind, but no one was saying anything, and I wasn't going to look like a chicken. I would rather die first. . .

"Whew. . .scary, huh?" said Ted.

"I'm glad you said something. Are we sure we want to do this?"

"If we go back now, imagine what names your brother is going to come up with. . .just ask Sally Smelly Belly."

"This is all Dave's fault," said Chocolate Fingers.

We pressed on, our enthusiasm left behind by the fence. The tunnel ended just below a stone staircase straight out of a Dracula movie. Just stone steps going up, no railings, no nothing. Now I was really nervous.

"I am too big to do this, you need to be a small mountain goat."

"You can tell that to your brother."

Chocolate Fingers hugged the wall and started up.

My feet felt big and clumsy. I was having an intimate relationship with the concrete wall, kind of flattened against the surface, slowly slithering along like a slug.

"What are you doing?"

"What does it look like?"

"Well, you got me on that. . .is this some kind of erotic dance?"

"No."

"Your crotch itches?"

"No. . .I'm slithering."

"Really. . .and you want to do this? I'm sure there's a reason, but I don't think I want to know."

"I just don't want to fall off these stairs."

"Well, pick up the speed a little."

"Hey, we can climb in right here!" The excited voice of discovery came from in front of me.

"Good, because the stairs end up here!"

"At the top?"

"No, they just end."

Oh God. . .

"We should have brought some flashlights, it's kind of dark in here."

Oh God. . .

"Go in, go in. . .we can't stay on these steps."

"Speak for yourself." This came out somewhat muffled, seeing as my cheek was pressed up against the wall.

The stairs did indeed just stop. The stairs ended. . .and the wall ended, they had both been blown off by the same explosion that had left a jagged hole in the bunker, a hole we now used to get inside. We stood on a stone floor, light filtered down through the cracked and battered ceiling. Water dripped down the walls and everything felt clammy.

"This is great."

"Let's get to the top."

"Which way?"

"Follow the light."

We followed the fragmented light to a stairwell that went down, into blackness.

"See. . ."

"No, I can't. . .wish I could."

". . .I told you we needed flashlights."

Thank God we didn't have any flashlights.

We backtracked and found a stairwell going up, but a caved-in wall blocked it. I was ready to get the hell out of there right then, and for a brief joyous moment it looked like it might be the only thing we could do. I started to feel relieved.

"Hey, we can skinny through here. . . I see a hallway."

"Let's break up into teams and play hide and seek."

"Hold on, let's get to the top first."

We squeezed over and under broken concrete and stood in a wide hallway.

"This must be Main Street."

I wasn't noticing. I was busy trying to remember the way back out of there.

"We need to mark the way out," I said.

"How?"

"We can use one of these pieces of concrete."

I picked up a fist-sized chunk and scratched an arrow on the wall.

"You got it going the wrong way. . .we're going this way."

"It's pointing the way out, not the way in."

"Oh."

"Hey, look somebody's already drawn arrows."

"Well, now what?"

"I'll make ours with two lines."

"Have you done this before? Who are you? Daniel Boone?"

"I saw this in 'Mark Trail.' This is what he would have done. . .and he would also have brought along an otter. Wait until my mom hears that something from the Sunday comics was useful. . ."

". . .wait till your mom hears you were in here, and from you no less. . ."

". . .ah. . .I guess she'll just have to go on thinking the comics are a waste of time."

"Can you imagine getting lost and having to spend the night in here?"

We pressed on, walking down Main Street. The ceiling was intact, which was good, but no light was coming in, which was bad. The hallway just led into blackness so deep that it didn't matter whether your eyes were open or shut. Behind us the hallway was brighter, which was good, but that was because the ceiling had collapsed, which was bad. It hadn't broken up—it was in one piece and sloped gradually to the floor like a ramp.

"Which way?"

We looked back and forth between the two directions. I wasn't going to leave it up to these guys, and spoke up.

"I can think of a couple of reasons not to head into the dark. I think it's important we see where we're walking, just in case there are more stairs that lead to nowhere. And we won't be able to see the arrows any longer. Let's head toward the light."

"Hmmmmm. . .," they said. *Mark Trail may not be as stupid as he looks.* There was agreement that this sounded like a good idea.

We followed the corridor, passing evenly spaced doorways on both sides of the passage, until the ceiling became so low it was impossible to continue. When we could go no further, we started looking into each of the rooms. Most were in ruins, they had become concrete rubble storage rooms.

"What do you think they used these rooms for?"

"I don't know. . ."

"Barracks maybe. . ."

"Maybe we'll find a skeleton."

I had forgotten about the skeletons.

One of the rooms had enough open space for us to get inside. It was one of the last doorways before the ceiling met the corridor floor. We had to crawl on our bellies to squeeze through. Once inside, there was bright sunlight coming in, and we crawled over to a gaping hole. There we sat looking at a catastrophe, and at the reason why the ceiling had caved in. . .the whole top of the bunker had been hit squarely in the middle. The top had completely collapsed to the bottom, but inexplicably had remained mostly intact. It looked like a concrete whirlpool that descended into an opening in the center, then dropped into a jagged dark pit. We sat around the opening, looking down into a caldron of broken concrete and twisted steel support cables that snarled back up at us. It must have been a hundred feet down into the abyss.

"Looks pretty nasty."

"If you're looking for skeletons, I bet there's plenty down there."

"No thank you, I'm happy sitting right here."

The collapsed roof had exposed other rooms that ringed the broken rim, all with similar views overlooking the pit below us.

"I think we can get to the top from here. We can step onto this ledge and scoot up."

"You're nuts."

"The slope isn't too bad."

Before anyone really had time to think about it, one kid jumped up and scampered up the collapsed roof and stood on the top of the rim. Then a second one did it. Then a third. Then it was my turn. I could stay behind and be alone in this room; maybe there was another way to the top. And then again, maybe there wasn't, and I'd find another way straight to the bottom.

"Go! Go!"

So I started up, but that slope wasn't meant for a moose like me. I didn't make it.

I sprawled onto the roof and started sliding slowly back down. They watched me for a moment from the top, then yelled down to me.

"What are you doing!? Are you slithering again!?"

"Arrrghhhhhh! . . ."

"Is that your answer?" asked Ted.

"Aiiiiiieeeeee! . . ."

"I don't think that sounds good. . .," they concluded.

I dug my fingers into the concrete. There's very little digging you can do with your fingers on concrete. Falling into a cesspool suddenly looked like a walk in the park. For a moment I was terrified, then calmness came over me. I was going to die. I was going to fall into the pit and be killed. I was going to be a skeleton for some kids to find someday, and they could take it home because it wouldn't be a Nazi skeleton.

Tony stood on the ledge below, he would be next to try the climb. When he saw me sliding down he braced himself and lay against the sloping roof.

"I'll stop you."

Now, Tony was a fairly substantial guy, and maybe he could do it. . .it was a desperate thought, of course he couldn't do it. There were going to be two skeletons for kids to take home someday.

My sneakers brought me to a stop just a scant few feet from the edge. Thank God for Converse. Like a scene from a Road Runner cartoon, my feet began to move like Wile E. Coyote. I left a skid mark and a smoke trail as I blasted to the top. I collapsed into a heap.

"That was pretty scary," a voice above me said. "It was like out of a movie."

"Who's talking? Is this God? Am I alive? . . . Is everything okay? You wouldn't happen to have a spare pair of underwear on you?"

"No. . .God doesn't need underwear. Could you use a hat?"

"God wears hats?"

Everything after that is a bit hazy. I know we played some games, but I don't remember much. I kept feeling myself slipping down the concrete. I walked out of that bunker like a ghost. I did the half-climb, half-swim fandango around the fence. I didn't care.

When I finally got home I grabbed a dictionary.

"What are you doing?" My brother was shocked, having never seen me actually use a dictionary.

"I'm looking up a word."

"Really? . . ."

"Yes, I've done it before."

"Really? . . . I didn't think you knew we had a dictionary. What word?"

"It begins with 'v'. . .I think it starts out 'verb'. . .and means something like look out, stupid."

"Verbum sat sapienti."

"What? . . ."

"A word to the wise."

"What is that?"

"It's Latin."

"So, the Jesuits were right. . .it is handy for more than addressing the Roman Senate."

"Yeah, but if anyone asks, I'll certainly deny it."

"Of course. Well, it sounds close, but it was only one word and it was German."

"And knowing this, you've decided to look it up in an English dictionary. . .interesting. Try a German dictionary."

"Yeah, like we have. . ."

"Here."

And he threw me a German-American dictionary.

"Wow, how'd you do that? Where'd this come from?"

"You get one when you take German."

"You took German?"

"Everyone in high school has to take German, even you."

"No. . ."

"Yes."

"I barely know English."

"I know."

"I'm doomed."

"I know."

I found "verboten."

"Here it is, verboten. . .forbidden, prohibited, restricted, banned, taboo, off limits, out of bounds, perilous, hazardous, dangerous. . ."

"It says all that?"

"Well, I've added a few. . .from personal experience."

★　　★　　★

So, I ALMOST didn't make it to my freshman year, which would have been a pity, maybe, depending on who you talk to. It certainly would have been better for the music department if I hadn't. But I did make it, and entered the converted Nazi army barracks that was the high school, ready for anything. Bring on the women. . .I've got the smokes.

"We only get four minutes between classes to get to the next one? This can't be right. What if I'm in shop class down in the basement and I have to get to the third floor, I'll never make it," said Ted.

"What? . . . Are we practicing our excuses already? I'm not prepared. . .why didn't anyone tell me to bring excuses with me on the first day?" I desperately tried to think of an excuse. "Jesus, I'm not good at making these up on the fly. . .how about 'my leg got caught in the stairs?'"

"Well, you certainly weren't kidding about not being good at making these up."

"Someone pushed me into my locker and left me there?"

My brother came by with his retinue of Older Guys.

"You chumps are all pretty lame. . .you want a good excuse? How about 'a senior came along and pounded me.'"

"I'm sure that would work, but that's okay, we'll stick with our lame excuses. I'm sure that's all they expect from us anyway. I wouldn't want to set any high expectations on the first day." I smiled at my brother, knowing full well that he couldn't pound me right there in the hall in front of witnesses. . .maybe.

"I don't think anyone has to worry about that from you," he said.

And then they were gone.

"Boy, we're going to have to be on our toes around here."
The bell went off.
"Shit. I'm using the locker excuse!" yelled Ted as he ran off.
"I got pounded by your brother," yelled Steve.
"So. . .I'm left with 'my leg got caught in the stairs?'"
"That's okay, from you it sounds good."
We were woefully out of shape for the four-minute hallway dash between bells.

★   ★   ★

THE SENIORS HAD a designated smoking area, and if you were "in" with the seniors they would allow you to sneak a smoke with them. I reviewed the freshman section of the senior 'in' list, and much to my surprise, I wasn't on it. It must have been an oversight. The freshman section was actually completely blank.

"Do you realize the freshman section of the senior 'in' list doesn't have any names at all?"
We were all shocked.
"Do they know who we are?"
"Apparently, they do."
We checked the sophomore section. There was only a girl listed. We jotted her name down on our private list.
"They must have taken a break or something, right after her name."
We all agreed there must be some plausible explanation for the oversight, after all, we were all part of the same Tobacco Brotherhood, right? We would investigate this whole thing, right after lunch.
So, we confidently strolled into the senior smoking area to share a cigarette and inquire if they had ever finished making up their 'in' list. Minutes after being pounded into dust, we rose like the Phoenix from the ashes, collected our various body parts that had been strewn about and began looking for a new place to have a smoke. The bandstand seemed like a good choice. We immediately designated it the freshman smoking area, and began compiling our own 'in' list.
Under the bandstand there was a storage room where the field markers and other supplies were kept. We casually strolled across the football field, and slipped unnoticed into the room. Inside, the ceiling was slanted from the inclined band seating above us. It sloped downward, and the only spot you could stand up without crouching was at the rear, where the highest back

rows raised the ceiling to almost normal height. The floor was dirt. In the middle of the room was a wooden support column with a pair of workman's clothes hanging from a nail. Richard sat on a stack of field markers with his back resting against the column. He was one of the most popular kids in the freshman class, and a twin.

Sometimes twins are the same, do the same things, like the same things, share everything. Sometimes twins aren't the same, sometimes there's the good twin and the evil twin. Robert was the good twin. Richard was with us.

Everything seemed to go well though, we got in and out without anyone really noticing. . .or so we thought. Lunch ended and we were all back in class. What we hadn't noticed was that Richard had snuffed out his cigarette on the workman's clothes. . .or so he thought. Sitting in chorus class I was peacefully oblivious when a voice cut through my afternoon fog. . .

"The bandstand's on FIRE!"

Did someone just stab me in the heart with an ice pick? Why yes they did, here's the handle sticking out of my chest. Pandemonium broke out and ran amuck in the classroom. Everyone flocked to the windows to get a good look. It was a fine late summer day, and the viewing was especially fine. Smoke was billowing out of the bandstand seating section, and from the storage room underneath you could just make out the flames from the workman's outfit licking at the ceiling, setting the seating above on fire.

There was yelling and cheering from every window in the school.

"Maybe, it'll spread! Maybe the whole school will burn down!!"

"Yes!"

"Burn! Burn!" yelled the chorus teacher.

"Hey! Why the hell isn't anyone getting a fire hose and putting out that damn fire!"

Did I just say that!? The shock of hearing myself yell this out was only matched by the shock of the people around me hearing it.

"What!!??"

"Er. . .ah. . .I mean. . . Hey! Stop anyone with a fire hose who tries to put out that damn fire!"

"That's better."

A major teenage fantasy was happening right before my eyes and I'm wasn't able to enjoy any of it!? I felt like Patton being kept out of the war. I was praying for a miracle to happen. As usual, if you need a miracle, start looking for a lawyer. Eventually, and I do mean eventually because by this time the whole building was up in flames, the school custodian walked slowly across the field with one lousy soda-style fire extinguisher in his hands.

Now if this wasn't the most farcical picture of modern fire fighting, then I don't know what is.

He passed the bandstand and pumped this pitiful stream of water on the press box next to it.

The bandstand was beyond help, there was no hope in trying to save it, and the building was now totally engulfed in flames. The fire engines finally arrived, and they ignored the bandstand too! They aimed their hoses at the press box, which was now completely saturated, and water was cascading out of its windows and doorway like it was part of a National Geographic show on the Mississippi flood plane. It was eventually torn down after being declared unsafe from water damage.

I was devastated and shaking like a leaf. I left the classroom amidst the confusion and went to my locker and took everything that even was remotely connected with fire. . .cigarettes. . .matches. . .Zippo lighter. . .flints. . .two wood sticks. . .Boy Scout manual, and threw everything out the hall window. They landed on the ground, right at the feet of the school counselor, who was sneaking his own smoke below. He looked around to see if anyone was watching, and then picked up the cigarettes and put them in his pocket. I ran back to class and tried to become invisible.

Within the hour a messenger arrived. He walked into the classroom, all eyes glued to his every step. *This had something to do with the bandstand. . .someone in this classroom was involved. Who? The name was on the slip of paper. With deliberation, the chorus teacher slowly opened the folded note, then took off her glasses. Everyone sat erect, and leaned forward for the announcement.*

"Georgy Porgy. . .you're wanted in the principal's office."

I went into cardiac arrest.

"That's not bad. . .it's certainly better than that leg caught in the stairs nonsense," she said. "Pretty convincing. . .but it won't work. It is an excuse worthy of a senior though, so it does show some promise for the future. . .if they ever let you back in school to have a future. Now off with you, to the principal's office."

"Hey! I might not be guilty."

"Sure. . .and God wears underwear."

I rose from my seat and took the long walk down the aisle while everyone turned to watch with looks of condolence, and at the same time a touch of admiration, although none of them would have traded places with me for all the tea in China. I wouldn't have either, who the hell wants a bunch of Chinese tea. . .they can't even give that stuff away in their own restaurants. Everyone knew I walked to my doom and watched my downcast exit from the classroom. It was all in slow motion. . .and the warden was waiting down at the office.

Outside his door stood the four of us. It didn't look good.

"What's the chance that it's just a coincidence that it's the four of us? . . ."

"The same as you having a smoke with the seniors."

Well, they had us. The informant network had fingered us only moments after the bandstand embers had died away, and we squirmed and lied our asses off for the rest of the day. We lied so much that our asses actually disappeared. In my case, having an Irish ass, mine was gone before we even started, so I was forced to write an IOU.

"Yeah, we were in there, but honest injun, we didn't do anything. . .we just looked around."

I'm not sure what an honest Indian has to do with convincing someone you're telling the truth, but we were willing to try anything. We didn't crack, and the day ended with the honest Indian story.

My mother was crying when I got home, she was shocked to the bottom of her Catholic roots. My father was willing to believe the lie.

"If he said he wasn't doing anything in there, then he wasn't doing anything in there."

I felt sick, knowing I was lying, but I couldn't tell them anything. I was in this with the other three, and locked into The Big Lie. The next morning the interrogation began immediately. The four of us were called out of homeroom, and we were kept isolated from each other. For a couple of hours we ran them around, and then they ran us around, in and out, chipping away, looking for a crack in our story.

We were out of breath and lying to beat the band, a band that no longer had a stand. I was lying so much that I lied about everything, even when there was obviously nothing to gain by it.

"Your name?"

"Fred. . .Jack. . .er. . .Dave. . .yes, that's it. . .Dave."

When the crack finally came, it went straight through the Earth and swallowed all of us. They convinced Ted that he might as well admit we were smoking in there because the rest of us had already said so.

I was shocked. "Ted, don't tell me your Eddie Haskell routine failed you?"

"Sorry."

"You're sorry!? I was counting on it!"

"You and me both."

It unraveled from there. I expected a deep depression, but relief settled over me. Lying that much in one day is exhausting, it hurt my head. I was tired of responding to any question asked of a Fred, Jack, or Dave, and I could no longer keep track of what I had lied about.

"Can someone please read me back some of my prior lies?"

The aftermath of it all was that the image of the "honest injun" had been tarnished once again, and we managed to get thrown out of high school on the second day of our freshman year. . .a new record for Bremerhaven High School. I tried reasoning with the principal.

"You know, if the seniors had only let us have a smoke with them, none of this would have happened. . ."

He was not sympathetic.

". . .so you see it's all kind of his fault. . ."

He was not sympathetic.

". . .he should be coming along with me. . ."

He never came.

Unfortunately for me, this set the tone for the rest of my checkered high school career. I am, of course, using "career" in its loosest possible sense.

And let's not forget about The Colonel. I could still hear his words hanging in the air. . . "*If he said he wasn't doing anything in there, then he wasn't doing anything in there.*"

BUZZ

I WAS SUSPENDED FROM school for a week, and my father had to go before a military Board of Inquiry with me in tow. The Bandstand Four were all there, with our fathers. The bandstand was U.S. government property, and they took a dim view of anyone destroying one of their buildings, unless of course, they decided to blow the shit out of it themselves.

In the end, they couldn't establish blame, even in light of our admission that we had been smoking in there. It was my father who had saved the day. After examining the pictures closely, he addressed the board.

"If you will look at the photo exhibits closely, you will notice that the seating and the roof are completely burned away. However, the walls of the structure are only scarred at the very top, where they meet the band seating above. It would appear that the fire started in the seating area, and not in the storage room below. If we are to believe that one of their cigarettes was the cause, then it was a truly amazing cigarette, for it was lying around, on a dirt floor, for an hour, then it ignited the dirt and set the band seating above on fire, while somehow missing the walls."

It was a damn good argument. . .I started believing it myself.

"The school grounds border a busy city thoroughfare. The press box and bandstand are separated from the sidewalk by just a few feet. It is far more likely for a passing pedestrian to have flipped a cigarette over the fence, which may have landed in the bandstand seating."

The military tribunal weighed his arguments and concluded. . .

"After reviewing the evidence and testimony, we cannot establish any fault with the loss of this structure. This board stands adjourned."

We would have jumped into each other's arms, but that's not the way things are done in the military, and we all know how it started anyway, and we were to blame. So, we slinked out of the courtroom, where we waited in the hall for our fathers, and where Richard apologized to us all.

"If anyone tells anything about this, I'll kick your ass."

"Eloquently spoken," we replied.

Our fathers remained behind to finish with the official duties and military courtesies, connected with a Board of Inquiry.

"Let's re-enact the Scopes trial. I'm Clarence Darrow."

"No, no, no. . .it should be the Billy Mitchell court-martial. . .this is a military courtroom, we should re-enact a military trial. I'm Billy Mitchell."

Knock. Knock.

We had started wondering what had happened to our dads and respectfully knocked on the door.

"Dad? . . ."

"Huuummpphh. . .and that concludes all the official duties gentlemen. . .see you this evening. . .at the club."

"Yes, sir."

"Yes, sir."

"Yes, sir."

"Yes, sir."

For that entire week, I sat in my room and waited for my father to deal with my lying, but he said nothing. And this weighed on my mind, causing me very neurotic dreams. . .dreams where I was the one who put the cigarette out on the workman's clothes, dreams where the pictures showed the walls had burned, and dreams where I was doing all of this in my underwear.

I don't know how anyone can be out and about dressed in their underwear, but I manage to do it quite a lot. On the face of it, it would seem pretty difficult to get out of the house dressed only in your underwear. Doesn't anybody notice?

"Bye Mom, I'm going out."

"Did you put on your good underwear?"

"Yes."

However, I notice that the "leaving the house" part never enters into a dream, you're already sitting there, and haven't even noticed it yourself. . .that you're in your underwear. It's like somewhere along the line, your clothes just suddenly disappeared. And now you just happen to spot it, and always before anyone else does, so it must have just happened in the last few seconds. I think we should exclude things like this from dreams. If it doesn't make sense awake, then it shouldn't get into a dream, unless of course, you actually have been out and about in your underwear.

My dad finally sat down with me.

"I know I've waited awhile to talk to you about all this, and with good reason. I had to calm down and be rational. . .or else I would have killed you."

"Thank you." I felt this decision should be rewarded with a solid positive acknowledgment.

"You know how I feel about lying, and you made me mad. . .at the beginning. After thinking this through, and at your mother's urging, I decided you probably should live past thirteen. . .although I don't know why. The situation was, no doubt, overwhelming for you. I know it overwhelmed your mother.

"Because of that, I'm not going to punish you anymore than you've already been punished by your suspension from school, and our restricting you for the rest of your life. However, again at your mother's urging, I've reduced it to one month. I'm not sure why she seems to be your advocate. I'm giving you your one break of a lifetime, so remember it. . .if something like this ever happens again, and we don't think it will, I'll expect, and you'll know, to stand up and tell the truth."

"Yes, sir."

"People will respect you for it."

"Yes, sir. "

"And if you don't, I'll kill you."

"Yes, sir."

Then he left me alone.

I was white as a sheet. I had been expecting the worse, and I think I got it.

★   ★   ★

ONE WEEK LATER, the four of us returned to school where we were greeted like a visit from the local leper colony. I would have climbed into my locker and stayed there for the day, and with those lockers I could have done it, and many of us actually did. The school lockers in Bremerhaven were not the traditional versions. These great big brown behemoths were more like a steel armoire than a school locker. A huge metal cabinet that could double as a tomb. It was what the army quartermaster came up with when asked to supply school lockers.

"Jesus, Charlie, they only have to hold books, not artillery shells."
They were too big.

Somehow, we all managed to fill them completely with crap. It was amazing that something so big, and so full, never had anything I was looking for, unless it was a week after I needed it. Finally, I had to get help just to close the door.

We needed a locker day, where everyone would have to empty theirs completely before going home. I discussed my idea with our principal.

"Everyone's grades are sure to improve. Imagine the homework that could be recovered." Or cleaning out the biological experiments that had once been lunch.

"I'm surprised."

"That the lockers are full?"

"No, that you had an idea I would even consider remotely passable."

"So, we're going to do it?"

"Well, since it was your idea, I am duty bound to say no."

So much for locker day.

I continued to be late, and semiunprepared for class.

"Where's your homework?"

"My locker composted it."

"You know, you've come a long way since 'my foot got stuck in the stairs,' and in such a short time."

"Well, I wasn't really prepared then, I didn't know we were supposed to do pre-work on excuses over the summer."

"Now, you've done it. I think you've actually made an excuse for your excuses."

"But my locker really did compost my homework."

"Oh, I'm sure you really believe that."

"It's true. . .have you ever looked in one of those lockers?"

"You're not going to drag me into your pathetic world. If you only put as much effort in your homework as you do these excuses. Let me savor this one for a moment. You've kind of combined a bit of biology and physics. . .nice touch."

"Thank you." And I hadn't even taken either course yet. "What about my excuse?"

"Locker composting?"

"Yeah."

"You're going to stick with that?"

"It's the best I've got."

"That's unfortunate, because I'm not buying it."

"You gotta admit, they're not your ordinary excuses."

"I always find you entertaining, but there's no credit for novelty."

"Well, there should be."

"Sit down."

I would have liked to put the same effort into my homework, but I couldn't control my teenage body and its raging hormones. I couldn't seem to focus on anything for more than ten minutes before my mind involuntarily shot off in another direction, no one could, except for the girls. Why is that?

Every one of my teachers got a ten-minute version of homework. They were not pleased with it. But what could I do? I was afflicted with Teen Angst Syndrome. But it wasn't a condition that anyone was able to find in the medical journals. The teachers conveniently claimed they had never heard of it.

"What'd you mean you never heard of it? You were a teenager once, weren't you?"

"No, we never were. I thought you all knew that."

"Well, we have our suspicions."

"I'll deny I ever said it, of course."

"Of course."

The four of us waited for time to diminish our status as the bad boys. In high school you never have to wait too long for something to overshadow you. Maybe a month of relative quiet had gone by when I came home to bump smack into a parental conference. This was a sure sign that Parental Decrees would follow, but for whom?

"Did I do something? Are they meeting about me?" I asked my sister.

"Dave was suspended from school today."

"Really. . .I didn't hear anything."

I felt somewhat elated, not because Dave was in trouble, but because, for once, it wasn't me. It felt like someone had just wiped my record clean.

"What happened?"

"From what I can hear, and the hearing isn't too good since they are being pains and speaking real low, he was building a still in the chemistry class storeroom. I haven't been able to find out what a still is."

"Really!?" I was impressed. So far, I had only been able to destroy things. I had never thought of actually building something.

"Where is Dave?"

"I don't know. . .he's not home. Do you know what a still is?"

"Yes. He must still be in interrogation."

"Well, you would know. Do you know what a still is?"

"Yes."

I left the house and waited at the bus stop to intercept my brother. It was nearly dark when he showed up, and we walked slowly home.

"What happened? Marcella says you were making a still in the chemistry storeroom. . ."

"Yeah."

"I'm amazed. Both that you actually did it, and that you also thought the school was the right place for it. Who caught you?"

"Mr. Conway. He came into the chemistry lab during lunch."

Mr. Conway was the school counselor. His only function was to alphabetize the college catalogues, and roam the halls, looking for, I suppose, more college catalogues. He was dangerous precisely because he was so unpredictable. There was no schedule to his whereabouts, he could show up anytime, anywhere. It's your worst nightmare, right in the middle of the perfectly planned bank caper, in walks the police chief to cash a check.

"He came all the way into the storeroom?"

"No, Gary was the lookout in the lab, the rest of us were in the back closet of the storeroom."

"What happened?"

"He asked Gary what he was doing in the lab during lunch."

"And. . ."

"He didn't accept Gary's 'ahhhhh. . .'"

"That was his function? To say 'ahhhhh'? And this from a senior? . . ."

"Yeah, no shit."

"Why did you build a still in the storeroom?"

"We didn't really. . .it just kind of evolved. Anders never goes in there, he always sends one of us. There's another little closet farther in back and we just started fooling around with the stuff back there, and before you knew it, we had the beginnings of a still. Then we wondered if we could actually do it. . .get it to work. I mean. . .think about it, who needs to build a still in Germany? You hold out your hand over here and someone will stick a beer in it. They really should give us an 'A' in chemistry, and then have suspended us from school."

"It doesn't work that way."

"Well, you would know. We've been suspended."
"For how long?"
"A week."
The bandstand sentence.
"Well, you've taken the heat off me, and I thank you."
"Don't mention it."
"And there's a parental conference in session."
"Great."
Dad once again had his restricted-for-life sentence reduced by Mom. This put a crimp in my brother's social life, and put his current reign as King of Buzz in jeopardy. He was proud of this position, and not wanting to get rusty he sat me down.
"I'm going to teach you Buzz."
"This isn't going to be like making me permanent set-up man for electric football, is it?"
"Probably. We'll need another chair."
"For who?"
"The third player, you need at least three, or the reverses aren't really reverses."
"I'm getting a bad feeling about this."
"All right, it's simple. We count off in a clockwise direction, when you get to a number that ends or is divisible by seven, say 'buzz' instead, okay? The direction reverses, whenever 'buzz' is said. Got that?"
"Yeah."
"That's why there's an empty chair."
"Okay."
"I'll play for the chair."
"Who's going to play for you?" I asked.
"This isn't going to be any fun, is it?"
"Well, not so far."
Dave looked a little frustrated. "Okay, I'll start. One. The chair says two."
"Buzz."
"Why'd you say buzz?"
"I forget which was the buzz number."
"In ten seconds?"
"Actually I can do it in less than ten seconds."
"I thought you had a ten-minute limit. . .that Teen Angst thing of yours."
"That's for whole concepts and school assignments, individual facts live for ten seconds or less."
"Let's start again before my ten minutes are up."
"So what was the number again?"
"Seven. You ready? One. . .chair says two."

"Three."

"Four. . .five."

"Six."

"Buzz." Dave whipped his head around and stared at the chair.

"Why are you staring at the chair?"

"That was the Double Fake Gambit, which you just fell for."

"Well, that's pretty easy to do with you flying your head around looking at empty chairs like a deranged idiot. So, staring at an empty chair is a Double Fake Gambit?"

"Yes, and you fell for it. You were the one who was supposed to answer."

"Oh. . .like the chair said something? . . ."

"I was just leading you astray by staring at the chair, which would have been a real person who might have said something. . .and then you both would have had to drink. . .thus the name Double Fake Gambit."

"You were leading me astray?"

"One. . .two," he replied. We got up to sixteen.

"Sixteen," I said.

"Buzz."

"My pants are on fire."

"Why'd you say that?"

"I don't know. I lost my composure. You were looking at the chair again. . .and the direction did reverse to the chair. . .I'm lost."

"That was a reverse Double Fake Gambit, to get the chair to think I was just doing a straight Double Fake Gambit."

"I was being lead astray again?"

"You're killing me."

"Restriction's a bitch, isn't it."

We finally made it to thirty-five. . .

"Now we add bang. . .for five's."

"You're making this up just because I know sevens."

"No, I'm not. And you still don't know sevens. Actually, no one starts with just sevens anyway, unless people like you are playing, just so we can watch you get blotto while we peacefully sip our beer and enjoy your predicament."

We struggled through Bang-Buzz. At thirty-five Dave released a giant gasp of relief from the frustration.

"Now we add pow. . .for three's"

"You're nuts, now I know this is a joke."

"With you, it was a joke from the start."

"How can you possibly want to do this, it's going to be incomprehensible. . .and I'm not even good with comprehensible?"

"Actually, with pow in the game it's not uncommon for several people to start drinking right in the middle of it, feeling with good justification that they must have screwed up somewhere along the line."

We finished, and I left Dave slumped over the third-man chair in complete exhaustion and with his eyeballs rolled up into his head.

I gathered my friends together to practice the game in the service club on the main base. I explained the rules, and since there was no beer available we used cups of water instead. We gained some proficiency, even with the Double Fake Gambit, and played for an afternoon, pounding down plenty of Dixie cups. We felt confident enough to take on my brother after that, and adjourned to catch the route bus home.

About ten minutes into the bus ride, we all discovered a side effect we could participate in, even without having used real beer. I had to piss like a racehorse. Surrounding me were six of my friends, we all had firm grips locked onto our crotches.

"Help!"

"George, you're an idiot! . . ."

"Hey, I didn't set you up! This was just stupidity! You guys know me. . .you know about stupidity."

"Aaarrrrgggghhhhh! . . ."

"I'm going to have to piss out the window!"

"You can't. . .we can't. . .I just got through with the bandstand. I can't be getting in trouble for riding the route bus with my dick hanging out the window! My father just wouldn't understand."

The ride from the main base first went across salt marsh flats, and it was a good ten-minute ride until we would hit the first stop in a housing area.

"I can't make it! . . ."

"We have to keep moving, we can't just sit here!"

We squirmed around furiously in our seats.

"This isn't working! . . ."

We all got up and milled around.

"Actung! Bleib sitzen!" yelled the driver.

"We can't!"

"There'll be a flood back here if you make us sit!"

"Was ist los mit der Amerikansch jungen!"

We were groaning and milling, jumping and stamping our feet, clamping our groins, and crying out in agony. To the driver we must have looked like an Apache war party. . .on the warpath to find a john. We worked ourselves into a frenzy doing the clamped crotch war dance around the bus. The driver's eyes were two giant silver dollars of disbelief shinning in his rearview mirror as he looked at us and almost drove off the road into the salt marsh flats.

"Look out!" screamed the other passengers.

The passengers were screaming, we were screaming, the driver was screaming, yelling German phrases we didn't understand, then he pulled over and threw us off the bus.

"Verruckt!" He yelled as he drove away.

"What the hell does 'yerook' mean?"

"I bet he wishes Germany won the war, then he could have had us all shot."

We ran into the high reeds.

"You know, it's supposed to be impossible to piss a quart."

"How do you know?"

"I read it. . .in *Catch 22*. You can't piss a quart. . .it's impossible."

"Not today. . ."

CARNIVAL

I WAS SITTING BY the window looking out across the football field, past the charred spot where the bandstand had stood, and watching the workers erect the carnival on the vacant lot across the street. It was October, and all across Germany it was Oktoberfest, even in the small port town of Bremerhaven, Oktoberfest had come. It had come to the vacant lot across the street.

Without the bandstand in the way, I had an unobstructed view of the carnival proceedings. All week long, I had watched their progress as the tents went up and the rides were erected. I was able to watch without my hormones getting in the way of my undivided attention. I had found a cure for Teen Angst Syndrome. . .Carnival.

"Allingham! Pay attention!"

"What? . . ."

"Pay attention."

"Can you repeat the question?"

"There was no question. . ."

"Great! . . ."

"I just want your attention."

"Do you know what's going on over there?"

"Yes, I do."

"And you still want my attention? . . ."

"Yes."

"That's going to be a little hard to do, don't you think?"

"No I don't."

"Really? . . ."

"Yes, really."

"Okay, but I can't really guarantee anything."

"But I can. I can guarantee a trip to the office."

"Another trip to the office? They weren't too pleased about the last one, you know."

"Really."

"Yes, really."

"Well, why don't you go down there and explain to them our little conversation."

"This was a conversation? . . ."

"Yes."

I made the familiar trek to the office following the well-worn path.

"Not you again!" I stood before the school secretary.

"That's what I said. I tried to tell her that you guys weren't going to be happy, but Miss Lindsford wants me to tell you about our conversation."

"Really?"

"Yes, really."

"Well, go ahead."

"I'll try, but I don't think we had a conversation."

"What happened?"

"Well, I was watching the carnival workers across the street, purely as an academic exercise in the laws of physics you understand. . ."

"Are you taking physics?"

"No. I'm only a freshman."

"Why do I feel you've been here longer? . . . Is it because you've been to the office enough times to be a junior?"

"I really don't think we should talk about what you feel. Do you?"

"What class was this?"

"English."

"Is that Allingham out there?"

"Yes, Mr. Denton."

"Send him in, I can't wait to hear this. . ."

"This is starting to get out of hand," I said.

"The principal wants to see you."

I sat across from Mr. Denton, trying to understand how watching some carnival workers could cause me to end up like this. I mentioned this to Mr. Denton.

"I don't understand how my watching some carnival workers across the street can end me up in here."

Mr. Denton didn't seem to hear.

"You know, the port commander has just released a list of the high school students he considers problems. Both you and your brother are on it," he said.

"That wouldn't be considered a good thing, would it?"

"I'll let your father discuss that with you."

"Who else is on it?"

"Most of your friends. Don't you want to know why you and your brother are on it?"

"Sure, why are we both on it?"

"I think you know why you're on it."

Why do they do things like this? It was like the principal turned into my mother, except I was actually allowed to sit on his furniture.

"Well," he continued. "It doesn't have any specifics, but I can guess it has something to do with the blackened ground next to the press box that we call our bandstand."

"It could have been worse. . .if we actually had a school band," I helpfully pointed out.

"We don't have a school band because the instruments kept turning up in pawn shops."

"Wow. . .I'm impressed."

"You would be. As for your brother and his friends, well, the still they built in the chemistry storeroom qualified all of them, don't you think? Ah. . .this is tiring." He rubbed his eyes and sighed. "Where are my pills? Mrs. Jones. . .have you seen my pills?"

"Which ones? The aspirin? The hypertension? The relaxants? The sedatives?"

Mr. Denton rifled through his desk drawer. "Any of them. . .all of them." I sat there quietly until he looked up rather surprised to see me still sitting there. "Go on, get out of here, go back to class. I'm starting to get a headache. Go compost your locker or something."

I left as he and the secretary were ransacking his office for pills.

That Friday night, Ted and I were off to the Oktoberfest carnival with our allowances jingling in our pockets. I had overheard from my brother's friends that you could get free passes on one of the rides if you brought some records for the attendant to play.

"*Good God! They're playing German versions of songs. . .'Tallahassee Lassie' with accordions!*"

"Hmmmm. . ."

I was now secretly carrying my brother's "Tallahassee Lassie" record inside my shirt. I knew I was risking Older Brother Pounding #372, but free rides are free rides. We took the bus to the high school, then crossed the street to the carnival entrance. The Snowball ride was first, a large tilted dish with cars rotating along its edge. For half the ride they went forward, then reversed direction for the finish. American rock-'n'-roll was blaring over the PA system.

"This is the one they were talking about," I said to Ted.

"I thought you said they played German versions?"

"That's what they said. Come on, let's find the guy."

The ride was surrounded by a walkway, its railing was crowded with German kids listening to the music. We climbed the steep incline to the top where the control booth was located.

"Hello," I said.

"Wie gehtes!"

"I was afraid of this, he's speaking German."

"Show him the record," said Ted.

"Not without some kind of explanation, this is Dave's record. I don't want him to get the wrong idea."

"I speak English, I can help you," said a towering, strapping, blonde Aryan lad, leaning against the railing.

"I'll take any help I can get," I replied, then lowered my voice aside to Ted. "Even if it means being shanghaied into the Bundesbahn by this guy."

"I have very good ears," he said. "And the Bundesbahn is the federal railway."

"You heard that over this music?"

"Yes, I told you I have very good ears, and you know very little about Germans."

"Actually, I know nothing about Germans." I pointed to the attendant. "Ask him if it's true that he gives out free passes for borrowing records."

"It is true."

"How do you know. . .you didn't ask."

"He has been doing it for years."

"Was ist los, Heinrich?" asked the attendant.

They talked briefly, and then Heinrich turned to me.

"He wants to see what you've brought."

I took the record out of my shirt and gave it to him. He looked at it closely, then smiled and reached over his head to a shelf behind him. He handed me a record.

"Talhausie Lausie," he said.

I took the record and looked it over. The artist name was Der Gunter Gerhardt Ziehharmonika Gruppe.

"Heinrich, what's this name in English?"

Heinrich read the name.

"The Gunter Gerhardt Accordion Group."

"My God, it's true. Heinrich, what's the attendant's name?"

"Roland."

"Roland. . ." I pointed to my record "This is the real thing, the Freddy Cannon version."

"Frede Canude? . . ."

"Yeah, Frede 'Boom Boom' Canude."

"Buum Buum? . . ."

"Yes, Buum Buum."

"Was ist Buum Buum?"

"It's. . .it's. . .it's because we like to sound as stupid as possible as a people. It's part of the American culture. . .part of our national heritage."

He seemed to understand that just fine.

"What'd you mean, 'we like to sound stupid?'" asked Ted indignantly.

And this from a kid whose nickname was Noodles.

"Quiet, I think he's getting us some free passes."

The ride came to a stop and emptied. The people waiting along the railing rushed to get on. When it was full, it started again.

"Excuse me," said Heinrich. "I must collect the tickets." And he stepped onto the spinning ride like he was taking a walk in the park, as casual and confident as you please. He moved from car to car, taking the tickets. Then he stopped between two cars and grabbed one of the safety railings in one hand, and then grabbed the second car's railing in his other hand. With his feet on the outer sideboard, and his hands grasping the railings, he lowered his body between the cars until his face was almost touching the spinning center disk.

"Holy shit! You see what Heinrich is doing?"

Roland handed us a fist full of passes.

"Roland! Heinrich is crazy! What is that, some kind of ticket taker gymnastics!?"

"Yah, danke," he said.

"Yah, danke, yourself."

We rode and rode for the next hour, and heard "Tallahassee Lassie" over and over.

"I guess he likes it!" I screamed to Ted over the noise of the ride as we sped around.

"She gut a hi-fi chaussie!" screamed Roland as we came by him. Heinrich catwalk'd around the outer sideboard to our car.

"You should try it out here!" shouted Heinrich over the mechanical clanging and clacking.

"No thanks, I like having all my fingers on both of my hands, and a face that resembles a face, even if that means it has to resemble mine!"

"You are too nervous, here I'll show you!"

He climbed into our car.

"Wait, there's only room for two in here!" screamed Ted.

"Sit on the railing!" yelled Heinrich. "Come on!"

"Heinrich, hasn't anyone told you this ride is spinning around? . . ."

"Come on!" he yelled again.

"I'm going to do it!" shouted Ted. He sat on the side railing next to Heinrich, his back to the spinning disk, and facing the crowded walkway. Heinrich grabbed my shoulder.

"Come on! Don't be a coward!"

I sat up on the railing. The crowd was whizzing by in a tilted blur.

"Now, lean back like this!"

He hooked his feet under the seat, held onto the side railing, and leaned backwards until his head was inches from the spinning center disk.

"Come on!" he yelled at us.

I looked at Ted for what I was sure would be the last time and leaned back. The centrifugal force was pulling more at my feet than at my head. I was able to hold myself in this position quite easily and watch the spinning disk coming at me, then go underneath me.

"Wow!"

"Sehr Gut!" yelled Heinrich. "Now we change position with each other!"

"What? . . ."

Heinrich rolled over the top of me, and stopped next to Ted.

"I'm not doing that!" cried Ted.

"We're going to die," I screamed. Heinrich just laughed and sat up, stepped out of the car and was back standing on the sideboard.

"Now maybe you listen to Heinrich!" and he was off to take more tickets. We flew around, still hanging out of the car, and could hear Roland singing away in the control booth.

"She loook lettle saussy!"

Hours later, we walked wobbly legged around the carnival, slowly losing our Snowball legs and regaining our land legs. Ahead of us, a group of our friends were walking together and stopping at every alleyway between the tents, then viciously attacking the empty space with bamboo canes they had picked up somewhere at the carnival. They yelled and screamed like a

Comanche war party. It was touch and go as they doggedly fought with the air in the alley, but they were tenacious, and prevailed. They did this until a curious crowd had gathered, then they would abruptly leave. The crowd would move in to take a look at the remains of whatever could have caused such a ruckus. There was never anything there, but by this time our friends had discovered another alleyway further ahead. And a new curious crowd would stop and watch.

"I'm on parole. . .let's keep out of this," I said.

"Look's like another diplomatic triumph to me," said Ted.

Ted and I thought a lot alike, that is, I thought we did, until the Freight Train incident.

I found my brother and after enduring the required barbs and punches from his buddies, managed to talk him into sneaking us some beer from the gasthaus tent. We made a tactical error by getting on the disappearing floor ride right after finishing these, and ended up on our hands and knees in the adjacent alley, to privately throw up.

"Attack!"

"Kill!"

It was the roving bamboo cane army.

"Shit. . ."

When they had finished battling the air, the curious crowd followed and discovered Ted and me, barfing away.

"At least they got to see something this time."

"Well, I don't think anyone recognized me, all they could see was my ass," I observed.

"What ass?" observed Ted.

Every time the carnival came to town, we went to the Snowball ride first, and Heinrich and Roland were always there. Roland would see us coming up the walkway and yell out. . .

"Down un F L A! . . ."

He still didn't know any English, so he had no idea what he was saying, but he was happy as hell to yell it anyway. Heinrich, of course, would try to kill us once again, with some new gymnastic feat. I think I saw him on the '62 German Olympic team, but it was hard to tell if it was really Roland from a small television screen. I definitely heard someone yell. . .

"Come on! Don't be a coward!"

GORPS AND DORFENBURGS

THE TEEN CLUB WAS our Mecca. . .and it was the same for every teenager on every American military base in Germany, and I suppose around the world as well. This teen nirvana is particularly strong overseas. You can't imagine how important it was to us, unless you build yourself a small building for, say, about two hundred, and then surround it with people wearing Lederhosen, and doing things that complemented wearing Lederhosen, and saying nothing you can understand. Personally, anyone wearing suspendered leather shorts was suspect enough.

The teen club was our sanctuary, our whole universe. I can still remember the excitement I felt on Fridays knowing that I would be there. It would have been even more exciting if I wasn't three months behind in dues. To be honest, a lot of that excitement was the fact that it was Friday. I still get excited on Fridays and there hasn't been a teen club in sight in years.

Almost everything began and ended from the club. Every dance, every romance, every trip, every good idea, every bad idea started and finished here. It was our total world. It was never far from our thoughts, even if we were standing on the high school football field for a Friday-night pep rally.

Someone came running through the crowd yelling. . .

"When the rally's over, we're going to snake dance to the teen club!"

"We're going to do what? . . ."

"We're going to snake dance to the teen club!"

He said this like we all knew exactly how to do the snake dance, and would also be happy to do it all the way to the teen club.

"Isn't this something the Sioux Indians would be more likely to do?" I asked.

"Well. . .I can't speak for the Sioux, but we're going to do our own version from here to the teen club."

"So tell me, what happened to walking?"

"I don't know."

Some of our bad ideas didn't always start at the teen club.

"How's this going to work?"

"Everyone's going to hold hands in a long chain, and snake our way along the street."

"You just made this up, didn't you?"

"No."

"We're going to do this snake dance right down Main Street? . . ."

"Yes."

"Through all the people? . . ."

"Yes."

"So, we're giving up on unwittingly looking like idiots in front of the Germans. . .and now we're actually trying to come up with ideas to make us look like fools?"

"I think so. . ."

"Well, count me in."

The seniors were in the middle of planning their class trip. . .to Paris. And they were going there because of the teen club. Since we were in Europe, senior class trips weren't just down the road to some museum. I would never get to be a senior in Germany. In three years, when our assignment was up, I'd only be a junior, and juniors go to. . .to. . .

"Hey, where do juniors go?"

"The juniors are going to a clock museum in Bremen."

I was going to a clock museum.

It's easy to say you're going to Paris, it's quite another to actually pay for it. Now, all the seniors needed was a good moneymaking idea. After sitting around the teen club for an afternoon, the only idea they came up with was to never snake dance to the club again. This was an excellent idea, but there was no money connected with it.

"How about Buzz Games to Benefit the Senior Class?"

"I'm not sure how that makes money, but I am sure it will cause a flock of Parental Decrees. . .and count me in."

The task was beginning to look insurmountable. Up until now, most of the seniors had never needed more money than it took to buy a pack of cigarettes, and sometimes that was insurmountable. They might as well have said they were raising money to buy an Atlas rocket. The bookies were giving better odds on the rocket.

We freshman only had to worry about coming up with the money to head twenty miles down the road to the town of Cuxshaven on the North Sea coast. We emptied the change out of our pockets, and covered that trip's entire cost. . .with money left over for cigarettes. It wasn't Paris, but we were excited anyway, and with great enthusiasm we ran out into the ocean, and ran and ran. The water never changed, it stayed three inches deep and freezing. We stopped from exhaustion, our cold blue ankles barely covered, and slowly we returned to the lava rock beach.

"Are there volcanos in Germany?"

"I haven't seen any."

"I wonder where they got this beach from?"

"From one helluva salesman."

"It's probably the same guy that sold my mother toilet water."

"What? . . ."

"I saw it in my mom's bathroom, a bottle of toilet water."

"Naw. . ."

"Yeah."

We sat down on a stretch of black lava beach and stared out at the North Sea.

"You know, the water has to get deeper out there, I can see ships," said Ted.

"Either it gets deeper or those are a very different kind of ship. Maybe if we just go out farther, we'll find the ocean. I know my ass is certainly tired of sitting on this lava rock."

"What ass?"

We all tried once again. . .and once again we returned with blue ankles, exhausted, and forced to carry back some of the weaker ones. We could still see the ships out in the distance, but we never were able to get close to them. This goes a long way in explaining the lack of any world-class surfers from Germany. However, if the Olympics ever have a one-mile ankle-water dash, watch out for the Germans.

★   ★   ★

It was a miracle. We all checked our mother's bathrooms, and sure as shootin', they all had a bottle of toilet water.

"We've gotta get in on this."

"Let's set up a toilet water stand."

"This is the idea that will get the seniors to Paris!"

"Why give them this gold mine?"

"We'll get in good with them, we might even be the first freshmen admitted to the senior smoking area."

It was too good to be true, an unlimited supply of toilet water right in your own bathroom, all you needed were some fancy bottles and you could make a fortune. We couldn't wait to tell the seniors that we had saved their trip with our astounding idea. Minutes after being pounded into dust, we collected our various body parts that had been strewn about, and gave up on ever having a smoke with the seniors.

"What happened?"

"I don't think they liked the idea."

"What's not to like?"

No one made a fortune in the toilet water business.

★   ★   ★

THE SENIORS ALSO needed chaperones for their trip. Chaperones to go to Paris. . .let's see, how could they convince someone to be a chaperone on a Paris trip?

"Let's just ask and see if anyone volunteers."

Prospective chaperones formed a line that extended to the horizon, ending in three inches of freezing water at Cuxshaven. But still there was no money. More ideas came in.

"An Indian Poker tournament?"

"Hmmmmm. . .maybe."

"What if we lose money?"

"Hmmmmm. . ."

"What about selling food to the troop ships?"

There was stunned silence. No one was expecting a real idea, especially a real good idea.

"Holy Christ, we're going to be rich!"

It was even better than toilet water.

The troop ships seemed to dock every week, and in a frantic twenty-hour period, several thousand GIs were processed onto troop trains parked dockside. These guys were tired and hungry. Need we say more?

Well, yes we do. After getting permission from the port authority to set up an area next to the trains, donuts and other assorted fine American cuisine was packaged by the hundreds. The entire teen club was enlisted to help. We all knew this ensured enough money for every conceivable trip the teen club could plan, and we were literally rubbing our hands together over the prospect of the killing that was about to take place. Soon, the senior class would be off to Paris on that Atlas rocket, with enough left over to cover clock museums for everybody.

"And we should banish club dues forever!" Well, you can't blame me for trying.

The GIs turned out not to be quite the pigeons we had thought. Imagine the shock when the sales were poor. The seniors were starting to get agitated.

"What's going on? This had better change, I've already been to the clock museum."

After several days trapped on a troop ship, and then being packed into trains, donuts didn't entice them.

What to do. . .what to do?

No one seemed to have an answer. Paris was slipping away, the chaperones pitched in with some fresh ideas.

"How about military salads?"

How my dad managed to become one of the chaperones is still a mystery. He's never to be underestimated when the chance to empty an entire city of all its booze presents itself.

In desperation and exhaustion, an unknown genius ceased crying out "Donuts! Get yer donuts here," and in a deranged moment shouted "Gorps! Get yer German Gorps. . .authentic German Gorps."

The heads began popping out of the train windows, and the Gorps began selling faster than we could bag them. We expanded on this success.

"Authentic German Wurstenbrat. . ."

"Dorfenburgs. . .Dorfenburgs. . ."

Those Dorfenburgs sold by the truckload. They sold so well that a permanent Dorfenburg stand was set up dockside. The senior class went to Paris, where one whiff of the general populace told them that the French really did use toilet water.

I returned to Cuxshaven, and the GIs rediscovered the donut.

"Goddamned little dependent assholes. . ."

★   ★   ★

THE TEEN CLUB had its own buses, well, they were still the army's buses, but on Friday and Saturday nights, at closing, they became the Teen Club Specials. Their destination markers had the word SPECIAL displayed. . .and they were, indeed, a different world from your ordinary route bus. For this dangerous assignment, the drivers were all handpicked volunteers with no traceable family. Inside, music was blaring from the early versions of the boom box. . .Grundig mini-reel-to-reel tape players. Several couples had already dropped below the level of the seats and out of sight in the darkness, under raincoats. Zippo lighters were impatiently being flicked opened and closed with one hand while we were delayed waiting for the last of the gasthaus stragglers to show.

"Wait. . .hold the buses!"

Here they come, a sort of human ball of tangled arms and legs rolling this way. Luckily the buses were parked in a natural depression and they rolled right up to the doors.

My brother extracted himself from the tangled ball and began immediately to lure a few of the latest unsuspecting junior-status members of the teen club in the pleasures of Trend, the "Mild Little Cigar."

"Remember to take a big drag, like a real man. . .and what about you kid? How about some wafer candy?"

Tobacco pipes were being readied and toilet paper rolls were being unsheathed. They say the pure products of America go crazy. I'd say my brother was proof of that.

My parents had given me one of the Grundig mini-tape recorders as a Christmas present, complete with an AC adapter. Back then an AC adapter was about the size of a small New England state, and I think it was only sold as a joke to gullible Americans. After you left the shop I'm sure they all had a good laugh over it.

I spent many an hour trying to record music using the microphone, never getting any worthwhile results. I tried everything, holding the microphone at every conceivable angle, attaching it directly to the front of the speaker, suspending it inside a shoebox, mystical contortions that brought rain, and still it never sounded good. The only time I managed to get a good recording was when my sister was taking a bath and absentmindedly singing "Go Down Moses." Song selection wasn't her strong suit. I stealthily crept to the door and slid the microphone noiselessly into the bathroom. Everyone, friend and foe alike, agreed it was a great recording, clear as a bell with excellent tone, everyone except my sister. I found it impractical to tape everything in the bathroom.

The buses started out, moving slowly through the dependents hotel complex where the teen club was located, and out into the city traffic.

In the final moments of calm before the storm, the only sounds were someone singing "Go Down Moses" and a conversation in Ubanghi.

"Tibime tibo ibunriboll tibhe tiboilibet pibapiber."

Ubanghi was a sort of Pig Latin, but without Pig Latin's obvious alliterative charm, and I don't believe it ever left Bremerhaven. Its secret? You place the letters "ib" after the first letter of each syllable of a word. For example the word sit would be sibit, you would be yibou, forget would be fiborgibet, and so on. Exception, wherever it becomes unpronounceable, you place the "ib" in front, e.g., ibunclibear?

The main attraction of Ubanghi was that it sounded ridiculous, and it was used effectively to pass along information right under the noses of our parents and teachers. The circle of those who knew its secret was kept small because most people thought sounding ridiculous was an undesirable trait. But not my friends.

"Time to unroll the toilet paper."

The toilet paper streamed out the windows on both sides. The pipes were then loaded with tobacco, and this group of specialists began blowing through the bowl, sending a dense plume of smoke out the stem. Other tape players started up, creating a sonic minestrone, the Zippo lighters were clicking open in time to the music. The bus soon filled with smoke so thick that the only person you could see was yourself. The toilet paper extended in long streams from several windows, forty to fifty feet behind the bus. The music was blaring, and the poor German bus driver could only grudgingly bear it as he vainly tried to clear his view of the road ahead and daydream that Germany had won the war. . .

"Goddamn little American dependent assholes."

The bus headed toward Main Street with toilet paper streaming behind it and smoke pouring out of the windows, "Go Down Moses" could be distinctly heard, since it was easily the best recording of the bunch. The only complement missing here would have been an approaching group of snake dancers. . .Little America.

"My father says we're all kind of like ambassadors for our country," said Ted as we bounced along the cobblestones.

"My father has never mentioned it," I said into the dense smoke cloud, in the general direction of his voice.

★   ★   ★

I MISSED ABOUT a month of Teen Club Specials when I went into the hospital. I had contracted a dreaded disease, not that I knew it was a dreaded disease. I thought the way I was feeling would pass all by itself, like a cold. . .but it didn't, it became worse. I felt like passing out, and would have, if I didn't feel quite so bad and uncomfortable. You know something is really wrong when you're feeling too bad to be able to pass out. I was woozy and tired, and I would have loved to sleep, but everything felt so lousy that it was impossible to find any position, sitting, standing or falling, that didn't feel awful.

I desperately tried my own home remedy. In our kitchen cabinet, my father had brought home government-issued vitamins. It was a bottle of 10,000 pills with a plain brown U.S. government label. You needed a forklift to get the bottle off the shelf. I took it to school with me. The pocket where I put the bottle was dragging on the ground.

"What's in your pocket, an anvil?" my friends asked.

"What are you trying to do, build yourself an ass?"

I was too tired to answer as I dragged along my vitamin bottle to my locker. Luckily, the locker was big enough for it to fit, and a couple of friends and I pushed it inside. Two of us, on opposing sides, unscrewed the cover, and I reached in and scooped up a handful, being careful not to lose my balance and fall into the jar. At the water cooler I began to gulp and swallow until I had consumed about a hundred. Within ten minutes I began to feel pretty good. I was in a netherworld of half okay, half dead, occurring simultaneously. I was like a pinball being bashed up. . .down. . .around. After thirty minutes I began to wind down like my mother's chime clock, until there wasn't enough wind left for me to strike one o'clock.

Between classes I was back at my locker for another fistful. I did this all day. And wouldn't you know it, I was right in the middle of trying to get a school projectionist license, something I really wanted. If you had a projectionist license you could get out of class to run the school theater projector. Only those with a license were allowed to pilot an army projector. So, I was trying to listen and learn in this class, sort of a first, and my head was reeling. I couldn't stand for very long, and had to find a chair. My head immediately fell over to one side. Since I was too tired to hold it up, I let it collapse onto the desktop.

Clunk.

From this position I was only able to thread the film properly around my navel. I struggled to the fountain for more vitamins and returned with my head back on top of my shoulders. I was again threading film right along with the rest of the class.

"Fine job, son," said the instructor.

Thirty minutes later I was hanging on the projector with film wrapped around me, bundled up like a mummy.

"You weren't the one I said 'fine job' to, were you?"

I couldn't answer him, I was too tired and the film had gagged me anyhow.

"I think we're going to have to cut you out of there."

If the jaws-of-life had been around back then, they would have used them. I took another fistful of vitamins at a break and. . .

"*Toota toot toot toot a toota toot toot,*" *Popeye the projectionist was back.*

"Today's our final class, and after reviewing your work, you all pass. Some of you owe me money for damaged film, but you will still get your licenses today."

With my license in hand I went home and collapsed on the couch.

"Help. . ." I said.

"What do you think you're doing?" said my mother. "You know you're not allowed on the couch."

"Help. . ."

"Roll onto the floor."

I rolled. She stepped over me, and began to stroke her couch smooth.

"Poor baby," she said. You would have thought she was talking to me, but I knew better.

"Help. . ."

"What's wrong with you. . .coming in here and sitting on the furniture like that. . .and in those clothes?"

"Help. . ."

Later, at dinner, my father asked my mother. . .

"Where's George?"

"Help. . ."

"He's over there lying in front of the couch. I don't understand kids today. Do you know that he actually came in and sat on the couch?"

"No. . ."

"Yes."

"Help. . ."

Finally, in the morning, as my father tripped over me. . .

"Maybe we should get you checked out."

"Help. . ."

I sat in the hospital corridor after being subjected to a battery of tests. A doctor came over with a metal clipboard in his hand.

"Your son is a very sick boy."

"What's wrong with him?"

"He has mononucleosis. . .and jaundice."

"Ohhh. . .," my mother gasped. "And he sat on the couch!"

"He's going to have to stay with us for a while," said the doctor. "Probably three or four weeks. He'll be in isolation, so you'll have to wear gowns and masks when you visit. In fact, you should begin shunning him right now."

I was immediately abandoned like I was radioactive. They stood across the corridor and talked about me in the past tense.

"I get his records," said my brother.

"I get that damned tape recorder," said my sister.

"We'll have to get the couch disinfected," said my mother.

My friends thought it was really cool that I was in isolation. They had a great time dressing up in the gowns and wearing the masks, and spending very little time at the entrance of my room. Rather, they wandered the ward corridors pretending they were doctors and stealing cigarettes from any unguarded room.

"We'll be glad when you're out of here," said the nurse. "Your friends are stealing everything that isn't nailed down. Yesterday I was missing a box of rubber gloves. Now what can they possibly do with those?"

She was telling me this as she tucked in my bed sheets so tight I was virtually flattened. My feet were pushed outward like a circus clown. Meanwhile, in my bathroom, a rubber glove attached to the faucet was just reaching the size of a small planet.

Boom!

"What was that!?" she cried.

"I don't know, I don't get around much these days."

Water started flowing under the bathroom door and spreading around her feet.

"Arrrggghhh! . . . Those little bastards!" She ran to the bathroom door and opened it.

Whoossshhh!

The water that had been backed up behind the door came rushing in.

"When I get my hands on those little shits, I'll show them what I can do with a rubber glove!"

She charged out of my room.

"Wait! Don't leave me here like this! I'll drown!"

The hospital had a movie theater, well, not a real theater, but they did show movies. Part of the cafeteria was set up with a projector, and couches were brought in from the various waiting rooms. You could smoke and watch a movie for free. When this news got out, I suddenly had a lot of friends. There were several rows of white-clad figures sitting on the back couches, all dressed in masks and gowns, wearing rubber gloves and smoking hospital cigarettes, while I remained in my room, flattened under the covers.

"Help. . ."

Eventually I got out. Not many of my friends showed up for my hospital discharge since you no longer got to wear the masks and gowns, and the head nurse had taken to chasing them wearing a rubber glove on one hand.

"Oh boys. . .come here, I have something I want to show you."

Only Earle and Ted were there on my last day.

"Boy, I can't wait until you get mono again."

It was the first time on record that Earle had his own cigarettes, and the first time the Red Cross had none.

I wasn't back on the Teen Club Specials for more than a couple of weeks before I landed back in the hospital. You should never give a thirteen-year-old a key, any key, unless you no longer want it. I had an apartment key, somewhere, usually not anywhere I could actually put a hand on it, and never when I was standing in front of our locked apartment door. I was locked out again, no key and no one home. We were on the first floor, so I tried one of my old standbys. I climbed onto the balcony and tried the door. It was usually unlocked. . .usually. Not this day.

I walked around to the back, checking all the windows to see if any were open. Not this day.

At the back of the apartment, the dining room window was slightly ajar. These were European-style windows, they had a handle you lifted up to unlock, and then the window could swing open. It was a two-step handle, the first step allowed the window to open a crack, and then it hit a stop position in the handle. This allowed the window to be slightly open without unlocking the whole thing.

Hmmmm. . .

Maybe I could bang on the frame and cause the handle to pop open the rest of the way and free the window.

Hmmmm. . .

I looked around for something to pound with. . .nothing. I have found that whenever you need a tool, there's never a handyman's toolbox nearby. I began to pound on the frame with the side of my fist. . .banging lightly at first. The handle didn't move. I pounded a little harder. . .then harder. I thought I saw the handle move slightly. This might work after all.

I kept banging away, watching the handle, using more force until. . .

CRASH!

My hand went through the window.

"Shit!"

I looked at the broken pane, the shattered glass was lying inside the apartment on the dining room floor.

"Well, I guess that's one way in. . .and I'm in for it now."

I was about to reach through and unlatch the window when I noticed one of the jagged shards of glass that remained in the frame had a telltale droplet of blood lazily meandering down the surface.

"Oh shit. . ."

These kinds of things never turn out good. I didn't want to look, but forced myself to raise my hand and turn it toward me. My little finger had been neatly filleted to the bone, slicing in at the base and slashed almost to the fingertip. One half of it dangled from the tip, exposing the white bone, blood was rolling down my arm like a tidal wave, and my arm was coated in crimson. My third finger had been deeply pierced, and was spurting blood like Oklahoma crude.

It made me sick to look at it, but I knew I had to do something quickly, so I ran, until I remembered you didn't want your heart pumping harder, and I slowed to a brisk walk, stopping at our neighbor's across the hall. I knocked on the door.

"Who is it?"

"Your neighbor across the hall!"

"Well, how nice of you. . ."

Boom. She fell to the floor in a dead faint.

"You can't do this! I need your help! Wake up!"

She sat up groggily. "What? . . . Oh my! We have to get you to the hospital!" She quickly went into the bathroom and returned with a soaking wet towel and wrapped it around my hand.

"Hold your hand up high, over your head."

We drove hell bent for leather, as fast as hell-bent leather can travel on cobblestone, and screeched to a halt in front of the emergency room entrance.

We got out and she grabbed the first white hospital uniform that passed. "We need help!"

"Follow me!"

I was rushed into an operating room, where a corpsman nonchalantly removed the towel and placed my hand over a stainless steel bowl, then left the room.

I was alone.

"Shouldn't someone be in here doing something? What happens when the bowl is full? Hello?"

The ward nurse from my mononucleosis stay walked by the door, stopped, looked in at me for a moment with a stern face, then briskly continued on her way.

"Hello?" I said again. "Man in here bleeding in a bowl. . ."

The hospital public address crackled to life.

"ATTENTION! ATTENTION! Secure all rubber gloves and Red Cross cigarettes immediately! That is all."

It's funny how she would associate me with that, after all, I was the one in isolation, trapped in my bed, with bed-sheet-compressed Barnum and Bailey feet. My friends had done it all, and had gotten away with it all. . .no one could recognize any of them behind the masks.

A doctor finally arrived.

"Well, let's see what you've done to yourself." He removed the bowl, pulled a table filled with implements right up next to the bed, picked up my arm and placed my hand on the table and snapped on the attached light. "My, that is nasty. How did you do this?"

"Put my hand through a window."

"On purpose?"

"No."

"Nurse, I'll need some #10 sutures and a syringe with 20ccs of mixolcaine. Did your parents bring you in?"

"No, my neighbor."

"Do they know what happened?"

"They will when they find that their dining room window is now part of their dining room floor."

"Doctor, his parents have been notified and are on the way. They have given their permission to perform whatever procedures you feel are necessary."

"Well, they must be old hands at this. Thank you, nurse. George, I'm going to numb your hand."

"Am I going to lose my finger?"

"No. But you're going to require a lot of sutures, especially in the little finger. I don't think there's been any tissue loss, but the healing process will cause some tightening and reduction, and may pull the finger down a bit."

"What's that mean?"

"You may not be able to straighten the finger fully."

"Just as long as I still have one, Doctor."

"Yes, that would be nice."

When the bandages came off, my finger was bent down. The doctors measured the degree of bend.

"Ninety degree deflection."

"Can it be straightened?" asked my father.

"We can do a skin graft. We'll make an incision across the middle of the little finger, straighten it out, remove a plug from the forearm, and suture it in place," replied the doctors.

"Well, what do you think of that George. . .George? Someone get some smelling salts in here."

My father expressed his deep concerns. "Go ahead."

So I ended up on the operating room table counting backwards from one hundred, with several doctors from MASH attending me. When I awoke in the recovery room, I had a massive Rube Goldberg contraption on my hand. There was a cast on my forearm that started just above the bandages that covered the skin graft wound and extended up to my wrist. Protruding out of the cast was what suspiciously appeared to be a wire coat hanger, bent closely together. It rose gently upward from the cast and ended just above the tip of my little finger, which was now encased in a massive bandage. There was a small amount of plaster with a hook embedded in the form of a "C" stuck onto the end of the dressing. Rubber bands were attached to the hook and connected to the hanger rod above, forming a miniature traction system.

"We want your finger immobilized during the next few weeks as the healing takes place. Then we'll remove the steel sutures. . ."

"Steel sutures?"

"Yes, the graft is held in place by surgical steel sutures, twisted at the ends. This may cause a small problem with removing the bandages, as they tend to get entangled. . .George? Nurse, get the smelling salts in here."

I endured weeks of ice cream stabbing, as I was never able to open up the flaps fast enough with one hand before a fork plunged into the carton. Unopened ice cream flaps in the cafeteria were not tolerated in my group. By the time I got to my seat, there were about eight forks protruding from the carton in an irregular fan shape, sort of resembling an Indian headdress.

The rubber bands in my Rube Goldberg contraption were not your ordinary household variety. They were far thicker, with amazing elasticity. Clearly these were the War Department's version, and I could see the corridors of the Pentagon buzzing with slingshot projectiles being launched by a thousand hostile actions, especially between the army and navy corridors.

This thought was crossing my mind as the projectile I launched was crossing the classroom and impacting Ted's butt.

"Owwwwww. . .!"

"What's going on behind my back?" said the English teacher as he diagrammed a sentence on the board.

Everyone looked about the room for the goings on behind his back, including Ted as he rubbed his sore butt, but by this time there was nothing to see, with the possible exception of me, cradling my injured hand with a painful and pathetic expression on my face.

"Surely it can't have anything to do with that injured boy? Why look at him, he can barely stand the pain as he gingerly holds his hand."

After a few moments of looking around, everything settled back down.

"Who wants to diagram this sentence for. . ."

"Owwwww. . .!"

"People! What is going on!"

I never let on to any of my friends what was going on, because that would be the same as posting it in the cafeteria, and I never got caught at it. It was, possibly, the only thing I didn't get caught at in Germany. I judiciously fired missiles for weeks, extracting full retribution for the ice cream mauling, and it was finally, and officially, chalked up to the ghosts of dead German soldiers who had once billeted in these former barracks.

I went back to the hospital for the unwrapping.

True to their word, the dressing was entangled in the steel sutures surrounding the skin graft. The nurse wanted to just rip it off in one quick, blood-curdling tug.

"One quick pull and it would be all over," she said.

"That's supposed to convince me? Listen, you just get me one of those blood collection bowls of yours, and put some water in it. I'll tell you when it's off."

I worked the dressing out of the sutures like a Swiss watch-maker over the next half-hour. No screams, no blood. The doctors came in, slightly depressed that there had been no screaming, and removed the sutures with a small pair of wire cutters they borrowed from the electrical shop. There we all sat, looking over the results, measuring the fruits of two months of their work.

"Forty-five degree deflection."

"Halfway there."

"Well, one more time should just about do it then, what do you think George. . .George? Someone get some smelling salts in here."

My father at least knew when to get out of a room.

"That's it gentlemen, after all it's just the little finger, and I can't see letting you loose on it once again. Two months is enough."

I was left with a bent finger, physical therapy got me to about thirty degrees, and that was it. I now had the burn scar on my left hand from the grenade at Fort Lewis, a bent and scarred little finger on my right, which to add insult to injury was growing hair out of the skin graft that had been taken out of my forearm. Both of my thumbs had half-formed first joints from birth, and would not bend at all. I had the hands of a plumber at the age of thirteen. I became self-conscious of them, and began to favor keeping them out of sight.

I was back for a brief hospital stay when I began to get that old familiar feeling, and returned with a mild second bout of mono. This time I didn't need to be isolated, so I got to watch the movies, smoking hospital cigarettes and wearing gloves, gowns and masks that I pilfered from the ward. It would have been better if some of my friends were there with me, because I made rather a bizarre solitary figure in the back of the movie cafeteria all by myself. Everyone went out of their way to give me plenty of room, letting me have an entire couch, not wanting to chance catching whatever it was that I had.

My final visit to the hospital was benign. . .the football physical, and I would hesitate to mention it at all except. . .

"One of the doctors in there is a women!" screamed Earle.

"So?"

"She's doing the hernia test."

"The hernia test?"

"Yeah. . .turn your head and cough."

"Really?"

"Really."

"Which line?"

"The one everyone's in."

GODDAMN IT FRANK

MR. COLEMAN TAUGHT DRAFTING, and had the world's worst bad breath. I doubt there's any connection between the two, but I'm not acquainted with any real drafters, and for all I know they may be leveling the walls, and each other, with their breath. It may be an occupational hazard of drafting. It was a new discovery for me. It was the first time I had encountered bad breath. But encounter it I had, and in spades. It made Dave's cauliflower farts seem amateurish, which depressed him. I suspect it was caused by Mr. Coleman's cigar habit, but I can't be sure, since his cigar smelled infinitely better than his breath.

"I think he's been gargling with the toilet water," said Ted.

In his class, your worst nightmare was to be called to the blackboard, for he would hover close by, replacing all the normal smells of the world with his breath.

"What happened. . .is the world rotting?" you would say, as you began to black out. You had to wonder what would happen if aliens ever abducted Mr. Coleman. . .

"Awcckkkk! . . . Bezflib!"

Which is alien for "This world is rotting," and they would have flown off to never return, thereby killing a future billion-dollar book and movie industry.

Anyone trapped at the board tried to turn their face and breathe out of the side of their mouths in a vain attempt to dodge the fumes.

The effort almost made you burst out and scream. . .

"Please, your breath. . .first you killed off all the aliens and now you're killing me. I'll do anything, just let me breathe!"

But no one ever did, all we managed to do was grimace and squirm, which would cause him to become even more attentive.

"Is there something wrong with you?" he would ask.

Well, of course there was, but we didn't dare move a muscle and force ourselves to take a breath. So we continued to squirm while we tried to hand signal that everything was just fine.

"I'm beginning to believe the teenagers of today have some kind of nervous disorder. All of you dance around like you have ants in your pants," he would say.

I would have preferred the ants.

Mr. Coleman was single. This didn't come as a surprise to any of us. We also thought he liked to drink, but this was only a guess, since any drinking he did, he did alone. He was also the coach of the soccer team. He was chosen because none of the real coaches wanted anything to do with it. Years before, in one of those teacher meetings held behind closed doors, he ended up as the high school soccer coach. We all assumed that bad breath must have been one of the top qualifications for the job.

My brother was on the soccer team, and it was at one of Mr. Coleman's practices where he nailed me with an errant soccer ball to the side of the head, spilling me right into the middle of the cheerleaders' practice pyramid. I became an unwelcome fifth member of the bottom tier, which instantly became the only tier still standing.

I heard him laughing back there, but I wasn't that mad because I know he didn't do it on purpose. To hit me deliberately would have required some skill, and he didn't have any. He couldn't have hit the side of the gym, unless he wasn't aiming at it. The entire soccer team couldn't have hit the side of the gym. I know. . .I saw them try. They hit everything and everybody except the gym. People were dropping like flies from errant soccer balls, but the side of the gym remained untouched.

Every junior and senior tried out for Mr. Coleman's soccer team, it was very popular. He was a legend in the school for more than just his breath. The soccer team trips were famous. The team would arrive at their destination on Friday morning, and he would get the players to their assigned barracks and then announce. . .

"All right men, game time is two o'clock tomorrow, see you then."

. . .and he was gone. They were suddenly men, and not teenagers with a nervous disorder. Nobody knew where he went, nor did anyone really care. He managed to get away with this for years. Except for the final undoing on The Berlin Trip.

Several members of the team, my brother included, rented a Volkswagen van and loaded it up with beer. They were last

seen heading off the base and into the city. When game time
rolled around, the team rolled in, Mr. Coleman rolled in, and
the van rolled in. Our team was spending a lot time trying to
sober up while the game was in progress. This was causing a lot
of strange behavior that didn't seem to fit in with a soccer game.
They didn't have to worry about hitting anyone, or anything,
with errant shots, they no longer seemed to be able to actually
kick the ball. The wind currents created by their misses were
kicking up a good little breeze on the sideline, which was helping revive some of those who had assumed a more comfortable
prone position. This wasn't an official position on the soccer
field, but it was popular that day. Others had staggered off behind the bleachers to throw up. This was eventually noticed
by everyone, including the entire Berlin high school commu-
nity. . .everyone except Mr. Coleman.

He prowled the sidelines, chomping on his cigar, slightly
aware that something was wrong with his players.

"It's these goddamned teenagers. There's just something
wrong with them. They've got ants in their pants."

Except for those who are lying unconscious on the ground,
whose pants were now completely free of ants.

Well, Mr. Coleman might not have known what was going
on, but the opposing school principal was getting a pretty good
idea as the number of bodies piled up around him.

"Mr. Coleman! Your team is drunk!"

Mr. Coleman turned around to face the Berlin principal.

"What!? . . ." The wind currents were just right to carry the
full impact of his toilet water cigar breath into the Berlin
principal's face.

Boom. The principal fell to the ground.

"He's dead. . .he must have had a heart attack!" someone
yelled.

Mr. Coleman went back to coaching the game.

"Come on now! Let's everyone start playing the game and
quit leaving the field. What the hell is the attraction under the
bleachers anyway?"

The Berlin principal was revived in time to read everyone
the riot act. This would have to be repeated later to several players on Mr. Coleman's team who were wondering why the principal of Berlin was giving the post game pep talk. Not really
comprehending anything, they smiled politely nonetheless.

Mr. Coleman sat there stunned. "What? It's not ants in their
pants? . . ."

When I heard what had happened, I knew immediately I
had to get in on these trips as soon as possible. My freshman

year ended, and for the most part, everything came out okay. And anything that didn't was all Dave's fault.

★   ★   ★

I WAS READY for my first summer job in Bremerhaven. I looked forward to having some money jingling in my pants.

"I think we want more than just jingling. I want the rustle of folding money in my pants," said Ted.

"It was just a figure of speech."

"Well, just as long as the figures are large amounts."

"I just want someone other than my dad to have jingling pants."

The job was at the car processing center on the main base. It was here that everyone picked up and delivered their cars for the Atlantic crossing. The cars coming out of the cargo holds of ships looked like they had been stored in a field behind a circus for a year. An area had been set aside as a car wash. It was an unofficial summer jobs program. Cars were washed for a buck, and anyone. . .any age, could show up and make some jingling cash. There were no job interviews, or residency requirements. The army had been kind enough to provide the location, we would handle the rest.

"Get out!" The Older Guys had unilaterally decided that this cash cow was under their exclusive control.

It had been placed off limits to us by order of an Older Guys Pounding Decree. Now, we had already been victimized by the lack of a smoking area at the high school, and here we were again, faced with practically the same thing. We pointed out to the port authority that our group was under employable age, and our job choices were limited. We could be pin boys at the bowling alley, carry out groceries at the commissary, or wash these cars, while the Older Guys had a lot of options. They weighed our arguments carefully, which we could tell by the annoyed looks on their faces, and then they passed a Port Authority Pounding Decree against the Older Guys.

With this many Pounding Decrees flying around a confrontation was sure to follow.

"We said get out!" said the Older Guys.

"But we're supposed to be able to wash cars. . .we have a Port Authority Pounding Decree right here that says so."

"We don't care about no stinking decree. Get out!"

We left with our tails between our legs, and with an apparently worthless Pounding Decree in our hands.

"I thought all Pounding Decrees were ironclad. At least my brother's are. . .what happened in there?"

We sat on the curb in our car washing clothes, which were indistinguishable from our regular clothes.

"We need bigger guns on our side."

"What can we do?"

"We can go to the MPs."

"The MPs? Aren't they the guys that usually come looking for us?"

"Yep."

"This appears to be a valid Pounding Decree," said the desk sergeant. "And you say they totally ignored it?"

"They said, 'We don't care about no stinking decree. Get out!'"

"Really. . .hmmmm. . .have a seat right over there."

In minutes we were back at the car wash with an MP escort.

"Gentlemen," said the desk sergeant, who decided to handle this himself. "Am I to understand that you ignored this decree?"

"No, sir!"

"No, sir!"

"No, sir!"

"No, sir!"

"Really. . .hmmmm. . .why don't you explain to me what happened when these boys arrived here this morning."

"We told them all the spots were taken, they were just too late. You have to get here early."

The sergeant handed them the decree.

"Have you read this?"

"Well. . ."

"Then read it now."

The Older Guys took a few moments to read it, then handed it back to the sergeant.

"So, gentlemen, was there any mention of 'spots' or 'getting here early,' or that you were running the show, or anything like that?"

"No, sir."

"So, then we understand each other. When I come back here at noon, I should see these boys busily washing cars, yes?"

"Yes, sir."

"I think we have an understanding. Then I'll see everyone at noon."

Our protectors left and the Older Guys stood there glaring. Then they handed us their decree.

"Have you read this?"

"Well. . ."

"Then read it now."

We took a few moments to read it, then handed it back to the Older Guys.

"So, gentlemen, was there any mention of 'blood' or 'bruising,' or anything like that?"

"Yes, there was a lot of that in there."

"Then we understand each other. When we turn around you will be gone, yes?"

We almost ran then, but we didn't. When they turned around we held up our decree like a shield, with our knees shaking. They were shocked.

"What are you still doing here?"

"We're going to wash cars."

Well, not expecting anything like this, they weren't sure what to do next. After a quick conference, they put all the supplies back in the locker, snapped closed the combination lock, and left us standing there.

"What do you think this means?" asked Ted.

"That we own the place!"

"Yeah!"

We hopped around screaming out self-congratulatory battle slogans.

"We won!"

"Yahoo!"

"We get to wash cars!"

"Yipee!"

"We don't know the combination to the lock!"

"Yah. . .what?"

Hmmmm, seems to be a hole right there in the middle of one of our battle cry yahoos.

"So, this is their big plan. . .wait for us to give up because we can't open the locker?"

"Well. . .we can't."

"Let's break it open."

"With what. . .it's an army locker." Built by the same people who made our school lockers. We would need a blowtorch and an armor piercing shell to break in.

"Then what are we going to do?"

"Let's try guessing the combination."

"Who do I look like? Willy Sutton?"

"Well, let's give it a try anyway."

The lock was the type that had four tumblers on the bottom. Our first guess was the obvious, all nines. It didn't open. Second-guess. . . all zeros. Third. . .all ones. . .the lock opened. It was obvious the Older Guys weren't Willy Sutton either.

"This is rather incredulous," I said.

"I can't believe it."

"I know. . .they're not the most inventive bunch."

"No, that you were actually able to use the word 'incredulous' in a conversation."

We broke out the supplies and faked knowing what we were doing. Still, it was just washing cars, and how hard could it be to throw water over a car? After the first couple of times with the car owners telling us what some of the stuff was used for, we were just fine.

"What is this thing again, sir?"

"A chamois."

"Chamois. . ."

"It's named for a European mountain antelope, but these are probably made out of sheepskin."

"Really, a naturalist lesson. . .and we're wiping a car with the skin of a dead animal."

"Yes."

"Incredulous."

"Ted, don't use words you've just heard until you know how."

That night we flashed our car washing dollars around the teen club, letting the Older Guys know that we had cracked the code. . .we had washed. This successful rebellion broke the back of the Older Guys Decree, and ripples were felt all the way down to Older Brother Decrees. A way of life was passing from our lives. Parental Decrees, however, remained immune.

The next summer they did amend the Port Authority Pounding Decree to include spots and getting there early, which I was never good at, so I moved on to the bowling alley, and stood in the ranks facing our leader. . .Jack the Pin Setter.

He stood there, looking us over, wearing professional bowling gloves and shoes, his cigarettes rolled up in his tee-shirt sleeve, and a towel attached to his belt with a bowling-pin belt buckle. We were simply summer help, setting pins for ten cents a line, and in awe of Jack the Pinsetter. Whenever he walked by, we cleared a path for him.

Jack called the back alley of machines Broadway, everything else was Out Front. We all fell into calling it the same thing, just to please Jack, he was our hero. Referring to these metal contraptions as a machine is stretching things. I think a blacksmith might have appreciated them, we certainly didn't. The main section was shaped like the triangular pattern of the pins, with ten slots, and a push bar extending across the back. When filled with pins you had to jump up and lean your weight against the bar to get it to come down. You pushed down on the bar to set the pins up vertically, and then let go of it to have the machine rise back up, barely missing your chin in the process.

We sat in our pin boy cubby slot, keeping feet and legs tucked out of the way. When a ball came through with the accompanying flying pins, I waited until everything stopped moving, then jumped into the pit, grabbed the ball and put it on the return ramp slope, and picked up the pins and placed them into the slots over vacated positions below. It was important to remember to place them over the empty spots, otherwise when you pushed down the set bar you'd knock over the pins still on the alley with the pins occupying their slots above. This would usually jam the machine at the same time, to the audible groans from the bowlers Out Front.

"Goddamn it, Frank! Get us a pin boy who knows what the hell he's doing!"

All the yelling would fluster us, and we would combine the jammed machine with an anemic push down the ball return ramp, so the ball failed to make it up the incline at the bowlers end, and came back down.

"Goddamn it, Frank!"

We usually did this in combination with returning another ball from the second alley, so they collided in the middle of the ball return runway.

Crack!

"Goddamn it, Frank!"

Frank, the alley manager didn't like to be referred to as "Goddamn it, Frank!" and would come storming back onto Broadway.

"Goddamn it!" he would yell, justifying his name. "What in the hell is going on back here!"

Frank was a "what in the hell" versus a "what the hell" kind of guy. I think "what in the hell" is the more formal version, and appreciated his using it when referring to us. Jack would settle Frank down and then get him out of there because he didn't want Goddamn it, Frank! on Broadway. This was Jack's place.

At the end of a grueling shift we were paid in cash.

"Nice job," Frank would say, and give me my $2.40. Down the line he would go, saying "Nice job" and handing out the line money, until he got to Jack.

"Amazing," he would say, and hand Jack $14.50. Our jaws would drop open.

Some of the GIs liked to play the game of Hit the Pin Boy, sort of like pin the tail on the donkey, but instead of being blindfolded, they were drunk. Jack taunted and teased them. He dangled his legs behind the pins so they could see him, but they never could hit him, they tried so hard that they'd throw the ball halfway down the alley, sometimes bouncing it across to another alley, prompting Goddamn it, Frank! to yell at them.

"Goddamn it! Keep the ball on your own alley, and don't loft it!"

Jack would purposely hold back the balls, and then send them all back without enough push to make it up their ramp, the dead roller train, as he called it. Then we'd all laugh as the drunk GIs stumbled along, trying to walk down the gutter to get their balls.

"Goddamn it, Frank!" the GIs would yell.

"Goddamn it, Jack!" Frank would yell.

My alleys were much calmer, and things moved much slower. The GIs were waiting on me like they were stuck in a bank teller's line, and they finally passed out. . .dead drunk. Two games bowled and each had consumed eight beers. Frank didn't mind, the alley made more money on beer than bowling anyway.

Then calamity struck. Automatic pinsetters were installed. Jack was visibly shaken, and stood there unable to move or say anything. In a week it was finished. . .automation. The cries of "Goddamn it, Frank!" dropped considerably.

After the elimination of pin boys at the bowling alley, I was forced into the commissary, becoming a carryout boy for tips. Thus, my stage of jobs ending with "boy" continued. Working for tips is not a good occupation in the service. The military are notoriously lousy tippers. You couldn't blame them, the Department of Defense is a notoriously lousy paymaster, unless of course you had a missile in your back pocket. Then you could have billions, easy. Unfortunately, I didn't have a missile in my pocket, so I got ten cents a carriage load.

Twice a month, Mrs. Lingstrom came into the commissary. For some unknown reason, Mr. Lingstrom was stationed about two hours away, and the only time she came into the port was to do her food shopping. I believe she bought groceries for a family of twenty, and a carriage train began to form behind her as she shopped. Most of us tried to hide. The checkout took forever, and she was known as a notoriously lousy tipper by the entire field of notoriously lousy tippers. Apparently, she thought we did this for our health and exercise. Sometimes she gave you an apple or an orange.

"What is this, Halloween?"

I never knew what Mr. Lingstrom did, but he must have had a paymaster considered lousy by the field of lousy paymasters.

In three years of summer jobs, I made a grand total of five hundred dollars.

I watched my brother at his summer job. He was in the laundry room at the U.S. Army Dependents Hotel, the transient bed and bath. He sat there smoking Camel cigarettes, reading a book, and shooting the shit with his friends who had come to visit. And wouldn't you love to know how that saying got started.

Blam!
"Whoa! Man, Look there's shit everywhere!"
Blam!
"You know, this is reminiscent of casual conversation. . ."

I marveled at the way he smoked those Camels. He'd suck in a gigantic load, and open his mouth wide as he inhaled. You could see the dense smoke disappear down his throat, then followed by a blast back out that would blow some of the papers off the desk.

Dave was one step away from giving up Camels and actually started to smoke Trends, "The Mild Little Cigar." He always carried them with him to sucker in overbearing little twerps that liked to emulate his smoking style.

"Here, try one of these. They're very mild and you won't even know you're smoking unless you take a big drag."

Same old line.

They would do it, of course, to prove their manhood. Their eyes would widen as the smoke caught at just about the Adam's apple. Now they were stuck, unwilling to look the fool and unwilling to retreat in defeat. And Dave would sit there smoking and treating them like equals for the duration of the torture.

Same old results.

"Enjoying your smoke?"

A weakened voice would respond, "Yes."

"Well, let's see you make a smoke ring."

By the time it was over, they would walk away unsteadily, some never to smoke again.

"It's my civic duty. Too bad I'm out of Tide Wafers."

Dave seemed to have a lot of civic duties just like this one. I took civics later in high school and never saw any of the duties he claimed as his responsibility.

Obviously another one of his duties was to sit around smoking and shooting the shit with his friends in the laundry room. Occasionally, a load of wrapped-up laundry would come flying down a shoot in the corner and land on the floor. Whomp! Dave would get up, untie the sheet, and separate the contents. Sheets in one pile, pillow cases in another, towels in another. Then he'd go back to smoking, reading, and talking. Dave is the only person I have ever known who could read and carry on a conversation. At the end of the week, he got an actual check from the U.S. Army. It was almost two hundred dollars.

"Wow!" I said. "What kind of job do you have?"

"I'm the laundry man."

"I have to stop doing these boy jobs."

Goddamn it, Frank!

LOOK TO THE SKY

In June, my parents went on their one and only grand European vacation, and left for a two-week journey around the continent. How my father talked my mom into doing this is a real mystery. We went to see them off, and she became train sick before her butt hit the seat. The conductor was bundling her up in a blanket even before the train had actually moved. As the train left the station, he was forced to stand in and wave good-bye to us in her place. Together with my father, they made the original odd couple. We stood on the platform watching until they were out of sight.

"Mom was looking rather handsome there in her uniform waving at us, don't you think? I especially liked the hat, better than her usual ones."

"My guess is there isn't a drop of booze left on that train by the time they get to Bremen," said Dave.

"I wonder which one Dad will choose to take on the rest of the vacation? That conductor was looking pretty good. If he picks Mom, I don't think they'll make the week," I said.

"They better. I've got plans," said Dave.

When we returned to the apartment the first thing Marcella did was use the phone. She called a friend who lived in the apartment two floors up.

"Can you believe it, they said I could use the phone while they were gone! Yes, they did! But this is an emergency! Do you know how long it's been since I could just pick up the phone and call someone whenever I wanted? I was losing my sanity, so I think this qualifies as a sort of emergency, don't you? You're the first one I called. . ."

She talked for quite a long time, then called another friend on the third floor.

"Can you believe it, they said I could use the phone while they were gone! Yes, they did! But this is an emergency! Do you know how long it's been since I could just pick up the phone and call someone whenever I wanted? I was losing my sanity, so I think this qualifies as a sort of emergency, don't you? You're the first one I called. . ."

"I need to use the phone, Marcella," said Dave.

"What!? I just got on!"

"I only need it for a minute, then you can have it back."

"Is this an emergency?"

"It will be. . .if I don't get the phone."

"Barbara, I'll call you right back, don't go anywhere."

Dave called the city brewery and had them deliver cases of beer to the apartment. I didn't know they would do that, I thought only the milkman delivered.

"This is Germany. . .this is milk," said Dave.

Somehow he had convinced Marcella to be on his side, and not say anything to anyone about what was going on. I don't know what the bribe was, but it had to be substantial. . .the *Sibling Handbook* didn't even have an entry for this one.

For two weeks his friends lived there, drank there, played cards there, and blew smoke down their girlfriend's throats. Lucky guys. There was, of course, the usual private couple activities going on. I didn't even have to be told.

"That's all right, everyone keep your seats." And I lit up a cigarette and stayed out of the back bedrooms.

"Smart kid," they said.

"Yeah, he's been trained," said Dave.

"Older Brother Poundings?"

"Several."

My parents returned to a spotless apartment. All the rugs were vacuumed, dishes cleaned, rooms aired out, and the brewery had picked up the mountain of empty beer bottles. Several of the salesmen received bonuses for exceeding their sales quota that year.

My mother was a bit bewildered.

"I. . .I'm pleasantly surprised."

"So am I. I was sure Dad would bring home the conductor," I replied.

This lasted until the phone bill arrived.

"Aaaarrrrgggggghhhhhhh!!!"

"I see you've noticed Marcella's emergency calls," I said.

"Aaaarrrrgggggghhhhhhh!!!"

★   ★   ★

IN JULY, DAVE and a friend left on a motorcycle for a summer tour of Europe. They got their international driver's license, bought a second-hand motorcycle, and took off for Hamburg. I'm not sure how he swung this deal, but he did. They returned with entirely different clothes than they had left with, I mean, nothing was the same.

"What happened?"

"Don't ask."

"Nice bonnet."

"Thanks."

Just before the start of my sophomore year we said good-bye to Dave. He was off to college, and I bought him a Dorfenwurst at the dockside stand as a going away gift. He was going to Connecticut by himself, first to New York City by ship, and then to catch a bus for the university.

I gave him the Dorfenwurst. "I wish it could be some Tide Wafers, I know how you love them."

"This is fine, besides, they may have some on board."

"We'll see you in June, and don't forget to stop by Bristol and play Name That Relative."

"George!" admonished my mother. "We, at least, trust him far more than you to talk with our relatives."

"Why? He's the one that taught me douchebag the last time we were there."

"George! You don't say those kind of things in polite company."

From the sound of it, polite company never has any fun. The ship sailed, my mom cried, my father went to the club, and I went home and moved into Dave's vacant room.

★   ★   ★

I STARTED OFF my sophomore year by trying out for the football team. It was late summer, and I discovered that football uniforms are not good summer attire. It was quite a sensation having leather and plastic parts stuck onto your body from head to toe, with a layer of sweat adhesive. They are also not good winter attire. In fact, I can't think of a season when they are good attire.

"Why am I doing this again?" I asked Ted.

"For the love of the sport and for your school."

"Heh, Heh."

"Ha, ha, ha."

"Ha, ha, ha, ha ha."

"HA, HA, HA, HA, HA, HA."

"HA, HA, HA, HA, HA, HA. . . .whew. . .hold on a second, I'm dying."

Football uniforms are also not good attire for laughing.

"What are you two girls laughing about back there!?" shouted one of the football coaches.

"Girls? . . ."

"Is he talking to us?"

"I don't know. . .are you talking to us?" I asked.

"All right! Give me five laps!"

"Is that your answer?"

"Give me ten laps!"

Football uniforms are also not good attire for running laps.

"I feel like *The Man in the Iron Mask* in here. Tell me again why I'm running around the track in this medieval outfit."

"Because you want to go on the trips. . .and you want to get laid."

I determinedly ran around the track.

"Son. . ."

"Yes, Dad."

". . .every time I drive by your football practices, you're running laps. I don't remember your brother doing this. What's going on?"

"I wish I knew. Every time I ask, I get more laps, so I don't ask anymore."

"Well, I'll stop by tomorrow afternoon and talk to the coach."

The next day, when we took the practice field, my father was doing laps around the track.

"Looks like things didn't go too well for your father," said Ted.

"Well, I'm not asking anyone, anything."

Ted came over that Saturday afternoon and picked me up for a quick stop at the little bahnhof.

"Good afternoon, Mrs. Allingham."

"Good afternoon, Ted."

"It must a little lonesome around here with David off to college."

"Yes, I haven't gotten used to it yet," my mom said with a note of sorrow in her voice. I, on the other hand, was now free from Older Brother Decrees, and had a bedroom twice the size. My old one was converted into a broom closet.

"You're looking very fit."

"Why thank you, Ted. I just had my annual physical at the clinic last Friday."

"Really? You don't look like you need to have an annual physical."

I stood there, admiring this genius at work.

"The doctor said the same thing, in fact, he said that I was in remarkably good shape for a woman my age."

My father put down the paper. "Did he say anything about your big, fat ass?"

"I don't recall your name coming up."

Ted and I weren't sure we had heard this correctly, but you should never have a joke explained to you, takes the heart out of it. . .ask someone about it later.

"Well, it was nice talking to you Mrs. Allingham. We're going for a walk around the neighborhood."

"And it was nice talking to you, Ted. I wish my son were as polite as you."

"Maybe, the two of you should do some laps around the neighborhood," added my father.

"Are your parents some kind of comedy act?" asked Ted as we went out the door.

"Sometimes, but mostly unintentionally."

"It's kind of true though, your father really does have a fat ass."

"Well, I don't think that was her intended meaning, Ted, but you're right, he has a big ass, which is kind of amazing considering he's full-blooded Irish. Look at me. . .and I'm only half Irish."

"Oh my God. . .you might have been completely disabled had he married an Irish women."

"And all these laps around the football field aren't helping."

★   ★   ★

DON'T EVER MAKE the mistake of thinking that people like the same things as you. They don't. They don't like the same paintings, they don't like the same movies, they don't like the same music—it's almost as if they don't like anything you like. This is something everyone learns on their own sooner or later, usually after they do something really dumb.

I still believed we all thought alike, and saw everything the same way. . .felt the same about everything. When I made a new discovery, I wanted to share it.

There is a song called "Freight Train" by Rusty Draper; it was a minor hit in the fifties on Mercury Records, when the label was still red. The chorus painted the most serene picture of clouds on a summer day. I was young, so I thought everyone saw these serene clouds passing by on this summer day. In fact, I was sure it was the only reason anyone bought the record.

That afternoon, I just knew Ted would love to see the serene summer clouds. After we returned from the little bahnhof, I gave him his chance.

"Ted, come here."

He came right over.

"Sit down and look out the window into the sky."

"Why? . . ."

"Just sit down here, and look out the window."

He sat down.

"What am I looking at?"

"Look at the clouds, just relax and look at the clouds in that blue sky."

"There aren't any clouds. . .or a blue sky."

"There will be." I put on "Freight Train."

"What's this music for?"

I should have smelled a rat right then.

"Don't talk! Just keep looking for those clouds."

"This is weird."

I really did this, no fooling.

"Just shut up, and keep looking."

The chorus part came on, and I quickly sat next to Ted, looking up into the sky with him.

"Now, what do you feel?"

"I feel like an idiot."

"No. . .no. . .look back at the sky. . ."

The song was back into the verse.

". . .wait. . .we have to wait for the chorus."

"You are so strange."

"It only works during the chorus."

"Yeah, sure. . ."

The chorus came back on.

"Quick. . .look. . .up into the sky."

"It's a bird, it's a plane. . ."

"Shut up. Be serious."

"You want me to be serious? While I'm doing this? . . ."

"What do you feel?"

"I feel really queer. . ."

"You. . .er. . .just exactly how do you mean that? . . ." as I moved over to give Ted a little extra room.

"I feel peculiar when you ask me what I feel. . .that's what I feel."

"Nothing else?"

"I feel like not being alone in your room with you."

I started the record again.

"Oh no. . .," said Ted. "I don't have to do this again, do I?"

"This will work, believe me, you just have to. . ."

"This is too weird, this is starting to feel like we're dressing up in girl's underwear."

". . .listen to the voices."

There were no serene summer clouds on this day, at least not for Ted.

"I'd rather dress up in girl's underwear than have to sit looking out the window into the sky with you next to me. . .moony eyed and all."

"Moony eyed!?"

"Yeah, like you're about to have a climax or something. It makes me very uncomfortable. Can I get out of here?"

"I. . .I. . ." I had nothing to say, but I did wonder if I could develop this into a climax.

"Can I leave?"

"Yes, please go."

For the next week, Ted ducked me. I was sure that everyone had heard about sitting and looking out the window, staring at clouds. I don't think anyone knew what I was trying to do, I'm not sure what I was trying to do anymore myself.

Trying to explain any of it was out of the question, for it just got dumber the more I thought about it. I felt like I was walking around the school dressed up in girl's underwear. It wasn't until I got older that I learned that dressing up in girl's underwear can be fun.

★　★　★

IN SEPTEMBER OF 1961, Ted and I made the football team. Being an upside-down year, the first since 1881, had a lot to do with it. It's the only explanation I have for the two of us making the team. The coach said we were both in the best shape of any two guys he had ever seen.

"Even better than your mom."

By my calculations, Ted and I had run over a hundred miles during the tryouts. I was on my way. . .on my first team trip. I felt like I had been accepted into a secret society.

We boarded the train at the main bahnhof, with half the school coming out to see us off. Half the school always came out to see off the teams, and then went directly into the gasthaus when the train left. Some went directly into the gasthaus before the train left. I personally know of a few people who went down to the bahnhof for every team departure, and never actually saw a team train leave the station. I believe Ted and I were in that group. So, here I was, standing in the train corridor, watching the station leave the train.

"Wow, this is really cool."

I stood in the corridor for a long time, mesmerized by the rocking of the train and by the passing countryside. Mikey came up beside me, singing the old Marlboro cigarette commercial.

"You get a lot to like in a Marlboro, filter, flavor, flip-top box."

And as he sang he pulled out a crumpled piece of tinfoil containing two battered cigarettes. . .not exactly what Marlboro had in mind.

He noticed me staring at the cigarettes in his hand.

"You really have to work at getting cigarettes to look like this," he said.

"I imagine so. Most people don't usually keep 'em around that long."

"I just got these at the station."

"Then it's quite an accomplishment."

He fished a pack of matches out of his pocket, and struck one ablaze as he continued to sing like he actually had a voice I wanted to hear, and lit one of those battered cigarettes. He inhaled with a flourish, exhaled, and crooned away. He was really starting to put some feeling into that jingle, and began posing. . .James Dean in Marlboro Country. You probably shouldn't sing and pose while smoking, too many things to do all at once for Mikey.

With a flick of his wrist, he launched the spent match out the train window and put the matchbook back in his pocket. At least that's what he thought he did. Unfortunately, he launched the matchbook, and put the burning match back into his pocket. He was crooning away, really enjoying himself, then his shirt pocket started to smolder. He still didn't know it, and he was still singing.

At first the smoke coming out of Mikey's pocket startled me.

"Uhhh. . .your. . .heh. . .your. . .heh. . .heh. . .your pocket. . .ha. . . ha. . ."

This was actually pretty funny. I only wish I could have told Mikey about it before he became a Roman candle. I wondered how he couldn't see the smoke coming out of his pocket?

". . .pocket. . .hee. . .hee." Now I had the giggles and was gasping for breath, and started to crumple to the corridor floor. I was convulsing with laughter and could only point.

"What! What's wrong with you?"

". . .not me. . ."

It's too bad I couldn't tell him because Mikey liked a good joke. Then a flame licked out of his pocket.

"Owww! Shit! Ooooo! Owww!"

He started hopping around. . .James Dean doing the Saint Vitus' dance. He ran screaming down the corridor to the bathroom and doused himself. Mikey was mad at me for a while, he didn't buy that I couldn't say anything.

"I tried."

"Not hard enough."

"I hope you brought another shirt."

"I was going to wear it to their teen club."

"You still can, it's a conversation piece now. It might actually attract a girl." You never know what's going to attract a girl. So far, all I knew was that calling them douchebag sure didn't.

Yep, cool Mikey, standing there with his shirt pocket on fire. Unluckily for me, my own moments are usually captured on film. Like that picture of me posing with the other neighborhood kids, dressed in our fathers' army equipment, and I'm the one with my fly open. It's the kind of picture my mother likes to show whenever I bring over a girl. Why is that?

I remember this part of high school rather clearly. However, I couldn't begin to tell you anything about the Articles of Confederation.

★   ★   ★

OUR TRAIN WAS heading for Frankfurt, the largest city in the southern American zone, and the hub for getting to the many bases that surrounded the town. It would take all night to get there. We would arrive early the next morning. I found it difficult to get to sleep at first, everything was too exciting, but eventually I dozed off.

The city of Hanover had a large switching yard where the trains were coupled to other trains in a giant mix and match process, and finally sent on their way. You arrived there sometime around two o'clock in the morning. By this time, everyone had been lulled into a sound sleep by the gentle rocking of the cars and the rhythmic click-clack of the train tracks. Once you got to Hanover, you woke up. The sound of the tracks had stopped, and you couldn't sleep without it. For what seemed like hours, the cars were pushed and pulled around the yard, as a new train was assembled for the rest of the journey. Slowly, everyone began to wake up, and then congregate around the windows, staring out at the eerie early morning scene. Under the harsh yard lights, engines and cars continually moved back and forth, their steam trails lingering in the night sky.

Everyone woke up in Hanover, it was an unwelcome nocturnal ritual on all the journeys south. No one ever slept through it. You just expected to wake up and hang out of the windows with everyone else, looking out over what appeared to be a maze of hundreds of tracks that crisscrossed the mammoth switching yard.

Paul, a strapping kid of limited common sense, which really doesn't distinguish him much from the rest of us, brought along a coconut for the occasion. He planned to break it open over one of the rails, and then drink a bleary-eyed coconut-milk toast. It's a mystery why Paul would want to do this, but at two in the morning it seemed to make some sense. This should tell you all you need to know about making any decisions at two in the morning.

We jumped off the train in our special Hanover coconut-milk toast underwear outfits and began to pound this coconut against the railroad tracks. It was a tough old nut, and just bounced off the cold metal with no damage done, except to the rail. One by one, we became arm weary, but still the coconut wouldn't crack.

"Hey, the train's leaving!"

"Shit!"

Sure enough, our train was being pulled away. Would it be just across a few tracks, across the yard, or was it on its way to Frankfurt? Paul grabbed his coconut, and we all ran after the train. Some yard workers caught sight of us, and they began screaming and running after us. So here we all were, in a scene that rivaled the snake dance to the teen club. The trains were moving back and forth, the ten of us and a coconut were running back and forth, and several dozen yard workers were running back and forth, yelling unknown Germanic phrases.

"I bet they wish that Germany had won the war!" I yelled to Paul.

"I only wish one thing," panted Paul.

"What's that?" I replied running alongside.

"That I wasn't in my underwear."

"Yeah. . .well, I don't even like coconuts."

My first trip. . .and already it was great. Ted watched us from the compartment window.

"Hey, you guys make good-looking ambassadors!"

Especially Mikey, running in his shorts and wearing the shirt with the burned-out pocket.

"Hey George! You're not going to try and blame this on the upside-down year again, are you!?" yelled Ted.

THE MANNEQUIN MAN

SHE WAS THE CHIEF's daughter, and something of a minor celebrity in the high school. The chief was a chief petty officer in the navy and he was in charge of the teen club. We all respected him. He was addressed simply as "Chief." He was largely responsible for Gorps and Dorfenburgs, as well as the senior class trip to Paris, so you know how everyone felt about him. His daughter's lofty standing came largely from being. . .his daughter. She wasn't particularly good looking. She was usually sour faced whenever you saw her, like she just discovered she was wearing her kid sister's girdle.

Everyone liked Chief, but you could tell he had a rough side that he hid well and never showed to us, at least I never saw it, but we knew, in his time, a few sailors sure had. Margaret had gained a certain status, and she only went out with seniors. We lowly sophomores were a little awed by her, which I believe was the intended effect.

So it was with great surprise to everyone when she broke up with her current senior and started hinting around that she wanted me, lowly little me. Wanting to go out with me was the surprise, breaking up is something she did rather often. I started hearing this rumor from my friends. . .it sounded like a rumor I would have started.

"She says she's interested in you."

"There's obviously been a mistake, I don't remember starting this rumor. Something must have been garbled in transmission. A lot of good rumors have been lost due to garbling. This just doesn't sound right."

"Well, one would certainly think so, wouldn't one," agreed Ted.

"Let's not be so positive, you're hurting my feelings."

"Well, let's hope so," finished Ted.

I continued to refuse to believe it. Why would Margaret be interested in me? After all, I was a sophomore like her, and had no particular status at all. If you added it all up. . .it didn't add up.

"This must be what you get when you're one of the Bandstand Four. Women want you," I concluded.

"They don't want me," said Ted. "And I'm one of the Bandstand Four."

"Well, that shoots my theory. If you had gone along with it, even though there was a hole, there might have been a date in it for you."

"Maybe she likes Rusty Drooper."

"That's Draper. . .and I thought I had lived that down."

"What could possibly give you that idea. . .there are a lot of things that can be lived down, but that's certainly not one of them. I'm surprised she'd even talk to you after that, in fact, I'm surprised I'm talking to you."

"It was a mistake. . .let's drop it before my brother hears about it. I don't need to provide him with any ammunition."

"He's gone to college. . ."

"So what. . .he has ears everywhere. . .don't kid yourself. I'm expecting a letter any day addressed to Moony Eyed."

"Are you going to go out with her?"

"Why do you want to know?"

"Why do I want to know? Jesus. . .you have a chance here. . .to do something no other mortal sophomore has done. . .turn her down."

"She hasn't asked me anything."

"Well, she will. . .it's only a matter of time."

"This is just talk, and mostly you doing the talking. I'm just going to wait and see. If she expects some kind of move out of me, she's going to be disappointed."

"We usually are."

"I'm talking about her. I don't particularly care if I disappoint you. . .especially after wasting Rust Drooper on you."

"Drapper," corrected Ted.

I didn't have to wait long.

It was after football practice. The field was empty, everyone had gone except the players and cheerleaders. A bus waited to take us home. I could see her through the visor of my medieval football chamber-pot helmet. She was standing by the grandstand with the other cheerleaders.

"Ted. . ."

"What?"

"Look who's over there."

"You expect me to turn this whole suit of armor around just to look at somebody?" Creak. . .clatter. . .clang. . .groan. . .lurch. "Ahhh. . . someone to see Moony Eyed I suspect. The moment of truth."

"Truth is not going to be involved, if I have anything to say about it."

"Are you ready?"

"I'm always ready."

"Sure. Okay, Moony Eyed, show us what you got."

We changed and clambered aboard the bus. I slid across an empty seat to the window. The black and gold skirt of a cheerleader slid next to me. It was Margaret. And now I sat looking at her. . .with my mind gone totally blank. . .and my mouth full of marbles. I didn't remember putting marbles in my mouth when I got on the bus, but they were there nonetheless. Things were looking pretty desperate. This would all soon be in my dreams, sitting together on the bus, she in her kid sister's girdle, and me in my underwear. . .high school couple of the year.

I looked around for some help from Ted. All I could see was the furious betting action in the rear of the bus. I just stared at Margaret and rolled the marbles around in my mouth. It was the best I could do, although I could probably muster up a dumbfounded look if really pressed.

"Hi," she said.

"Burferlinger. . ."

"What?" she asked.

It was the same question I had. I smoothly collected myself, confidently looked her in the eye and said, "Bahaberaher. . ."

She stared at me for a moment. "Hi," she said again.

Oh, we're going to start this all over again, hey. . .well, I've got a burferlinger or two left.

"Hi." Well. . .an actual English word, and it even fit.

Silence.

Well, that may have been it.

I hoped she had something else, because I sure didn't want to go back to burferlinger.

"Are you going to the teen club tonight?"

"Yes," I said confidently.

That was good. If we kept to yes or no questions, I might have been able to work my way up from imbecile.

"Will I see you there?"

What did this mean? Was she asking if I'd be with her when I got there? Or was it just an innocent question about whether I was going? I was overthinking this. I decided not to say anything! I stopped talking. . . which might have been good. I was blowing the one-word answers. What happened to the yes or no questions?

"Uhh. . ."

What happened to English?

She'd slipped her hand into mine!

"Aiiieeee. . ."

The tilt signs rang up in my eyes. The fuses were starting to blow.

"Will I see you there?"

"Burferlinger. . ." Oh, nooooooo.

"I'll see you later." And she was gone.

"Come back. I can talk, really, you'll see. . ."

I stood up and called after her.

"Bahaberaher. . ."

Ted came up and sat down in her empty seat. "That was really smooth, Rusty."

"What happened? I don't remember a thing."

"How convenient. You really impressed her."

"I did?"

"Yeah. . .it was a sight to behold. I think you may have something new to live down, but not with me. I made ten bucks on those burgerlingers of yours."

And thus, our brief courtship began. . .emphasis on brief. It didn't last more than a few weeks. I was inexperienced at this whole boy/girl thing. I was expecting something different, you know, like in the movies. . .we'd be a couple. I didn't see her very much, even when I saw her. She was always moving along, from one group to another, doing her socialite thing. I would be towed along behind her. She was Cleopatra. . .I was the barge. I believed I was strictly for display purposes. . .see bottom for disposal date. . .if you could find my bottom.

My expiration date came quickly.

I had lost track of the time for our date to a dance and showed up an hour late. She had already left. The chief answered the door and drilled me with a look that turned my feet to stone. We had the briefest of conversations.

He said: "Asshole. . ."

I said: "Bahaberaher. . ."

I was pretty frantic.

When I got to the dance, Ted met me at the door.

"Ted, is she here?"

"Ah, Burferlinger. . .who are you referring to?"

"Come on. . ."

"Good God! Have you seen yourself!?"

"What! What!"

"You've left home without your nose ring."

"Funny man."

"She's in there, and she's been forced to mingle without you along in your customary role as mannequin man, so I'd watch out."

I went into the hall and peered around as I walked across the darkened room. There was a cold icy wind blowing across the dance floor that led right to her. The closer I got the more my legs began to seize up, and I veered off and made for the lobby instead. I was safe there.

"What are you doing back here?" asked Ted.

"I don't know, I think I blacked out."

Margaret blew in on the Arctic wind.

"Well, time for me to go," said Ted.

Margaret started yelling.

"Where were you! I've been here for an hour!"

"I got the time. . ."

"You made me feel like a fool! No one stands me up!"

Well, I could see I wasn't supposed to say anything. But that was fine, I didn't know what to say anyway. She yelled, I stood there. She kept going and going. I had stopped listening. I was just standing there in amazement, it was like watching some kind of medical demonstration. How long could she keep this up?

"What are you staring at!? Don't you have anything to say!?"

"I didn't think I was allowed to speak."

The band picked this moment to take a break. We became the sole entertainment.

"*Is that Burferlinger out there? . . .*"

Everyone could hear her.

"I'm not staying here. . .or with you for another minute! Call me a cab!"

I guess I didn't move fast enough.

"What are you standing there for, get me a cab!"

"Do you want me to call you one or you get one? I'm a little confused over the difference." I thought she was going to explode, her face was all puffed up and red.

"What!? What. . .What!?"

She turned her back on me and stormed out of the lobby. It ended with her roaring away in a cab, which I neither called nor captured.

"Whew. . ."

I walked back into the hall, where everyone was staring at me, including the band. . .and they were German. They all thought Burferlinger had really stood her up, and after a while most came by to pat me on the back and give me a thumbs up. They should have given me a watch.

★　★　★

MARGARET AND I ended just about the time soccer began. I had never heard of soccer before I went to Bremerhaven, and even after I was told about it, I didn't believe there was a game where your arms were strictly used as counterweights.

"It's true," said Ted.

"Says you. You expect me to believe that people actually play a game where they run around with their arms tied to their sides and kick a ball around? Why it's darn un-American."

"It's not an American game."

"I should say so, it's something you just made up."

But he hadn't. It was true. I really wasn't interested in a game where you also used your face to hit the ball.

Boink!

"Yeeeooowwwww!. . ."

Catcher's forehead again.

It didn't seem natural for everyone to be jumping up for the ball with their arms stuck at their sides, like a bunch of porpoises trying to snag a fish at Sea World. Ted put it in perspective.

"Team trips. . .get laid."

Just call me Flipper.

Since soccer was the national sport of Germany, all the American high schools were required to play. Wherever you were, you had to play the national sport of the host country. . .some sort of U.S. Army American Dependents High School Pounding Decree. Somewhere out there, the Kurdistan American High School is playing polo with the head of a former local village chief.

The soccer season started with a few pre-season games against the German high schools, sort of an ass-kicking desensitizing program. Although we stayed pretty close, and actually won a game since we had several half-breeds raised in both worlds, we usually succumbed with ambassadorial grace.

"Fuck you!"

This was okay, since they really didn't understand English, and we really didn't understand German. Both sides stood there yelling out misunderstood obscenities until the coaches came over and broke it up. It was more going through the motions anyway, since years before everyone had gotten pretty tired of post-game swearing. But tradition is tradition.

Before our soccer practices officially started, and before the coach came onto the field, we played "smoccer." It was very popular. We held smoccer practices where the gym building formed a little protective cove, hidden from view. The goalkeeper took up his position, recessed in the cove, while the rest of us appeared to be taking practice kicks. The wall behind him did a nice job of returning our kicks without the need for a goalkeeper at all. He was free to lounge about and have a smoke, completely out of sight. His main function was to keep the cigarette going while we kicked balls at a furious pace. We looked to be working hard at improving our game. The balls were returned at a pace almost as furious as our kicks. You might have thought we had a helluva goalie. . .we actually had a helluva wall.

"We oughta just move this wall into the goal."

"I think that would be cheating."

"Who cares. . .it's not an American game."

To an observer it must have looked to be tiring, because the goalie position was frequently rotated. Goalkeeper in smoccer was very popular. We never got caught, mostly because it's hard to burn down a concrete wall with a cigarette. And not to denigrate our athletic prowess completely. . .we were quite good at smoccer. If any team wanted to take us on in a smoccer match, we were ready.

Our main athletic interest was, and remained, to make sure we were on those team trains leaving on Thursday night. Past that, well, there wasn't anything past that.

★   ★   ★

BREMERHAVEN WAS ACTUALLY in the British sector. We were there only because a port was needed to process the troops. Otherwise, we would have been in southern Germany with the rest of the Americans. The only other base outside of the American sector was Berlin. We shared that in common with them, and it fostered a kind of bond between us, so we saved our best screwing up for when we visited each other. There's something about knowing you're isolated that makes you prone to doing stupid things, at least that's the excuse I always used.

The British have an entirely different take on things. You might think they're like us, but they really aren't, and I'm sure even mildly suggesting this irritates them. I don't think they enjoy having children. I think it's something they bear with English resignation. They left all of their kids at one central boarding school when they arrived in Germany. The school was about twenty minutes up the road from us, in Cuxshaven.

They must have heard about our ass-kicking desensitizing program, and they wanted to get in on it, so they invited us over for a quick game. It was a thinly disguised opportunity for a pay back. We had held an international high school basketball ass-kicking desensitizing tournament with Canadian, German, and British teams. They had represented Britain, and now they wanted their chance to get even.

Were we humiliated? You bet we were. I can still hear the cries from the stands. . . *"This ain't basketball Yank."* I think they were expecting a real soccer team, and you already know about our soccer teams.

We thought we were going to a British military base, just like Bremerhaven, and not this large boarding school. There was a small city of kids there. And in true British style, it was a pretty severe and authoritarian kind of place. And in true American style, we brought out the worst in everybody. . .our main ambassadorial mission.

We took our soccer shellacking gracefully, having successfully completed our German desensitization program. Our training was so thorough that we sat there wondering why the British seemed to be taking the game so seriously. They left the field so quickly in celebration that they completely forgot the post-game swearing ceremonies.

"Say, isn't this a breach of etiquette?"

So, we swore at each other, but it wasn't nearly as satisfying. At dinner we were busy with our main mission. . .trying to figure out where we could go in this town. Much to our chagrin, we learned just how dependent we had become on GIs telling us where all the action was.

"What's in this town?"

"What is this town?"

"What town?"

"Town? . . ."

The coach came over.

"They're having a dance in your honor tonight."

"Our honor!?" We were stunned. We had never been honored before.

"Shut up, and listen. I want everyone to be there and show some respect."

"Do we have to go, really?"

"Do you want to keep playing smoccer?"

"Smoccer, coach? What's smoccer?" asked Vinnie.

"I have informants. Remember that."

"Is nothing sacred?"

"No, not here, not now, and I want every one of you at the dance. This team will not repeat The Berlin Episode."

As if we could ever approach the legend of Berlin.

"What Berlin Episode?" asked Vinnie.

"It's the dance, or in your rooms for a nine o'clock bed check."

So we went to the dance they organized for us. It was one of the few chances these kids got to mingle with each other, since the boys were strictly segregated from the girls by tank trenches and minefields. These kids were starved for fun. . .starved for love. . .starved for us. . .starved for me! Set up the banquet table and serve me up!

It started off slowly, the boys on one side, the girls on the other, and us in between. . .in the no-man's-land minefield.

"Why are we in the middle?"

"I don't know. Frankly, I don't know what's going on here at all."

"On no! . . ."

"What? . . ."

"Accordion alert!"

It was another one of those German rock-'n'-roll polka bands. They began setting up their equipment. Things were looking pretty grim.

"How'd we get into this?"

"Let's go outside for a little smoccer."

"Coach will be pissed if we leave."

"Hey, we aren't leaving, we're just going out for a cigarette."

"Do you want to tell him that or should I? Coach, the team is going out for a cigarette. . ."

"We'll go a few at a time so he won't notice, in groups of four or five goalies."

Outside we talked it over.

"What are we going to do?"

"We're trapped here."

"We're going to have to make the best of it."

"Maybe we should get up there and play something."

Several of the guys could actually sing. . .not me, of course.

"Listen, we'll ask if they don't mind us doing a few songs. Tony can play the piano. What'd you think?"

"Who's going to play the accordion?" I asked.

They looked at me like I was insane.

"I was kidding."

"With you, we never know."

"What can I do? I need to do something," I said.

"Hmmmm. . . ."

This was a problem, what could I be? I couldn't sing, didn't know an instrument. . .yes I had a guitar in the corner of my room, but everyone had a guitar in the corner of his room. I knew one chord. It had taken me a year. It was a good chord. If I knew a second, then I could have joined a band. A third would have made me a virtuoso, any more than that and I would have had to start wearing a beret and grow a goatee. . .and I look ridiculous in a beret.

"I know one chord. . ."

"Stop. . .stop. Don't even think it."

"I've got it, you're the manager. You'd be good at it, managers don't do anything."

"You're right, I would be good at that. I'll keep the girls from rushing the stage. . .and I'll be a listener. . .I will be your main listener."

"Just don't do anything you'll be denying tomorrow."

"Are you nuts, that's exactly what I hope to be doing tomorrow."

Well, the ice was still hanging in the air, and the teacher's barricades were still holding fast when the band finally took a break. There was a general round of applause for that decision. It was then that everything changed.

Tony went up and asked very politely, in the best Eddie Haskell tradition, if it would be all right to use the stage while the band was on break. The headmaster, Dr. Doolittle, didn't see any harm in it, and asked that the accordions be cleared.

After a few throat clearings, and tinkling warmups on the piano keys, the boys released all their pent-up teenage hormones into a vicious, no-holds-barred, no-tuning-required, version of "Mary Lou."

The change in the auditorium was immediate. The barricades came crashing down, the guys charged the girls, and the girls rushed the guys. I was in the middle. Lust was all around me.

"Hey! Take me! Use me! I'm the manager! Give me a reason to lie tomorrow!"

Our stock went up enormously, including the managers'. Even the girls fawned over us. We were taken outside and fondled, even by the girls. . .repeatedly. And since we were in limited supply, each one of us was surrounded by a lot of fondlers. Personally, this was my favorite part.

"This is amazing."

"Yeah, they even like us."

"They love us!"

"I'm getting to first base with everyone. . .even the guys."

"I'm way past first base."

"No one's going to believe us back in Bremerhaven."

"So? Let's not tell 'em."

"I wonder if my dad can get assigned here?"

"And leave the officer's club and the golf course?"

"Long shot, huh?"

They extended the dance hours. We were charming and roguish, as Americans can sometimes be when not streaming toilet paper out of bus windows, but we never took advantage and were never less than completely honest.

"Why, yes, I know Elvis."

"Why, yes, I knew James Dean."

The timing couldn't have been better. Americans were new to them, fun was new to them, and most importantly, I was new to them. I've never been fondled as much before or since, even by people to whom I've given money. From one to another, all through the night, spinning and dancing, intoxicated by their smell, stimulated by their touch. . .we were all falling in love with everyone for the night.

All too quickly it was over, and we were rushed off to spend the night in the well-guarded staff quarters.

"Do you believe this night? Why they even liked George— and he didn't even pay them."

"Hey! . . ."

At breakfast the next morning we were all quiet. Was last night just a dream? The coach came in and said the bus was ready to go.

We slowly walked outside, and there, in the parking lot, were hundreds of kids waiting to say good-bye. I was astonished. We hugged and waved and swore we would return. We hung out the windows until the school was completely out of sight.

We never went back.

NIGHT OF THE HUMMELS

TED LEFT. WE WENT down to the port and said our farewells aboard one of the MSTS ships. These were U.S. Navy versions of an ocean liner. You can imagine what they looked like. All I'll say is the navy really should take a trip on a real ocean liner sometime.

I would miss Ted's good counsel and sensible advice. . .that sounds like he resigned from the president's cabinet. If you know anything, then you know that Ted never had a piece of advice other than *"team trips. . .get laid"* in him. It was possibly the best advice I ever got in my life. Nobody I have known gave counsel.

It was a sad day. We all had a Worstenbrat at the dockside stand, where Margaret was helping out. . .her new senior was close by. I thought at first he was a cigar store Indian, but then he moved and scared the hell out of all of us.

"Man, don't do that!"

Margaret handed me a Worstenbrat.

"You should have gotten her that cab," whispered Ted. "That looks like a Worstenbrat your brother would give you."

It looked like decomposed animal droppings. "Yeah, with a Tide Wafer on the side. . .funny thing about this."

"It doesn't look that funny to me, that's a seriously nasty-looking Worstenbrat."

As the hour got late, I gave Ted the "Rusty Drooper" record as a going away gift.

"What's this?"

"A gift."

"Won't you be needing this?"

"Naw, I figure you can use it at your new high school."

"For what?"

"It may come in handy."

"For what?"

"You can use it with the girls."

"For what?"

We left Ted standing on the deck, and we stood on the dock as the big ship was pushed away by the tugboats.

"So long, Burferlinger!" Ted yelled from the ship's railing.

"So long, Douchebag!"

"George!"

"It's all right, Mom. . .Ted isn't polite company."

I thought I saw a small round disk fall from his hand into the North Sea. The ship sailed and we left for home. Ted was the first of my Bremerhaven buddies to leave. One thing you have to get used to in the military—people leave, and often. We all came out to see everyone off. It was both to say good-bye and a chance to run around the ship like lunatics.

"Goddamned little dependent assholes!"

You can never know anybody more than three years, and for that to happen, they had to arrive on the same day as you. There is no such thing as a childhood friend, all my childhood friends are swimming in Lime Creek and playing Deep Fielder.

My new compadres were Earle, also known as Babycakes, a nickname that as far as I know had remained dormant for nearly a decade before Earle grabbed it, and Steve. Steve wanted to be Elvis Presley. The rest of us wanted to look like Elvis, but Steve actually wanted to be him. He also had a huge collection a paperback books in his room. I don't think he read them, he just collected them. Earle was strictly a profit kind of guy. If there was a buck to be found, you'd find Earle. He had another nickname for that, but in good conscience I won't reveal it. Babycakes is bad enough.

"What happened last night over at Diane's apartment?" Babycakes asked.

"I didn't know anything happened."

Diane Brew was known to all of us, and she was reputed to be advanced for her age, or so the rumors said. She had a nickname that rhymed with her last name. It was such a natural that I think the reputation was started just to support the name, which I also think would be a great name for a beer.

She was our age, and since we weren't really doing anything other than clumsy attempts at what we read in our father's copies of the *Playboy Advisor*, how could she? *Playboy* didn't really help us—we didn't understand the vocabulary.

"What's this mean. . .fellatio? I can't find it in the dictionary, not even the German-American dictionary."

"I think it's a kind of opera singer."

"Really? So, he wants her to sing to him?"

"I guess."

"I think you guess wrong. This is no help at all."

Earle had misinterpreted one of the columns so badly that
he got another nickname I also can't reveal. All I'll say is that it
was the result of mistaken identity or very poor aim. *Playboy*
should really include a young reader's vocabulary section in
the back.

Diane was really too young for any of it to be true, so I was
pretty skeptical. I'd had some experience with girls my age,
and they weren't doing anything. Doreen was my age, and she
wasn't doing any of this. . .yet. I think Doreen and I were on
the same schedule. I know we were reasonably close. She proved
it to me one day, in the back of the route bus, riding alone to
the teen club. I was sitting directly across from her, in the two
facing rear seats. One thing lead to another and before you
knew it she fell for an old ploy. Or I fell for an old ploy. It's
really not clear who was doing the ploying. I told her she was
too young to know anything about sex, let alone have any experience with it.

"How do you know? I may be the most experienced person you've ever met, you can't tell from just looking at me."

"Oh, yes I can."

"How?"

"Because you tremble and shake every time I say 'sex'."

"No, that's you trembling and shaking."

"Really?"

"Yes."

"Well, it could be, however I still think you've *neevveeerrrr*
done *anything*."

This raised the ante considerably.

"I have too."

"Prove it."

"I don't have to prove anything."

"I knew it."

"You don't know anything."

She looked at me for a moment and then let out a little
sigh. I took this to be a good sign. I was wearing her down.

"What do you want to do?"

So, after some intense negotiations, I was able to slide my
hand under her skirt and up her leg until. . .

"Just on the outside." Until she said that.

"Outside of what?"

"You know."

I probably should, but I don't think I do. This had never come up in the *Playboy Advisor*.

It could mean so many different things. Outside the panties? Inside the panties but still outside? This was also at a time when silence was an integral part of fooling around, so I didn't want to ask any questions. If you didn't say anything, then they might not notice what you were doing, and as long as they didn't notice, you were free to move ahead. Saying anything at all could break the spell and. . .

"Hey, how did I get naked?"

. . .would be the next thing you heard from someone.

"Gosh, I don't know. Maybe you came that way. I find myself in my underwear a lot. . .with no explanation at all."

At least that's the way we thought things were supposed to work. Her breaking the silence broke the spell and put an end to everything.

I went to Diane's apartment one evening with a couple of friends. We were so inexperienced we didn't know that bringing along a couple of friends wasn't a good idea. She was doing the laundry while a friend of hers was ironing. Nothing at all happened. Her friend did chase us around the apartment with a hot iron, but I don't think that's what we came for. More than ever, I thought it was all a lot of bunk, and mostly started because of her name.

"Well, Rickey has got a giant dent in his forehead, and I heard he got it over at Diane's," continued Earle.

"We'll, it could've been from a soccer ball, but I'm totally in the dark, and I'm much better off left right there, otherwise I'd probably be the one with a soccer dent in my forehead," I concluded.

Steve was practicing his. . . "Well thank ya, thank ya very much," but took a break to tell us.

"I know what happened."

"Really? How did you find out?"

"I asked Rickey."

"What a novel idea."

Steve told us what he knew. It seems that Rickey had been visiting Diane, without bringing any friends along, for some time. One of these visits ended with her parents making a surprise return. They had some suspicions about Diane.

Rickey took off on a dead run, just managing to miss them as they entered the apartments. He escaped through the basement passageway, which ran the entire length of the apartment building. He bypassed the middle stairwell, and made for the last stairway at the very end of the corridor. He came full tilt to the end, took the turn at high speed, leapt for the first step, and cold-cocked himself on the exposed plaster-covered pipes that ran along the length of the basement. He bounced off the pipe, fell into a pile, and was unceremoniously covered with falling plaster debris. The building custodian found him with a dent in his forehead, delirious, and covered in plaster.

"Was ist los mit du?"

"What. . .where am I?"

It was like a Hercule Perot mystery. *Why was this body lying at the foot of the basement stairwell, covered with plaster debris?*

"Hercule, I want to know if there's a connection between this photograph of a person lying on the basement floor, covered with plaster, and my daughter," said the beautiful Mrs. Brew.

"Pleaze," thought Hercule, *"let her finally be zee one who finds this ridiculous Belgian mustache arousing so I can finally get zee girl."*

So, it had been true about Diane all along, and it turned out that silence was involved. But it wasn't keeping silent while you were with a girl, but keeping silent about a girl. We were close, off by one preposition. "Keep thy mouth shut and thou shalt be rewarded". . .my new eleventh commandment. . .who am I kidding. . .it's my only commandment.

After that, bodies were regularly found lying on that basement stairwell floor, covered with plaster debris. . .but nobody was talking.

Diane left just as I was ready to be found lying on the basement floor. I never got to dent my forehead on the corridor run. When she left, half the guys in the port came out to see her off, most with bandaged foreheads. Margaret was serving up the Worstenbrat at the stand. They ran out for the first time ever.

"Looks like a Worstenbrat your brother would give you," said Earle.

"Damn, doesn't that girl have anything else to do? Where does she find these?"

Steve almost collided with Margaret's latest senior. "Whoa! Man, don't do that! Tell somebody before you move, I thought you were a statue."

"Sorry, I'll try and give some warning."

"Well thank ya. . .thank ya very much."

"I just saw the chaplain here, what do you think that means?"

"Nothing."

"Nothing?"

"You're here, and it means nothing, so he can be here, and it can mean nothing."

Actually, it meant nothing for all three of us.

That New Year's Eve we still had no real reason to see any girl off at the dock other than for a chance to run around the ship like lunatics.

"Goddamned little dependent assholes!"

Butch couldn't go out on New Year's Eve. . .he had to baby-sit. He was from one of those strange homes that had two teenagers and a two-year-old. It wasn't until later that I found out how those kinds of things happen. But anyway, someone was going to have to stay home that New Year's, and after drawing straws with his sister, Butch found out he lost. He was grousing about it all week, not only was it going to be New Year's Eve, but it was also a Friday night. The more he thought about it, the more he grumbled.

"New Year's and Friday night. . .jeezus. . ."

Yeah, that's about all he said all week.

"New Year's and Friday night. . .jeezus. . ."

"Hey, Butch, you got that five bucks you owe me?"

"New Year's and Friday night. . .jeezus. . ."

There was no way anyone was going to hear much from Butch until after. . .

"New Year's and Friday night. . .jeezus. . ."

He was inconsolable, until someone hit upon an idea.

"Hey, Butch, listen. We'll stop by on New Year's, play some cards, keep you company. . .have some laughs."

Sounded pretty good to him, it was better than anything else he had heard up until then.

"Yeah, that would be good, yeah. . ."

The teen club was having its own New Year's party that night, and we were all having good clean fun. The pipe tobacco and toilet paper rolls had been stashed for the Teen Club Special, and Chief was in an especially good mood. I knew that because he actually talked to me. I even got a seminormal Worstenbrat.

Some of us ducked out for a quick beer or two at a local gasthaus. The Germans were even in a good mood—they didn't seem to mind us being Americans that night.

"Ya, tonight we haben ein exchange special. . .2.75 marks to ze dollar."

"Well, only a thirty percent screw job instead of the usual forty. Danke, mein Herr."

Some of them were even beginning to believe that Germany had won the war. Twenty years later that turned out to be true. We left them as the lines were beginning to form for a good view of the passing of the Teen Club Special. The best seats went early.

Somewhere around ten o'clock, we headed over to see Butch. By this time no one really wanted to, but we had all promised.

"Hey, it's about time you guys showed up."

"Well, we didn't realize when we told you we'd come over that there would be so many other things we'd rather be doing. But we're men of our word, even if it means missing whatever it is we're missing."

I fiddled with the radio, trying to get Radio Luxembourg— AFN was stuck in a time-warped perpetual Guy Lombardo medley. Then Pat Boone came on. . .

"Stop! Stop! I'll talk. . .I did it. Whatever it is, I did it, it was me. Just take him off. . ."

"Hey George, what are you yammering about. . .can't you get anything on that radio?"

"I'm trying. . ."

Radio Luxembourg wasn't around the corner; when you got it at all, it would fade in and out. I eventually stumbled onto it and we settled down at the dining room table. Butch had obviously been at his old man's liquor cabinet. He was already pretty well sloshed.

Well, one thing led to another, and pretty soon Butch wasn't in any condition to play cards, or anything else, which left us in kind of a dilemma. His two-year-old brother was asleep in the bedroom, and we couldn't leave with Butch like this, so we had to call his parents at the officer's club and give them the news that their son wasn't feeling so good.

"What do you mean he isn't feeling so good!?"

"Well, sir. . ."

"Who is this!? What are you doing at my house!?"

Butch was semiconscious at the dinning room table, his head lying on his folded arms. He peeked out of the only eye that was still working.

"Who are yoou talkithing tooo!?"

He sounded just like his old man, except he was drunk along with being coarse. Butch lifted himself up, and swung around.

"Whoo are yoou. . ."

He fell right into a bookcase, which toppled over with a loud crash.

"What was that!?" screamed his father.

I was stuck holding the phone between these two. I put my hand over the mouthpiece.

"Why am I the one calling? Just because I tuned the radio I get all the electrical jobs?"

No one answered me.

"I asked what was that noise!?"

"I said whoo are yoou talkithing tooo!?"

"Oh shit," said Earle as he picked up the cabinet. There on the floor were the broken ruins of German Hummels. You could see their little arms and legs, and little broken heads. I didn't know they were so expensive until my mother enlightened me when I touched one of hers.

"Don't move. You're holding a year's allowance."

"What? This little thing."

"Just put it down, then put you hands on top of your head, interlace your fingers, and back away slowly."

It was a statuette about four inches high of a waiter carrying a wine bottle. It didn't look like much to me. I thought it came from the five-and-dime. Little did I know it actually came from the vault of the five-and-dime.

The baby brother started crying, and Rickey With The Dented Forehead went in to check on him. I was still holding the phone.

"Sir, I think you better come home."

"None of you move! Everyone stays just like they are, understand!"

"Yes, sir. . ."

Butch lunged at me, and I pressed the receiver into his hand.

"Butch, it's your father."

His face went white.

"BUTCH! WHAT HAVE YOU DONE!"

I could hear his dad's voice straight through Butch's head and coming out his other ear.

"Oh shit. . .he's on his way," said Butch.

He dropped the phone and fell to the couch—the color had drained from his face.

"He's going to kill me."

This was the first thing Butch had gotten right all night. Rickey With The Dented Forehead brought out the little brother and was holding him in his arms. We righted the bookcase and then made little piles of Hummel Rubble where each figurine had once stood.

"You ever notice how things start out one way, and end up totally different from what you thought?" I asked Earle. "Right about now I expected to be on the Teen Club Special, streaming toilet paper out the windows, instead I'm making little piles of Hummels. I had no intentions of doing anything wrong. I mean, I didn't go out to rob a bank or anything, did I? Although these Hummels might qualify. From what I heard on the phone, Butch is a dead man. The question is, are we?"

"Well, of course we are. . .I knew that the second the bookcase hit the floor," said Earle.

"You're very comforting, thank you."

"You're welcome."

Earle tried to put the individual pieces into their respective piles. "Maybe we can glue some of these together or something. . .maybe they won't notice."

"So, I guess Butch's parents are blind. Well, we may have a chance then. . .they might not find their way home."

"So, you're saying we don't have a tinker's chance."

"I don't know anything about the Tinkers, but if there's money to be made here, Earle, you would think of something that might actually work."

"I'm not good under pressure."

"Like who is? The last time I was under pressure, I told them my name was Fred, Jack, and Dave."

"I need some time to think."

"I would say, go out and buy replacements, but from what I know about Hummels, all of our combined cash would buy a. . .well here. . ." I picked up a broken leg. "One of these."

When Butch's father came home he stormed right passed all of us without a word, grabbed Butch by the scruff of his neck, and dragged him into a back room. Butch's mother was close behind, pleading with her husband to control himself. From the back of the apartment we could here a struggle and then Butch flew out of the room, soared across the hall, and crash-landed onto the floor of the opposite room. His father followed, then there was another momentary struggle, and Butch flew out of that room, soared back across the hall, and crash landed in the first room. They were an air force family.

Butch was getting a whole year's worth of flight training in one night.

"Jim! Jim!" his wife screamed. "Please stop!"

She had obviously left the club in a hurry, her coat was barely on and she must have had to run to keep up with him, because she was out of breath. She was trying to save Butch, who was just now sailing. . .sorry, that would be a navy family. . .flying back across the hall.

Her eyes darted back and forth, looking frantically around the room as if she might find something that could stop all of this, and then her face went cold when she saw her Hummels.

Her voice became low and bloodless. "I think you boys better go now."

The next morning, my father got a visit from Butch's father. I stayed in my room and had serious thoughts about jumping out of the window and hitting the road. I figured one of my mother's Hummels would pay for a year on the lam. I really hadn't done much of anything. As I sat there and waited for my father, I thought back over the night. All I really did was tune the radio and work the phone. If you knew Butch, then you'd know it was all inevitable, and this was neither the first nor the last time that Butch flew back and forth across his hallway. Less than a year later, he left high school and joined the service. It was either that, said the judge, or serve some serious time.

THE BASEBALL TRIP

LIKE MOST THINGS OF this nature, the sports trips were beyond the control of their participants. It was a series of events that combined to create a presence, like some electromagnetic monster from another dimension. It was propelled along by its own inertia. Like a tornado, it gathered in every ants-in-their-pants teenager that came near. All inhibitions and common sense were lost under its spell, and you were powerless to stop it. It was one chain reaction after another, and before you knew it, you were running around a train yard in your underwear, with a coconut in your hand.

The actual games had very little impact on any of this—mostly you spent time trying not to get into a real game. Having to wear a medieval football outfit was bad enough.

"Allingham!"

"Me, coach? . . ."

"How many Allinghams do you see here?"

"Is this a trick question? I'm not good with trick questions."

"Get your helmet on, I'm putting you in."

"I was only heading to the water jug, Coach. I wouldn't want you to interpret my walking by as a desire to get into the game. Besides, I'm only good at running laps. You've never actually let me play another position. Perhaps if you wanted me to run somewhere. . ."

"Where's your helmet?"

"It should be around here somewhere."

"You don't know where your helmet is?"

"Well, I only need it at the beginning and at the end of the game. . .for the players parade, so I don't see any reason to be stuck hanging on to it all the time, do you?"

"Never mind, go sit down."

I went back to the bench and sat down next to Ted.
"That was close, the coach almost put me in the game."
"No! . . ."
"Yes, thank god I didn't have my helmet. Can you imagine? . . ."
"Maybe he just wanted you to get him some coffee or something."
"He wanted me to put my helmet on."
"No! . . ."
"You'd think he'd know better than to get us confused with the real players."
Luckily these kinds of things happened rarely.
Still, the entire school was willing to risk being told to put their helmet on, just so they could get in on the trips. Everybody tried out for every sport.
"I'm going out for track. . .the high jump!"
"You weigh three hundred pounds."
"Pole vault?"
"You think three hundred pounds is an asset in the pole vault?"
"Football. Three hundred pounds is good in football."
"It would be. . .if you were taller than five foot two."
"What. . .what then!? What can I be?"
"Each team has a trainer-manager. . ."
"That's it! I'll be both!"
"Which sport do you want to be trainer-manager for?"
"All of them!"
"Well, baseball is going on now."
"Just throw me the old pigskin. . ."
"That's the old horsehide. . ."
"Am I still the trainer?"
"Luckily for you, no one expects the trainer to know anything"
"That's good! I'm perfect."
This was also how most of the other positions were filled.
"We need someone to play first base."
"Just throw me the old pigskin."
Luckily no one expected much from the players either.
The real tryouts should have been. . .
"Let's hear your German."
"Herr Ober, ein bier."
"There's sixteen people on this team."
"Herr Ober, sechzehn bier."
"You're on the team."
"Herr Ober, hundert bier, bitte."

"You're starting."

Earle's response to this was always. . .

"Who's paying for the beer?"

On some really bad advice, we had once taken a bus on a baseball trip. Why anyone thought this was a good idea, I don't know. Despite its vaunted reputation, our Mercedes bus broke down in the middle of the night. We had nothing to do until we were rescued but try and help the driver figure out what was wrong. So, we got out and looked for the engine hood.

"Well, here's the problem, the engine is missing."

"It has to have one, how'd we get this far?"

"Hey guys, the engine's back here."

"We are in serious trouble, the engine has moved all the way to the back of the bus."

The engine cover was off and the German driver was standing rubbing his chin with his hand and quietly musing to himself.

"Ach der lieber. . .was ist los?"

"Hey, George. You know German, find out what's going on."

"No, you're confused. I was thrown out of German. . .thanks to Rickey With The Dented Forehead."

"That's close enough."

"Well, I'll use what I know. . .Ist Post fur mich da?"

"Was!? . . ." replied the driver.

"What'd he say?"

"He said 'What?'" I translated.

"What'd you ask?"

"I asked if there was any mail for me."

"How long were you in that class before they threw you out?"

"Ich hatte gern die Speiskarte?"

"Now what'd you ask?"

"If I could see a menu."

"So, they threw you out when they got up to the M's? . . ."

"Verruckt. . .," mumbled the driver under his breath as he reached into the engine compartment and pulled open a small hatch cover.

"What'd he say?"

"I think he's formulating his answer."

". . .idioten."

"He thanks us for our help, but he feels he can handle it from here."

We climbed back on board, congratulating ourselves for helping out.

"That went rather well, don't you think?"

It was the last time we ever used a bus. The next day, our teams on field performance suffered from the lack of a midnight chase around the train yards in Hanover.

"We won't make that blunder again," said the coaches.

The next trip was to Berlin. It started out very peaceful. The yard workers met us in Hanover.

"Captain Jim, this is Captain Gerholdt, they'll be defending the south goal. . .your team will receive the opening coconut. . ."

Things were proceeding smoothly.

We violated the prohibition against opening the window shades while in East Germany, and traded cigarettes with the Russian guards at the checkpoints. We always did this, and it was expected. The Russians would stand facing away from the train with a cigarette held in one hand behind their back. We would make the exchange in a single swift motion.

Then we stopped at one of the checkpoints for a very long time.

The coaches came by.

"Why have we been here so long?" we asked.

"There's a problem. Someone has scratched a swastika into the paint on the side of this car. Coincidentally, it happens to be the car with the Bremerhaven baseball team in it."

"Hey, it wasn't us," we said. "It must be somebody's idea of a joke."

"Sure, tell it to the Russians."

"We don't think they would find it amusing." The Russians weren't noted for their sense of humor. "What are they doing now?"

"They've confiscated the train. . ."

"What? . . ."

". . .and everyone on it."

"Don't tell me I'm going to have to learn Russian!?"

"George. . .shut up. It was probably you who did it."

"It wasn't me, Coach. I swear."

"Why do you think swearing will make me believe you?"

"Don't confuse me. This is just not my style. . .the bandstand, yes. . .I admit that. . .and a few other things. . .mostly not my fault. . .but this is not me. It's not even a good likeness of me."

"Well, somebody did it, and they think it's someone on this team. Maybe you were out there having a smoke. . ."

"Coach, don't even say things like that. Somebody is going to hear you and the next thing you know, I'll be branded with it. . .and do you think I'd be smoking on a train to Berlin? Do you think I would flash American cigarettes in front of some Russian guards? Do you think I want to start a stampede?"

"What the hell is he talking about?" he asked his assistant coach.

"The Russians prize American cigarettes."

"They do?"

"Yes, they can't grow tobacco in Russia."

"So, what's in their cigarettes?"

"They taste like burned potatoes."

"You can't smoke potatoes."

"Apparently, the Russians can."

The train was moved off to a siding and we sat for seventeen hours while Washington and Moscow bargained for our release. Eventually we were let go. The news wires said it was for several thousand cartons of cigarettes and a few hundred bushels of potatoes.

When we arrived at the Berlin train station, the MPs came through the car before we got off the train.

"Listen up! If you're asked any questions in the station you are to tell them 'no comment'. Everyone got that?"

"Tell who no comment?"

"Could be our parents."

"God, are they here?" The color drained from Butch's face.

As soon as we stepped onto the platform, flashbulbs started going off and voices came from every direction.

"Excuse me! . . ."

"Entschuldigung! . . ."

"Can you tell us what happened!? . . ."

"Is there any truth to the rumor that this was caused by the Americans? . . ."

"Konnen sie mir geben die informationen! . . ."

"No comment."

"No comment."

"No comment."

We said it so much on the way through the station that the words lost their meaning, and became hard to even pronounce.

"No commender. . ."

"No commandante. . ."

"No cannendder. . ."

We were hustled off to an isolated barracks on the main base.

"What the hell was that all about? Hey, where are the GIs!?"

The next afternoon, after the game, I came out of the barrack's shower, getting ready to go out on the town. . .and invade the Berlin Teen Club. Several guys were huddled around the radio.

"What are you doing?"

"Shhhhh. . .."

Independent news sources are reporting that the Russian action was precipitated by an incident on an American military train traveling the Berlin corridor. A Russian military spokesman claims that inflammatory symbols were found on one of the cars of the train. This reportedly led the Russian high command to believe that the American military was testing their resolve to support a fellow socialist state. The U.S. State Department has issued a statement saying that they believe the Russians are using a minor incident as a pretext to heighten tensions in the divided city. . .

"What's going on?"

"Shhhhh. . .the Russians have brought up tanks at Checkpoint Charlie, and now we have too. It's because of that swastika you scratched on the train."

"I didn't scratch a swastika on the train! Why won't anybody believe me? I want a real swastika, not a drawing!" The coach came into the room. "See, Coach. . . see what you've started. . .I told you when you said it. . ."

"Listen, everyone stay in the barracks. There's been some trouble. Don't anybody leave here until I find out what we should do."

We all immediately left. The room was empty before he finished the sentence.

"Where'd everybody go? . . ."

We hit the street and headed for the U-bahn.

"Where are we going? . . ."

"To Checkpoint Charlie, of course. . ."

"But the coach said to stay in the barracks. Should we be doing this?"

"Who are you again?" asked Earle.

"Bill. . ."

"You're new Bill, so watch and learn. We won't be alone for long, half the city is probably already there. I just hope we haven't missed anything. . ."

"Why are you carrying a pair of jeans?"

"Never question me, Bill."

By the time we arrived the street was jammed. The tourists mingled among the monuments and the machine-gun nests. The tanks were all lined up two abreast, and facing each other across the checkpoint.

"This is pretty cool. I'm not sure what they've accomplished besides the first tank traffic jam I've ever seen, but it's still pretty cool."

We hung around for about half an hour and nothing happened. The GIs were eating K rations on their tanks, the Russians were eating potatoes on theirs. Earle managed to sell his jeans behind the Russian war memorial to an East German guard.

"Should we stay here or get a beer?"

"What do you think? . . ."

"Well, I'm done," said Earle.

"Why did you sell your pants to an East German guard?" asked Bill.

"Because I have all the potatoes I need."

"You know, I'm sure they'll start selling beer here pretty soon."

"It'll be at least an hour before the vendors can push their carts all the way here."

Berlin trips always seemed to be our downfall, and to be fair, Bremerhaven trips always seemed to be theirs. If we hadn't ever gone there on these trips, then I'm sure I could have been accepted by Harvard, at least that's what my mother says.

With all the commotion in town, and with trains being commandeered left and right by all the brass that weren't going to get caught in the city if the Russians did decide to take all of Berlin's potatoes, things got very screwed up. We were stuck in Berlin with no train space to take us back to Bremerhaven.

"How could this happen?" said the military travel clerk at the station. "This is the army, we never screw up. I don't have any six-man compartments available."

Six-man compartments were de rigor for traveling teams. They came with nice, soft, Naugahyde-covered, ironing-board, pull-down bedslabs. Coaches were usually in the four-man versions, but sometimes they had the plush two-man compartments.

"I can get you coaches into a two-man compartment. . ."

Naturally.

". . .but all I got left is one four-man compartment."

"Maybe, some of us could bunk with the coaches," came a voice from the rear.

The army clerk and the coaches had to support each other to keep from falling over with laughter.

The clerk wiped the tears from his eyes as he regained his composure. "Good one. That leaves twelve of you stranded in Berlin," he said.

"I speak German," I said. "I'll stay behind."

The coaches again convulsed with laughter. "Stop it! Stop it! We heard you on the bus trip. You guys are such cards, whew! If we have to look at any menus, we'll call you. Everyone goes, or everyone stays."

"I have two four-man compartments available on the midnight train, and a compartment for the both of you. If you'd like to squeeze the team into these two compartments, I can get you on that train. We'd have to sneak around the German train authority to put eight men in them, but if you're willing. . .or you can wait until Monday. . .or Tuesday."

"Midnight, that's five hours away. . ." The coaches looked at their watches.

Kid's aren't the only ones capable of making stupid decisions. . .

"All right."

"Understand that we're taking a chance here, I'm only doing this just to get your team home. Even though these cars have U.S. Army written on the side, the railroad still belongs to the Germans, and they run it. So if you get caught with eight men in those compartments, there will be hell to pay."

From what I've heard in my life, hell makes a lot of money on these deals.

"They're going to have to duck the conductor when he comes around for tickets. If he finds eight guys in there playing grab ass, they'll put all our asses in a sling."

A second chance for the coaches to reconsider the first chance. . .

"No problem."

"Okay. See me an hour before the departure time."

The coaches huddled us around.

"You heard him. Everyone stay close by and be back here an hour before we leave."

Within ten minutes we had dispersed throughout the city. We interpreted "close by" to include the bar district surrounding the train station. Four hours sounded like a whole night to us.

The coaches walked up and down Berlin's large train station mall.

"Do you see any of them?"

"No."

"They wouldn't have left the station, would they?"

"We said to stay close by."

"I hate to think George is out there using his German. . ."

That's exactly what I was doing, setting back foreign relations and using my German. By eleven o'clock we had seen every menu in the city, visited all our regular spots, lost at several rounds of buzz, and loaded up with supplies. Lewis and Clark had started out with fewer provisions than we now carried.

"Tell me again. . .why do we need this coconut?"

"Tradition, Bill."

"It's after eleven, we've got to hurry."

"We could take a taxi."

"I've only got dollars left, they'll kill us on the exchange."

In the train station, the official exchange rate was four to one, by the time you'd hit the street, been through the bars and caught a cab, somehow the dollar and the mark became equal.

"If we don't have any marks. . .then no cab."

Earle was sensitive to exchange rates.

"Someone run ahead and tell them we're on our way. . ."

The coaches were on the platform as we came into the station.

"Come on! You're late!"

We jumped aboard.

"Four of you get in each compartment, the rest of you get lost until after the conductor goes through."

We scattered through the length of the train with our tickets in hand. Usually the coaches kept all the tickets and you sat in the compartments like it was bed check at Alcatraz, while the conductor counted everybody. We hid out in the dinning car waiting for the conductor to finish his rounds. I ordered from the menu. . .

"Ich wunschte essen von der Grill."

"Sehr gut!"

"Entscheiden Sie fur uns."

"Wunderbar!"

"What'd you say?"

"I ordered for the three of us. I left it in his hands."

He returned with the current state of German-American relations arranged on a plate. An orange, beets, and a bread stick. . .all grilled.

"Dibs on the bread stick!" we cried out simultaneously.

Meanwhile, the coaches were checking on where everyone had gone.

"Where's Allingham?"

"He's with a bunch that went to the dinning car."

"Don't let him order! . . ."

"You'll be eating a fried prune pit. . ."

"And feel damn lucky you had first dibs. . ."

When we returned to the compartments, the trainside vendors were at the windows, hawking everything and anything. They reminded me of our dockside Worstenbrat stand.

"Hey, look. . .*real* Gorps and Dorfenburgs."

"Call them over here."

"We don't have enough of everything already?" asked Bill.

"You are really new. . .you never have enough of anything."

"Good thing the coaches compartments are in the next car."

"I can't breathe in here, there's no room!"

"This really is uncomfortable for eight guys."

"Well, I need some room." I jumped up into the luggage space over the compartment door.

"The way I figure it, two in the luggage space, and two under the bottom bunks should cover it."

"Who's going to be where?"

"We'll figure that part out later."

By 2:00 A.M., we were too stuffed to eat the rest of the food or finish the beer. So, what do you do with all that leftover food? Well, it would look mighty good on Johnny's face. . .splat.

"Are we now deciding who sleeps where?" asked Johnny.

"Is this more tradition?" asked Bill.

Thwack!

"Wow! What was that. . .blueberry? It's really thick. I can't see a thing."

I shook up a bottle of beer and hosed him off.

"Thanks!"

"Don't mention it." I then voluntarily hosed off several others who hadn't asked, but seemed to really need it.

"Hey! . . ."

"Look out! . . ."

Splat!

Flommp!

Squisshhh!

"Watch what you're doing with that coconut!"

Soon, we all resembled a confectionery version of Swamp Thing, sitting in a compartment decorated to match. All the linens and pillows had mysteriously disappeared out the window.

"So, who sleeps where?"

"It's amazing how all these different foods can homogenize into this thick gooey stuff." A rainbow ooze.

From the companion compartment next to us we could hear voices.

"Hey! . . ."

"Look out! . . ."

Splat!

Flommp!

Squisshhh!

"I think the boys next door are deciding who sleeps where."

"Amazing, it's like parallel worlds."

"You read too much."

Splat!

"Hey!"

"Duck! . . ."

Flommp!

Squisshhh!

By morning we stepped off the train in dried, crusty rainbows of food-colored clothing. The coaches looked us over as we stood on the platform.

"Why do you people look like this?"

"Well, he wanted the bottom bunk. . ."

"It was not my fault. I was just sitting there when suddenly the world went blue. . ."

"It's his fault, he brought the coconut."

"And he should watch where his feet go."

"So, that's why there's cheese dip between my toes?"

"Shut up! Go home!"

★   ★   ★

THE GERMAN CLEANING crew opened the compartment door.

"Act der lieber!! Ist Post fur mich da!!"

"Ich hatte gern die Speiskarte!!"

We can only imagine what the fastidious German character thought of the condition of those two compartments.

Monday morning we were all called down to the principal's office. . .Mr. Coleman. He had been recently promoted, bad breath had finally risen to the top of the qualification list for principal.

"Why is it always Berlin?" he mused to himself. "Didn't I have some of your older brothers on the soccer team?"

The words rolled over us. . .with his breath.

Boom!

Four kids went down. Several more turned green, the rest of us were turning blue from holding our breath.

"It's the same thing every time I talk to teenagers."

Boom.

The coaches went down.

"Don't any of you think before you do something?"

Silence, then. . .

"I can answer that," came a voice from the back. "My father has told me several times that I never think before I do anything, so the answer is no, we didn't think at all."

"Yes, he's right."

"It's true."

There was almost universal agreement among all of us.

"You're new here," said Mr. Coleman to Bill. "Do you think this is any way to start a high school career?"

"I think we all just admitted that we don't think at all, sir. Is this a rhetorical question?"

"The German railroad has condemned the car you were in, and pulled it off the line. This reflects badly on all of us, especially on me as the new principal of a high school that has had more than its share of problems. We have an unenviable reputation in the USAREUR school system. We must have a punishment that fits the crime and shows our commitment to improving this school's tarnished reputation."

Mr. Coleman moved around his desk to directly face us. We, including the coaches, as a group, stepped back.

"What are you doing now? Stand still. What was the punishment the soccer team received?" he asked his secretary.

"They were flogged." She and Mr. Coleman had a good laugh.

"If only. . .obviously we will have suspension and detention, repayment for the refurbishing costs, public apologies to the student body, to the port commander, the city of Bremerhaven, the German people, the German railroad, the German-American Club. . .have I left anyone out?" His secretary thought a moment, then her face brightened joyously.

"Their parents!"

"Of course. . .their parents! I will personally contact each of your parents. Many of your fathers believe in the army way of doing things." Mr. Coleman moved back around his desk, then saw Butch.

"And in the air force way. . ."

He whispered to his secretary, his breath enveloping her. "Matilda, this is where the flogging comes in." Matilda gagged and fell unconscious to the floor.

Poor Butch. . .more flight training.

THE PIRATE'S ANSWER

BILL DIDN'T REMAIN THE *new* guy for very long. His stock went up considerably from being involved with The Baseball Trip, and asking Mr. Coleman if the "Don't you think before you do anything?" was a rhetorical question—it confounded Mr. Coleman and drove the rest of us to the dictionary. The coaches told him he wouldn't be allowed on any other teams if he insisted on using authentic English.

"We have enough trouble with Allingham's German, so don't annoy us."

New generations had been inspired and were already saying. . .

"Did you see what they looked like when they came back? We've got to get in on these trips."

We apologized to everyone, and anyone, who came anywhere near us for the next two weeks. Standing in front of the German train authority, we listened to the train master berate us in German. We didn't understand a word he said, but listened politely until he stopped talking and stood there looking directly at us.

"Warum? . . ." he asked.

"I think this is where we're supposed to give a response," I whispered to Earle.

There were whispers among all of us.

"He wants an answer."

"To what? What'd he say?"

"Didn't we say we were sorry at the beginning?"

"Somebody should say something."

It was touch and go for a moment until. . .

"I can answer that," came a voice from the back. "My father has told me several times that I never think before I do anything, so the answer is no, we didn't think at all."

Bill prepared himself for a reprise of his rhetorical question addendum, but the train master said nothing, then turned his back on us, and we were duly dismissed.

"I think that went rather nicely, don't you?" I said to Earle.

"Yes, I do."

We were all satisfied.

Bill turned out to be a very smart guy. His only dumb move was hanging out with us, but then there were few alternatives, and none that sounded any good. He was the prototype nerd, which in those days was known as a "square" as in. . . "*He's a square, he just didn't dig me at all*" (Bill Parsons, *The All-American Boy*). I say this with the deepest respect and affection. . .er. . .make that admiration. I liked the guy. Being in the small American enclave in Germany may have been the best thing that could have happened to him. I say may because there are a lot of different views on this, especially among the parents. Being so small in number, we accepted everyone. You do that when you're completely surrounded by people who don't say anything you can understand. We would've learned more of the language, but we were already playing soccer, and adding anything on to that would have been viewed suspiciously. You might as well have gone all the way and grown a Belgian detective's mustache and worn leather shorts. . .not attractive features in our high school. The only guy to do it, Bob, was instantly tagged Booby. . .and he actually liked the name. Draw your own conclusions.

So, Bill was on a football team for probably the first and last time in his life, and he quickly adapted to the trips, maybe too quickly for the good of the rest of us. He sat there in the train compartment with a coin-changer attached to his belt and his Las Vegas dealer's hat pulled low over his forehead. Bill peered over the top of his cards through his giant Coke-bottle eyeglasses, playing nickel-dime poker with what only minutes before had been our money. He was very good at it, so good that Earle was forced to become an ally. Earle had no loyalty when it came to money.

It was obvious that Bill didn't really fit in, and he proved to have qualities that the rest of us had only heard about from attending our school counselor's mandatory College Catalogue Public Readings. Things like resourcefulness. . .where do you find a Las Vegas dealer's hat in Bremerhaven? Soon, he proved that the Mr. Coleman rhetorical question rebuttal was no fluke. He started *The Pirate's Answer*.

The official high school newspaper was called *The Port Call*, and Bill, being the intelligent and literary kind of guy, had joined the newspaper staff. Mary Milkolodian, affectionately known to us all as Mary Milktoast, had rallied the staff around her and against Bill, usurping his rightful position as editor. This was from Bill's perspective, of course, but we all agreed with him. We had to, he had all our money. Mary was shaping the paper in her own image, a kind of Bobbsey Twins style of sludge that everyone was managing to ignore quite nicely, which is the time-honored tradition with most high school newspapers. Everyone, that is, except Bill.

He resigned from the staff, brooded for a while, then single-handedly founded *The Pirate's Answer*. Earle went along for the money.

"What are you guys doing by yourselves up in the maid's room?" I asked.

Earle, not wanting to let on to anything just yet, but not wanting to start any strange rumors about what they were doing up in the maid's room all alone (obviously he had forgotten all about the Rusty Drooper Incident or he would have told me to take a hike), said. . .

"What room?"

"Don't try that with me, I invented that defense."

"No wonder it doesn't work."

"What's going on up there?"

"We're working on a project."

"You've never worked on a project in your life."

"This isn't a school project."

"Well. . .that I can believe. So what is it?"

"I can't tell you."

"Well, I know money has to be involved here somewhere."

"I'm not at liberty to say."

"We'll see. . ."

Money was the truest test of Earle's liberty. His palms would sweat, and the adrenaline would flow whenever billfolds opened. His heart would start to pound so loud you would've thought the Mohegans were on the warpath.

"Is that thunder?"

"So, you're not ready to tell me. . ." I placed a one-dollar bill on the table."

"No. . .er. . ." He loosened his collar.

"Really. . ." I placed a second dollar on top of the first.

"Ah. . .my blood pressure. . .where's my medication?"

A third bill was placed on the stack.

"Ah. . .stop. . .I can't. . ."

A fourth bill was added.

"Oooohhhhh. . ." Earle started to rub his chest. "This is inhuman. . ."

I straightened the stack and placed a fifth bill on top.

"A paper! . . . We're writing a newspaper." He broke down and sobbed. His head dropped onto the table and into his folded arms. . .but his hand managed to simultaneously creep out and take the money.

"What!? . . . That's it! A paper? I've been cheated!"

"No refunds."

"Yeah, that I'd like to see. . .a refund from you."

So Earle let me into their inner sanctum for five bucks. There sat Bill, wearing printer's sleeves.

"You know Bill, when you first arrived I didn't think you were going to make it, and look at you now."

"Who let you in!? . . ."

"You really had no choice. . .even if it was Earle who told me. I knew something was going on, and if I knew, then you can bet your bottom five bucks others know."

Earle nodded in agreement. I sat down in a corner chair and lit up a cigarette.

"Please, go on with whatever you're doing. Your secret is safe with me. . .as much as any secret has ever been safe with me."

"We're doomed," said Bill.

A third member of their group arrived.

"Craig, you're in this too? Just how many of you are there?"

"What are you doing here!? . . ."

"Well, I'm not Jimmy Olsen."

"It doesn't matter, we go to press Friday anyway." Bill put a sheet of paper in the typewriter.

They were prepared. They had their own mimeograph machine, typewriters and Bill's inexhaustible supply of costume accessories for every occasion.

"Remember," said Bill to his staff. "Check two sources before making the whole thing up."

By Friday they were ready with the first edition of "*All the news that fits we print.*"

"How much are you going to charge?" I asked.

"Five cents," said Bill, wearing his Perry White, editor-in-chief white shirt with rolled-up sleeves.

"Five cents!?" Earle almost passed out.

"Five cents," repeated Bill.

"What do you care," I said to Earle. "You've already made five bucks."

"What's he talking about?" asked Bill.

"Nothing." said Earle.

They hawked the copies at the teen club that Friday night and sold out quickly. Bill's creation was not only witty and fun, but actually contained some rather interesting and bizarre stories masquerading as news, and above all, included a gossip column that had the real dirt on almost everyone. He soon had a roaring success on his hands. Here he was, the editor and chief correspondent of an underground high school newspaper before there were really any such things. For the first time in my life, I actually read a school newspaper.

I'd like to think I had a minor role in this, nothing that could be tracked back to me. But then again, I've thought I've had a lot of minor roles, and when it was tracked back to me, I found out I had suddenly been promoted to major, and sometimes colonel. The role of editor suited Bill. Earle saw it all as strictly a business venture. He became the business manager, and handled the day-to-day operations, the money, the money, the money, the money, and the coercion of lower-class students. To be honest, this last task was shared with a lot of others who had nothing whatsoever to do with the paper.

The Pirate's Answer became the highlight of the school week, and founded some of the most time-honored yellow journalism techniques ever seen in Bremerhaven High School, and that was doing something considering some of the people who had gone before him. This was an accomplishment right up there with any of *The Mr. Coleman All-Time Top Ten Ants in The Pants High School Career False Starts* listed in the inaugural issue. The "Burning Down of the Bandstand" still occupied number one. Adding this to my other accomplishments, I had been associated with four of the top ten. Not bad. . .but I did get an early start.

Bill was obviously going somewhere with his life, and at the moment, as he slyly played cards, he was on his way to Frankfurt with the rest of us, and most of our money.

One day, the unthinkable happened. Rumors were flying around the school about a deal that had been worked out between the school paper and *The Pirate's Answer*. The entire PA staff vociferously denied this, but on press day the headline read "PA SELLS OUT!" There was a drawing of two hands ex-

tended in the handshake of compromise. True, the hand labeled "Port Call" was full of a cash bribe, but it was still a major
shock. Bill had successfully started his own paper, vanquished
his foes, ascended the throne of editorship of the school paper, sold us all out for his own gain, lied to us, took our money,
and countless other qualifications that all added up to one
thing. . .United States congressman.

★   ★   ★

OVER THE CHRISTMAS holidays of 1962 we received new orders,
and began packing to leave Germany.

"We're going back to D.C. again?" asked my mother.

"Yes," replied my father.

"And in the middle of the school year?"

"Yes."

"I'm too tired to try a find a Catholic high school."

"Yes! . . ." Marcella and I said.

Back to the land of the round doorknobs. After we had
finished all the packing, we moved out of the apartment and
checked into the transient hotel, waiting for our ship to be
ready for boarding. Only one last tribal rite remained. . .the
sacred Last Night in Germany. This task was performed by The
Guys. A task reminiscent of Sherman's March To The Sea.

This was not a last nostalgic look at the city. I was too young
for nostalgia, and I would have needed Bill to give me the word's
definition anyway. It was a thinly disguised excuse for taking
advantage of Germany one last time, a roving review of the
town, giving our hosts one last chance to screw me on exchang-
ing Dollars for German Marks.

"Come on, Herr Schmidt. . .I'm leaving the country in the
morning. I won't be back to the bahnhof ever again. . ."

"But you haf bin gut customur, I give you four marks to
dollar."

"Come on, Herr Schmidt. . .you've never given me more
than three the whole time I've been here. . .make my leaving
memorable. . .please. . .screw me."

"Was? . . ."

"Take advantage. . .I'm begging you."

"All right. . .if you say. . .one dollar to Deutsche Mark."

"You can do better than that. . ."

"Two dollar to Deutsche Mark."

"Now we're talking!"

Earle was on oxygen.

"Why'd you do that?"

"That was his going away gift."

"He should get you one."

"If you could have seen what Ted and I looked like three years ago when we first came in here, you wouldn't say that. He never batted an eye, just served up the beer and handed it down to the two little twerps that were about as tall as his German Shepherd."

Herr Schmidt's German Shepherd was about the size of a small horse. Rommel mostly stayed behind the bar, and I didn't even know he had a dog until I saw its back just peeking over the top as he walked around back there. It was like a sighting of the Loch Ness monster as the huge shoulders moved along. Nobody screwed around too much in Herr Schmidt's gasthaus.

"Now that I'm a big twerp, I'm showing my appreciation," I was beginning to slur my words.

I was drinking way too much, and I crossed the line somewhere along the route back to the teen club. I knew something was up when I found myself looking up into the night sky. I had expected to be seeing some faces, since I had just turned around to say something to someone behind me. Now I was suddenly lying on my back, draped over a hedgerow. It was a beautiful night sky, full of stars. Then faces appeared in that sky, staring down at me. I didn't feel the fall at all. My legs were draped over a sidewalk hedge, and I was sprawled in someone's yard.

"Are you all right?"

"Yeah, I think so." I sat up. "Help me out of here."

Hands grabbed me and I floated onto my feet.

"I think we'll help you the rest of the way."

"They'll be no thinking about it. . ."

And there were still a couple of drinks down below that hadn't hit me yet.

"Let's get him back to the hotel."

Steve and Rickey With The Dented Forehead helped me up.

"Well, thank ya, thank ya very much," I said to Steve.

We pressed on.

There's nothing quite like being carried into a hotel and being deposited on the counter of the front desk, a night delivery for the night manager. I was hoping to be inconspicuous, but with all the people in the lobby stopped in their tracks and staring at me, I took the "in" right off inconspicuous. Who could blame them for staring? I would have done the same thing. I tried to manage a dignified smile as I was being dragged by, but I fear I looked more like a grinning nitwit.

"Why are you grinning like that?" asked Steve.

"I'mmphh. . .can't."

"That's your explanation? . . ."

It was obvious that speech had now left me. I wondered what I would lose next.

As I was being carried across the lobby, I began to feel a sense of déjà vu. It was one of the few feelings I had left. What was it about this scene? I couldn't have done this before, could I? Had I actually been dragged across half the hotel lobbies in Germany and I just don't remember? It wasn't the hotel, but something in the way people stared at me.

"Spastic tennis. . ." I mumbled.

"What?"

". . .spas. . .tennis."

"You wouldn't think it was possible he could get worse," said Earle.

Steve shifted his grip on me. "Yeah, and all in about twenty feet. I'm afraid to ask about this tennis."

The people were staring at me just like that day my brother, a friend of his, and I were walking across town, heading for the tennis courts. Somewhere along the way, my brother's friend decided to start dragging his foot. Then he contorted his face, hunched his back, paralyzed his hand, and shuffled along the street as this grotesque apparition. Another American diplomatic triumph in post-war West Germany.

"What are you doing?" asked my brother.

"Off to play spastic tennis," he answered.

Whoa. . .from what deep recess of the *Coleman Top Ten* did this inspiration spring from? Now please, this was not my idea. I didn't wish to offend anyone then, and I don't want to offend anyone now. I'm sure there are many good spastic tennis players out there, so please don't write me any nasty letters.

The Germans didn't seem to appreciate his efforts. I don't think they knew what this was all about, however I'm sure they had us pegged as Americans. I don't remember seeing that many tennis courts outside of the American housing areas, and the Germans probably thought this guy was carrying some kind of high-tech boat paddle. Please, I'm sure there are plenty of good spastic boat paddlers out there, so again, don't send me any nasty letters.

The people on the street just stared at the three of us as we came by them. I was really embarrassed. It's one thing to stream toilet paper out of buses and run around train yards in your underwear, but walking down the streets of the city with Quasimodo as your tennis partner was really too much for me. I smiled politely to the passing people while their eyes bugged out at us. I wished I could have disappeared.

Now I was being dragged across the lobby and wished I could disappear again. Life is a series of events punctuated by wishing you could disappear. And now here I was lying across the hotel front desk.

"Ah, young Mr. Burferlinger, nice to see you again. . .Front!"

"Would you like something?" asked the night manager.

"What'd you got?"

"Everyone be quiet."

I couldn't tell who was speaking or what they were saying, it all started to sound like it was underwater.

". . .rooomff. . .ahhhh," I said.

These sounds, however, made perfect sense to me. But they didn't make sense to anyone else, although that "roomff" was pretty close.

"May I have that again, please?" asked the night manager.

"Mmmm. . .keyhh."

"Excuse me?"

I slid off the countertop to my knees and stopped with my chin hanging on the edge.

"We need his key," said The Guys.

"What room number?"

I responded by crumbling to the floor.

"We don't know."

"Could you please pick him up, and give me his name."

They got the key and I was dragged back across the lobby, past all the same people, and out to the stairwell leading to my room. I wasn't any help at all, and proceeded to collapse on the stairs. The Guys weren't in such hot shape either, and together we crawled up the stairs to my door. They managed to get to their feet, but I was much more comfortable on my hands and knees. There really wasn't much of a chance I could do anything else anyway, so I crawled along behind them and into the room.

They were trying to get my clothes off when my parents showed up. They were only moments away, coming up the stairs.

"What'd we do with him now?"

"Hide him. Shove him in the closet."

"And if we do that. . .it will be just us standing here."

"So?"

"So. . .if he's not here, then why exactly are we here? Robbing the place?"

It might have been trouble, but my mother had her own hands full. Around the corner crawled The Colonel.

"Whaatiiff. . .," he said.

"Wellumph. . .," I replied.

His eyes lit up with recognition.

"Humphh wiff velcin. . ."

"Ahhh. . .," I answered.

"Ahhh. . .," he replied.

Finally, someone to talk to. We chatted amiably.

It was the most we had ever spoken. It didn't last very long. It was then that I lost the last thing I had. . .consciousness.

The next morning my mother took me to an early breakfast, sat me down, ordered for me, and then watched while I forced down eggs, for God's sake. She pretended not to know anything had happened the night before, and sat there full of herself while I was dying.

"My, what nice country air," she said.

My solace was that we were about to board our ship, and it was the same one we had arrived on.

"Wait 'till the ship's doctor sees you!"

"Waiter, some poached eggs for my son."

We sailed late that morning, and I again looked for shipboard romance. The result? One hundred and thirteen chicken sandwiches and 323 Cokes later, we docked in New York. Dad waved good-bye to the throngs lining the ship's railing and Mom was carried down the gangplank.

She hit the solid Earth, and was up and fit immediately once again. "I called Dave at the university and he will meet us in Bristol."

"Noooo. . .not Name That Relative again!"

"And don't you dare call Aunt Jenny a douchebag. I've worked for three years to smooth everything over from our last visit."

"Then why ruin it, let's just go on to D.C."

"No, I want to see my sisters."

"Then I should go to D.C."

"You'll come."

I won't bore everyone with the details, the less said the better, suffice it to say I had a few more conferences with my mother in most of the kitchens in Bristol. . .and I was disinherited by Uncle Tony.

THE GREEN MONSTER

We were back living in the Virginia suburbs of D.C. The Colonel had been assigned to Cameron Station. If the name of your post doesn't start with Fort, then you know you're in big trouble. Cameron Station couldn't even qualify for a camp. There wasn't anything on this station! No quarters, no barracks, no troops. . .just several large warehouses, a giant PX and commissary complex, and a gas station. We drove through looking like a moving birdcage of stunned canaries with our beaks stuck through the bars in astonishment.

"This is a joke on us, isn't it Dad? It's the army having some more fun, isn't it. . .where are we really assigned?"

"I'm afraid this is it."

"But there's nothing here!? Where's your company? Where are you going to work? In one of those warehouses?"

"No. . .I'll be in there."

He pointed at a small brick building set behind the warehouses.

So, Cameron Station has several large warehouses, a giant PX and commissary, a gas station, and a brick hut.

"Where are we going to live? I'll tell you right now, I'm not going back to Deep Fielder."

"What are you talking about? We have a nice place, right next to the high school."

We finished our riding tour of Cameron Station in our DKW. Remember the Play-Doh-encrusted wringer washing machine noises that came out of our Buick on the trip to Washington State? In a DKW, these are normal. A DKW is supposed to be a car. . .at least those were the rumors. My father had selected it, and brought it back from Germany. I don't blame you if you've never heard of it. We all would have preferred to have never heard of it. It was small, like most of the European cars of that day, and ugly, like most of the European cars of that day. It was very much like an old Saab, if that helps you. In fact, it was an old Saab with just a different body. It had the two-cycle engine that sounded like a popcorn machine, and you had to mix the oil with the gas just like an outboard motor. The oil had to go into the gas tank first, into some mysterious mixing bowl. Those were the days when there were real gas stations, with real gas station attendants, that actually knew a thing or two about servicing cars, but not when it came to DKWs. They just assumed it was a regular car. . .a small, ugly regular car. You had to pull into a local boat marina to find somebody who knew something about a DKW.

"Hey boy, why is there a boat motor in here?"

"It's those crazy Germans."

I had to leap out the moment I stopped at a station to make sure they didn't start pumping the gas before I could get the oil into the mixing tank. Then they would have to wait as I measured out the right amount of oil for the amount of gas. This seemed to amuse them for a while, then it would just annoy them. All and all, no one was too happy about going to the gas station. They gave me another set of directions to the boat marina with my change.

This car would never start. The dashboard was caved in from where my brother had hammered it with his fist whenever the engine refused to start up. And, since this was every time, the dashboard had been beaten distinctly concave. The speaker grill for the radio was twisted and mangled from a summer of being on the wrong side of a standing Older Brother Car Starting Pounding Decree.

"I see that Older Brother Pounding Decrees encompass more than just me."

"This fuckin' car."

I'll say one thing for the DKW, it had a helluva starter motor. It would whirl and whirl to beat the band, it just never actually started anything.

"This fuckin' car."

"That's where we've got it wrong, I don't think this is a car at all. I think the Germans had all those leftover V-2 parts lying around after the war, and turned them into this. It's our mistake for assuming it was a car. I'm sure they're all laughing it up back there. . ."

"They may have won zee war, Mein Herr, but now we have zem! Let zem sit in zee V-2mobile all day with zee starter gafunken spinning round und round."

Pound!

"This fuckin' car."

"I wonder if the starter motor is actually hooked up to anything? What do you think, Dave?"

Hammer!

"This fuckin' car."

Dave didn't think so.

So the DKW became known as "This Fuckin' Car."

My father wouldn't even try to start it. He would put the car in gear, turn the key, and use the starter motor to propel himself along until he reached enough speed for the car to jump-start itself to life. Then he was off in a cloud of oil smoke and a cacophony of two-cycle popping.

On Sunday mornings we would all pile into The Shitbox (this was the more formal name for This Fuckin' Car, and intended for my mother's polite company) and head to church. People waited in the parking lot until we arrived, just to witness us getting out of the DKW, for we were all very tall, and it was well worth the wait to see us popping out of it.

"They actually got out of that car thing. . ."

At the end of services there was a mad scramble to get the best views to see how we got back into The Shitbox. It was like a Chinese box puzzle. And like all good puzzles, I'm not going to give away the solution.

My brother and I never took The Shitbox anywhere without a pit crew. Once we managed to get the engine started, then our real troubles would begin. Everyone had to deal with the mystery gear. . .first gear. It was a mystery because no one could ever find it. The shift pattern on the column said it was supposed to be right there, next to second gear, but you needed the touch of a surgeon to locate it, and you had the duration of a traffic light to do it.

"Those Germans, they're a lot of laughs, aren't they?"

Pound!

"This fuckin' car."

By now the dashboard was so beaten inward that it looked like a dazed smile.

The last-ditch starting alternative was skipping first gear altogether and using second gear instead. The EPA frowned upon this option. It required revving the engine up to about a gazillion RPM, which would effectively blot out that section of the Earth in two-cycle oil smoke exhaust, and ride the clutch up to speed. And this was the car I was going to use to make my reputation in my new high school, to impress the girls, to join the school car club?

Popity. . .pop. . .popity. . .pop. . .pop. . .billow. . ..billow.

"Hey guys, check it out. German engineering! Where are the women?"

Popity. . .pop. . .popity. . .pop. . .pop. . .billow. . ..billow.

There were never any women, and unfortunately for me, it was also no longer 1959. It was 1963, but I still looked like the day I stepped off the boat in Germany back in '59 in my skinny belts and white socks. These two eras did not mix well. Everyone had gone collegiate and I. . .hadn't. Everyone, that is, except the real hoods, who thought a new felon had just walked in the door.

"Gee. . .did I happen to mention this is just a fashion statement?"

"What? . . ."

The DKW and I were a matched set.

"Come on, let me show you my car. . ."

A few months later, Earle's family returned from Germany and moved outside of Baltimore. He called me up. . .

"Somehow I'm in a teenage gang!" he cried.

"Yeah, same thing happened to me. I can get you out."

"How?"

"I'll borrow the car and drive up."

"And then what?"

"Believe me, that'll be enough."

Taking the DKW to Baltimore was daring of the highest order. It was my first trip of any distance. I was nervous as a kitten, prayed every mile and sweated out every noise.

I made it to Baltimore and we found Earle's new gang buddies. . .

Popity. . .pop. . .popity. . .pop. . .pop. . .billow. . ..billow.

"Hey guys, I'm here! Where are the women?"

They didn't say anything, they just stood there with their mouths agape, and that's the way we left them.

"Thanks, I think," said Earle. "I hope nobody else saw me."

"How do you think I feel? I have to drive it all the time."

"God, what was your father thinking?"

"He wasn't."

"And I thought it was only us who didn't think before we did something."

"Let me tell you, it ain't funny being on the other end."

Returning to D.C., I was again nervous as a kitten, praying every mile and sweating out every noise. Prayers had their usual impact, so on the way back to D.C. the DKW broke down. I stood on the roadside with no inkling as to what I should do next when a car pulled over and stopped. The door opened and out stepped my brother.

It was high order improbability, for my brother had started out the day in Connecticut, some eight hours earlier. He had left college for semester break at about the same time I left for Baltimore.

"Is it dead?" he asked.

"The radiator light came on."

"Too bad."

"About the radiator?"

"No, that it's not really dead."

The driver of his ride from Connecticut got out and opened his trunk.

"Good God, look at all this stuff." I was stunned. It was loaded with enough survival gear to have kept Patton's Third Army rolling.

"Let's see what we've got here," he said.

He took a rag and opened the radiator cap.

"Well, there's no water."

He went back to his car and returned.

"Here."

He handed us a five-gallon water can. We handled filling the radiator.

"Start it up."

"Well, this could take awhile. . ."

Before the words were out of my mouth, he got into the DKW.

"Where are the keys?"

"Here."

He took them, turned the ignition on, and. . .waarruuummm, the DKW started.

"What!? . . . How'd you do that?"

A hose started sprinkling water.

"Is it raining?" we asked.

"There's your problem, split hose."

We were off again, my brother and I, in the DKW, after patching the hose with some magic tape from his trunk.

"This fuckin' car. . .," said Dave to himself.

★   ★   ★

Dave took to wearing disguises he bought at a costume shop to limit his embarrassment of being seen behind the wheel of The Shitbox. I thought it was a futile exercise.

"How so?" asked Dave.

"Do you think they really believe that Jackie Kennedy is driving by in her DKW?"

"Why not?"

"For the same reason they don't believe it's Jerry Lewis when I drive by."

Most people thought I didn't need a mask to be mistaken for Jerry Lewis.

★   ★   ★

THAT SUMMER THE Colonel brought home The Green Monster. It complemented the DKW, in fact, it could have been a premium giveaway that came with the DKW. It was a green imitation Naugahyde-covered monstrosity that my father placed in our room.

"What is it?" I asked my brother.

"I don't know."

We looked it over. It was like a refrigerator cartoon turned on its side. There were two drawers on each end with an opening in the middle.

My father watched us from the bedroom doorway. "It's a desk," he said. Then he left us alone in the room with The Thing.

"This can't be a desk," I said. "I've seen desks before, and this is nothing at all like them."

"This is what you get when you let a man who brought home a DKW, bring home a desk."

"It could be one of those *Popular Mechanics* home projects; they put plans in the magazine to build things like this."

"No one would buy a magazine that had plans to build something like this. The plans were for a real desk and someone turned them into this, after all, look at the lamp you made in shop," said my brother.

On our nightstand was the lamp I had built in junior high shop class at Fort Lewis. It was four pieces of wood nailed together that resembled a cube, sort of, with a lamp socket sticking out of the top. Fate determined that it would survive both Atlantic crossings to once again stalk me. My mother always put it in our room, like she was proud of it. I noticed it never went in her room, like she was proud of it.

"This would be a *Popular Mechanics* project gone terribly wrong," said Dave.

"It could be a piece of abandoned army furniture he found on the post."

"I've never seen anything that looked like this, even in the army. . .even abandoned in the army. I don't think you call this furniture. I think it was an abandoned crate and they covered it with abandoned imitation Naugahyde." Dave stood there with his bottom lip curled over his teeth, looking intently at the Naugahyde crate. "I've got it! It's a test! The old man is testing us. He puts this thing in our room then waits to see what we'll do. Like *Candid Camera*." Dave was proud of solving the mystery.

"Are you sure? He's never tested us before."

"We'll it's the only thing it could be."

"I hope you're right."

We went into my father's bedroom.

"Dad, we figured it out, we know it's a test. There is no such thing, not even a *Popular Mechanics* project, that looks like. . .whatever that is in our room," said Dave.

"Yeah, Dad. You had us going there for a minute. . .a desk. You're a card, Dad."

"Yeah, quite the joke. Where did you ever get something like that? Did you have the wood shop on the station make it up? They must still be laughing."

My father put on his uniform jacket and walked into the living room with us following along behind him.

"Dad, you can have it taken out now, we know you were just testing us."

He walked to the front door and opened it.

"There is no wood shop on the station. . .it's a desk," he said. "It's not a test. I got it for your room. And I was lucky to get it before it was snapped up by someone else."

He closed the door and was gone.

"Lucky? . . ." my brother said.

"Snapped up? . . ." I said.

We went back into our room and looked at The Green Monster with an entirely different perspective. It was ours, it was going to stay, it was a desk, it was a nightmare.

Out the window we could see The Colonel driving away in the DKW. . .popity. . .popity. . .billow. . .billow.

"What are we going to do?" I asked.

My brother ran his hand along the green imitation Naugahyde covering.

"We live with it."

"But it looks like it's covered with pressed grass clippings. Do you think he would notice if we sold it?"

"If you can sell this, then I'll take the blame for whatever story we come up with."

My brother tried opening one of the drawers, but it wouldn't budge. He tried the others, same thing.

"I think these are decorative."

"Decorative? . . ."

"Either that or they're nailed shut."

"How can you write on it? It's covered with these little bumps."

"I think it's supposed to be like that. . .it's texture. I believe it's even considered an appealing feature."

I looked at him like he was crazy. "Do you expect me to believe that?"

"Does it matter?"

That evening, The Colonel brought home a large piece of Plexiglas.

"For your desktop," he said.

"Thank you," we said.

We placed the Plexiglas on top of the desk.

"Maybe we can cover it with something. . .like a sheet," I said.

"Maybe. I've got it! Let's paint it!"

"Good idea."

The next day we went down to the basement, found a can of white paint, and brushed it on.

"It looks worse," I said dumbfounded.

"It looks like a hideous, overgrown, dressing table."

"Maybe Mom will like it, she likes my lamp."

"She doesn't like your lamp, she just likes making you put it your room."

"Well, what do we do now?"

"Let's see what other colors we can find."

We painted it brown.

"Ugh, white was better."

"Maybe a car color, like metallic red," said my brother.

"Where are we going to get that?"

"From an auto parts store."

"This will cost money?"

"Do you want The Thing in our room the way it is?"

We bought two cans of metallic candy apple red.

"This is going to be great!"

We both began spraying from opposite ends.

"What's happening!?"

As we sprayed, the surface began to wrinkle and crack open, exposing the original green. It was a scene from a horror movie. It was a wrinkled-red, cracked-brown, fractured-white, bumpy-green desk collage.

"This is horrible, Dave."

"We have managed to make this desk worse. You wouldn't think that was possible, but we've found a way." My brother's matter-of-fact tone betrayed no emotion, just stating the facts, ma'am.

"We can't put it back in our room like this, we have to do something."

"One thing is for sure, we won't be on the Mr. Craftsman show."

"Maybe we should take off the green covering?"

"What more harm can we do?"

"I'm sure we'll find something."

A tug and a pull, then a rip and a tear. The cover was glued down, and wasn't going anywhere. We had only managed to pull up a small corner where the glue wasn't holding.

"We'll be here the rest of our lives," I said.

"We have until dinner. . .until Dad gets home."

"Can we go back to the green covering? Get the paint off?"

"We'll have to get paint remover."

A trip to the hardware store, and another couple of dollars later we had a large can of paint remover.

"Okay, it says to brush it on."

We spread the liquid over the top, and waited like the can said.

"It looks like it's working."

The paint was liquefying.

"Let's wipe some away and see what it looks like."

We took some paper towels and wiped. The towels had the red, white, and brown. . .and green smeared on them.

"It's dissolving the green covering!" I yelled.

"Why is this happening? Quick! Wipe it up as fast as you can!"

We ripped off long reams of paper towels and wiped the top furiously. It began to harden as we tried to clean it off. We wiped until the paper towels stuck to the top, and we could wipe no more. We had a new look. . .a swirling tapestry of all the original colors, and all their combinations, none of which were attractive.

"Who said what more harm can we do?"

Dave walked around the desk. "It's almost better than the wrinkled confetti look, if it wasn't for some of these new colors we've invented. I'm particularly fond of these bits of torn paper towels stuck in it."

The sides were still the cracked collage from the metallic paint debacle.

"Maybe we should call someone."

"Like who?" I asked.

"I don't know. . .we can't bury it in the backyard, it's too big."

"How much time do we have?"

"It's 3:30 P.M., a couple of more hours."

"Okay, let's think."

"That hasn't been our strong suit."

"Then, what do you suggest?"

A voice came down the stairs. "What are you boys doing down there?"

"Mom!"

"Nothing!"

"Don't tell me 'nothing,' I've heard you. . ." She came down the basement stairs. "You better not be making a mess down here. I've just cleaned and. . .aiiiieeeee!"

"Now Mom, it's not as bad as it looks."

She looked at the desk, brought up both hands to her cheeks and said. . .

"Aiiiiieeeee!"

"We're working on it, Mom."

She looked at us and said. . .

"Aiiiiieeeee!"

"We still have some time to finish it."

She looked at the clock and said. . .

"Aiiiiieeeee!"

"We had good intentions."

"Boys, it was his favorite color." My brother and I looked at each other, perplexed by this.

"His favorite color?"

"Well, it's still in there. . .in some spots," said Dave.

"In some swirls. . .," I said.

". . .some flows," said my brother.

". . .some cracks."

". . .some crevices."

". . .some fissures."

We both were laughing.

"Chasms. . .ha. . .ha."

"Troughs. . .ha. . .ha."

"Eddies. . .ha. . .ha," said Mom. "All right, stop it. It's not funny." Mom wiped a laughter tear from her eye. "Maybe we can bury it in the backyard with his golf trophy."

"It's too big, Mom, we already thought of that."

"You buried his golf trophy in the backyard?" I asked.

"You don't think I was going to live with that in my house?"

"Now you know how we feel. We don't want to live with this desk in our room," said my brother.

"What about my lamp, can we bury that?"

"I like your lamp. We need to do something about this desk."

"We've been trying all day. . ."

"And this is your result? . . ." she asked.

"Well. . .yes. . .it is," I said.

"Let me see what I can do."

My mother was the queen of furniture antiquing, and she brought out all her talents and chemicals.

"We'll have to sand," she said as she put on her antiquing rubber gloves. "I figure three grades should do it." She put on her antiquing overalls. "Maybe four, depending on how it goes." She put on her respirator. "Color selection is important." She hooked up her paint gun. "We should be done before your father gets home." She flicked on the belt sander.

Two hours later, the desk was finished. . .green.

"We're back to where we started," I said.

"No," my brother replied. "Now we have these squiggly little lines that are supposed to be. . .what are they supposed to be?"

"That's the wood grain, the essence of the antiquing process," she proudly announced.

"It kind of looks like camouflage," I said.

We carried the desk back up to our room, while Mom turned the basement back into a NASA clean room.

"He's coming!"

Popity. . .popity. . .billow. . .billow.

"Quick, assume innocent positions."

I left the room.

"Where, are you going?"

"My innocent position is outside."

"Oh, no you don't, you're going to be in here with me."

"If you can show me an innocent position anywhere in this room, then I'll stay."

"Too late, he's here."

Dave grabbed a magazine and sprawled out on his bed.

"I need my tank," I said.

Dad was happy with the antiquing. He had a soft spot for camouflage.

★ ★ ★

MY SISTER TURNED sixteen about the same time the desk turned camouflage. Marcella got her learner's permit to drive, but before the week was out she had been barred for life from ever getting a driver's license in the state of Virginia. This is some kind of a record for someone who had a learner's permit for about a week. I don't know if this ruling is still in effect, she no longer lives in Virginia, and life sentences these days are down to about five or six years. Life sentences for driver's licenses must be down to about the same length of time as she had a learner's permit, a week. So, on some strange level of comparison, she was even.

She did manage to squeeze one quick driving lesson out of my father.

"This is how to start the car." Car in gear, motor engaged, crank up to speed, pop the clutch. . .popity. . .popity. . .billow . . .billow.

I'm not sure how this would work if she ever wanted to use someone else's car.

"Aiiiieeee. . .what are you doing!?"

"Starting the car."

"Just turn the key!"

"Wow, what will they think of next. Where's the popping and the smoke?"

"Get out of my car."

On a warm, early fall night, she sat on the front step of her girlfriend's townhouse with her learner's permit stuck in her jeans back pocket. An idea began to form, slowly at first, causing her head to hurt somewhat.

"What? . . ." she said to herself.

"What? . . ." said her girlfriend.

"What? . . ." she said to her girlfriend.

"You started to say something. . ."

"I did?"

"Yes."

"Well, no matter."

"I thought I just saw your car coming home," said her girlfriend.

"By itself? Well, it was probably my brother. Was he beating on the dash and screaming 'this fuckin' car?'"

"I don't think it was him, it looked like Jackie Kennedy."

"I've been thinking," said my sister. You have a license, and I have a learner's permit. I can drive if you're in the car." Her face beamed with the impulsive thought. "I can get a lesson tonight."

This idea would end her very short driving career, and land everyone in court.

"I don't know, this doesn't sound like a good idea," said her girlfriend.

"You're not doing anything, I'm not doing anything, I have a learner's permit, you have a license, there's the car. . .this is kismet."

Everything she said was right, except the part about the DKW being a car, and possibly the kismet thing.

They both silently thought it over for a while.

This doesn't sound too bad. . .does it? Why not do it?

It's their car, if they let her take it, then I'll come along.

"Listen, if your parents say it's okay. Then I'll come along."

"Okay."

Marcella's plan did not include asking anyone if it was okay.

As far as I knew, the evening was like any other, taking its usual slow course. I was sitting at the camouflage desk in my room, unaware that anything extraordinary was occurring outside. Then the doorbell rang. The Colonel got up from The Chair and answered the door. I remained engrossed in the antiqued wood-grain lines painted on the desk, they interested me more than the chemical formulas in my textbook.

I heard a commotion in the hallway. Angry voices and the sounds of a scuffle filled the apartment. I peeked into the living room. The Colonel was struggling with two Virginia state troopers. I was frozen in shock at the scene. I had never seen The Colonel struggle with anyone before, let alone with a couple of state troopers. If he was going to be in a struggle, I envisioned it would be with Russians holding out in their fire-power demonstration hut.

"Hey! Hey! Whoa! Achtung! Halt!" I heard myself yelling. This had no effect whatsoever, but I felt like I was doing something. It didn't seem wise to jump into the middle of this, so I just repeated. . .

"Hey! Hey! Whoa! Achtung! Halt!"

Well, the struggle ended, and I'd like to believe my Hey! Hey! Whoa! Achtung! Halt! had something to do with it.

"What's this all about!?" yelled my father.

"You're under arrest!"

"What for!?"

"For a hit and park."

"Hit and park!? What!? . . ."

They escorted The Colonel outside where two police cruisers were parked at the front and rear of the DKW. Their flashing lights were still on, and the red pulsating beams reflected
off the buildings and the cars, creating a kind of glaring and
surreal scene. The DKW seemed to be drooped in shame, the
fact that both the front and rear were bashed in had something to do with that.

"What happened to my car!?" yelled The Colonel

"I suppose you don't know anything about this?"

"Of course I don't, I was in my apartment all evening, just
ask my son."

Gulp.

"Actually, I was in my room and didn't see anything. . ."

"Thanks a lot, son!"

"Have you been drinking tonight? Your neighbors say that
you drink a lot, and that you tend to drive erratically. They're
afraid to be on the streets when you come home. Does your
son care to comment on that?"

Gulp.

"Well. . ."

"You're killing me, son!"

My mother came out of the apartment in her Inca Ceremonial Cold Cream mask.

"What's happening here!? Why do you have my husband!?"

"Your husband was involved in a motor vehicle incident,
Ma'am."

"Wait until you hear what kind. . .," said my father.

"Has your husband been drinking tonight?"

"Well. . ."

"I already said that, Mom."

"Who's been driving your car tonight, Ma'am?"

"It couldn't be us, we don't have a car," I said. They pointed
to the DKW. "Oh. . ."

"No one's been driving this car tonight!" yelled my father.

Unbeknownst to us, while my father sat in the living room,
while my mother was bathing herself in cold cream, while I sat
staring at my camouflaged desk, my sister had set her impulsive idea into motion. It might have worked out okay, I guess,
but it was also the kind of idea that a sixteen-year-old can really
screw up. This may sound like a bad movie script, but I'll swear
to it, and the Virginia state court records will bear me out.

The DKW was parallel parked out on the front street. My
sister stealthily spirited the keys out of the house without be-

ing detected. Once inside the car she made another bad decision, she was going to drive right away, none of this waiting for a deserted stretch of road nonsense.

Since her first lesson had mostly to do with the various starting methods employed by DKW owners, the clutch was a total mystery to her.

"Why are there so many pedals down here," she asked her girlfriend."

"I don't know. This car is a lot different from any that I've ever been in before." That goes without saying.

"That one is the gas pedal, I know that, and that one is the brake, maybe that one opens the trunk."

"No, I watched my dad, it has something to do with starting the car. It must be the starter pedal."

"That sounds right. I know there are a lot of things on a car that are called 'starter' something. How does it work?"

"Let's see if I can remember. You push it in and move this lever into one of these slots. Then you push this button. . ." The starter motor began to turn.

"I hear some whirling, but nothing is happening," said her girlfriend.

"I know. Then you let the starter pedal back up. . ."

They lurched forward, crashing into the car parked in front of them.

CRUNCH.

"Oh, no. . ."

Panic set in, and instead of leaving bad enough alone, she moved some more levers and proceeded to ram the car in back of her.

CRUNCH.

There were more crumpled fenders. Now she was truly frightened and in a state of frenzy, she pushed buttons, moved levers and stepped on pedals.

Her girlfriend took to screaming, as my sister jumped the curb, slicing the side of the DKW and coming to a stop on the front lawn.

As she realized the full impact of all she had accomplished, and at such a tender age, she became very calm. Her girlfriend stopped screaming, and through many combinations of pedals and levers, they managed to return the DKW back to the original parking spot.

"At least we didn't hit the building. . .at least I don't think we hit the building. Did we hit the building?"

"Shut up," said my sister. "Did anyone see us?"

"I don't know, I had my eyes closed."

"I don't think anyone saw us."

"Don't you think someone may have heard all that twisting and tearing and screaming? . . ."

"It's not too bad, maybe no one will notice."

Unfortunately for Marcella, everyone wasn't blind, and someone eventually noticed and that's when the state police entered the picture.

"No one's been driving this car tonight!" yelled The Colonel.

The air crackled with the police calls on the squad car radios. A crowd had formed, a third cruiser pulled up and officers began to string out yellow crime scene tape and push back the people. It was high drama and worthy of a *Perry Mason* courtroom scene my mother loved so dearly, unfortunately we were living it. The Colonel was being handcuffed, my mother was yelling and pushing the police.

She was arrested.

My sister burst from the crowd, breaking down and confessing.

"It was me, not my father!" she sobbed. ". . .too many pedals. . .too many levers. . ."

She was arrested.

My brother just happened upon the scene, dropped off by some friends at that very moment, and he jumped out of the car. He handed out Tide Wafers to the police.

"Bllaaaagghh!"

"Bllaaaagghh!"

"Bllaaaagghh!"

He was arrested.

I slinked around in the background, peering over the crowd and trying to avoid being associated with my family. . .

"There's another one. . .the tall Georgy Porgy in back of the crowd!" a voice cried out that sounded suspiciously like my brother.

"There he is over there!" I yelled and pointed off into the darkness. It didn't work and the crowd drove me out into the hands of the waiting police.

"Are you part of this family?" asked the trooper.

"What?"

"I said, are you part of this family?"

"Where?"

"Are you deaf?"

"What?"

I was arrested.

We all went down to the police station, where we were unceremoniously booked.

"I would like to point out to the court that the car was never actually started," said our lawyer, on our day in court.

"What's that have to do with anything?" answered the judge.

"I'm not sure, but it has to have a bearing on something, wouldn't you think?"

"Hmmmm."

The court adjourned for an inspection of the DKW. The judge got into the car with the keys and turned the ignition switch. The starter began whirling to beat the band. After about five minutes the judge began to beat on the dashboard and scream obscenities.

The judge dismissed the charges against all, except my sister.

"Barred for life," said the judge.

"What was that about a bar?"

"Easy, Dad."

★   ★   ★

THE DKW FINALLY died, and it wasn't a pretty sight, nor was it, as you might suspect, at the hand of my brother. Everyone had their own small parts in hastening its death, but it was I who finally killed her. She had survived earlier attempts, like Dave accidentally forgetting to put oil in with the gas and having the engine seize up. There was some suspicion that this wasn't an accident. My father actually found someone who could fix a DKW, if you can believe that. He had to search several boat marinas, but eventually he came up with Fritz, a German boat mechanic.

"Perfect," said my brother.

The DKW returned. It was like a horror novel, no matter what we did, The Shitbox returned.

However, there was no return from wrapping her around a telephone pole. She sat in the her final resting place, with her nose pointed into a ditch, a telephone pole protruding from the backseat, and a Jerry Lewis mask lying on the front floor.

"What'd you suppose this means?" asked the investigating policeman while holding up the mask.

"Could be it was used in a robbery. . ."

"No," my brother said. "The robbery took place on the day the car was bought."

It was over. There would be no more Sunday rides to church, no more crop dusting starts from traffic lights. . .Jackie Kennedy would never drive her again.

My brother and sister both agreed they owed me one. There was some suspicion that it wasn't entirely an accident.

THE PRINCE OF COOL

CHRISTMAS. THE MOST indelible image of Christmas isn't the presents, which I'm sure is another shock for my parents. . .

"All that money and he doesn't remember a damn thing!"

And from my father's perspective. . .

"Another martini my dear? . . ."

I can clearly see my mother emerging from the kitchen in her ceremonial Christmas apron at around one in the afternoon, and serving Christmas dinner. One o'clock is not a good time to expect kids to be ready to eat a big holiday feast, especially when all year long one o'clock was actually bologna sandwich time. So we picked at the food.

"Don't pick at your food. Eat it."

Around six we would tug at my mother's skirt, and point to our mouths.

"Please sir, more."

"We've already had dinner. If you're hungry, get a carrot."

"A carrot?"

"A carrot."

So Christmas dinner turned out to be a diet day, unless you were Bugs Bunny.

Mom changed everything when we were in our teens. She retired her ceremonial Christmas apron and announced.

"One o'clock is again bologna sandwich time."

"Yea!" we said.

"We are going to midnight mass and you can eat what you like after that. . .as long as you make it yourself."

"Yea!" said Dad. We all knew what he was going to make.

"When we get home from mass you can open the presents." And that was that, her ceremonial Christmas apron disappeared.

Holiday high masses are purposely designed as an ordeal. This is so you don't get the idea that a holiday comes cheap, and you are properly grateful by the time the mass is over. The priests perform the Latin chant and polish and examine the bottom of the chalice many times during the service, and you get to count the holes in the church ceiling panels to pass the time. There is a Latin phrase about two-thirds of the way through. . .Eta mesa est. . . "Go, the mass has ended," but no one ever leaves. Dave said it was legit to go right then, that it is the original finish of the mass, and the rest was added because priests don't have anything better to do with themselves on a Sunday. Whenever we tried, Mom would collar us. She was unimpressed with Dave's interpretation.

"But Mom, he's been taught by the Jesuits!"

She was equally unimpressed with my argument. All that Jesuit training, and none of it of any practical use.

Once we returned home, we sat around and opened the presents while eating bologna sandwiches. . .and some of us were drinking martinis. By four in the morning it was all over and we straggled off to bed.

In a few days the good cheer had stretched thin, then snapped, and my mother resumed calling me a heathen. I've always assumed this was for learning what eta mesa est actually meant. Life settled back to what passed for normal in our house.

For The Colonel, normal would be an evening of making himself a drink, then making more drinks, then trying to find The Command Post Chair. From there he passed easily through the various stages of his life, the bourbon stage. . .the scotch stage. . .the vodka stage. I have no idea what signaled the beginning or end of a stage, but while in one, that's all he would drink, with the exception of the martini.

"There's always room for a martini," he would say.

"That's what they say about Jell-O," we replied.

"That's what who says about Jell-O?"

"Never mind."

"Are you saying someone would rather have Jell-O than a martini?"

"Never mind."

"Hmmmm. . .maybe a Jell-O martini? I'm going to have to mention this to the club steward."

"Never mind."

These stages only applied to the home, when away he would drink "the cabinet."

We never bought him liquor as a present. Mom would have skinned us alive, and it was too expensive. We bought golf balls. No matter what the occasion, a golf ball was always the answer. And if he couldn't get booze from us, then golf balls were a close second. From what I've seen, the military really runs on booze and golf balls. Recruiting posters should show the army advancing in golf carts with a martini glass insignia on the side.

Once The Colonel actually located The Command Post Chair, he was settled for the night. It is from here that several command decisions were issued throughout the evening.

"George, be a good boy and bring me the paper."

This was the only known time he ever thought of me as a good boy, and the only time I was given the chance to be a good boy several times during the course of an evening. It was from this Command Post Chair that such famed decisions as the $50 heraldry search began, and also the buying of a Renault Dauphin to replace the DKW. The Renault decision was a master stroke. Who would have believed The Colonel could actually have found a car that was less reliable than a DKW? In French, dauphin meant "heir apparent". . .having this car as the heir was like handing over the English throne to Leo Gorcy and the Bowery Boys, but it somehow made sense in the context of replacing the DKW. Hanging in our hallway was the result of the extensive heraldry research conducted for The Colonel's fifty bucks. . .a family crest that looked like a 1955 Buick hood ornament, although not nearly as nice.

Over time, The Command Post Chair began to take on the shape of The Colonel, so it really wasn't very comfortable for anyone else to use. It reminded me of Norman Bates' mother's bed in the movie *Psycho* (I guess that would be Mrs. Bates), where her body impression was permanently pressed into the mattress. They say dogs begin to resemble their masters, or vice versa, and it's true of Command Post Chairs as well.

Dad jealousy guarded his chair as though it was the pinnacle of luxurious comfort, but it was very hard to sit in and pushed your butt forward, eventually forcing you to slide out of the chair and crumple to the floor.

"Dad, is this the way this chair is supposed to work?"

"Who said that? . . . Oh, I didn't see you down there."

The only reason we wanted to sit in it at all was because my father had positioned it directly in front of the television, the choicest location in the living room. Everyone else was seated on the living room perimeter, and had to peer around the chair in order to see the set. There was a clear view over the top until my father sat down, and blotted out the entire screen, and that portion of the Earth as well. My mother, a lifelong professional martyr, had been leaning forward to see *Perry Mason* for so many years that it became her permanent chair posture wherever she went.

Through industriousness, my father had built a moat around his chair. He was completely ringed by cigarette burns in the rug. Some of these were so deep that entire colonies of unidentifiable rug creatures had taken up residence. I assume they all had their own versions of uncomfortable Command Post Chairs down there, with a great view of the TV.

The Colonel would make himself a Command Post Chair Martini, and it was a drink worthy of the title. I don't know if you can really call them martinis because all he did was get a brandy snifter, a large, heavy duty one, and fill it with gin. I think there may have been an ice cube in there, but it wasn't a requirement. When my mother began to complain, he would point out. . .

"I've only had two martinis."

He was fond of saying he only had two martinis. . .and we were fond of trying to understand what it was he was trying to say.

From the Command Post Chair, he was now ready for his evening to begin. . .martini snifter on his right, the automatic moat ejection ash tray on his left, and the television set straight in front of him, tuned to *Perry Mason*. Before Act III, he's out like a light, form fitted into his chair. Twenty years of tuning in and he still doesn't know how Perry solved a single case. The beauty of it is that there are no such things as reruns in his world.

And don't think my mother's peripheral perch or her martyr's posture has dulled her television skills. She won't admit it, but she likes westerns. This comes after *Perry Mason*, of course. . .only the Pope comes before Perry.

On one show, where the water was mysteriously disappearing from a group stranded in the Mojave Desert, she piped up.

"It's in his leg."

After the out of control, incredulous laughter of her entire family had subsided, she said.

"You'll see."

And, damned if they didn't find the water in this guy's wooden leg.

"I can't believe it. . .," we all said.

She beamed with righteous satisfaction.

My father died a few years after the "miracle of the water leg" show. They say it was a stroke, but my brother and I have a theory that he was attempting to light a cigarette after a second martini and he exploded. The first thing my mother did was get rid of the Command Post Chair, and get one of her own. After that, the rest of us were forced to perch on the perimeter trying to see around her.

"Does this have anything to do with our laughing about the water leg?" we asked.

Three weeks later she came home with a new Renault.

It would be years before all these events transpired, so I sat there now, on the living room periphery, eating a Christmas bologna sandwich, trying to see around my father, and starting to think about my coming freshman year of college. Dave would be entering his senior year, and we would be at the university together. The last time this happened, the world lost a bandstand.

I sat there wondering how everyone at college managed to get themselves up in the morning without the Mom Alarm Clock. As you can see, I had few wonderings of any great importance.

"Dave, how do you get up for class at college. Do they have a wake-up service or something?"

"Where do you think I'm going to school. . .the Hilton?"

"So what do you do?"

"You get an alarm clock, dolt."

"Hmmm. . .an alarm clock dolt. Is this different from an ordinary alarm clock?"

"The alarm clock hasn't changed, you're the dolt."

"Is that good?"

"For you it is."

"Do women find it attractive?"

"No one is going to get you up at college, so you better start learning right now," interjected Mom. Actually, she said this about everything, just replace the "get you up at college" with anything you like. . ."make you eggs in the morning". . ."clean the lint out of your belly button". . .it was a multipurpose declaration.

So, I started learning for myself right then. I got the most annoying alarm clock made. At first, I thought about getting a clock radio, but found them to be a paradox. And who wants a paradox for a clock? They appear to be designed for everything but getting up. I think there's something fundamentally wrong with an alarm design that has buttons labeled "snooze" and "sleep." These buttons should have been labeled "crack of noon." The only buttons it seemed to be missing were "wake" and "up."

I finally picked a simple alarm clock, with a buzzer that sounded like a dentist drill excavating a granite tooth through a public address system. A sticker on the front said *World's Most Annoying Alarm Clock!*

Still, it wasn't enough. Through diligence, I was able to sleep through it by dreaming that I actually got up. I was forced to augment my clock with a feature of my own design. When the alarm went off, I immediately headed straight for the shower. This can have a few drawbacks unless you simultaneously open your eyes. I have ended up more than a few times in the utility room groping around for the shower fixtures, and once falling into the utility room sink/tub. If you couldn't find the shower, then this was a pretty close second. It certainly was better that finding yourself standing on the front stoop as a religious apparition for the milkman. If I managed to find the shower, and to set the spray to "African killer bees," it was a somewhat effective way of waking up.

It's really too elaborate of a method, and fraught with places to go wrong. I am accepting any advice and all offers for a good alarm system, although you will probably have to wake me up to get me to listen.

★   ★   ★

THE DKW DIED at about the same time I was trying to learn how to shower in the utility room tub/sink. My father had since bought the Renault, and was lamenting a lost opportunity.

"If we still had the DKW, you two could have taken it to college with you."

"You wouldn't have really made us take the DKW to college, right?"

"Why not, it was a good car."

"Heh. . .heh. . .ha. . .haa. . .whew. . .Dad. . .you're a card. I want you to tell Dave that when you see him, but wait until he's having something to drink. Then we can watch him snort through his nose."

I don't think I've seen a good snort from Dave since the Bicycle Hockey days.

I left for college on the bus, with my World's Most Annoying Alarm Clock tucked away in my suitcase. All in all, a step up from a DKW. This was college in the sixties, the time of fraternities. . .and sororities, a time to get down to the serious business of academic pursuit. And pursue I did, although the women turned out to be a helluva lot faster than I had imagined. . .had they been in training or something?

The Connecticut University campus was picturesque. It was located way out in the country, set in the hills, with lots of old ivy-covered buildings reminiscent more of a small college town. There were two lakes on the campus, and an old abandoned row of fraternity houses that the university had bought up during the forties. The street was left untouched, and I'm not sure to what use they put the houses other than waiting for *Life Magazine* to happen by and take pictures. It looked like a campus should look, serene and wise. . .stately. It felt comforting, like a Sunday afternoon, just walking through it—crossing the wide expansive lawns, half expecting to see gown-clad professors strolling along the walkways. It was a timeless kind of illusion that lasted until you came into the newer areas, with their sterile high-rise buildings and the sharp angled architecture of the modern factory-style campus.

The old library was very cool, built in the Jeffersonian style. The oldest section housed the "stacks," several smallish floors crammed with bookracks, connected by wrought-iron stairways. You could get lost in seemingly endless narrow passageways. Iron railings guarded the stairwell, and looking down from the highest floor, the passageways disappeared into darkness, dropping to the basement below. There were a handful of study cubicles tucked into corners for the use of those with enough courage to brave the back passageways of a place so at home in an Edgar Allen Poe story. Or in my case, someone pretending he was in a submarine.

"Captain Nemo, here. Where are the native women?"

There were never any native women.

★   ★   ★

IT WAS FRESHMAN week at the college, we were required to wear beanies and nametags. Yes, we really did have to wear beanies and nametags, a practice that was abandoned just a few years later when someone finally woke up and said *"What the hell am I doing?"* and ripped it off in front of a stunned upper-classman Freshman Week Marshal.

They handed me a beanie.

"Great. Now all I need is a DKW." Then the humiliation would have been complete.

My nametag was causing me all kinds of problems. Here was, at last, a chance to pick whatever name I wanted with just

a simple pen stroke. . .a chance to finally get the yoke of Georgy
Porgy off of me. The pen kept darting back and forth to the
paper, again and again, as I decided, then rejected, and then
re-decided on my new name.

The problem? Any name I chose became meaningless after repeating it over and over to myself, trying to get a sense of
its identity. At worst, it conjured up some pretty ugly images.

"John. . .John. . .John. . .Gotta hit the john."

"Joe. . .Joe. . .Joe's a schmoe. . .Hey Joe, you got gum?
Say it ain't so. . .Joe. . .G.I. Joe"

Sometimes it helps to say the female equivalent to understand why you don't like it. "Ed. . .Ed. . .Edwina."

"Fred. . .Fred. . .Fredwina."

"Charles. . .Charlie. . .Chuck. . .bo-buck banana-fanna fo-. . ."

"Richard. . .Rick. . .Rich. . .Richie. . .Dick. . .Dickey. . ."

And would you believe it? I wrote down George. In about
twenty minutes I had reduced the entire lexicon of English
names to sounding ridiculous, meaningless, moronic, obscene,
or like various breeds of dogs and cats. I was sticking with
George. At least I knew most of its offensive possibilities.

So the first line of my nametag had taken about a half-
hour to fill out, and now for the second line. . .hometown.
Good Lord, I knew college was going to be difficult, but how
can you get stuck signing in? Where is my hometown? Should I
write down where my parents are now? Where I remembered
best? Maybe our permanent "home address?" I do have it written down here somewhere, somewhere in my wallet, let's see,
yeah, here it is, a place where I've never actually lived, and
loaded with relatives who have disinherited me. Well, it seemed
like a logical choice, so I wrote down the Bristol Street address
that my dad had given us. For the next hour I ran into kids from
Bristol. . .who all wondered why they had never run into me.

I next tried where we were now living. . .Alexandria. I was
bombarded with questions about Virginia, and I had no answers for that either.

"Where are you from?"

"That's not an easy question."

"How'd you get here. . .to school in Connecticut?"

"By bus."

"No. . .why did you come to Connecticut if you're not from
any of the places you crossed out on your nametag?"

"That's kind of complicated."

"We're seventeen, how complicated can it be?"

I was fixated on my nametag, trying to come up with a
town in America that I could write down and actually answer a

question about, when someone said hello.

". . .what!?"

"I said hello. What are you doing?"

It was a native woman, and I didn't even have to chase her.

"I'm thinking of getting rid of this nametag." A few years ahead of the Beanie Rebellion of '66.

"Why?"

"You can't believe the trouble I'm having."

"You should be glad. . ."

"About what?"

"Everyone should be outrageous."

"Are we in the same conversation, or have you moved into another dimension?"

"Everyone should be outrageous about everything! . . ."

"So, you've decided to go with the 'other dimension' explanation." No wonder I didn't have to chase this one. "I haven't followed anything you've. . ."

"No one should."

"Should what? Follow?"

"Look at mine."

"Look at your what?"

"Nametag, silly."

"Diesel? Your name is Diesel and you call me silly?"

"It's my nickname."

"Why?"

"Because when I get mad, I'm like a runaway train."

"Tell me, do you know where they keep the normal girls?"

"What do you mean by that? I'm a normal girl. I believe in free love."

"Who ever told you that you were normal. . .and the hell with the normal girls anyway."

"Well, good-bye."

And she disappeared into the crowd.

"Wait. . .wait! . . ." She was gone.

I was left standing there, the tall kid with a nametag that had an unsure scrawl of the name George and whose hometown was crossed out several times, and finally read NONE. And I had already lost Diesel. . .if you know where she went, please call. One last thing, some people actually came up to me and seriously wanted to know where the town of None was located.

★ ★ ★

A COUPLE OF weeks into the semester, with the smell of summer still lingering in the air, strong biological forces were at work on this very late Indian summer day. These are irresistible forces that take some time to adjust to, and until you do, there is a real chance of turning into a Drooling Spazmozal whenever you see a Young Bronze Coed strolling along the campus walkways in her wafer-thin, semitransparent dress. The hormonal jolts can dissolve you into an unrecognizable heap of moans, while you clutch wildly at your loins.

Such a coed was just ahead of me—several clutched loin-moaners littered the sidewalk.

I sped up. No one wanted to miss the opportunity to be down, clutching wildly at his loins. Loin clutching has its own intrinsic rewards. I reached my classroom building without spotting her.

"Shit!"

I looked all around.

"Shit!"

I saw another body crash to the sidewalk near the end of the building just ahead. I ran around the corner, but no one was in sight. I was close, fresh moans were everywhere, but I was out of time and reluctantly went to class.

It was impossible to concentrate while suffering from a case of Sidewalk Moaning. The professor insisted on asking questions during the lecture. I considered this highly unfair and unethical, and it violated every known definition of a lecture. A young coed sitting in the first row shifted in her seat, her summer dress rising high against her thigh.

"Would anyone care to try and. . .oooooo. . ."

Down the professor went.

He struggled to a sitting position right in front of the young coed. She had begun to rise from her seat to try and help, but her dress had caught on the desk as she parted her legs to stand, her gleaming bronze thighs and white panties were directly in front of the professor.

". . .aaaaggggghhhhh. . ."

Down he went again.

"You've killed him!" we shouted. Chaos broke out. She tried to apologize and turned to face us with her blouse open down to her perfect summer breasts.

". . .uuuuoooooooo. . ."

Another one fell at my feet.

She whirled around. "I. . .didn't. . ."

Bang! Two more down.

"Stop it! You're worse than Lizzie Borden."

She started to walk towards the rear of the classroom. Her dress was still caught on the desk, and it pulled off right in front of me. . .

Boom! Flop! Crash!

There wasn't a man left standing.

". . .oooooooo. . .aaaaahhhhh. . ..aaaaagggggghhhhhh."

The groans and tumbling desks brought out an Emergency Moaning Medical Team. We were revived and order was restored. The instructor nervously wiped his forehead and weakly announced.

"Remember. Papers are due Friday."

"What. . .what paper? What Friday? This Friday? How long have I been out!?"

"No make-ups. No late papers accepted."

"When did this paper thing happen?"

Nobody answered me. There was no time to worry about it. There was barely enough time to get to the student union for a gathering of the Clans Of The Snack Bar.

So far, I had avoided relapsing into the Pool Girl At Fort Myer Effect, probably because there wasn't a pool around, but it was only a matter of time. Sooner or later I would do something that would etch itself forever on my mind. I would get to relive the hellish moment over and over, grimacing in eternal embarrassment at the thought of it. But you can't bend time to change the way things turned out, I've tried. . .

"Why are you scrunching up your face like that?"

"This is not how you bend time?"

"I don't think so. I believe you need some sort of machine with large rotating disks and Olympic torch levers for that."

It was a heavy load to carry and almost worth doing something stupid right away to get the whole thing over with.

There I stood in the doorway of the student union snack bar, which was the social hub of the campus during the weekday afternoons. I surveyed the packed house from the stairway entrance. There wasn't an empty seat in the place. It was full of all the right people, the campus kings and queens. The trick was to get them to notice you. They were so busy trying to impress each other that it was easy to go unseen. This wasn't going to be easy.

I stood momentarily on the top step of the small staircase that led into the snack bar. Not too long, mind you, pausing there too long and you risked losing that cavalier look that was so important. I peered around the room as if I were looking for someone, stalling as long as I dared, before I allowed my face to light up with recognition. Ah, yes, there are those mythical people now. I could almost hear the announcement of my entrance. . .

"Hear ye, Hear ye. His majesty. . .The Prince of Cool."

I grandly descended the stairs, confident that I had the right combination of *savoir-faire* and attention. I was ready to make my entry into the den of the campus elite. A little less attention to the kings and queens and a little more to the grand descent was required—for I went ass-over-tea-kettle as I missed the first step and transformed myself from *savoir-faire* into a tumbling human sphere of jumbled legs and arms frantically groping for the railing. My momentum carried me across the tile floor and I sailed by several stunned tables of people before disappearing completely under one of the tables. The noise and chaos of toppling chairs and scattering people rang in my ears as I vanished from view. A trail of spilled soda cups and paper plates strewn across the floor was all that remained of my entrance. It was fairly spectacular, I just wished someone else had done it. It appeared this was another one of those mom"

"Captain Nemo here, I am presently submerged."

SWINGEN BARREN

I HAD BARELY PLUGGED the World's Most Annoying Alarm Clock into the wall of the all-freshman male complex of dormitories known as the Jungle—and barely found out that a "grinder" doesn't sharpen knives in New England but is actually a submarine sandwich—when I made my first class selection blunder. . .Math 104.

"That's why they took all the upper classmen out of here, so we could make blunders like this, and actually pick classes that no one has taken in years," said my roommate Stu From New Haven.

"That's not the worst of it," I said. "I also have to take three years of a college language."

"Why? Didn't you take any language in high school?"

"I tried, but Rickey With The Dented Forehead got me thrown out."

"Who?"

"Rickey With The Dented Forehead. Apparently 'Das automobile ist rude' doesn't mean 'The car is red' in German."

"What does it mean?"

"I don't know. I was thrown out right after I said it. I never did find out what was wrong with it. . .I thought it sounded pretty good. I tried telling the college admittance board that I was fluent in Ubangi, but you know colleges, they expect the languages to be listed in some book they have."

"Ubangi?"

"Yeah, Ubangi. . .don't tell me you've never heard of it either?"

"Did Ramar of the Jungle speak that?"

"Could be. . .I don't remember much about Ramar, outside of them all running back and forth along the same jungle path every week. I always expected a few head-on collisions, but I'm sure those ended up on the cutting room floor. I do know that Ubangi is spoken in Bremerhaven, Germany. That may be the only place left using the language."

"I can see why you had trouble."

"Hey, if they can speak French in New Orleans, then they can speak Ubangi in Bremerhaven. It doesn't matter anyhow, those pre-admissions people said they never heard of it. . ."

"We can't seem to find Ubanghi listed on any of the known languages of world civilization."

"How did you spell it?"

"Ubanghi."

"That's high Ubanghi. I learned the common people's version, low Ubangi. . .U B A N G I."

"Hmmm. . .that doesn't appear either."

"Don't tell me I spent three years studying an unlisted language!?"

"I'm afraid so."

"Someone should really tell the kids still in Germany before this happens to them too. So what does this mean?"

"I'm afraid you are going to have to take three years of a college language, unless there is some other language that you failed to put down on your application."

"I know German."

"You took high school German."

"Well, it wasn't formal classroom credit. But I lived in the country for three years, and learned the language on the street."

"Would you like to take a proficiency bypass exam?"

"This doesn't involve surgery, does it?"

"No."

"Okay."

I was placed in a classroom, alone with the National Collegiate German Proficiency Exam.

"There must be a mistake, this test seems to be in hieroglyphics."

"Let me see that exam."

He took it from my hand and looked over the test.

"No, this isn't the Ancient Egyptian Languages Exam, it's the German exam."

"You actually have an Ancient Egyptian Languages Exam?"

"Yes, it was my major, would you like to take that as well?"

"One joke at a time, please."

After two hours of turning the paper at various angles, looking for words I recognized, I wrote. . .

"Herr Ober, ein bier. Herr Ober, sechzehn bier. Herr Ober, hundert bier, bitte. Ist Post fur mich da? Ich hatte gern die Speiskarte? Fraulein, rasch mit die hosen, and every German beer company name I knew."

And finally. . .
"Thibis tibest sibucks."
"I'm afraid you didn't do well on the proficiency exam."
"No? How shocking. . ."
"Well, outside of a few tourist phrases, and something we can't seem to translate. . .the test was virtually blank."
"Maybe I should try that Egyptian exam."
"I don't think there would be anything to gain in that. . .do you?"
"So, I'll be taking three years of college level German?"
"Probably longer."
"Let's hope they've cleared up the problem with those red cars."
So Ubangi and Ubanghi have proved to be totally useless outside of Bremerhaven. . .three years of work down the drain.

"Grinderman in the lobby! Grinderman in the lobby!" The public address shocked me out of my trance.

"Quick," said my roommate. "Before we get stuck with tuna fish,"—and he ran out of the room to join a human stampede headed for the lobby.

"Ham! Salami! Tuna grinders in the lobby!"

"I'm too depressed for a grinder."

I took Math 104 because everyone assured me it was harmless. . .and also because it was held at ten o'clock. I had hoped it was my salvation for fulfilling the freshman math requirement. I stink at math. I think it's fundamentally wrong to mix in letters of the alphabet with numbers. Nobody else seemed to agree—not even my roommate Stu From New Haven.

"That's how math is. . .," he said.

"Would you write a paper and mix in some numbers with the letters in a word?"

"That's different."

"How so?"

"Would there be any point to my explaining this?"

"None at all."

"Math 104 isn't really math."

"That's what they told me. That's why I took it."

It was called the Logic of Math. I soon found out that I also stink at logic. I was totally lost almost immediately, while the incomprehensible facts continued to pile up, burying me deeper and deeper. . .and deeper. Math 104 had started out like it was going to be almost understandable, but soon I felt like I was back in high school chemistry. At least with chemistry, one look at that first formula and I knew I was in trouble. I believe chemistry formulas are interchangeable with ancient Egyptian hieroglyphics.

My first exam score was a seventy. I didn't know a damn thing, but somehow I'd gotten through it. Maybe I knew more than I thought. My next exam score was a sixty-six. So it was true, I knew exactly what I thought. I figured I was losing 11.2 percent with each exam. At this rate my next score should've been around fifty-eight, and the final around an even fifty. The classroom discussions didn't even sound like English anymore. They sounded like Ubangi. . .

"Tibodibay wibe wibill ibe diboibing libogibic pibairs."

"Whibat?"

My third exam was an eleven. I asked the professor for a meeting.

"See me in my office. . .eight o'clock tomorrow."

"Eight o'clock!?"

"Eight o'clock!"

He left the auditorium. "One of the reasons I took this class was so I didn't have to go anywhere at eight o'clock," I said as he disappeared out the door.

I stopped by his office the next morning at eight o'clock, as requested. I wanted to get everything straightened out, and to get him to like me. It's essential that, when final grades are dolled out, the professor likes you. . .at least it is in my world.

"I have calculated, at my current rate of decline, that my third exam score would be a fifty-eight. . .," I began.

"I guess you stink at real math as well. . ."

"Thank you. I didn't think it was possible to get an eleven," I said.

"Neither did we, but you proved us all wrong on that one."

"I don't get any of this stuff. . .a trunk full of black and white socks. . .pairs of twins within twins. . .I'm kind of lost."

"It's probability sets. . .you have to use your noodle."

"No one told me to bring a noodle."

"Well, maybe you'll do better on the final."

"That's a joke, isn't it."

"Yes, it was. . .ha. . .ha. . .ha. . ."

"You know, I wasn't bad at math until you guys started mixing in the alphabet."

"Says you. . ."

For the final I filled in the exam paper with a mishmash of Math 104 key words and phrases that I thought might or might not have had anything to do with the questions, and handed in the exam paper.

The day the final grades were posted in the physical science building, I took the long route to get there, and waited until the hall was empty. I stood in front of the computer listing of the final grades posted on the wall. I waved my hand over the list with my eyes closed, trying to conjure up some Caribbean magic. I didn't know any Caribbean magic. I mimicked some bad B-movie hocus-pocus gestures in desperation, and massaged the paper with the palm of my hand. Finally, I opened my eyes and. . .

"What are you doing?"

. . .looked into the eyes of a janitor.

"I thought I was alone."

"Well, it will certainly stay that way if you keep doing things like this."

"Thanks for the advice."

"Just hurry it up, I've got a hallway to clean."

"Okay."

I gave one long exhale and then found my name. I ran my finger over to the grade column. . . 'D'.

"'D'! Hey, look, I got a 'D'!" I looked around for the janitor, but all the hallways were empty, he had disappeared into thin air in a flash. Then the heavens opened up, angels' voices rode the sunbeams down from above. I was blinded.

"You must talk to a priest right away. . ."

"Yes. Yes. I have to talk to a priest right away."

I sat in the confessional at the campus chapel, and told the priest everything that had happened.

"Son, I don't think God had anything to do with this. It's most likely a clerical error. You can try and have it corrected if you like. Personally, I think it would be much harder to get an eleven on a exam, than a 'D'."

"You would think so, wouldn't you? Well, I certainly don't want a grade I don't deserve, Father."

He smiled and laid a hand on my shoulder.

"Who are we kidding, of course you do. Keep the grade and say ten Our Fathers and ten Hail Mary's. Light a candle before you leave."

This was far more than I was used to receiving for an American Standard Catholic Confession, but this did seem like a genuine miracle so. . .

"I'll do it, Father! You can count on me."

"You're a 'good boy.'"

"Good-bye, and thank you, Father."

"Gibood-bibye."

I joyously returned to my dormitory and discovered I had forgotten my key to the room.

I knocked on the door. "Hey! Open up! I got a 'D'!"

I could hear someone scurrying around inside.

"Who is it?"

"It's me."

"We already have one of those in here."

"One of what?"

"Me."

"You?"

"No, not you, we have me. You isn't here right now, you could be you, if you play your cards right."

"I thought you were we. At least that's what you said."

"How could I be we, when I'm me?"

"You said we already have me. Therefore you must be we, and so we is already in there, and you can't be me. So there really is no me in there at all, that was just a lie to keep me out."

"I was sure I was me."

"No, I am me, as we have just proved."

The door opened.

"I thought you were me. . .now you are we? Are you saying you're already in here?"

If you followed any of this, then Math 104 is for you.

★   ★   ★

MY SECOND BLUNDER wasn't quite so obvious. I had overlooked that Connecticut was in New England, and that New England bordered Canada, and that Canada bordered the Arctic, and that after fall comes winter. Be careful of what college you pick, for you'll have to live there, so choose well, my friend, and don't come to Connecticut. UCONN doesn't rhyme with Yukon for nothing, and choosing a husky for a mascot wasn't just co-incidental.

As I walked along, popular local campus colloquialisms that needed no New England translations came to mind. . .

"Colder than a well-digger's ass." I'm not sure how cold that would actually be, since I'm not that familiar with well-diggers or their asses, but since I've heard it often, I assume a well-digger's ass is mighty cold. Still, there seems to be some sense to it, never having given it much thought, but you can imagine that a well-digger's ass is probably cold. Then we have "colder than a witch's tit." Obviously, I have a lot to learn about witches and their tits. "Colder than a son of a bitch?" This is not very descriptive because I know for a fact that it can be hotter than a son of a bitch.

"Colder than an Eskimo's dick." I'm going to leave that one alone. There are more, but they all seem to involve more anatomical parts of arctic dwellers. In Connecticut, most of us settled on my personal favorite. . ."I hate this fucking place."

★   ★   ★

CHRISTMAS BREAK.

Earle called to tell me he no longer wanted to be called Babycakes.

"Gee, what a surprise," I said.

"I'm more of an entrepreneur now, and I need something more respectable. . .professional."

"How about Mancakes? So, this is why you called?"

"No, but it's something I felt I had to say."

"Why are you calling?"

"I've managed to get myself invited to a hotel New Year's Eve party in D.C. . .and they said I can bring whomever I want."

"What kind of fools are these?"

"Professional fools. But you can't bring the DKW, or wear any of those Halloween masks."

"The DKW is gone."

"Really?"

"We bought a Renault."

"For just a moment. . .there was a glimmer of hope."

"Where did you meet these people?"

"Through the real estate company."

"What real estate company?"

"I'm working part time for a real estate development company."

"So. . .this entrepreneur crap is for real?"

"Yes, it's real crap."

"Well, I certainly wouldn't want to miss this."

We all went, my sister, my brother, and I. As long as I have known Earle, he has been hustling, an impatient bundle of energy. Cigarettes were made especially for people like him, and he must have gone through three or four packs a day. A perpetual cloud of cigarette smoke hovered around him. Earle also didn't need an alarm clock at all. He was already sitting on the bed fully dressed waiting for the time to roll around when he could begin annoying the normal people. He had a hard time coping with the nuisance of being a teenager while waiting to head his own company and build his financial empire. Earle was also frugal. . .cheap. He still had the first bag of potatoes he fleeced off the Russians.

Somehow he had wangled an invitation to this New Year's party being held by preemie-yuppies, which I guess would make them puppies. This was before yuppies had fully developed beyond their embryonic stage. We could tell because they were still driving Buicks. We were sorely out of place, except for Earle, who was sucking up pretty good. The three of us were quickly identified and segregated into the Alarm Clock Group.

We held a quick backroom family huddle.

"This sucks."

"What should we do?"

"We could leave, but what would be the fun of that," said Dave. "I wish I had some Tide Wafers for that punch."

"Earle seems to be enjoying himself," I said.

"And the surprise would be?"

"Well, I guess we're going to have to come up with a surprise."

"Something the three of us can do," said Marcella.

We emerged from the room as The Flying Von Hamies, the famous Austrian high wire act. We practiced our accents for a few minutes before rejoining the party.

"Yes, we were with the Hamborg circus, you know, and we've just begun a tour of your country, and we know very little English."

We all sounded like Austrian body builders—even my sister.

"Ya. . .ze Hammborg curcus."

Boy, things turned around fast. We were surrounded, and the more we gestured and struggled with English, the bigger our admiring crowd became. It was a real struggle not to sound like a bad imitation of a Swedish chef.

"Ya, ya. Ze high wire ist dannger. Ist not zat so, Helmut?" asked my brother. Dave had reinstated a unilateral Older Brother Decree and named me Helmut.

"Ya, Booobie," I replied. He glared at me briefly.

"Wee practice each day vary, vary hard. To. . .ooh vhat ist English vord. . .to. . .to. . .perfective!" he continued.

"Perfection," corrected the crowd.

"Ya, ya. Perfection. Tank you. My English ist not so goot."

Earle was stunned.

He made a quick recovery and instantly became an Austrian high wire act impresario, a close relative of an entrepreneur, and also our manager. Dave was off and running. . .who needed Tide Wafers?

"Please, more ze horses' ovaries."

His diction improved dramatically for horses' ovaries.

For years, he has delighted in calling hors d'oeuvres, horses ovaries. It never failed to amuse him, and he never failed to use it whenever the opportunity came along. It was a Von Hamie family tradition. . .like a cauliflower fart.

"You speak very well," said the crowd.

"Ya, tank you. But ve must leave now to more hard work on ze GerZumpen."

"GerZumpen?" replied the crowd.

"Ya. . .ze GerZumpen," I said.

"Ya, ya," said my sister.

A round of ya's for everyone.

"What is the GerZumpen?" asked the crowd.

"Ya. . .tell zem was ist GerZumpen," I said.

"Ze GerZumpen ist zie masterpiece of zie act, unt most dannger," continued my brother.

It was dangerous because he hadn't the slightest idea of what to say next, and he was starting to sound more like Sergeant Schultz (*"I know nozzing."*) than an Austrian high wire act. The crowd became attentively quiet.

"Ve all zump from ze platform unt ze same time, unt land in ze net, ya? Unt bouncen vay high, unt graben ze swingen baren, ya?"

"Zump for ze swingen baren?" I said.

"Ya, swingen baren, dummkopf."

"All together!?" gasped the crowd.

"Ya, ve zump togesor," said my sister.

"Ya, ya, zumpen togesor," repeated Dave.

Another round of ya's for everyone.

"Zumpen?" I said.

"All three of you at the same time!? . . . ." said the crowd.

"Ya, but careful, or zie GerZumpen ist zie GerCrashen!" He finished with a flourish.

"Swingen baren?" I said.

We left right after Earle signed us up to do three shows on Sunday. . .and then stiffed us for the cash advance.

I stole the punch ladle.

"Herr Ober, more horses' ovaries fur alles!"

MOON OVER MIAMI

ONE OF THE RESULTS of creating an all-male freshman "jungle" dormitory complex was that the fraternities had the biggest spring rush in their history. During pledge week, the entire jungle lived over at the fraternities, and after the bids went out, the fraternities doubled in size overnight. That was why I was now looking at an egg in my hand. . . imagining all sorts of perverted uses one might put it to, given the time to think about it.

"What do you think they're going to want us to do with this egg?" I asked Stu From New Haven, who had pledged along with me.

He looked at the egg in my hand, then at the one in his.

"I don't know, but it can't be good."

"Why do you think we each have one?"

"I'd think it would be far worse if you were the only one with an egg."

"Good point." I returned to examining mine. "If this involves the use of any kind of lubricating creams, then I'm going to have to quit the fraternity. I only joined to meet women anyway."

"I don't think you can."

"You're probably right. . .I haven't met any women yet."

"I mean, quit the fraternity."

"Why not?"

"I don't know why, I just know you can't."

I looked at Stu From New Haven. "It's exactly this kind of thinking that's caused us to end up holding an egg in our hand in the first place. . .instead of a women. Of course you can quit."

"Maybe you should look around. We're locked in the basement. We have a mattress, some clothes, and a raw egg. If we ever get out of here, I don't think it would be a good idea to ask to quit. . .you might just end up needing that lubricating cream."

"Hmmm. . ." I thought he may be right about this. "What do you think they're going to want us to do with all this stuff?" I held up several sheets of paper stapled together.

"Memorize it."

"Memorize it!?"

"Weren't you listening when they dragged us down here?"

"I can't understand anything. . .or even hear anything other than the tired blood rushing through my head. . .at three in the morning. I just thought it was more Mystical Greek Drivel, which I tried to sleep through."

"Well, it is more Mystical Greek Drivel. . .but you can't sleep through it, you have to memorize it by morning. We all have to know it perfectly, as well as all these instructions."

"What instructions?" I leafed through the papers. "Well, I'll be damned. . .instructions." They were actually Fraternal Directives, which have a lot in common with Older Brother Pounding Decrees. We had to memorize the first two pages, and recite it perfectly whenever we returned to the house from class. There was also something about a Changing of the Log that made very little sense, but there was nothing about the eggs.

"You know anything about this log they're talking about?"

"No."

"Have you read any of this stuff we have to memorize? Listen to this. . . 'Oh mighty rulers of all the lands and masters of the desert sands, allow this pig of humility to. . . pig of humility?' What is this. . .Ali Baba and the Forty Thieves?"

"I wouldn't let them hear you say that."

"Let who hear. . .we're the only ones down here, but it is a bit much, don't you think?"

"It doesn't matter what we think. . ."

The basement door burst open.

"Welcome to Hell Week, gentlemen!"

"Well, this certainly doesn't sound good. . .Stu? Stu?"

The Pledge Master was greeted by everyone standing up and shouting at once.

"What's with this egg!?"

"Why are we down here!?"

"I can't memorize this by morning! I can't even memorize my classwork. . .and it makes sense!" This guy obviously wasn't in Math 104.

"Yeah! He's right!" And neither was he.

"Everyone shut up!" And the Pledge Master pulled out a rather large wooden paddle.

"Would you like that egg scrambled?"

"Why yes, I can memorize this. . ."

"I could live down here. . .some curtains, a new rug. . ."

"I said. . .shut up!"

Silence.

"All right. Sit down."

We all sat down on our mattresses. "No mysteries, gentlemen. The eggs will go into your front right pants pocket. No hard-boiling them, no putting them into a plastic bag. We will check, and if we find anything like that, then all the brothers get to break one over your head. That's forty-two brothers and forty-two eggs over the head. So, go ahead and do it. We have lots of eggs, and we need the diversion. Once you leave the house for a class, the only way back in will be a perfect recitation of the Pledges' Oath. Going to class is the only reason not to be down here with the rest of your pledge class. If you muck up the oath, you will back up ten paces and start over, and if you screw it up again, another ten paces until you get it right or you reach the state border, whichever comes first. I've got all your class schedules, so, if you think you're getting out of here to go hang out at the sororities, forget it."

"Why do we have an egg in our pocket at all?" I asked.

There was a gasp from the pledge class inmates. The Pledge Master held up his hand for quiet. "It's all right, it's a reasonable question. Tradition, that's the reason for the egg."

"This fraternity has a tradition of carrying an egg in their pants pocket?" It was an innocent reaction to his answer. Another gasp went up from the inmates.

"You have something against tradition?"

"No, not at all. In fact, I used to be part of a tradition that carried a coconut around, not in my pants mind you. . ."

"Shut up."

Before long I had to go to class, and learn a new way of walking. . .the "careful with that egg, Eugene" saunter that resembled the gait of the boys trying out for the chorus line. Several of us returned to the house together, swishing in unison across the quadrangle.

"We look ridiculous."

"Tradition, gentlemen. . ."

We joined the long line of pledges jammed up at the front door, stumbling through the Pledges' Oath. The brothers hung out of the windows and stood around the front door, yelling and screaming what they would later claim was encouragement. They menacingly tossed a raw egg in their hand like they were flipping a coin. It took steady nerves to recite a perfect version that met their ever-changing standards.

"Oh, shit. Look at the line to get in!"

"Look at all the eggs!"

They whittled their way through the pledges, and then it was my turn to step up to the firing line.

"Begin!"

"Oh mighty rulers. . ."

"What. . .what was that? Pretty weak, back up! Start again!"

"Oh. . ."

"Oh? . . ."

"Back up!"

"Oh mighty. . ."

"Christ, did you hear that mighty? Back up!"

"Oh mighty rulers of the desert. . ."

"Stop! Rulers of what? Get it right!"

A hailstorm of raw eggs pelted me.

"Back up!"

"Oh mighty rulers of all the lands. . ."

"Better, but I just don't like it! Back up!"

"Ohmightrulersafallthelandsandmaster. . ."

"Stop! What are doing? Do you think you'll get something by me!"

Another egg hailstorm.

"Back up!"

"Oh–mighty--rulers–of–the–"

"Not funny! Back up!"

"Oh might rulers of all the lands and masters of the desert sands,"—I'm going good now—"allow this pig of humility. . ."

"I didn't hear that pig quite loud enough! Back up!"

"Oh. . ."

"Oh? . . ." I'm back where I started. "Back up!"

I was alone. Everyone else had managed to get inside. It was now lunch and I had been out there for about an hour. I was backed up past several adjoining fraternity houses. I had to scream to be heard, and the brothers were watching me through binoculars. My only hope was they would get tired or bored, and let me off the hook. I was standing in front of another fraternity, and still yelling away. Whoops. . .back ten more paces. I couldn't even make out who was standing by the doorway anymore. Well, they couldn't hit me with an egg while I was this far away.

The front door opened and several of the brothers carried out an object and placed it on the ground. People began screaming and running for cover.

"What is it!?" I yelled. "Why is everyone running away!?"

"Egg canon!" they screamed.

"Egg canon!?"

Boom.

Splat.

Then I was alone on the quadrangle. I was now standing in front of the last fraternity house on the row. The windows were filled with faces all looking out at me. It would have been more flattering if I wasn't covered in egg. At least I could see these guys, so I faced them to recite.

"Not funny! Back up!"

"Well, these guys thought so!" I shouted back.

"Which house are you pledging!?"

"At this distance, it could be almost anybody."

"What was that!?"

"Phi Sigma!"

"Right! Back up!"

There was no hope of making it in for lunch.

"Hey! How about a box lunch!"

The response was an egg howitzer'd across my beam.

"How about hard-boiling one of those eggs!"

"Back up!"

Then the front door of this last fraternity house opened, and the All-Collegiate Catering Team emerged. A caravan of people carrying a table, chair, tablecloth, dishes, candelabra. . .the whole works emerged.

"Well, thank you, how kind."

"We've seen this all before. . .and we can make a pretty good guess about your chances."

"I guess they'd be pretty slim for getting lunch today."

"You're way past slim. . .you'd make a good couple with Twiggy. . .and she'd be the fat one. We're now taking bets on dinner."

I sat and ate, a solitary diner in the middle of the fraternity quadrangle. I finished the lunch and looked over to their front door.

"Coffee?"

A moment later a cup of hot coffee was served.

"Thank you."

"Will you be requiring a bed for the evening?"

"Depends. Are you bringing it out to me, or does that come with a room?"

"No promises. I must leave you now. . .your house has the best egg canon on the quadrangle."

"Say, you wouldn't happen to need an extra pledge? . . ."

"Oh no, you're not getting off that easy."

Loyalty was not one of my strong suits.

As soon as I finished my coffee, the doors opened once again, and it was all whisked away as quickly as it was set up. I stood back up to face the egg canon.

"I hope you've enjoyed your meal!" the Phi Sigma brothers yelled. "When, and if, you ever get in here, the brothers have a present for you! Did you ever see Captain Blood?"

"Christ, they want to kill me. . .and Twiggy."

All this just to get laid.

★   ★   ★

THEY DIDN'T KILL me, but, that summer, Columbia Van Lines almost did.

I was so good at making tactical blunders that I continued it right on into the summer. I took a job with a moving company. . .Columbia Van Lines. This may come as a surprise, but van lines do not attract the creme de la creme of the general working populace. Generally speaking, the creme had curdled with these guys. Their idea of an early breakfast was a bottle of beer to cure the DTs from the night before.

I reported for work and completed the morning training class.

"Okay, pick up this box and put it over there. . .okay. . .good. As you can see he has the THIS ARROW UP pointing up. . .this is acceptable. . .normally we like to see a good amount this way, however we're not fanatical, so arrows pointing down are also acceptable."

We progressed to the advanced afternoon session.

"Okay, pick up both of these boxes and put them over there, good. As you can see he has the box marked FRAGILE on the bottom. Excellent."

Some of us were assigned to the warehouse, and these lucky few left to learn how to puncture storage crates with forklifts, while the rest of us were turned over to the trucks.

"Okay, men, now you're going to put to use what you've learned. Dismissed."

We left for our assigned trucks and a life of carrying furniture into and out of houses, packing boxes, struggling with a washer or dryer, and God forbid you heard. . .

"Bring the piano board."

Football practices could use this one. A board with straps and handles was attached to the piano, and six men hoisted it up, and off you went, directly into the nearest wall. We looked like the losers of the bat race at a baseball game, the one where you spin around a bat standing on its end with your forehead placed on the knob until smoke starts to rise from your head, then try to run across the field.

There were no scheduled work hours other than the starting time. You worked until the truck was empty or loaded. The big jobs had a driver, a foreman, and a couple of us galley slaves.

I fell into a mindless rhythm, "Dayo. . .dayaaaaaoooooo. . .daylight come, and me want to go home. . ."

"Allingham. . ."

"Yes, Barge Commander."

"Quit singing. . .you're on a local."

The death sentence. A loadup and unload in a single day.

"You're with Jacobs."

"Yes, Barge Commander."

Jacobs. . .the king of the beer breakfast.

Off we went, directly to a twenty-four-hour package store. Then off to the customer's home. It was located on the second floor of an apartment building.

"Oh, God. . ."

"Let's go, boy. . .time to hump."

"Just exactly how do you mean that?"

Well, it was better than carrying everything up two flights. The morning went okay. By lunch the truck was full and the apartment barren.

"We'll meet you at the new address, right after lunch," said Jacobs to the customer, and we drove off.

He passed several lunch spots until he found what he was looking for, one that incorporated a package store. I was skeptical. I doubted people stopped here for the food. I bought my lunch, he bought his. . .two pints and a six-pack. The first pint lasted about as long as my burger. Jacobs wasn't in any hurry to leave and sat there sipping on the second pint from its paper bag until it was late in the afternoon.

"Shouldn't we get going pretty soon?"

"Whaaa? . . ."

"Shouldn't we get going?"

"Sure kid. . ."

We were off again. Jacobs popped open a beer and sipped as he drove. The truck was weaving in the lane, and twice we hit the median. He didn't seem to notice. If you have to hit a median, I recommend using a moving van, unless they offer you a tank.

We stopped in front of the new address. Somehow we had made it in one piece and with the trailer still attached. The homeowner was standing there with an angry look on his face. When he saw what kind of shape Jacobs was in, the look turned into one of despair. I could only apologize to him.

"I don't know what to say, sir, but I'll get it unloaded."

"I. . .," and his voice just trailed off.

"Come on," I said to Jacobs. "You have to get closer to the curb." The truck was stopped practically in the middle of the street.

"All right, college boy, let's see if you can do any better. . ."

Never tell the working world that you're home for the summer from college. It just tends to annoy them. It is far better to tell them your parole officer got you the job.

So, I jumped up in the cab and started it up. The DKW was good for one thing, this gearbox was easy compared to "mystery gear." I managed to park closer to the curb, began to unload the truck while Jacobs finished his last pint, and then opened a beer.

The homeowner couldn't believe his eyes, and started helping me unload.

"Don't worry about unpacking anything, just get it off the truck," he said as we began to run everything off the trailer like a couple of movers on an overdose of amphetamines.

A truck never got unloaded so fast. Any hope of getting back to the warehouse evaporated when I came out front and found Jacobs passed out on the front lawn.

The homeowner was relieved.

"Thank God."

There he lay, right under the Columbia Van Lines slogan painted on the side of the truck. . ."We treat your home like our home."

The homeowner and I both looked at each other, and broke out laughing.

"I guess his home is the drunk tank," I said.

"This is so pathetic it's funny."

"And he's one of the better ones."

"Ha. . .ha. . .you mean I got lucky?"

"Ha. . .ha. . .looks like you've got a guest."

The homeowner stopped laughing at that.

I locked the truck, called the van lines and told them they could pick up Jacobs off the front lawn whenever they liked, called my brother for a ride, and left the homeowner sitting on his front porch. He was watching over the body. . .with a baseball bat in easy reach.

Don't take any summer jobs with van lines. . .unless they really do treat your home like their home. . .but check their home first.

★   ★   ★

I SURVIVED THE summer and returned to campus. The frat was immediately plunged into the Fall Campus Carnival to raise money for charity. This escalates quickly into a competition between all the frat houses, all the independent houses, all the dormitories, and all the various other student groups. There were a lot of different contests involved, including radio marathons, dorm-versus-dorm donation challenges, a circus midway in the field house, float building for a campus parade, cash pledges for lots of bizarre group behavior, and campus-wide activities that impact practically everything for a two-week stretch.

Everyone gets involved, but involvement is relative since my fraternity, having been on the low end of ambitious, decided to just ride on the coattails of anybody who'd let us get anyway with it (our specialty). It wasn't like we weren't trying, we were just waiting for something to come along that sounded like we could actually do it.

"You'd think with all the things going on, there would be something we could do."

"Forget it, Stu. I can't recall seeing anyone in here doing anything that would be worth money. . .or involves any effort. It is one of the reasons I chose this frat in the first place."

Stu From New Haven was a little guy, barely over five feet, and barely over a hundred pounds, we were the Mutt and Jeff of the house. I was comfortable with it from my years of experience being Laurel and Hardy with my brother.

During the first week, no carnival activity materialized that we thought suited us. We waited. . .and waited. There was an emergency frat house meeting.

"We've got to do something before the carnival ends."

"I've got an idea. . ."

"Careful, this is where we usually get in trouble."

". . .what about bizarre behavior? I'm sure we can do that."

"You'd think so."

"So what's your idea?"

"That's it. . .to do something with bizarre behavior."

"Actually, that's not an idea. . .that's a category. Coming up with the actual bizarre behavior would be an idea."

"That's as far as I got, let someone else do some work."

With time running out, we capitulated and used the traditional approach.

"We'll build a float."

"Jeezus. . .we really have fallen on hard times guys. . .a float?"

"It's a little late to start one of those."

"It doesn't have to be a good float."

There was instant laughter that someone thought we would be building a good float.

"We couldn't build a good float even if we started it last year."

"So, then we're agreed, we'll build a lousy float."

Everyone was agreed.

We were able to entice a girls dorm to help build the lousy float. We had enough girls to qualify as a gaggle, and enough guys for a bunch.

The float was slow to take shape. We didn't have any plan, as that would have violated fraternity rules on ambition, so we just waited for inspiration to emerge from the wire mesh and papier-mâché as we went along. We liked to think this was the more creative approach. Like the Trans Continental Railroad, we started in two groups from opposite ends, progressing slowly towards each other with our only design direction being to make a lot of paper flowers as we went along.

"Floats have lots of flowers, that's what's important."

"Should it resemble anything when we're done?"

"I don't think that matters."

We expected to meet in the middle with something we could all be proud of and even recognize. The gaggle was very skeptical of this approach to float design, creative or not.

"Nobody builds a float this way."

"Well, then we're the first."

"I always wanted to be first at something."

"But it can't work, you have to have some kind of idea."

"We're not really good with ideas. Anybody who knows us can tell you that. We've had ideas before, and I can't say it's ever done us much good. So trust us, have a pioneer spirit, and some of these rum spirits as well."

Things weren't going well and we grudgingly began to accept the fact that the gaggle may have been right. As a last-ditch effort to salvage the float, we assigned a committee to try and decide if anything recognizable was emerging. We were willing to do anything except have a plan. The committee was given carte blanche, and several other kinds of blanche as well. It could comment whenever it felt it was appropriate, and anyone could answer if they felt something should be said, and this was directed at no one in particular.

"So what do we have?"

"A giant mound of paper flowers."

"That's good. . .isn't it?"

"What's the parade theme again?"

"Camelot."

"Maybe we should just declare this a glen. . .that's close enough for Camelot."

"I'm afraid I'm going to have to agree with the gaggle on this one, guys. This is pretty bad. . .even for a lousy float."

"Well, you were the one who said to have some rum spirits and see what comes out."

"That may have been a mistake."

"At this point, do we care?"

"So we lose the float competition, so what. . ."

"She has a point. . .so what?"

"Maybe someone will pledge money not to have our float in the parade."

"And how would anyone know to do that?"

"Put it on display. . . Pledge money NOT to see this float in the parade."

"That's not a bad idea."

"Just shows you how far we've fallen, if that's considered a good idea."

"Not a good idea. . .just not a bad idea."

"Let's make it so we can ride in it."

"And now insanity completely takes over."

"We can change it. We'll make it something we can ride in."

"A big flower volcano."

"The amazing Camelot flower volcano? And what does it do, spit us out like human cannon balls?"

"No, we can have someone inside throwing flowers out the top."

"I hate to admit this, but that doesn't sound too bad to me."

"That doesn't sound too bad to you!? . . ."

"Is this another not-a-bad-idea category, or have we started a new category. . . doesn't sound too bad?"

"I think we're all missing the point of this parade. There's supposed to be some connection between the theme and the float."

"At this point, the fact that there is a theme is really immaterial."

"Well, what can we make it?"

"I think we're going to have to adjourn for a float design session."

"See, if we had done this at the start, we wouldn't be in this mess," said the gloating gaggle.

So, the design session was organized. And what better place for a design group to meet than Diana's?

Diana's was a state park conveniently located just south of the university, or southeast, or southwest, actually I have no idea which direction. . .I wasn't driving. It was named after Greek mythology's Diana's Pool, and indeed, it did widen into a pool fed by a mountain spring. Here, lounging about the surrounding rocky cliffs and crevices, we gathered to design the Great Carnival Float. During the first week of the fall semester it was warm enough to dive into the pool for a brief chilling swim, but this is Connecticut, and now the water was suitable only for well-diggers, witch's tits, or as a refrigerant.

Here we formed into design committees and passed out responsibilities.

"Your group is to ensure there are enough cups to go around at all times."

"And we'll make sure the cups are kept full," volunteered a second group.

"An equally important function," we noted.

"Our group has decided to do nothing."

"Well, an honest group. I'm not sure how to respond to honesty, I have so little experience with it. I don't know what to say. . .makes the rest of us sound ambitious."

"And we have rules against ambition."

"All right, then, our group is amending its purpose. . .as soon as we find a purpose."

"I don't know if it's possible to amend doing nothing. You can add to nothing, subtracting is another matter. Then you're getting into negative numbers, and I never understood how you could have less than nothing. Math is not my strong suit, ever since they started sticking letters of the alphabet in it."

"Still smarting over Math 104?" said Stu From New Haven.

"Smarts has nothing to do with it."

"I've been sitting here, and I think I have an idea about the float."

"Good Lord, and I was having so much fun. Who brought this person?"

"Is it a good idea? Because I'm only interested in good ideas. I don't want to have to think about anything but good ideas."

"I didn't know you went in for thinking."

"Occasionally, but I don't recommend it. I've never had good results. I usually end up here."

"I have a good idea," said another.

"Two ideas in one afternoon? I believe we've set a precedent."

"What's your idea?"

"Let's put the beer in the water to keep it cold."

"Our first good idea! A toast!"

There was general agreement among all the groups that this was a good idea.

"We're on our way."

"Now, since we're doing so well, what about the float?"

"Someone said they had an idea."

"I did."

"Well, I'm ready to take a chance. Let's hear it."

"A castle. It's easy, fits the theme, it's just a big cube that we can also ride in."

Musing remarks came from all the groups.

"To get us all inside, it would have to be pretty big."

"I don't want to get involved with lumber. . .or building codes."

"Let's keep it small, a small castle with two or three inside, and the rest of us can just dress up and ride around on the outside."

"I like the idea of a cube, we can get a milk carton as a working model to follow."

The afternoon drifted by.

"I have a bad thought." This is technically not on the same level as an idea, and usually employed to avoid the formality of real ideas.

"What is it?"

"Trying to get out of Diana's in the dark after drinking all day."

There was drunken understanding among all the groups as dusk settled firmly over the park. The Bataan Death March was easier. I don't have many of the details since this was all done in the dark. I could only hear what was going on, but you can rest assured the Three Stooges were there, the Keystone Cops joined us, and most of Gilligan's Island came along. We finally ended with a Chinese fire drill.

"Thurston. . .where are you?"

The mile trek back to the entrance lasted for several hours, and required the assistance of most of the state's emergency rescue teams and several Saint Bernard dogs.

We made it to the cars, and Derelict, one of the bunch, added to the proceedings by barfing into the lap of the girl sitting next to him. I was wondering what I could do to help things along when High Pockets, another of the bunch, dumped his beer in my lap. It was becoming obvious that the bunch, and not the gaggle, was the group mostly responsible for this chaos.

"If we work at this, maybe we can all have something in our laps."

★ ★ ★

PARADE DAY.

The parade marshals wouldn't let us all ride on the float.

"You are above maximum float capacity," they said. "You'll have to get your group down to six."

"How do you determine maximum float capacity?" we asked.

"From years of experience with crappy float designs." And they left us, going on to berate the next float.

"Oh yeah, well this ain't no crappy float, it's a lousy float . . .a lot you know!"

"So, we have designed a float from the House of Crap."

"What!? . . . You're agreeing with him?"

"Actually, I'm happy about it. At least we're in a category. If you recall, it was just a day ago that we had a possible flower volcano."

"Yeah. . .now we'll be judged against other crappy floats. We might win something."

We tried appealing the marshal's capacity ruling, and after some intense negotiations, we were allowed two inside the castle, and six riding on the outside.

"How come the two inside are both guys?" asked the gaggle.

"It'll be funnier if the damsel in distress is one of us dressed as a woman."

"Why? We can be funny too."

"Please. . .as funny as Derelict? Why, he makes a terrible-looking guy, just imagine what kind of girl he'd make."

"This is the guy who barfed in my lap!"

"He has the best qualifications," we said.

"Like what?"

"Well. . .barfing in your lap for one, and he holds the record for Fastest Post-finals Drunk By A Future Ex-student Not Influenced By A Wager." He had this category to himself, since everyone else found it too long to even say. He was found passed out in the john, with an empty six-pack of Colt 45 malt liquor at his side, and his legs protruding from under the stall door. . .twenty minutes flat, start to finish. Why he went to the john is anyone's guess, only he knows and he wasn't talking. He was barely breathing.

This confused the gaggle long enough to get Derelict inside the castle.

"We have to get something out of this deal or we'll cause a scene."

"Why would you expect anyone to recognize you are causing a scene in this crowd? I still say that if you want to win the Crappy Float Division, then we should have Derelict inside."

"Give us the six spots on the outside and we'll agree."

"Hey, it's cold in here," said Derelict.

"Here, have some brandy."

"Leave the bottle."

The deal was settled. The gaggle wasn't happy about it, and sat by themselves sulking. We, of the bunch, were left without women. . .and left to talk among ourselves.

"And to think I carried some of them out of Diana's on my back."

"Actually, I believe they carried you out."

"Well, I would have been willing to carry some of them. . .not that one though. . .some of the lighter ones."

"What should we do now, run alongside the float and try to keep up?"

"You know, I can now see why you were the one who came up with the flower volcano idea. It'd serve you right if you did run alongside the crappy float. . .around the whole campus."

"Wait a second, let's think about that for just a minute. . .the crappy float surrounded by a bunch of crappy guys running alongside. Let's try and visualize that. You know, it just may give us an edge with the judges."

"And just how is that enhancing our crappy float?"

"I don't want to run anywhere or visualize anything, getting out of Diana's was exhausting enough. Let's just find a good spot and watch the parade."

We settled on the grassy slope in front of the fraternity quadrangle. The parade was a major event, and the slope was crowded with students and families from the town out to enjoy the day. A clown was handing out balloons and hard-boiled Easter eggs to the kids. They were running around and losing their balloons at a furious pace. There was a brightly colored balloon armada floating towards the center of the campus.

"It's a little nippy out here."

"Speaking of nips, I gave Derelict my brandy. Did anybody bring some?"

"I gave him mine too."

"All right, how many gave Derelict their brandy?"

All the hands went up.

The parade was coming down the boulevard, passing the life science building and slowing as they approached our crowded corner. The lead floats were magnificent, multicolored and intricate in their design. Many carried the letters of a fraternity or the name of an independent house. They passed in slow review. The kids ran in circles around them, ignoring every parade marshal's attempt to get them off the street. The families applauded each float as it passed. Various groups of students cheered for the floats they had helped create.

"Ah, here comes the Crappy Float Division."

Following the Magnificent Float Division trailed the Crappy Float Division. The parade turned at the traffic light and the lead floats were almost at the student union by the time our float came into view.

"There it is!"

"You know, now that I see it from this vantage point, it looks more like the turret of the *Monitor* than a castle, or is it the *Merrimac*? I get the two confused."

"Leave it to a history major to confuse history."

"I think it looks like a wedding cake."

There was a jam-up somewhere ahead and the parade came to a halt. Our float was stopped directly in front of us. Inside the castle, Derelict stuck his head out the window, acting the damsel in distress. His wig fell off, landing on the street in front of the children. They screamed in delight, then Derelict screamed in delight, and began a chase scene inside the castle with our Camelot knight. The children began running around imitating them. Derelict stuck his head out the window again, his inebriated eyes gazing out at the crowd on the grassy slope. Then he pulled down the top of his dress, flashing a brassiere. A gasp went up from the families. Derelict interpreted this as approval. The two of them resumed the chase.

Derelict threw off more clothes. The two of them were into the roles now, and the castle was rocking back and forth as they stumbled around inside. The crowd became restless. Derelict's dress came flying out the window, followed by the knight's costume. The crowd howled in disbelief. The children stood in dumbstruck entrancement. People from the other side of the street came streaming across to see what was causing all the excitement.

For a moment, the two of them disappeared. An edgy anticipation grew in the crowd.

"I hope they've passed out."

It would have been nice, but instead, the castle window now framed two perfect sets of butt cheeks, mooning the crowd.

"I think Derelict has his own carnival theme going on here."

"I wonder what it is?"

The children screamed and parents went running to gather up their kids. Grandparents shielded their eyes in disbelief. The college students roared their approval. The parade marshals ran around like they were trying to get out of Diana's after drinking all day. The clown took aim, and hit a perfect bull's-eye on Derelict's left butt cheek with a hard-boiled egg. A campus police cruiser pulled up to investigate, and got a face full of full moons. The girls on our float jumped for it, and disappeared in the confusion. The float behind rolled forward and rammed ours, causing the castle to topple. Derelict and our knight rolled out into full daylight. In their current costume it was readily apparent that neither was a real damsel. Empty rum bottles rolled down the street. A second cruiser blocked off the front of our float, but not before running over a bottle and blowing out a tire. Derelict took off for the life science building, an appropriate choice for a naked man I thought. Our knight gathered up some streamers and wrapped them around himself. Then he jumped off the back, collided with the clown, and they both fell to the ground. Hard-boiled eggs went everywhere. The campus cops jumped on both of them. Kids picked up the eggs and pelted each other and then pelted the campus cops, who tried to arrest them. Their parents jumped into the fray, trying to save their children. The rest of the floats behind were abandoned as the numbers running around in the street swelled. The students and families on the hill began throwing their pack lunches at the campus cops, then at each other. Food filled the air. Then the Magnificent Float Division attacked the Crappy Float Division, yelling "Mongrels!". . . "Peasants!". . . "Debasers!"

"I like a parade that keeps to the theme even when insulting you, don't you?"

More police cruisers arrived. Derelict had found some balloons and was last seen being pursued across a parking lot while holding balloons at the fore and aft. We just sat where we were, and watched the parade come unraveled.

"You know, for my money, you just can't beat the Crappy Float Division for excitement."

"I wonder if this will affect donations?"

"I'm wondering how long we're going to be on probation."

"See, this is what ambition gets you."

"Actually, this is what Derelict gets you."

The headline in the campus newspaper on the following day read. . .Moon over MyAuntBee.

"Hey. . .I think we had that carnival theme all wrong. According to this headline, Derelict may have been right after all. It must have been some Floridian. . .tropical kind of thing."

The accompanying picture was fuzzy and I didn't think it captured the true spirit. However, there were far better ones exhibited at the inquest. All this and we didn't even win the Crappy Float Division. No one got laid. Derelict carried a bright red egg scar on his left butt cheek for the rest of the semester, which for him lasted until the inquest.

"And to think I actually believed things like this would stop happening to me, once I left Bremerhaven."

"Is that the place where they speak Ubangi?" asked Stu From New Haven.

ALL POTATOES DAY

WATER FIGHTS IN COLLEGE take precedence over everything, except sex, although that's never been put to a real test as far as I know, so it's mostly conjecture on my part. Once you're in college you're out of the amateur ranks and into the PCWFF, the Professional College Water Fights Federation. The water rains down the stairwells in sheets like a scene from a navy training film, and cascades over each step, picking up speed with each descending floor. It's reminiscent of a national park where you drive your car over roads that are submerged under streams.

I have returned from class many an unsuspecting time and upon opening the front door, encountered a raging water fight in the fraternity house. There in the rising mists I could faintly see figures moving about each of the floors, clad from head to foot in yellow rain gear, struggling under the weight of large garbage cans filled with water. They looked like New England seafarers in an Atlantic Ocean storm.

Others carried converted fire extinguishers to drive back any inter-floor assaults. . .or to settle some old scores on their own floor. A solitary individual dressed in red passed through the barricades with complete impunity. . .The Orchestrator. This was a much-coveted executive position in the fraternity house, for he was responsible for judging the caliber of all fraternal intramural activities. . .and he got free beer. A tote board with the cumulative points for the current year was posted in the dinning room.

And here I was, back from class, sneaking through the battle lines, working at being invisible, and trying to make it to my room unscathed. Good fortune was with me—I stood in my room completely dry. Stu From New Haven was cowering in the bottom of the closet. Only his rump was visible.

"Open warfare has broken out," came his muffled voice through the hanging row of clothes. "No one's safe."

"Well, well, a talking butt. Stu, you look ridiculous."

The words were barely out of my mouth when a four-foot stream of toothpaste streaked past me and plastered the opposite wall. A narrow miss that made me quickly strip off my shirt. The last time I got hit with one of those, my clothes foamed for days. The nozzle of the spent tube still protruded into our room from under the door. You only get a single stomp with one of those babies.

"Move over, Stu!"

Too late. "Knock. Knock," said a hallway voice. Our door opened and an object was hurtled into the room.

"Shaving cream bomb! Hit the deck!" screamed Stu From New Haven. (Shaving Cream Bomb: One of an array of weapons comprising the complete college arsenal. Especially effective in close quarters. Consists of one food store, paper shopping bag, with a medium yield explosive device, placed with the fuse protruding through the bottom of the bag. Fill the bag with shaving cream, light and serve. [See the Oxford Companion to College Armaments.])

Boom!

Splat!

"That's worth fifty points. . .and a beer for me, of course," yelled The Orchestrator, as he popped open another lager.

We stood there, enveloped in Burma Shave.

"Look! It's the Abominable Snowman. . .and his son," called out the New England seafarers. Abominable Mutt and Abominable Jeff.

Now, this was college!

★ ★ ★

WE SPENT A lot of time in front of the mirror getting ready for Saturday night in the old fraternity house, primping like Spanish bullfighters in slow preparation for the evening matches with our dates. There were gallons of Canoe and English Leather flowing on every floor. It was a lengthy and exhausting effort, and I took frequent breaks to visit other rooms, each with their own Spanish primpers standing in front of the mirror.

"What's going on in here? Why are you gagging?" I asked.

"Canoe fume alert. . .run. . .get out while you can!"

"Aaarrrggghhhh! . . ." Too late, I was blinded. "Help! I can't see. I can't. . .aarrrgggggghhh. . .I can't breathe!" I careened off the walls holding my throat, rubbing my eyes. I stumbled back into the hallway and collapsed.

The alarm was sounded.

"Quickly, men! We have cologne casualties in the hall!"

I could hear the sound of running footsteps, and then felt hands grabbing hold of me.

"Here, drink some of this. . .and hold this towel over your eyes. You! Check and see if there are any others in there. Stay close to the floor! Block the stairway! Close off this corridor! Get these people out of here!"

I was whisked away to a hastily prepared field hospital room and placed on a bunk bed. Soon there were others being brought in, until the room was full. I was feeling better and sat up.

"Stu! When did you get here?"

"I don't know. . .I think I blacked out."

"What happened out there?"

"It was High Pockets, he opened a new barrel of Canoe."

High Pockets' motto was. . ."*You can never wear enough.*"

"How's everyone doing in here?" asked our rescue team.

"We're okay."

"Great, then you won't mind this. . ."

"No! . . . Shaving Cream Bomb!"

Boom.

Splat.

"Look, it's an Abominable Snowman convention."

Now, this was really college!

WHEN I WASN'T visiting other rooms and being overcome by fumes, I spent my primping break time leaning out of the window at the end of the hall. I watched the roadway that looped behind the fraternity quadrangle. The jocks from Sigma Chi were releasing the emergency brakes of the cars parked on the hill, rolling them down to the stop sign below. These weren't their cars, of course, although with jocks you can never be certain.

"Hey. . .duh. . .that was my car."

Since their species was significantly bigger than the normal human populace that surrounded their breeding pens, not much was said about this little game they played. A subspecies interpreter had been provided free by the university, but the attempts to communicate with them had not gone well. In their world, "duh" had as many meanings as the Eskimos have words for snow. Besides, most of us knew better than to park our cars anywhere near them. I didn't have to worry at all. . .I didn't have a car. Actually, if you know anything about our family car, then you know our family didn't have a car.

As the pile accumulated at the bottom of the hill, Noah came up to me.

"What are you doing?"

Noah has to be the first person to have been stuck with that name since the original guy managed to park his ark on a mountaintop in Turkey. I don't know about you, but if I had been driving, I would have parked it in Southern California, and made a killing in real estate. I mean, he was on a first-name basis with God, so I don't think it should have been too hard for the two of them to figure it out. I'd be a little suspect of a God that drops you off on a mountain in Turkey, anyway.

"I'm just watching the Sigma Chi Valet Parking. It's kind of quiet around here without Derelict around. . .watching this kind of reminds me of him."

Noah had an open textbook in his hand.

"Noah, it's Saturday night. . .why are you carrying around a textbook? I'm sure this is against several fraternity bylaws. I'd put it away before you get caught."

"I'm studying."

"Sssshhhhhh. . .quiet! Jeezus. . .what are you trying to do, get us both in trouble!? It's bad enough you're out here in the hall carrying a book, don't add blasphemy."

"You're a pretty weird guy."

"I'm weird? Do you see me carrying around a textbook on Saturday night?"

"I don't think I've ever seen you carrying a book."

"Exactly. So who's weird now? What class is that book for?"

"Medieval Poetry."

"Ladies and gentlemen of the jury, I rest my case." I looked at the front cover. "This isn't one of those joke textbooks that's meant to scare people like me, is it?"

"What'd you mean. . .joke textbook?"

"The bookstore is full of joke textbooks. And this sure looks like one of them. I'd check with your professor, and make sure he's not laughing behind your back, but don't mention my name or you'll be meeting with him at eight o'clock"

"No, it's not a joke."

I took the textbook and flipped it open to about the middle.

"No, I'm pretty sure this is a joke. . .people actually study this?"

"Not really."

"Why are you taking it?"

"I was ambushed by my advisor."

"I know the feeling."

"At the time it sounded kind of scholarly. . .well, to make a short story even longer. . .I made a bad decision."

"Tell me about it. . .I took Math 104. This is your major? Medieval Poetry?"

"I'm an English major."

"I'm an Economics major, but you don't see me taking The Study of Micro Economics as a Mathematical Model."

"That's one of your joke textbooks, isn't it?"

"Well, it would be, if it were a real course, but since I just made that up. . ."

"It sounded good."

"Well, it would to someone taking Medieval Poetry."

I stared at him for some time I guess, with my mouth slightly agape, prompting Noah to say something to end the silence.

"Would you like to hear a medieval poem?"

"Ahh. . .no. I think that would be incredibly dangerous and you'd be wasting your time. . .I thought 'Leader of the Pack' was good poetry."

"Well if you change your mind. . ."

"I don't think you'd want to be in the deli line waiting for that to happen."

". . .let me know."

I stood alone at the window with only the sound of the campus radio station drifting across the quadrangle, punctuated now and then by breaking glass and crumpled fenders.

★   ★   ★

THE DAYS HAD warmed up, but the nights were still plenty chilly, and they would be until the semester was nearly at an end. The coeds began to emerge in their spring outfits during the day. The color was starting to return to their dormant white bodies after a winter's hibernation in New England well-digger's attire. I crossed the square behind the student union. The south campus women's dorms were sprinkled with young coeds sunning themselves on the lawn. I felt a quiver in my loins. . .Springtime Sidewalk Moaning was almost here.

Write this down. . .if you want to attend class more frequently than Punxsutawney Phil's appearance on Groundhog Day, don't take classes at eight o'clock. . .A.M., or at nine o'clock, if you can help it. Did you know they actually hand out schedules and give clues as to what's going to be on the exams in these classes? They call this a lecture, and although I've become quite a fan, I don't get to see much of it. It's supposed to be better than Cliff Notes, if you can believe there's anything better than Cliff Notes.

Then, just to compound my problems, my wake-up system completely broke down. There in my mailbox was a blue slip. . .an Attendance Warning Slip. Class attendance was mandatory in the early sixties. After three cuts in any one class a blue slip would appear in your mailbox.

I was shocked.

"Haven't I been going to class?" I asked Stu From New Haven.

"Occasionally."

"Which occasions?"

"Well, you went the day hell froze over, remember?"

"Hell always freezes over in Connecticut, Stu. So, I would have been going to class a lot, and I wouldn't have gotten this slip."

"Well, maybe you didn't go then either."

"What else could I have been doing?"

"As near as I can tell, you've been dreaming that you have gotten up, dressed, and went to class."

"Damn. Why didn't you tell me?"

"Because you were doing better in those classes than in your real ones."

So, in spite of the World's Most Annoying Alarm Clock, I had missed a few classes. I felt I was blameless. However, I had trouble convincing anyone else, especially since the mandatory attendance policy had blame as an integral part of the system.

"What's my defense?" I asked Stu From New Haven.

"Defense?"

"Yeah, what am I going to say?"

"You have no defense. What can you say. . .that you dreamed you were in class?"

"Do you think that might work?"

I sat in the attendance office with a pathetic look on my face and hung my head, begging like a stray dog for mercy. Cowering and whimpering were accepted for a first offense. If you moved on to an Attendance Warning Slip Second Rank. . .the pink slip, then they expected something better than just a pathetic look, which is too bad because I was really good at pathetic looks. A pink slip was waiting for me when I made it back to the dorm. I should have just hung around the office.

"Why are you still here? We bought your pathetic puppy dog routine."

"Actually, I did leave, and I have since returned. . .with this."

"Dear. . .dear. . .dear. . ."

A three dear rejoinder. As rejoinders go, this was pretty serious.

Back and forth we went.

"How can I tell I'm not in class if I'm dreaming I'm in class?" I asked them.

"What?"

Then it finally happened. I dreamed I wasn't in class. . .and I got a pink slip.

It was a hit and run fight, slips were flying and pathetic looks were everywhere. And now, with the spring semester beginning to quiver in my loins and a bevy of pink slips in hand, I had a premonition that I was probably in my last semester at college, so it really didn't matter what excuse I came up with at the attendance office. I crossed the campus and entered the main administration building.

"Hey, George! How are you?"

"I'm fine Mr. Jamerson."

"Hey everybody, look who's here. Well, come on in. I heard your fraternity was given the death penalty. . .social forfeiture for the rest of the year. It was a helluva parade though, the best I've seen."

"It wasn't my fault."

"Naturally."

I was very popular in the administration building. I was here so often they had to add to their staff, and the original group had all been promoted.

"So, what brings you here?"

"Attendance."

"Shocking. . .have a seat. We've just hired a new woman in the office and I think you would be perfect for her."

"Will I get some extra consideration for this?"

"Sure. Sure. Can we film this? We want to start a training series and it would be an immense help to us to film you. . .and for Miss Parker, this is a real opportunity."

"All right. . .but just remember, someone had better put in a good word with the warden."

"You bet. Wait here, I'll get Miss Parker. Now go easy on her, she's new. . .but don't be a pushover, okay?"

"Okay."

I sat down in my usual chair and waited. Miss Parker came in with the Resolute New Recruit Look on her face.

"Good afternoon. I'm Miss Parker."

Mr. Franks was beaming as he closed the door on us.

"Good afternoon."

"Please, have a seat."

"I have."

"Yes. . .so you have. Well, shall we begin?"

"Certainly."

"So, you have received a blue slip. . ."

"Pink slip. . .slips."

"Oh. . ."

"Oh, indeed."

"Excuse me?"

"I said, it's a pink slip."

"Why have you missed so many classes?"

"I hurt my leg."

"Why didn't you go to the infirmary and get a medical excuse?"

"I'm a Christian Scientist."

I could hear stifled laughter coming from the room next door. Miss Parker sat a little straighter in her chair.

"I see. So you're claiming your religious convictions kept you from going to the infirmary?"

"I'd certainly like to."

She checked my record and found that I wasn't a Christian Scientist.

"Have you no shame?"

"Yes, if you must know, I have plenty of shame. In fact, I have more than enough for the both of us."

She checked my record and found I had plenty of shame.

"So, why have you missed so many classes?"

"Some of those were bona fide holidays."

"Which ones. . ."

"Well, here for instance. . .March 15th. That's All Potatoes Day in Ireland. . .and in Russia also, I believe. You can check my record, I am Irish. Here, see, I don't have an ass, that should prove that I'm telling the truth." I turned around so she could verify that I, indeed, had no ass. "See, I can't even shake my booty, which is a real detriment at fraternity parties." I tried shaking my booty for her. More stifled laughter came from next door. Miss Parker shook her head and set her jaw into a resolute pose.

"Have you no self-respect?"

"Haven't I already admitted to shame? Don't you think that's enough? Besides, I don't think you can have self-respect if you admit to shame, or shake your booty during an office interview, do you? Being high on shame kind of means you'd be low on self-respect. Just one of life's contradictions, being high and low at the same time."

"Don't you ever get tired of being wrong?"

"Not yet."

See dropped her gaze down to her lap.

"Your education is important to us."

"Since when? Look, I'll level with you. This whole thing has been blown way out of proportion. I didn't mean to skip any classes, honest, I just have a medical condition. . ."

"So you said. . .you're a Christian Scientist with an injured leg."

"No, I didn't injure my leg, you know that. . .and I'm not a Christian Scientist, that was just for the boys in the back room. Truthfully. . .I dream I go to class—that's the whole problem—and I'm doing a lot better in those classes than the ones I actually attend. Except when I show up in my underwear and then spend the whole class time trying to figure how to get out of there without anyone noticing me. Say, you wouldn't happen to know how you can actually get all the way to the classroom without noticing you're in your underwear, would you? That's the part that's always skipped in my dreams. I really would like to know how that happens."

"Well. . .er. . .can we get back. . ."

"I'm not talking about dreams that start out with you fully dressed and somehow you lose all your clothes without remembering how. . ."

"I need some help in here. . ."

". . .like it just happened in a tornado or something, and they just flew off you without you knowing it. I'm talking about the ones where you just materialize out of thin air. . .in your underwear. I admit it's a helluva transit system, instantly appearing someplace, but obviously you can only be in your underwear to use it. If I do actually make it to class, and I'm actually wearing clothes, then I'm okay. . .I mean my dream classes, of course. . ."

"Stop the film, someone get in here!"

"Do you think I could get any credits for my dream classes? I think I'm doing real well in them, at least that's what Stu says, but I don't know if you can really trust him. He's partly at fault for letting me go to dream classes. Next time I'm there, I'll ask what classes I'm taking, because that seems to be another problem. I'm never real clear what the class actually is. . .and we better do this pretty quickly because I've started to dream I'm cutting those classes too. . .if you can believe that. I'll probably start dreaming about coming here, and then how will we know which one is the real you. You can tell which one is the real me, if we're having a dream meeting. . .I'll be in my underwear. . .will you? So, what do you think?"

"George. . .George, slow down there," said Mr. Franks as he entered the room. "Take it easy on the poor woman."

"Well, you said don't be a pushover. You know, I'm always answering your questions, and you guys never answer any of mine."

"Go to a class sometime. . .a real class, they'll answer all your questions."

Miss Parker was nervously wringing her hands, probably worrying about ending up in my dreams wearing her underwear.

"Miss Parker, I'm sorry, I thought you were ready. Forgive me." Mr. Franks looked over at me. "You and I are going to have a serious talk."

"Okay, but remember the last time we tried to have a serious talk? You ended up looking like Miss Parker. No offense intended, Miss Parker."

My midterm grades were all Incompletes.

I tried explaining to my professors that the attendance office and the making of their training film were monopolizing my time.

"That's not bad, I've never heard that one before."

"So? . . ."

"Well, you're high on the novelty scale. . ."

"Yeah. . .yeah. . .I've heard it all before. . .no credit for novelty."

I was being pink-slipped to death by the attendance office. I feverishly poured over the calendar for every Irish holiday I could find, finally capitulated, and officially withdrew from the university. The attendance office sent me a fruit basket and a nice card signed by the entire staff. . .except for Miss Parker. I sent a return note thanking them, and told them I wouldn't actually be leaving the campus until the end of the semester. They sent someone over and took back the fruit basket. The university abandoned the mandatory attendance policy the next year, and the entire attendance staff was let go.

So, I officially became an Ex-Student In Residence, a nice title. I was completely relaxed and comfortable. I said nothing to my parents, other than I felt I was making good progress in all my classes. I was now on the proverbial road to the local military recruitment center.

Derelict was gone, High Pockets was on his way out, and now they had me. . .Dirty Moose.

THE CLAY PEOPLE

So, you didn't know I was Dirty Moose, heh? For a long time, I didn't either, it was sprung on me the same way I just sprang it on you. I didn't pick it. I would think that's fairly obvious. I held off mentioning it until the last possible moment, for reasons I also think are fairly obvious. The dynamics of nicknames mostly leaves you out of the choice. I think my results demonstrate that. You never seem to be able to suggest your own, which is why I ended as Dirty Moose.

At first, I was just Moose, which was a bad start in itself. Then, some people started calling me Dirty because I had a campus radio show where I called myself Dirty George, so I have myself to blame for some of this. These names were left unguarded for only a scant moment or two, and just like an unguarded backseat of a '55 Chevy, they cross-pollinated, and I ended up as Dirty Moose. I never thought I could ever be called something that would make Georgy Porgy sound good. I was wrong. . .again. You can imagine how thrilled any girl was to meet. . .

"What was that again? . . ."

"Dirty Moose."

"Oh. . ."

They would have preferred to kiss Georgy Porgy, regardless of the consequences, than go out with someone called Dirty Moose. No matter how hard I tried to convince them that the name really didn't mean anything, they never believed me.

"You must be some kind of grubby, sexually perverted, mountain man," they would say.

You can see why it was important for me to get into a fraternity.

"I'm not grubby or a mountain man," I replied. "I should be called Tripod," I continued. "Nobody listens to me. . .they all thought Dirty Moose sounded better, but I don't see any of them going around calling each other unwashed animal names."

"No, I suppose you don't. . .," they said.

Later on, I learned you don't have to use any of the nicknames your so-called friends stick you with, and you're free to say anything that comes to mind. So I was eventually able to switch to Tripod, and I was suddenly in great demand with the girls. . .well, certain kinds of girls. . .my favorite kind of girls.

During the final days of that last semester, I lounged around the frat house until all hours of the morning, and slept late, to the complete annoyance of the World's Most Annoying Alarm Clock, as well as everyone else in the house.

"We'll be glad when you're gone. You're like The Phantom of Phi Sigma, and you're starting to scare off the women. They say they're afraid of the grubby, sexually perverted, mountain man who lives in the lounge. You've become our own bad version of a Grimm's fairy tale."

There were never any women.

"If you can manage to bring any women in here, then I promise I won't scare them off."

"Uh. . .well. . .okay. Now, how do we get women in here?"

No one seemed to know.

The semester ended without anyone providing me with a single woman to scare. I packed my bags, leaving the Connecticut well-diggers to fend for themselves.

★ ★ ★

I ARRIVED HOME and before the sun had set on that first day, I was sitting across from an air force recruiter. I would tell my parents about everything, as soon as I finished telling everything to the air force.

"Someone *was making good progress in their classes, folks. . .but it turned out not to be me, sorry for the mix-up. However, the good news is that I'm now in the air force.*"

"*I guess that would explain the blue hat.*"

It was going to be a one-two knockout punch that would leave them dazed, and they would barely recover in time to see me leaving for basic training.

"*Say, wasn't George just here? Is college over for the year?*" my mom would ask.

"*Another martini, my dear?*" my father would inquire.

The recruiter was very friendly.

"I have some experience in broadcasting," I said. "I'd like to get into that field in the air force. I'd like to be able to show something for being called Dirty Moose."

"Certainly! Who wouldn't." He was comforting, and most enthusiastic about the whole idea. "My God, we always need people for broadcasting, we can't keep 'em in," said Sergeant Bamboozle.

I took all their tests, had all the qualifying scores and went home.

"Well, I've dropped out of school, and I've joined the air force, my plane leaves in an hour. . .good-bye."

I left two bewildered and motionless parental mannequins sitting at the family arbitration table.

"Wasn't George just here? Is college over for the year?" asked my mom.

"Another martini, my dear?" inquired my father.

★　★　★

I LEFT FOR basic training at Lackland Air Force Base in San Antonio, Texas. I remember very little of these four weeks. I had the life baked right out of me, with most of the memories, by the Texas summer sun. . .except for those memories associated with *The Air Force Versus The Electric Shaver Case.* I had brought my shaver with me, and I wish somebody had told me the service had a thing about electric shavers at basic training. It seemed the shaver was okay, but the case wasn't.

"You mean I can have the shaver, but you don't want to see the case."

"That's right. I find that case and there will be hell to pay."

Hell, once again, cashes in.

"Well, what can I do with it?"

"You can shove it up your ass for all I care, just don't let me find it!"

"This will fit up my ass?"

"Are you tying to be funny?"

"No sir, Sergeant!"

"Don't call me sir! I work for a living!"

"No, Sergeant! I'm just confused about all this."

"Well, it's simple. If I find the case, it's your ass, understood?"

I suppose I could have put it up my ass, but the difference between having the shaver case up my ass, or the sergeant having my ass eluded me. I once saw a movie called *Papillon*, where

Louie the Forger apparently kept his money up his ass for months. Even though air force basic training was only four weeks long, I just wasn't up to it. I just wanted to find a good hiding place.

"Why don't you just throw it away?" said my bunkmate.

"Where would you suggest? All the trashcans are inspected hourly to make sure they're clean and sparkling. I don't think we can actually put trash in them."

After spending hours looking around the barracks and failing to come up with a place the sergeant wouldn't find my shaving case, I was faced with the real prospect of shoving it up my ass, until I spied my laundry bag hanging from the bunk bed post.

"I've got it!"

"What?"

"I'm going to suspend it in the middle of my dirty laundry."

"Jeez, that's not bad. Who'd go digging through your dirty underwear?"

The next day as we stood in formation, the sergeant came up to me and. . .

"Why'd I find a shaver case in your laundry bag, Airman!?" The veins stood out on his neck as he craned forward and blasted me. It started to appear that the sergeant would indeed have my ass. The next words spoken would determine if I lived or died. . .and if I kept my ass.

"Sheer stupidity, Sergeant!"

His head cocked slightly to the side, and a genuinely satisfied look came over him.

"Son, I don't know how, but you've managed to come up with the only answer I'll accept." He wheeled quickly back to the front of the formation.

"That. . .gentlemen, is the only answer I ever expect out of any of you! You don't know anything! You don't do anything unless I tell you! And since today is such a balmy day. . .we're going to do a little marching."

A balmy day in a Texas summer hovers around a hundred degrees. We were dressed in our balmy air force summer outfits, long-sleeved, heavy-weight, dark green fatigues, with the salt deposits around the cuffs.

"My God, look at this! My body is shedding all its salt. . .I'm dying."

Around and around the concrete parade ground we went, depositing salt along the way. The Bonneville Salt Flats have nothing on the Lackland Air Force Base parade grounds. From what I remember, this is about all we did, march, take salt tablets, then deposit the salt on the parade ground, and then start it all over again.

When it was over, I was assigned to technical school, and just like my recruiter said, they assigned me to the air police.

What? Is this right? Could I have been lead astray by my recruiter? Air police? Let's jump into the Wayback Machine and replay what he said. . .

"My God, we always need people for broad. . .(cough). . .olice, can't keep 'em in."

I clung desperately to the hope that I was in the broadcasting branch of the air police. *Click. . .* "*10-4*". *. .click. . .hiss. . .click. . .* "*That's 10-28 on the 10-4, I'll be 10-80 at the 10-20*". *. .click. . .hiss . . . click. . .* "*Okay, I'll 10-30 that 10-80 and raise you a 10-20*". *. . click. . . hiss. . .checkmate.* But we all know what was going on. . .I had been Sergeant Bamboozled.

At least I knew I had been screwed, the guy next to me enlisted for photography and he was convinced he was going to be photographing crime scenes for the air police.

"My God, we always need people for photo..(cough). . .olice, can't keep 'em in."

The photolice—from the same group that brought you the broadolice. I told him to buy himself an Instamatic, because that's as close as he was going to get.

So we were whisked away to Air Police Training School where, if any were left, all these misconceptions were laid to rest. We were carrying rifles and slogging through the summer dirt of Texas. These memories are clear to me, in spite of the heat.

It was starting to seem like the ultimate screw job.

"Didn't I join the air force? How'd I get in the army? When I came back from Germany. . .I ended up in a teen gang without knowing it. And now it's happened again! I think it's going to take more than a DKW to get me out of this one," I said to Frank Photolice.

"What's a DKW?"

"Never mind. Why don't you take my picture."

"I don't have a camera."

"Yeah, no shit."

"Hey, I just have to get through this, and then it's off to the photolice for me."

You had to admire Frank.

It truly was just like the army, with the exception that we were going to do it for four years. The training went on and on during the long Texas summer down in San Antonio. And then one day they actually took us off the base and gave us to the army.

"Wow. . .now we really have been screwed," we all said.

For the next two weeks our training was in their hands. I knew we were in trouble when they said we would be bivouacked. Bivouac is something only the army does, the rest of the world calls it camping out. We referred to it as the bushwhack.

We were now in the army world, where everyone was called a grunt. As we were run across the Texas plain in the hot July sun, we pondered this. . .

"Why. . .(grunt). . .do you. . .(grunt). . .think. . .(wheez). . .they call. . .(hack). . .them. . .(grunt). . .grunts. . .(phlegm)? . . ."

At the beginning of the second week we disembarked the trucks dressed in full combat gear. You haven't lived until you've worn full combat gear in Texas, in July. It was my very own personal sauna outfit.

We were in formation next to the firing range where a group of army nurses were qualifying with pistols. Why the army felt that nurses should have to do this is a mystery. The army used the Colt .45 automatic, actually a miniature artillery piece that can double as a field cannon. It's very heavy and the nurses were struggling to keep it from dragging down their arms as they attempted pointing it toward the targets. Several of them actually had their arms stretched completely to the ground, like plastic men, with the gun lying at their feet. Everyone who didn't have to be there had abandoned the range, and they were all cowering behind a bulletproof barrier.

We remained in formation. . .waiting, which is a highly developed specialization in the service. It even has its own career code assigned to it. When our sergeants saw the huddled masses behind the bulletproof barrier, and the nurses with .45s pointed in various directions, they knew exactly what to do. . .

"Everybody back in the trucks, before you get shot."

The only thing hotter than a personal sauna suit is wearing that suit sitting in a canvas-covered truck in the sun, in Texas, in July.

"Please Sarge, I'd rather get shot."

Another sergeant came screaming down our ranks.

"Move 'em out, down the road!"

We moved down the road and looked around for our own bulletproof barriers. We were standing in formation, in our sauna suits, in the sun, in Texas, in July.

"Is this part of our training?"

"Someone poke me with a fork and see if the juices run clear."

"Shut up! Everyone drink some water and take your salt tablets!" yelled one of the sergeants as he passed by the ranks.

Hot canteen water and salt tablets, mmmm. . .mmmm. . .good.

"Is this lunch?"

The firing range erupted in gunfire as the nurses shot the shit out of everything in sight.

"Everyone off the road and find some cover!"

The nurses blew away the wind sock and took out a few of the target mounts, one even managed to explode the target line pulley five feet in front of her. The instructors were busy doing the Mexican hat dance to avoid the stray shrapnel flying around, and disarming some of the more exuberant nurses.

We were now lying on sun-baked ground, in our sauna suits,. in the sun, in Texas, in July.

"How long does this go on?"

"Until we are all blackened, rotting corpses."

There's always an optimist. . .and from the smell, we were already rotting. Another volley of shots, and now the firing range sign was swinging from its last remaining hinge.

"Enough!" yelled a range instructor. "You all qualify! Congratulations! Just put the weapons on the ground and step back!" The nurses cheered and applauded each other.

By now, a steady steam of sweat poured like a waterfall out of the cuff of my sleeve, and hissed as it struck the ground. My God, the juices were running clear!

"I'm dying," I said to the guy next to me.

"You wish," he replied.

The range was clear, and the instructors were ready. "All right, let's bring the air force in here, that should just about take care of what's left of our sign."

When we were finished, not a target was left standing. None of them had any bullet holes in them mind you, just all the mounts had been shot away. There wasn't a target pulley left intact, and the range sign had fallen and impaled itself into the ground like a dart, just as the instructors predicted. Its direction arrow prophetically pointed to the center of the Earth.

I no longer could hear anything, incessant gunfire right next to my ears caused me to go deaf, so I had to try lip reading as the range instructors waved for us to stop.

"You guys make the nurses look like Annie Oakley."

We cheered and applauded, for none of us could hear anything and we really stunk at lip reading.

"You all qualify."

This was during Vietnam, everyone qualified. They even gave us marksmanship awards to wear on our uniforms. I suppose if we had actually shot one of the instructors we might not have qualified. . .or maybe just not have gotten the marksmanship badge.

"Fine work, men."

Our own sergeants seemed genuinely pleased. I don't know if it was with us, or the fact that they had actually survived once again. We were marched down the road until we came to a series of bleachers. They looked out of place sitting alongside the road in the middle of nowhere, looking out over desolate Texas countryside, baking in the summer heat.

"Fall out, and take a seat!" yelled our sergeants.

This wasn't the perk it would seem. The bleachers were just about the temperature of the surface of the sun, and felt about as comfortable as sliding onto the vinyl seats of a car parked on the sun. . .while wearing shorts.

"Ow!"

"Ouch!"

"Shit!"

"Everyone shut up and sit down!"

We sat in our sauna suits, with our butts being cooked by the oven bleacher seats. From out of the surrounding woods appeared army instructors wearing red armbands. They seemed to have materialized from thin air, just like the Clay People emerging from the rocks in *Flash Gordon*. They remained silent as they approached and took up positions around the bleachers. One was standing right next to me. I was awed, I had never seen Clay People up close.

"Men, this is the warfare simulation area. I don't think you can really hurt the place, but after the job you did on the firing range, I can't be certain. However, we're here to try and gain a little experience with ground maneuvers. I know we're air force, but since you are all air police, you will need to know this in Viennnmmmmm. . ." And his voice trailed off.

"Excuse me, Sergeant. . .can't hear you back here!"

"In Vietnam!"

We were better off when we were all going to Viennnmmmmm.

I looked down for some reassurance from the Clay People. They remained silent.

"The army personnel are here to instruct us. . .and they will be the referees. They have the final say on what happens out here. Behind us, there is a fortification some distance away. That is your objective. You will be broken down into four-man squads. . .aggressor and defender. The army instructors will explain further."

The Clay People came to life again, and walked out to face the bleachers. They explained the concept of four-man diamond-shaped formations and how to approach our objective. When we came to any clearings, we were to pick a spot halfway, sprint to that spot, and hit the ground. Then sprint the remaining distance. Whenever we were "engaged by enemy forces," we were to hit the dirt and crawl, maintaining our diamond formation.

When the instructors finished we were given ammunition clips containing blank cartridges. The squadron was broken down into four-man teams, and the defenders chosen. They left with several of the Clay People and melted into the woods. After a short time, we aggressors followed, walking slowly along. Before that day I thought this was called going for a hike, but I soon found out we had actually been going on maneuvers. Won't the Boy Scouts be surprised.

The woods afforded no real relief from the heat. In fact, the trees stifled what little breeze there was, and produced no shade from the scrubby branches. These weren't leafy maple trees, they were stunted and barren, with no leaves and plenty of sharp protrusions that grabbed at you, scratched you, and got caught on your sauna suit. They were army trees, for the army surely had them planted special. The ground was dusty and strewn with the dried dead branches that had fallen. For the life of me, I didn't see how we were supposed to sneak up on anything when every step produced a snap, crackle, and pop. It was as if a giant bowl of Rice Krispies was moving through the woods. Then the first major problem occurred... .a clearing. Our diamond formation collapsed into four guys waiting on the corner for a bus. We were jammed together in the starting gate for the Mid-Clearing Dash Event.

I took off for the mid-clearing spot and found out immediately what a woman goes through trying to run. Like a bra full of bouncing boobs, my backpack was bouncing up and down, the web belt was dancing around my waist, the canteen was slamming into my butt, the helmet was banging up and down on my skull coming to periodic rests at various skewed angles—none that let me see where I was going—and for this whole time, I was holding onto this damn M-16 rifle. And let me tell you, combat boots aren't jogging shoes. I came to a rolling, tumbling, falling, crashing stop at the mid-clearing spot. I was lying on top of my canteen and had kicked up a cloud of dust, which my lungs instantly rejected, filing an immediate protest along the neural network that, in the future, this stuff really shouldn't be confused with oxygen.

Gunfire erupted all around me. Clay people! I began crawling. Our diamond formation disintegrated, it was now just an army concept. I couldn't locate anybody, friend or foe. I wanted to dump everything I had, but figured I could only get away with claiming the backpack fell off. I left it behind and crawled into the woods past the clearing. Now what should I do? I wasn't sure about what direction to go. Should I try to find the rest of my squad? Should I become Audie Murphy and take the objective single-handed? I decided I needed a shot of hot canteen water and time to think this over.

In the brush just ahead, I could see something moving. I put the canteen back in the web belt and aimed my M16. Someone was crawling towards me. I quietly waited, not sure what to do. He steadily closed the distance. I felt like yelling and asking who he was, but I was sure that wasn't how things were supposed to work. The shoot-now-and-ask-questions-later policy of Wild Bill Hickok seemed a better choice. By now he had stopped crawling and was looking at me. For a frozen moment in time we just stared at each other. Then we both activated the shoot-now policy simultaneously. We waited for one of the Clay People referees to appear and declare a winner. No one showed up. We were forced to determine the results ourselves.

"Got Ya!"

"Missed me! I got you!"

"Oh no! I got you right in the heart."

"Oh no you didn't, I'm wearing Superman's suit."

"Oh yeah, well, I've got Kryptonite bullets!"

Neither of us would give in, and no one came to help us out, so we both eventually crawled our separate ways. Can you believe that guy claiming he was wearing Superman's suit? I crawled into another clearing. By now I was covered from head to foot in branch debris, and coated with choking dust. I rose up and took off for the mid-clearing spot, boots snapping and crackling across the ground, canteen slapping my butt, and helmet clanging on my head. The mid-clearing spot came and went, I was too tired to stop. I decided to try and traverse the whole clearing in one mad dash, and made for the woods beyond. Two steps past the mid-clearing spot the sounds of gunfire exploded from all directions. Clay people appeared immediately.

"You're dead!"

"Oh yeah. . .now you show up! Where were you guys ten minutes ago?"

"Why didn't you stop halfway like we told you!?"

"Do you know there's a guy out here who thinks he's wearing Superman's suit?" A little misdirection to try and save my butt from an ass chewing.

"You are a @%%$@%*&%@$#@#@$$@$$!!!$##$#$$#. . ." Everything after the "you are" was lost in an amazing stream of obscenities that put our own training instructors to shame.

"That was masterful. . .very impressive," I said admiringly.

"Shut up!"

"Shut up? That's it?"

"Shut up you @#@@@&**@$#@$$$@@###@##@!%@#&!"

"Thank you."

They told me to head back to the bleachers and wait. As I got close, I could see everyone lying stretched out on the seats with their equipment off, their sauna suits open to the waist, and guzzling fresh water. How come I didn't know about this sooner? I would have been sitting here before our diamond formation had snapped, crackled, and popped their way to the first clearing. I wouldn't have made it ten yards before having my own squad shoot me.

One by one, everyone straggled in and sat in the bleachers. The Clay People said we did all right. Sure. What did they have to lose? They melted back into the woods. We were loaded into trucks to be driven back, hopefully, to the bushwhack. We drove past a sign that said DANGER! LIVE FIRE AREA AHEAD! . . .followed by. . .MAIN OBSTACLE COURSE. I wondered if they had a SECONDARY OBSTACLE COURSE. . .the air force obstacle course. Would this day ever end?

"Fall in!"

"But Sarge, we're air force. . .this is definitely an army thing."

"Shut up you @#$$#@#!"

It was a pitiful display, and luckily, no one from the army was around to hear him.

There we were, facing the obstacle course in our sauna suits, in the sun, in Texas, in July. Over hill, over dale (my first dale by the way), fording streams, climbing strange army structures placed in the most annoying places and jumping off cliffs and into a large trench where the Clay People waited.

"Keep moving!"

I crawled out of the trench, under barbed wire, around explosive pits, with my face buried in the dust and my canteen under my belly where it had worked around once again. Who designs these things?

"Keep your ass down, soldier!"

"My canteen. . ."

"Then get rid of it!"

"I didn't think I had an option."

"You want to get your ass shot off for a canteen!? Oh. . .seems your ass has already been shot off. . .well. . .er. . .you want to get shot for a canteen!?"

I took no comfort from the fact that it was not possible for an Irish ass to get shot off. I unbuckled my web belt and let it fall away. I started making good progress. It must have been too good, for the Clay People began throwing M-80s in my path.

"Is this about the canteen? Because, if it is, I can go back and get it."

"Shut up!"

Ahead was a section of narrow barbed-wire tunnels. Only the army knows what they were supposed to represent. They were so narrow you had to push your rifle ahead and undulate your body like a snake to move. My helmet fell across my eyes and continued to work its way down until I was pushing it along like a plow.

"Now what are you doing!?"

"What? Aren't I doing it right? Don't tell me this isn't the way helmets are supposed to work?"

"You are the sorriest excuse for a soldier I have ever seen!"

"I'm really an airman. . .which may have something to do with it."

"What are we going to do with you?"

"We don't crawl very much on an air base. . .really."

Finally, I reached the end and sat with the rest of the sorriest excuses for soldiers, rejoicing that we had made it through and toasting our finishing the course with canteens of hot water and salt tablets. What joy! We were relaxed as dusk settled over the countryside. Then several army trucks pulled up and began to unload equipment.

"Maybe these trucks will take us back when they finish unloading."

We watched as the Clay People assembled machine guns and blocked them into the gun mounts just behind us. As the sun set, they began to fire at targets just above the trenches at the start of the barbed-wire section. We could see the tracer bullets flash to the targets and hear their distinctive whine as they split the night air.

"Look what the poor bastards in the army are going to have to crawl through," someone said.

Our sergeants showed up.

"Okay, everyone up to the trench!"

Surely they were joking. We may be in the air police, but this was still the air force. Wasn't it? I say, wasn't it? We don't do things like this. . .do we? Do we? Hello? . . .

"Move it! Move it!"

We slowly moved up the hill in stunned silence and back into trenches. The guns began to fire again, and the sound of the bullets was closer than ever.

"George, you better keep your head down," said Frank Photolice.

"You know what's amazing? . . ."

"What?"

". . .that you think you have to tell me that."

"All right!" screamed the TI. "No matter what happens, don't anyone stand up!"

Well, I guess I was wrong again, I guess someone does have to say it.

"Someone always stands up!" continued the TI. "And someone always gets shot! All right you candy asses. . .first wave, move out!"

Like we're really going to move out after he says that. . .we all became frozen candy asses. I guess no one figured they were in the first wave. I knew I wasn't. He couldn't have been talking to me. . .you must first have an ass in order for it to be candy. I was in the last wave, the very last wave. . .Big Kahoonas wave.

"First wave! Move out! I better see some butts moving real quick or you'll be sorry sons of bitches!"

We were already sorry sons of bitches, but nobody mentioned it to him. The first wave suddenly remembered who they were, and began an agonizing crawl out of the trenches.

"And remember! No standing up!"

Thanks again, Sarge.

Back over the top, I followed the first wave. The streaks of the tracer bullets were white against the night sky, and left there after images criss-crossed in my eyes. The bullet's whine was very close, seemed like an inch or two from my nose. We crawled along in the dirt, spitting out the dust that coated our mouths and throats. I plowed my helmet into the boots of the guy ahead of me more than once, and had to resist the temptation of untying his laces. I doubt the army would have found it funny. But I did, and I began to chuckle at the thought as I crawled.

"No laughing!"

God, there was no fun out here at all.

When I came to the barbed wire I rolled onto my back to push up the wire with my rifle. All I could see was white-hot tracers slicing through the black sky. There was no chuckling now. Oh Lord, what have I gotten myself into? I wondered.

As each bullet whined by my head, I could only think. . .what am I doing here? As a kid I thought this kind of stuff was great fun.

"I know what's wrong here, you guys should have got me when I was ten years old."

"Who's talking out there. . .is that you Airman Moose?"

NUCLEAR BASEBALL

Air police school finally ended, and I was still alive. I left Texas for my first assignment at Langley Air Force Base, located on the Virginia coast, north of Virginia Beach. The air police is broken down into two groups, security and law enforcement. Both are exceedingly dull, unless something actually happens. This was, thankfully, rare. It could mean real trouble and I was not real good with real trouble. Another benefit of air police work is that the rest of the air force loathes you. It soon became apparent this was a secondary and quite important function. . .with us to hate, everybody was much happier than they would have been otherwise, with the exception of those of us who were actually in the air police. All in all, it made for quite a satisfying military career.

Ordinarily, you were not permanently assigned to law enforcement or security, but traded off periodically whenever the commander felt you might be having some fun. Fun is much frowned upon in the service.

You are already familiar with the law enforcement group, whether you realize it or not. They are the ones who try to stop Godzilla from entering the base. Standing there dressed in white hats and white scarfs, they direct the traffic and snap off salutes with flashing white gloves and issue Godzilla a temporary base pass. They are also the first ones to get karate-chopped by invading spies. By my estimates, an APs life expectancy is about ten seconds when faced with secret agents or colossal reptiles on the lam.

Security is far earthier, dressing in fatigues and walking perimeter fences in the rain. It's the closet thing the air force has to being in the army, which was a nasty little surprise for all of us who joined the air force specifically to stay out of the army. The K-9s are a separate group altogether. They're usually found with their dogs, performing these bizarre rituals inside their own compound, while wearing what looks like Michelin Tire Man outfits. Even the dogs are suspicious of them and keep a wary eye.

I found myself walking the perimeter fence on the first night of my arrival. As I walked along my personal stretch of fence, I had a sobering thought. . .a six-and-a-half-foot guard walking the perimeter in Vietnam probably made a really good target, like some mechanical duck in a carnival shooting gallery.

Ping. . .Clink. . .Whirrrrr. . .Ping. . .Clink. . .Whirrrrr. . .

"What's that, Sarge?"

"Sounds like they got Allingham in their sights again."

This wasn't good. I was going to have to do something about it. So, the next morning I went to the squadron commander and asked for a transfer out of the air police. Of all the ways I know to get yourself in good with the squadron commander upon your introduction, this is not one of them.

"See the training sergeant. . .Sergeant Bamboozle," he said.

I took this as a direct order and went immediately to the training room, where I was greeted at the door.

"Please come in. . .always glad to see a new recruit."

"Say, didn't your brother recruit me?" I asked.

"I don't have any brothers. Sit down right over here and tell me why you want out of such a good career field. We need good APs, can't keep 'em in." He seemed genuinely concerned.

"Are you sure you don't have a brother?"

"Positive. So, why are you asking for a transfer?"

"Because I'm not a mechanical duck."

"I should think not. . .fill this form out. . .and this one. . .and this one. . .and this one. . ."

He was having quite a good time. He got to use forms he didn't even know he had. I was set up to take the bypass exam for the information career field.

"If you pass it, then we'll assign you a secondary career code, and then we can use it to apply for a transfer," said a smiling Sergeant Bamboozle.

However, there wasn't an exam for broadcasting.

"This is another of the air force's little recruitment jokes, isn't it."

"Sure looks that way," said the merry Sergeant Bamboozle. "The closest thing we've got is an exam for journalism. I think that's good enough, don't you? Do you want to take it?"

"Journalism? In place of a broadcasting exam? This may come as a surprise to you, but they're not the same thing."

"Really? How different can they be?"

"They're nothing at all like each other. Why don't we just make it an ancient Egyptian languages exam."

"Whatever you want. Hmmm. . .I don't seem to have a career code for ancient Egyptian. Looks like journalism will have to do."

So I took it. I didn't know a damn thing about journalism, and it was a good thing that the air force didn't either, because I passed. Sergeant Bamboozle lost his sunny disposition when he saw my score. He refused to even see me. I couldn't get past the front door.

"Go away. I'm not in."

"But I can see you."

"That's not me."

"You can't possibly think that's going to work, can you?" I stuck my foot in the way as he tried to close his door in my face.

"Yes, I can. This is the service."

He had a point. I was starting to think I wasn't expected to pass. . .what do you think?

"Hey, you should've given me the rocket scientist bypass test, if you didn't want to take any chances!" I yelled as he managed to dislodge my foot and slam his door closed.

"We thought we had, but it doesn't matter. Whenever it's you, I'm in when I'm out, and when I'm out I'm in."

"What? I can't understand you through the door."

"I should have listened to my brother. . ."

"What? Did you just say that you're out when you're in, and you're in when you're out?"

"What?"

Sergeant Barbarino.

I went to see the squadron commander.

"Go away. I'm not in. Actually, I'm out when I'm in, and I'm in when I'm out."

The wing commander.

"Go away. I'm in, so I'm out."

The base commander.

"Go away."

Base commanders don't care if they're in or not.

Stage Two, the Tom O'Bedlam School of Military Transfers. . .going psycho. I became confused and incoherent.

"What's supposed to be different about this?" asked my friends.

"You can't have a confused and incoherent person guarding the base."

"Why not?"

"Well, I'm sure the flight commander will know why."

I told the flight commander he couldn't cross the runway because the bridge was out.

"The bridge is always out," he said.

I countered. "Last night I dreamed I was an air policeman in my Maidenform bra."

"Yeah, so what? Last night I dreamed I was a Maidenform bra."

It seemed I was only convincing him his dreams were better than mine, and I was perfect for the air police. Psychos, as it turns out, are highly prized for walking the perimeter. I was getting nowhere. I needed a new plan, so I bided my time, and planned. . .and planned.

Winter was coming on, the nights were getting cold. My planning was disrupted by the K-9s, who liked to let their dogs fly around blind corners on long leashes to scare the hell out of us whenever we came out to relieve them. I lost my fondness for their game after the first time they pulled it on me, and I tripped over myself as I tried to grab my rifle off my shoulder, reverse my step and break into a run, all simultaneously. I can tell you now that all of these actions work smoothly when done separately. However, when performed together, they leave you in a pile of twitching arms and legs. I figured that out right after I fell to the pavement, all tangled up in my shoulder strap, with twisted arms and legs going in different directions.

"Wow, that's great! What else can you do?"

"Fuck you!" This is a far more effective response if you're not a tangled ball, spinning around on the ground. "You're lucky I didn't shoot your dog."

"Correct me if I'm wrong, but if you fire your rifle in your current position, you will shoot yourself in the ass. . .if you actually had an ass."

"Yeah. . .well. . .it would have been worth it to see you dragging a dead dog around on a leash for the rest of the night."

"Yes, it probably would have, if you had actually managed to aim at something other than your ass. . .er. . .bottom. . .er. . .say, what do you call that empty spot where your ass should be?"

"It's an Irish ass. . .and fuck you." Reduced to a snarling fuck you once again.

"That's what passes for an ass in Ireland?"

"I'm afraid so. . .actually, in Ireland, this is considered a good ass."

The dog trick stopped being much of a surprise, since the K-9s did it every single time we came to relieve them. It still worked on the rookies, and since we all liked a good joke, we didn't tell any of the new guys.

"Fuck you!" said the tangled ball of twisted arms, legs, and shoulder straps spinning around on the ground.

"Someone go out and pick up the new guy, and tell the K-9s to quit fucking around out there," said the flight commander. "Unless they want to start wearing their Michelin outfits on shift."

I made an appointment at the base hospital to see the psychiatrist. Under close psychiatric examination—that involved a lot of erratic movements on my part, some incoherent ramblings, a few admissions of hating all my relatives and ancestors, as well as all of his, and being hooked up to a small power station so that a lot of squiggly lines could run down a chart—he finally recommended that I be transferred. The squadron commander was in when he was in this time, just so he could laugh at me.

"These guys don't have any power. . .now get out of here!"

"But. . ."

"Go away. I'm no longer in. . .since I'm in. . .or when I'm in. . .or something like that."

"What? . . ."

On one very cold night while guarding the alert hangar I was close to giving up. It had been six months, and I had nothing to show for it except everyone on the base was out when they were in and vice versa. I seemed to have exhausted about every avenue, and I stood at the alert hangar bundled up in my parka, pretty much defeated. I was beginning to resign myself to forever being on the perimeter when the intruder alarm went off.

Glaring high-powered floodlights snapped on, followed by the sound of a two-thousand-pound version of the World's Most Annoying Alarm Clock. Scared the crap out of me! I fumbled and stumbled around, simultaneously trying to get my rifle off my shoulder and looking around for some intruder. Once again I was a tangled ball on the ground, all twisted up in arms, legs, and shoulder strap.

"Halt! Halt I say, or I'll roll right over there! I know where you are! I can hear you laughing!"

But there weren't any intruders, there never were. It was mostly birds flying through the photoelectric beams that guarded the alert hangar's runway entrance and setting off the alarm. The laughing was usually dependent kids who snuck through the tall grass to toss a rock through the beams.

"Goddamn little dependent assholes!"

Other times it was the shift commander who liked a good laugh as much as the dependent kids.

"Wow, that was really cool," he said to the other kids.

It was enough to jar me awake and to help me get my focus back on getting out of the air police. I had to come up with a plan, something as startling as a rock through the alert hangar alarm beams, and above all, something that worked. I already had plenty of startling plans that didn't work. . .and I had to find one before I became the largest mechanical duck to ever set foot in Vietnam.

I went inside the hangar to get warm and think. This was technically abandoning your post. Actually, it *was* abandoning your post, but we all would sneak inside, now and then, for some heat.

I jumped up and down on my toes to get warm, then walked around the hangar. The plane filled the bay, and I looked at all the red tags dangling from underneath its belly. I opened the door to the lounge area. It was the middle of the night and the crews were asleep upstairs. The room was empty. I closed the door and went back into the hangar just as the outside door opened and the shift commander came inside.

"What are you doing in here?"

"Ah. . .er. . .making sure the plane is still in the hangar?"

"You thought it might be missing? Shouldn't you be outside stumbling and bumbling around?"

"I was just out there doing that."

"Come out here."

We stood outside on the concrete runway in silence.

"What am I going to do with you?" he said to himself. "I'll be back."

He walked back to his truck and left. He returned after he felt I had stewed in my own juices long enough. His timing was good, I was completely stewed.

We sat in his truck.

"I know you want out of the air police, but son, this isn't the way."

"I didn't do this on. . ."

"Just hear me out. You don't want out with something like this on your record. A court-martial isn't the way you go about getting a transfer. . ."

The thought had never crossed my mind, and if it had, I doubt I could have caught it before it finished covering such a short distance.

"Actually, I was just trying to get warm. . ."

"You don't want to be sent to Bumfuck, Egypt. I'm going to handle your punishment myself. The major won't ever know. Your next days off are going to be spent cleaning the CP."

I think it's pretty obvious I don't want to go to Bumfuck, Egypt. I don't even want to go to Goodfuck, Egypt. I readily agreed the command post needed a good cleaning, and I was the guy for the job.

After turning the CP into the cleanest building on the base, the shift sergeants moved me to a new spot.

"Maybe we'll try you out on the entrance gates for a while. You might find it more to your liking."

I liked it just long enough to have myself banished from law enforcement, not immediately, just right after my first night on the main gate. I was rotated on the other gates for a while, until I gained a little seasoning. The main gate is reserved for the veterans. It's the busiest gate, the one used by the commanders, John Q. Public, all spies, and, of course, Godzilla. I finally qualified for main gate duty by successfully handling the rest of Langley's entrances, including the CIA gate, which wasn't even officially there.

"Excuse me, Officer. . ."

"I'm not an officer, I'm an airman. . .if you can believe that a service branch actually wants to call its members airmen. . .like we're all running around in a Buck Rogers serial."

"Excuse me, Airman, is this the CIA entrance?"

"I can neither confirm nor deny that this is the CIA entrance."

"Is this CIA Langley?"

"No comment."

"This is Langley Air Force Base, correct?"

"Yes, I can confirm that. . .it is Langley Air Force Base."

"So, are those buildings over there the CIA Headquarters?"

"I don't see any buildings."

"But they're right over there. . ."

"I cannot confirm nor deny the existence of 'right over there'."

"What? . . . Is this the CIA or isn't it?"

"I wouldn't argue that it is the CIA, and I wouldn't argue that it isn't the CIA."

"Well, thank you, Senator."

"You handled that masterfully, son. We think you're ready," said the shift sergeants.

The next midnight shift I was assigned to the main gate. It was a very quiet night, and I fought off dozing by doing a few laps around the gatehouse.

"What the hell are you doing?"

Shift sergeants didn't want the shift commander having all the fun, and they liked to sneak up on the posts as well, to try and catch someone doing something wrong.

"Halt! Who goes there?"

"It's a little late for that. What the hell were you doing?"

"Just a quick refreshing run around the gatehouse."

"There has to be something in the regulations about this. . ."

But there wasn't. They found this frustrating, nowhere in the manual did it say anything about doing laps around gatehouses. Without a regulation of some kind, they were lost. They looked in the index under laps, running, trotting, marathons, relays, races, sprints, short track, breeder's cup, and everything else they could think of, but there was nary a word. They viewed me suspiciously, thinking I had purposely outmaneuvered them.

"We don't like this."

"We're going to refer this to the HMFWIC. . ."

". . .and he's going to take a dim view of it."

"A mighty dim view."

"The HMSXYZ? . . ." I asked.

"You know who that is, troop?"

"That's like His Majesty's Ship. . .it's a Royal Navy thing, right?"

"You're an idiot. It's HMFWIC."

"Is that the lieutenant?"

They laughed uproariously. "That's the Head Mother Fucker What's In Charge!"

"And we can guarantee he'll take a dim view."

They looked at each other. "The lieutenant. . ." And they laughed again.

"Is that a military title?" I asked, but they were too busy patting each other on the back and laughing up a storm as they left the guardhouse.

"The lieutenant he says. . ."

Until the HMFWIC issued a dim view, they would just have to watch and wait, wait for me to do something wrong that they could find in the manual.

As they left, the morning rush hour began, slowly at first, but the traffic quickly began to back up at the gate. I checked the entering cars for a base sticker. Anyone without one had to pull off to the side and wait, like a special order at McDonald's, until I collected some pertinent information.

"Birth certificate, marriage license, and library card please."

"What? . . ."

"Did you use the valet refrigerator during your stay?"

"I haven't even gotten in yet. . ."

"That would be a no, then?"

I issued a temporary pass. The traffic increased, the number of cars without stickers increased. I was waving and saluting, and writing things down, and passing out the temp passes, and soon, just like Lucy and the chocolate candies coming down the conveyor belt, I was overwhelmed. I was saluting everything that moved, throwing temp passes by the dozen at stunned drivers, writing squiggly psychiatric chart lines in the base pass log. I was finally reduced to standing in the middle of the road with a permanent salute on one hand, and temp passes extended out with the other. My hat was askew, my boots had become untied, a white glove was stuck under the brim of my hat, my pistol hung from the holster, held only by the braided cord, my shirttail was out, my fly was open. Spies came in by the hundreds—Godzilla got by me. I was the automatic AP man. Cling. . .salute. . .clang. . .handout base pass. . .cling. . .salute. . .clang. . .cling. . .ping. . .clink. . .whirrrrrrr.

"Now, this is in the regulations," the shift sergeants said to one another.

"Whoa there, son. We think you belong back in security."

"Yeah. . .let's go to the storage site."

They took me back to the squadron, where I changed into fatigues, and just before I was sent out to walk the storage site perimeter they handed me a clipboard.

"You have to fill out the information you left off your log this morning. We need the names, license-plate numbers, destinations and the time entered for all the passes you issued. You see, you gave out 133 passes, and you only have entries for 26 of them, then a lot of squiggly lines, so we'll need the remaining 106."

"105," another corrected.

"107," said a third.

"Whatever," said the first.

"That makes 318," I said. The service is not much on humor, and we just looked at each other in silence for a moment.

"Is this a gag?" I asked, still not understanding the No Humor Rule.

"There are no gags in the regulations, son. An entry for each pass is required," said Sergeant One.

"Yes. No exceptions," said Sergeant Two.

"And an entry we will have," said Sergeant Three.

The No Humor Rule was now fairly clear in my mind.

"Okay." I took pen in hand. "Luckily, I remember it all," and I confidently tapped the side of my head to show them it was all still right up there. "Let's see, there was Airman Huntz Hall, he was going to the. . .base, his license was. . .GEZ123, then came Sergeant Bilko, he was going to the. . .base, license was. . .

"Don't forget the time."

"Right. . .time." I filled in the log.

"Good job. Now let's take you out to The Site."

The three of them seemed happy to have names for all the passes. They handed the clipboard to the desk sergeant as we left. I was dropped off and left to walk around the perimeter of The Site for the rest of the shift. The only change all morning was a flock of Michelin Tire Men rolling into The Site with their dogs.

★   ★   ★

INVENTIVE WAYS TO fight guard post boredom are left totally up to you. There are no suggestions in the AP manual. In fact, it's not even mentioned in the manual, there was no guard post amusement section at all.

If you are proficient with out-of-body experiences, you might try taking a trip. I usually ended up as an AP on another base, so I gave that up. Another way was getting orders to Vietnam. . .not recommended. If you were working a guard post that issued a pistol, quick draw was a perennial favorite. The service likes to call these sidearms, but I was always getting this confused with the arms that were already at my side, and preferred calling it a pistol. The shift sergeants said calling it a pistol also violated the No Humor Rule. Go figure. There was also a minor drawback of accidentally firing the pistol and shooting someone, thereafter allowing you to watch APs walk the perimeter around your new home. Also, not recommended.

You could try to sneak a transistor radio past the shift sergeants in the hood of your parka. They enjoyed this very much, since mowing their lawns was the punishment for anyone caught. Parka jacket hoods were favorite places to store things—snacks, coffee, books, chilidogs, floor lamps.

By far the best and most popular pastime was a game of my own invention. . .nuclear baseball. This required being assigned to guard duty at the nuclear storage site. Since it had, more or less, become my permanent home, I had plenty of time to devise the game.

We had managed to get a can of tennis balls into The Site hidden in the shift sergeant's own truck, a coup in itself. The rest was easy. . .M16 bats (with the ammo clips removed, please), fatigue hats for bases and four-man teams. The Site was conveniently laid out with a large center courtyard used for maneuvering the bombs into and out of their shelters. It even had lights for night games.

The only real intrusion came when they picked up or returned one of the bombs.

"Do they really have to keep coming in here all the time just to get one of these things? If they need them so much, why don't they just keep them back on the base, and quit bothering us? It really disrupts the flow of the game."

"Maybe they can call ahead, and we could have a bomb waiting for them out front."

"Like ordering a pizza."

"Yeah, like a pizza."

Before nuclear baseball, guarding The Site was like sitting on death row. It was located on the wooded outskirts of the base, desolate and isolated. Being assigned there caused more than a few audible groans. Now the groans had tapered off to an occasional unsatisfying moan.

"What's going on? You guys aren't groaning like you used to."

"Yeah, you're taking some of the enjoyment out of this. . .what are you guys up to out there?"

The shift sergeants threw their entire efforts into finding out if there was any fun going on out there. They made several surprise trips to The Site, but since they had to go through a series of entrance gates to get inside, they tipped their hand every time. The sound of those gates clanging open could be heard all the way to the CIA entrance gate.

"*What was that noise?*"

"*What noise?*"

"*That noise! . . .*"

"*I cannot confirm that there is a noise.*"

Sneaking up on the perimeter fence just set off the motion alarms, sounding horns and snapping on searchlights well before they could get anywhere close to us. It not only didn't work, but it also scared the hell out of everybody, including themselves.

With each failure they became more agitated. Their constant attention was getting to be unnerving. We gathered to talk it over.

"What are we going to do?"

"I can't stand this anymore. It's like someone reading over your shoulder. . .all the time."

"We're going to have to let them catch us at something. But what?"

"Cards," someone said.

"Cards!?"

"Sure. . .cards and gambling. This is a honorable and time-tested service past time."

"I thought that was drinking and golf," I said.

"Well, that too. . ."

"Listen, we can't be drinking out there and we can't be playing cards either. That would be abandoning your post, and you can only do that at the alert hangar."

"That's not what Sergeant King told me, he said I'd be going to Bumfuck, Egypt."

"Well, they're still trying to get even with you for passing that journalism exam. Keep thinking."

The race was on. We had to think of the reason to catch us, before they thought of a way to catch us.

Several days later, Joe From The Bronx came into my room and dropped an armful of balls.

"I bought every kind of ball they sell in the PX."

On my floor were balls of every sort, a football, a basketball, a soccer ball, a beachball, a volleyball, a rubber ball, a medicine ball, you name it, we had it.

"The answer is in here somewhere."

"This must have cost you a fortune."

"Everyone owes me. . ."

I had a braingust. I was incapable of a full storm.

"Let's bring them all. . .except for the medicine ball."

"All of them!?"

"Sure. This will overwhelm the sergeants, and nobody has to leave their post to kick. . .or throw. . .or heave these around The Site. They'll be everywhere."

"Hmmm. . .how are we going to get this many balls inside?"

"We'll deflate 'em and shove 'em down our pants."

"You can sneak in the football and the basketball, you have plenty of room where an ass should be," said Joe.

Jimmy With The Long Nose came in.

"What's all this?"

We pointed at the balls on the floor. "Nuclear Football. . .nuclear basketball. . .nuclear volleyball. . .nuclear beachball. . .nuclear spud."

"I think we've gone a little overboard on these games."

"No. This is for the sergeants to find."

"God, we'll be mowing their lawns till doomsday."

"It's for Nuclear Baseball."

We took off our caps in silent respect.

"All right, start letting out the air."

Now we just waited to be caught. We offered no resistance, but nothing happened. The sergeants were conspicuously quiet.

"What the hell's going on, first they're sneaking around out here every other minute, and now you can't even find 'em."

Now we were all edgy, right along with the sergeants. Everyone was so nervous that several people would have shot a hole in the ceiling if you had yelled Boo! at the weapons check.

The K-9 guys started complaining that it was hard to sneak their dogs around any corners with all these balls lying around. Every time one of The Site crews pulled out a bomb from its shed, a few balls came bouncing out with it.

"This is getting ridiculous, pretty soon everyone will know, except for our sergeants!"

I was on The Site entrance on the night when the shift sergeants hit us with a surprise readiness inspection.

"What's the fifth general order?" asked Shift Sergeant One.

"The fifth general order is to quit my post only when properly relieved. . ." I stood at ease with my arms folded behind my back. Shift Sergeant Two was looking me over as I recited.

"Where are your arms?" he asked.

I stopped in mid-sentence. ". . .er. . .my arms?"

I unfolded my arms from my back and extended them for him to see.

"Are you trying to be funny?"

"God, I hope not, because I know all about the No Humor Rule."

"Your sidearm."

"Sidearm!? You know, I knew this was going to get me in trouble someday. . .and believe me, I don't want to go to Bumfuck, Egypt. I just can't get it through my head about sidearms, arms, weapons and all that. If you guys just used the familiar names, like rifles and pistols. . .when you said arms. . .well, I just didn't make the connection, you know. I thought you were asking for my arms, not my sidearm. . ."

"Shut up and show me your sidearm."

I opened my fatigue jacket and exposed the holster.

"Let me see the weapon."

"I'm sorry, Sergeant, but you know I can't do that. A sentry is never to surrender his rifle-pistol-sidearm-weapon to anyone, unless I'm being placed under arrest. Are you arresting me?"

"Hmmm. . .maybe."

Shift Sergeant One was slowly moving towards the door while gazing out the window. "We'll see what the regulations say about someone who gets confused about arms."

"You are the one who used to do laps around the guardhouse, aren't you," said Shift Sergeant Two.

Shift Sergeant One left the building and got back into the truck.

"Open the gate," ordered Shift Sergeant Two.

I leaned over the desk and pushed the button. The gates separated. Shift Sergeant One started the truck and drove off.

"He forgot you."

"Don't worry about me. Close the gates."

I pushed the button again, and the gates closed.

"I'm just going to wait here with you. . .keep you company. You don't mind, do you?"

"Not a bit, Sergeant."

"I wonder how your buddies are doing out there?"

"Guarding up a storm, Sergeant."

"I'll bet."

A few minutes later, the radio crackled with static, then a low voice whispered, "Clear?"

"Go on, answer him."

"Answer what?"

"Just say clear."

I keyed the mike. "Clear."

"Let's give them a few more minutes, shall we?"

"A few minutes for what, Sergeant?"

"I don't know, you tell me."

"I don't know what you mean."

"Yeah, just like you don't know what arms are. There's something going on out here, and I'm going to find out what, and I'm going to find out tonight."

I stared at him for a moment. "Like some coffee?"

"No, I don't want any coffee, this ain't no social visit." He went to the window and looked out. "Can't see much from here, can you. I'm going inside, and I don't want to hear anything over the radio—not a whispered word, not a keyed mike—nothing. You got that?"

"You want me to come with you?"

"So, you're abandoning your post? Do you think this is the alert hangar? No, I don't want you to come with me. I don't want you to do anything, just sit here. . ." He went to the door and listened. ". . .sssshhhhh. . .you hear that?"

"Hear what?"

"It sounds like a truckload of basketballs coming down the road."

Whomp!

A football hit the side of the guardhouse.

"Jesus! What the hell was that!"

"Could be aliens. . .they're out here a lot." Which was true. Even though the air force and the CIA had both threatened us, and swore us all to secrecy, I'm giving away the secret. . .aliens stink at Nuclear Baseball.

"You stay put!"

"Yes, Sergeant."

He went into The Site, keeping to the shadows, then he disappeared around the end building. A minute went by, then finally the radio crackled again.

"I got 'em."

"Good work," came the reply.

The truck came back up the road to The Site entrance. I hit the button and opened the gates. Shift Sergeant One drove straight passed the gatehouse and into The Site. Everyone was rounded up and taken back to the squadron. We sat in the back, amidst an ocean of balls.

"I'm glad they finally came in there, I was getting exhausted heaving all these balls around."

"Me too,"

"Hesnonestratum," said one of the aliens rounded up with us.

"You can say that again."

"Hesnonestratum."

Aliens have no understanding of figures of speech. They're hell on wheels when it comes to figuring out numbers with letters, though.

"How are you guys at mowing lawns?"

"Neenmo!" He held up his tentacles in disdain.

"Figures."

"Shut up, back there!"

"Sarge, I'm not going to have to fill out another logbook, am I?"

"Shut up!"

The sergeants' lawns were immaculate for that entire summer.

I did manage to get myself transferred out of the air police, I won't tell you how, but it was around the same time as the Alert Hangar Hockey Incident. . .summer doesn't last forever, you know. On warm nights, whenever you drove past The Site, you could still hear. . .

"Out!"

"Neenmo!"

THE CAR GHETTO

ON A SPRING MORNING, I packed my bags, loaded my car, and left the air police squadron. I drove across the base to my new barracks. The next day I reported to a Lieutenant Corker in the information office.

"So, you're the guy who passed the Journalism Proficiency Exam and has never actually done any journalism. . ."

"Yes, sir."

"Doesn't say very much for the exam."

"Thank you, sir."

He introduced me around the office and then handed me to Jim, a young black guy slightly older than me, who headed the radio and television section. The rest of the office was divided into preparing a base newspaper, and sending out news releases. Jim talked nonstop and moonlighted at a black radio station, where he continued to blather away. I soon realized he had a medical condition, if he actually stopped talking he would have fallen into a coma. So I listened politely and never interrupted, so as not to trigger an attack.

"We think he's vocal cataleptic," said the lieutenant.

"Is it contagious?"

"I don't think so, but I wouldn't drink from the same glass if I were you."

During the day, Jim and I visited the radio and television stations in Newport News and Norfolk. We thought if we actually showed up there dressed in our uniforms they would be more inclined to put air force stories on the air. It needed more thought. If it wasn't a plane crash, they didn't want to know about it. Showing up in uniforms did nothing, other than having us being mistaken for the doorman at every station in town. I made five bucks in tips for the day, which was more than my air force pay.

There really wasn't much for service broadcasters to do in the States. We mostly waited for overseas orders to AFRTS stations around the world. AFRTS stood for the Armed Forces Radio and Television Service and was lovingly referred to as AFARTS.

"So Dirty Moose, what are you up to these days?"

"I'm in AFARTS."

"How appropriate."

"I think so."

I usually tagged along with Jim to ensure that no one would stop him from talking, and to call for emergency medical help if someone did cause him to fall into a vocal cataleptic coma. Sometimes I bothered the newspaper staff, but only during their most critical moments in setting up the weekly edition. This is where I met Tim.

Tim was a standard air force enlistee of the late sixties, a college drop out. . .hiding from the army. He had dropped out of the University of Maryland.

"I have a friend who goes there," I said when I met him.

"You're not going to ask if I know him, are you?"

"No."

"Good."

"It was just idle introductory conversation. I would have said the same thing even if I didn't know anyone who went there. However, in this case, I did actually know someone who went there."

"How can I be sure that you're not idly conversing a lie right now?"

"That's the beauty of it, you can't. . .I may be lying and I may not, but I usually reserve my best lies for women. They expect it, and I wouldn't want to disappoint them."

"So, if you are lying. . .then I'm getting a second-rate lie rather than one of the premium lies?"

"Unless I'm telling the truth, and I wouldn't assume it's just a second-rate lie. I have many grades of lies, so you could be getting a good lie or even a respectable lie, just not a premium lie. However, since it was an idle conversation lie, I wouldn't count on it."

This convinced Tim that we should become friends. Tim worked on the base newspaper.

"How'd you get into information? I thought everyone was being put into the air police," I asked him.

"Well, think again. . .some of us have fate and timing on our side, my friend."

"You obviously didn't have Sergeant Bamboozle for a recruiter."

"On the contrary, everyone had Sergeant Bamboozle."

And so began our symbiotic relationship. Tim had blonde hair, California surfer looks, and the luck of the Irish without being Irish. He had been assigned to information while the rest of us were being shepherded around the Texas inferno by the Clay People. His Langley squadron was overcrowded, and when they authorized a few lucky chaps to live off the base at the expense of Uncle Sam, his name came up. I was, of course, still Dirty Moose, living on the wrong side of the tracks from fate and timing.

Tim and I began an office hair competition that ran for the entire summer I was assigned to keep Jim from lapsing into a coma. You might think this was some minor competition between two souls with nothing much better to do. And that would be true. But it did require a little technique and some slight of hand. The service reacts to long hair the same way your mother would react to someone walking along with his fly open and Mr. Johnson swinging in the breeze. . .it attracts attention. This added an element of risk to our competition.

Another element of risk would be me actually unfurling Mr. Johnson in public.

Fuummmmppphhhh.

"*Aaiiiieeeee!*"

"Earthquake!"

"Monster!"

"*It's Tripod Man!*"

If only.

In the late sixties, it was easy to spot someone in the service. . .everyone else had hair. Since we ached to be just like everyone else, it was a social imperative for us to grow ours. The air force standards were slightly more relaxed when compared to the other services. So, we started with a leg up, we had a quarter-inch head start on the rest of the military pack.

Every day at lunch the rulers came out for an update.

"2.76 inches. . ."

"2.71 inches. . ."

These were finely scaled rulers we borrowed from the flight line mechanic shops.

"I'm still leading," I said.

Tim's face slumped in defeat.

"Damn."

To hide this massive amount of hair required massive amounts of grease, and not just Brylcreem style, but tubs of Vaseline petroleum jelly. I'm going to give away my secret. . .even Tim doesn't know it to this day. I never used Vaseline. . .that would take days to wash out. I used K&Y lubricating jelly. That's right—lubricating jelly, right out of the tube. I just had to suffer through the strange looks at the counter when I bought it. It's water soluble, and rinses out almost instantly.

"How do you get the grease out of your hair so easily, Dando?" Tim was particularly fond of this alias of mine, which I had stolen from the book *Dando Shaft. . .Everyman's Millionaire*. Tim washed his hair for a third time, and still he would have qualified as a decent bet for exploratory drilling by Texaco.

"Fate and timing, my friend."

"Blow it out your ass."

"Well, all right, but I have no idea why you'd want me to do that in your apartment. I wouldn't smoke too close to that head of hair of yours, oil fires are hard to put out. I think Red Adair is in the Middle East right now, so you would just have to burn for days, until he could get here."

We were able to dodge discovery with grease because the service has a time honored devotion to the redneck look. The closer you came to Johnny Cash, the better your chances for promotion. This was strictly limited to the enlisted ranks, the officers had Perry Como. . .except my father who preferred Jackie Gleason. In my estimation, Perry Como officers were promoted by more than ten to one over Jackie Gleason officers.

"3.1 inches. . ."

"3.01 inches. . ."

"Damn."

Tim was becoming more desperate. If only he could bring some attention to my hair without bringing attention to his own. . .

"I think Dando's collar is looking a little frayed. . .," he said while passing Lieutenant Corker's desk. ". . .no. . .I'm wrong. It must be the hair that's hanging over it just made it look that way."

Lieutenant Corker didn't look up.

"Damn."

"3.25 inches. . ."

"3.2 inches. . ."

"Damn."

Tim took to strolling by the lieutenant's desk every day. "I think Dando's hat is riding a little high, don't you, Lieutenant? Maybe his head is getting a little bigger. No. . .I'm wrong again. . .must be that pompadour he's got stuffed under it."

Lieutenant Corker took a memo from the in basket, stamped it with the date, then placed it in the out basket without looking at it, or looking up. . .work, work, work.

"Damn."

"3.75 inches. . ."

"3.40 inches. . ."

"Damn!"

Tim again strolled by the lieutenant's desk. "I was re-reading Robert E. Lee's farewell to the troops last night, Lieutenant, and noticed that Dando is starting to resemble some of those Civil War hair styles."

"What was that?"

"Robert E. Lee's farewell to the troops?"

"What about. . .say. . .isn't your hair getting a little long?"

"What!?"

"I think it's time for a haircut."

"What!?"

"Let's you and I visit the barber. I need one myself." He was right, I could see that at least one hair was actually touching an ear. He dragged Tim away to the barbershop screaming. . .

"Check Dando's pockets for Pomade! He doesn't even like Perry Como!"

The sound of Perry Como's name brought Lieutenant Corker to a stop. He looked over at me.

"You need a haircut too."

"Yes!" yelled Tim, still clutched in the lieutenant's grip.

"Get one by tomorrow."

"What!?" screamed Tim.

They left with Tim still in the lieutenant's clutches.

I went to an off-base barber who was knowledgeable of the Hair War Standards of '68. I waited behind two Perry Como's and one Johnny Cash.

"Trim anything over 2.15 inches," I said.

He pulled out his finely scaled flight-line mechanic's ruler and proceeded to go to work.

I had just entered the building early the next morning.

"Did you see Tim?"

"No, what happened?"

"They white walled him."

"No!"

"Yes! He's under sedation."

Lieutenant Corker passed by me on the way to check on Tim, and looked at my hair.

"All right. . .barely."

Tim returned the next day.

"2.15 inches. . ."

"0 inches. . ."

"Damn."

★   ★   ★

TIM PUT HIMSELF in hock up to his eyeballs to get an MGB, and consequently, we never made it anywhere we tried to go. To the relief of everyone involved, it expired in a pall of smoke one summer day while approaching a stop sign. It was one of those "What's that noise Tim?" moments, and before he could get his mouth open there was a shudder, a groan, a meltdown, and we turned into an MGB glider.

"Well, this stop sign surely is prophetic, don't you think?"

"Shut up."

The barracks parking lot had the entire spectrum of Cars Of The Service. And looking at them you could get a sense of some of their owners. . .Hopeful. . .Foolish. . .Practical. . .Broke. . .Gambler. . .Joker. . .Boob . . .Pigeon. . .Handsome. That last one was me.

At one time or another I had been in them all, and at one time or another, been a glider in them all. There was Jeff's '55 Ford Fairlane. The A-frame fell out while making a left turn at a traffic light at Buckroe Beach. His was the worst kind of glider, it didn't even make it to the side of the road, and you had to get out and push it off the street. He was Broke and his choice was strictly determined by cash, he paid a hundred bucks for it. . .making him Boob as well.

We had Deluded. His father didn't want him in the Broke category, so he offered to buy him a car. Deluded wanted one like Tim's, but his father laughed and said no sports cars. . .or no money. So he bought a Ford Cortina. This is an English Ford. Then Deluded proceeded to take it down to the speed shop and load it up with gauges, wire wheels, chrome engine parts, speed shifters, and anything else he could lay his hands on including a two-way radio. The inside was crammed full with all the new parts. A microphone and its cord hung down in the front passenger's face, and the fifty new dashboard gauges would blind you at night. He only forget one thing as he turned into a Cortina Glider. . .it was an English Ford.

"Ten-four good buddy. . .static. . .everything's gone quiet. . .static
. . . losing altitude fast. . .send in the pit crews. "

Then we had Pat's '55 Chevy. With his pegged pants and slicked-back hair, only a '55 Chevy would do for Pat. When he said yes to that fat, cigar smoking salesman's first price of a thousand dollars for a beat up Bel Air convertible, the cigar fell out of fatboy's mouth and landed in his shoe. Pat was Pigeon. The car never made it through the first month. Along the D.C. beltway it began a nauseating death lurch. First it would lose all its speed, then roar back, then lose it again and then roar back. . .

"Help!" I screamed.

Car loses speed.

"We can make it," he said.

Roars back.

"I don't want to!"

Loses it.

"This is going to go away."

Roars back.

"Please, I really don't mind pushing."

Loses it.

"Think of it as a rodeo."

Roars back.

"When's it going to go away?"

Loses it. . .and doesn't roar back.

"Right now."

We glided to the shoulder and got out. Opening the hood revealed gasoline pouring out the side of the carburetor and onto the hot manifold.

"Is that a new design?"

"Quick, get away from it!"

We jumped off the shoulder and rolled down the embankment. The gasoline softly ignited. No big explosion or parts of a '55 Chevy flying past us. Just the soft frruuummmmmppppp of gasoline going up in flame. The car was completely engulfed in minutes. Fire trucks arrived in time to douse the trunk. When it was all over, there sat a blackened Bel Air shell with a nice trunk lid.

"Well, at least we didn't have to push."

We had Ted's '58 Chevy with the 60/40 split reclin-o-matic front bench seat. American car bench seats of the period didn't recline and weren't split. Ted's was the first. I believe he's responsible for the modern-day option, which allows you to select the amount of recline. Ted's prototype operated on the potluck principal. The entire roof liner came down on us one day, like a collapsing tent, while driving across the base. We looked like a scene from the movie *The Blob*, as we struggled to push it off of us and to stay on the road. The auto manufacturers haven't picked up this option.

Then there was Fred's Austin-Healy. Its front wheel came off as he was pulling out of the barracks parking lot. It rolled right by three of us as we sat watching from the curb. The wheel rolled all the way to the mess hall, then disappeared down the open door of a loading shoot.

"And fuck you too," yelled Fred, sitting there with his front axle impaled into the asphalt.

"There's another one we won't have to push," we said.

"What'd you think the boys in the mess hall are going to make out of that?"

"I expect they've seen it before."

Bob pulled in with his '54 Ford, beating his own darkness curfew by scant minutes, for he had neither working interior nor exterior lights.

"This is kind of like a car ghetto, you know."

"Why, yes, I do know."

Jim's car actually ran pretty well, even though he had hit fifty thousand miles without a tune-up. . .or an oil change. He probably would have won the most reliable award if he hadn't driven onto an island highway divider. Truthfully, it wasn't really his fault. It was very foggy, and we all had to look out the side windows searching for some part of the roadway. The tip of the island glided silently underneath and began spreading out without being noticed while we continued to search for the side of the road.

"Hey, I think I see it!"

"What's it doing way over there?"

Sccrruuuunnnncchhhhhhh.

Nobody won the most reliable award.

We also had a dry-weather fleet. These were mostly English cars where electric systems quit when the moisture level rose above that of the Mojave Desert.

Frank owned a piss-yellow Karmann-Ghia, with the brakes-optional feature. There must have been some miscommunication between the Germans and the Italians on this one. When he got in, he would test the brakes to see if the option was in effect that day. It was all right though, Frank was a master at planning the brakes-optional route.

Then there was my own '59 Chevy, with its see-through floorboards. It was impervious to wet weather, except for the spray coming up off the road, through the floor, and providing a refreshing facial mist. But nothing really phased me. . .I was a veteran of the DKW.

This all became so familiar that I could tell in the first five minutes of looking at a car if there was even the smallest glimmer of hope that we would make it to where we were going. There has never been another collection in my life quite like the Cars Of The Service. I look back on most of it fondly now, but there's only so much fondness one can have for. . .

"Come on, get out and walk."

Which is better than. . .

"Come on, get out and push."

★   ★   ★

LANGLEY WAS RELATIVELY close to D.C., and I frequently went home on the weekends. Earle drove over from the University of Maryland for a visit. He came in his Mercedes. I had advised him to buy a Mustang. They had just come out, were fairly cheap, and seemed to be a cross between a sports car and a real car. Real cars are important to have, since they don't break down.

Naturally, Earle ignored my advice completely, since, in his world, real cars were meaningless. Image cars were everything for an entrepreneur. Since Earle was in college, the Image Mercedes he could afford had come over on the Mayflower, and been forgotten in a cow barn until being turned over to the dealer. However, it did pass Earle's rigorous inspection, which meant the radio still worked, and he bought it. . .Earle could have qualified as both Pigeon and Boob.

We were on our way to go canoeing on the Potomac. . .talk about not having anything to do. I slipped into the front seat, worn smooth by the many moons that had slipped across it before me. My butt settled down. . . down to about an inch from the floor, and my knees were just slightly above my head. This position impeded my job of tuning the radio, for which I had much prior experience.

"Earle, I can't reach the radio from down here."

"What's that? I can't hear you. Sounds like you're in a canyon."

"I can't speak any louder, my lungs are being crushed."

"What?"

"My lungs. . .I can't breathe. . ."

"Can't hear you. . ."

"Air. . .help me."

Instead he drove away as my butt settled closer to the floor, and I peered out between my thighs at the dashboard. It was a medical impossibility to assume the position I was now in.

"Help. . .," I said.

"What's wrong with you, and why are you down there like that? You're ruining my seat."

"There's a seat in here?"

"What are you talking about? Of course there's a seat there."

"No. . .no there's not. What I think you've got here is a toilet bowl. . .without the toilet seat. I sat in one of those before, and this is just what it felt like."

He helped me out and I sat on the rim gasping for breath.

"Thanks, I almost blacked out there."

I could finally see over the dash. Everyone was passing us.

"Why are we going so slow?"

"Not all of the gears are working yet."

"Yet? Are you expecting that they will?"

"When the transmission gets fixed."

"What gear are we in?"

"Second."

I looked over at the speedometer. We were doing thirty-five miles per hour on the D.C. beltway. Earle seemed oblivious to everyone and just waved at all the drivers that honked their horns and screamed obscenities at him.

"Thank you, Madam," he would say, as they offered themselves to him as they passed us. This was Earle's interpretation.

"Earle, I don't think that 'fuck you' is a sexual overture."

"What else could it be?"

I didn't have the energy to argue, since I was balanced on the rim of the seat with my face pushed up against the dashboard. All in all, an improvement over the toilet bowl without a seat position. Soon, we were off the beltway and on the city streets. Just past the Kennedy Center, we parked at a canoe rental place. Steve Monday was there waiting for us.

"Where have you guys been?"

"Just how fast do you think a two-speed Mercedes with toilet bowl seats can go?"

"What!? . . ."

Earle locked the car. I assumed this was a joke.

"Are you afraid somebody's going to put something in it?"

Steve was also a friend from Bremerhaven. His sister Donna was the thinnest girl I had ever seen. She was so thin that she could have actually been there with us now.

"Is Donna here?"

I carefully moved my hands through the air, probing for her presence.

"Am I getting close? Hotter? Colder?"

"Shut up."

"Let's get the canoe," said Earle.

Off we went, Lewis and Clark and Steve on the Potomac. Earle was at the front, I was at the rear and Steve was relaxing in the middle. The water was a nice shade of polluted brown, and I was enjoying the various chemicals and sludge odors wafting up on this summer day. I wondered if it was corrosive enough to actually eat through the bottom of the boat before we could get the canoe back. We quickly mastered the paddling technique, and glided silently along the river.

As we crossed under Memorial Bridge, a small beach area appeared along the shoreline. Here we parked, had a smoke and lay out in the sun. Earle wandered off to look around, returning out of breath and excited.

"Girls!"

"Where?!"

"Coming this way."

He was followed shortly by two girls in very skimpy bikinis, the best kind. They set out some beach towels and animatedly talked with each other in a foreign language.

"French," I said.

"How do you know?"

"I don't, but I'm going with French. What would you like them to be?"

"French is good."

"Yeah," said Steve.

"Should we talk to them?" Earle looked like he was ready to get up and go over there.

"And what language will you be using?" I asked.

"English is my only choice. . .and a little German."

"Let's hear your German."

"Herr Ober, ein bier."

"That's it?"

"No."

"What else you got?"

"Herr Ober, zwei bier."

"I can order up to ten beers," offered Steve.

"Well, I've got more German than that. I can order up to a hundred beers. . .and tell them to take off their nylons," I replied.

"I know. And let's not forget about getting a menu. . .that's how you got on the baseball team. However, I'm not discounting the value of telling them to take off their nylons."

They spread lotion on each other as we looked on. They seemed delighted to have us watch them, and we were delighted to oblige. Earle's tongue began to hang out of his mouth, saliva rolling off like Pavlov's dog.

"Let's go before you get sand on your tongue. Nothing's going to happen here anyway." We stood up. "You know, Earle. If you could get your tongue to lick an eyebrow instead of just having drool run off it. . ."

"Whose eyebrow?"

". . .yours. I don't think anyone is interested in seeing you lick someone else's eyebrow. If you could lick your own eyebrow, then we'd have a chance."

"You mean, I'd have a chance."

"You wouldn't share with your buddies?"

"What buddies?"

"Us."

"Where?"

Earle Barbarino.

As we rose up, not a word was spoken. Nothing had to be said, we all knew exactly what to do. Our chests were thrust forward, our stomachs tight, our biceps flexed, as we walked stiff legged with taut calf muscles to the canoe. The three-man Olympic Speed Canoe Team was ready to return to training for their middle distance event. Silently, we flipped the canoe into the water, displaying incredible strength and finesse. The two Frenchettes stopped applying their lotion and watched, enraptured by the big, strong American Olympians preparing to depart.

The canoe was a toy in our hands. We pushed off from shore with breathtaking power. Then, in masterful unison, we dug the paddles into the water and stroked forward. The canoe shot through the water with incredible force. This was a team to be reckoned with. . .a contender. The Frenchettes' eyes were wide with admiration. . .and desire. The canoe tipped slightly, enough for some water to enter and soak Steve, but he said nothing in his resolute Olympian pose. As the coxswain, I was about to inform the forward Olympian that we should be paddling on opposite sides, but was unable to pass on the message before another enormous Olympian paddle stroke.

Then we disappeared. The world went brown.

"Where. . .blub. . .could. . .blub. . .this. . .blub. . .be?" I wondered out loud.

Olympian capsize.

I stood up, the paddle still in my hands. Earle was floundering in deeper water. Steve had taken to what looked like bobbing for apples. In this case, he was bobbing for wallets and cigarettes. The canoe, still capsized, returned to the shore. The Frenchettes came down and pulled it onto the beach.

"Your canoe, Monsieur."

Later, as I sat in the toilet bowl seat of Earle's Mercedes, we tried to salvage a little dignity by pretending it never happened. The radio was blaring and we sat silently watching the road. Well, I was actually watching the dashboard, not being high enough to see much of the road. Suddenly, there came clanking noises, muffled at first, but growing louder quickly, until the clamor began competing with the radio.

"What is that?" asked Earle.

Then, every light on the dashboard came on, and we turned into a Mercedes glider. The Olympic Speed Canoe Team's final humiliation. We coasted to a stop on the shoulder, and just sat there for a moment. Finally Earl spoke.

"I can't believe how fast we went over."

"Like a whirling dervish," I said. "I blame France."

BEAM ME HOME, I'VE HAD ENOUGH

MY SISTER WAS FINISHING a college summer session around the time the Olympic Canoe Team collided with the French whirling dervish, and she needed a ride home. I offered her my services, something for which she still blames me.

"Hasn't she seen your car?" the fellow members of Cars Of The Service asked.

"Yes."

"What's the answer. . .yes, she has, or yes, she hasn't?"

"Yes."

She had violated a rule of thumb, and probably all of the adjacent digits as well. . .if you can't afford a car, chances are very good that your brother can't either.

I took my black '59 Chevrolet Impala, Detroit's final statement on fins, up to Connecticut. Most things had stopped working, no radio, no emergency brake, a hole in the floorboards that allowed a fairly unobstructed view of the highway rolling along underneath. To start it, I would short out the contacts on the solenoid with a screwdriver, which conveniently hung from my glove compartment. The latch had ceased to function, and the door refused to stay closed. The light inside burned continuously. I would have removed the bulb, but since it was the only interior light that actually worked, I felt obligated to leave it alone.

All in all, she was a real Babemobile, a charter member of Cars Of The Service.

I had just replaced the engine. The first one had a nasty habit of losing all of its oil. This would only happen on deserted stretches of an unknown highway. More oil had been sprayed on the road during her short life than Venezuela has proven reserves. I appropriated a small block V8 from a buddy of mine who had stopped his car on a dime. Unfortunately, the dime was lying behind a telephone pole. His engine survived unscathed. This little beauty was quickly spirited away and was now wallowing under my hood. The changeover had resulted in a gap of about one foot between the radiator and the engine fan.

"She needs a fan shroud," said the mechanic.

"How much? And what is it?"

"Twenty-five dollars. It's a fan shroud."

"Didn't anyone ever tell you that you can't define a word with the word?"

"What? . . ."

"Let me think about it."

Twenty-five bucks was serious money for a GI. Through the winter and spring, I never thought about The Gap. By that summer, I forgot I had The Gap.

I arrived in the early afternoon at the house my sister was sharing with two other girls. It was in a city neighborhood of Hartford, and I parked in a garage behind the house. When I walked in the front door a small brown dog ran underneath a chair and began an incessant series of growls, snarls, and bared teeth. I ignored this obvious fateful warning.

That night, I washed out the K&Y and unfurled my hair. I was busy romancing one of my sister's roommates, who was so impressed by the Babemobile that she actually wanted to sit in it. The romancing didn't get very far. I got drunk, barfed. . .which took the blush right off the rose. . .and then wilted it, and also filled the car with a fragrance the pine-scent mirror hangtag couldn't handle. Unknowingly, the car had been kicked out of gear during the scramble to abandon it.

"Sorry about pushing you out of the way like that," I said to Marcella's roommate's prone body lying on the back lawn.

"I think you broke my nose," she replied between gasps for air.

"Actually, that may be beneficial."

Weather forecast for tomorrow—very hot. I ignored all these fateful warnings.

★   ★   ★

IN THE MORNING, as we walked out the back door, my car began to exit the garage. . .without a driver. I leapt off the porch, flinging my sister's belongings onto the lawn, and ran for my fleeing auto.

"Hey, my stuff!"

"Hey, my car!"

I was able to jump into the front seat and hit the brakes before my car went crashing into the street traffic. Sometimes emergency brakes are nice to have. What if that had happened during the night? There would have been fins everywhere.

"What's wrong with your car?" yelled my sister.

"It's a much shorter list to find something right with my car. . .shorter, but a futile gesture. Let's see, I was in it last night. . .there were people making out. . .a hand was sliding along someone's leg. . .whose leg was that. . .whose hand. . .could they have been from the same person?"

"Please, spare me the details."

". . .a foot pushing against the floor shift. . .barfing. . ."

"Please tell me not in the car."

"Emergency exit. . .foot crashing against a floor shift. . . foot crashing against a floor shift. . .should that be in there?" I mused.

"I can't believe your car waited until now. It's almost enough to make you believe in God."

"Almost, but then again, God has provided you with the Babemobile for your ride home."

"Babemobile?"

"Yes. . .Babemobile."

I was able to ignore this fateful warning.

We finished packing up. The trunk and backseat were now loaded with my sister's belongings.

The early morning was peaceful as we cruised at our assigned altitude of zero feet. I liked to fantasize about piloting an airplane whenever I drove the Babemobile, and what else was one to do considering the size of those fins. . .and, after all, I was in the air force.

The temperature started to rise as we headed into the midmorning highway traffic. It was the beginning of the hottest day of the summer. It was starting to get stuffy in the car.

"Turn on the air conditioner," she said, totally serious. Ah, youth.

"Certainly," I replied.

I grabbed a convenient shoebox lid and fanned the air her way.

"Feeling cooler?"

"No air conditioning?"

"Well, that depends on what you consider to be air conditioning."

"Instant cold air at the push of a button."

"Instant. . .button. . .hmmmmm."

"And the answer would be?"

"The answer would be. . .no. But I find it delightfully refreshing that you would actually think this car had air conditioning. . .and thinking about it is as close to delightfully refreshing as it's gonna get in here."

We both ignored this fateful warning.

It was now miserably hot. I had been watching the temperature gauge rise steadily. She started to overheat. . .the car, that is. The needle had passed into the border of the red zone. The Gap was back as a full-fledged Cars Of The Service option. I was left with no choice. I turned on the heater.

For a few peaceful moments, the last of the peaceful moments, my sister didn't notice what I had done. When she started to feel the hot air blowing at her feet, she didn't have any trouble figuring it out.

"Aaarrggghhh!? What are you doing! Are you crazy!?"

"What are you yelling about, this is a standard practice with Cars Of The Service. We're overheating. . .this is the only way I can cool down the engine."

"I went along with no air conditioning, but you can't be serious about this!"

Explaining was fruitless. I no longer thought it was a plausible thing to do myself.

She wasn't really interested in an explanation anyway. That whole What are you doing? and Are you crazy? turned out to be rhetorical. The air coming out of the heater was beginning to melt the plastic snaps on my sandals. My foot was turning red where the scorching air was blasting across it.

"I need something to block the air from my foot," I said.

"Try your head."

"Interesting concept. . . and something that was actually possible in the front seat of Earle's Mercedes. . .come on. . .look around for something."

She rummaged around in the backseat.

"This really does work, this will cool. . .," I continued, figuring a good explanation always helps things.

"I don't give a damn!"

Explanations aren't what they're cracked up to be. . .even good ones.

"I don't care if it'll cure cancer! It's a hundred degrees outside, and you turn on the heater!" She slumped back in her seat. "Here!" She threw the shoebox lid at me. "Your air conditioner."

I drove along holding the wheel with one hand, bending down and positioning the lid with the other. I wasn't going to risk asking for her help. I needed that lid blocking the heater's air, not shoved up my ass.

My sister was wilting, the sweat matted her hair against her forehead. The air was becoming uncomfortable to breathe. I have no idea what the temperature was in that car, but my clothes were becoming a looser fit by the minute.

"Are you sure this really helps?" she asked while lifting her matted hair and fanning herself with her own shoebox lid air conditioner.

"Well, if you had bothered to listen to my explanation, you would know it does. Do you think I'm enjoying this? I'm cooking my foot, I've got sweat pouring into my eyes, and I'm stuck to this seat."

Another mile.

"I've never heard of this. It sounds crazy."

Another mile.

"Where'd you hear of this?"

Another mile.

"I don't think this does any good."

"Hang on, it helps to fantasize you're driving on the surface of the sun."

"I fail to see the difference. God. . ." She sounded demoralized. "I'm thirsty. . .I need a Coke. I need a lot of Cokes."

She was getting delirious.

"I can't. . .," I started to say.

"I will have to kill you if I don't get, at least, a Coke." She was serious. About the Cokes. . .and the killing.

"If I. . ."

"Either a Coke or you're dead. . ."

Her hair was plastered to her head and her skin gleamed with a mixture of perspiration and body oil, as she rummaged around in the backseat to get her gun.

"All right! The next rest stop."

She turned back around, not happy and continued grumbling to herself. I took the next highway restaurant exit. I didn't pull into a parking spot, instead I rolled to a stop in front of the snack bar. I kept the engine running.

"Jump out."

"What? . . ."

"Get out! I can't shut off the engine, it'll just get hotter. I've got to keep on driving. I'll pick you up as I come back around."

She looked at me with wide eyes and open mouth, then jumped out and ran inside. I circled once around the parking lot. No sign of her. Back around once more. Still no Marcella. The heat was causing me to hallucinate. Through the rising heat waves I was sure I could see her making obscene gestures at me.

No, I'm okay, that is her, she is making obscene gestures at me. I pulled up.

"Didn't Mom tell you anything about making a spectacle of yourself?"

"Look who's talking. . .look at what you're driving."

She jumped in.

"Watch out for the shoebox lid!" I yelled.

"Shove your shoebox lid!"

So, I had been right about that.

"No thank you, it's doing a great job down where it is. I doubt it would be as effective shoved up my ass. I realize, of course, this is nowhere near as satisfying for you."

I had to wrestle one of the Cokes away from her.

"Get away! Leave my Cokes alone!"

"One. . .just one."

We shot back onto the highway. I pulled out my roasted right foot, and switched to my left. With my right leg still dangling in the air, and looking for a place to cool down, I spied her invitingly open window.

"Don't you dare . . .," she screamed.

I suppose it was a lot to ask, having my foot dangling out of her window and right in front of her nose. So I left it up in the air, dangling by the rearview mirror instead.

"Mother, what are they doing in that car?"

"Never mind, dear. He's probably taking a dancing lesson, but we should mind our own business. . .unless we see a policeman."

Another mile along the Great Sauna Highway. As we disappeared over the horizon, Marcella said. . .

"The DKW was better than this."

"There's no reason to get nasty."

The sad thing is, this wasn't the last car of mine that required turning on the heater in the summer.

★   ★   ★

IN SEPTEMBER, LIEUTENANT Corker came out of his office, a semi-annual event. I thought he was coming out to tell us he was about to go into hibernation, and to not bother him again until spring. Instead, he came over to my desk.

"Dando, your orders are here. You must have friends in high places. . .you're going to Thule."

"Tulie. . .is that something like a Tulip. . .am I going to Europe?"

"Not exactly."

"Where am I going?"

"Well, let's look at the map, shall we. . ."

He pulled down a wall map and started with his finger at Langley.

"We're here. . .aaaannnnd. . ."

His finger started up the East Coast.

". . .you are. . ."

He went through Maryland. . .Pennsylvania. . .New York . . .Vermont. . . Maine. . .Prince Edward Island. . .Lapland (home of the Lapers). . .crossed Labrador. . .sailed across Baffin Bay. . .wandered up the coast of Greenland. . .crossed the Arctic Circle. . .and kept on going.

"Hold on there, Lieutenant."

"Here we are. . .Thule."

My mouth hung down to my shoes.

"Thule?"

"Thule."

Bumfuck, Egypt.

So, I was the one going into hibernation. While Neil Armstrong was moon walking, I was learning to do the indigenous form of ice walking. . .the Thule Shuffle. A one. . .two. . .yahoo onto your ass, as I trudged across the frozen tundra of Thule Air Base, assigned to the Armed Forces Radio and Television Service. Neil got the more cozy accommodations.

For the uninitiated, the Danes named this Arctic island Greenland to entice people into believing it was nicer that Iceland. That was their travel brochure slogan. . .*NICER THAN ICELAND!* How many places even think their competition is Iceland? You soon learned not to trust the Danes. Obviously they fooled no one, because no one lived here. If you really want to know what it was like, just stick your head in a freezer. . .and leave it there.

Thule did have a lot of unique qualities, but none that anyone welcomed. The air was so dry that we took our lives in our hands just reaching for the linen. Bolts of static electricity snapped out and drew blood whenever you picked up your blanket. Changing the sheets required wearing a thick rubberized radiation suit, or at least attaching a ground wire to yourself. I had tried wrapping a copper wire around my forehead and attaching it to the heating duct. All I managed to do was get Radio Luxembourg on my back teeth (and it came in clearer than it ever did in Bremerhaven) and blow every fuse in the barracks.

We were in a constant running battle with the Arctic Dust Balls From Hell that lurked under our beds where they grew larger and stronger with each passing day. Occasional scouting patrols would briefly roll out to see what they could seize and take back to the mother ship. Pulsating lightning balls of dust roamed the hallways, daring us to try and make our beds.

We fought a pitched battle through the barracks' corridors, finally losing and ending up standing outside, holding the clean sheets that were to have gone on the beds.

We met the guys from the barracks across the street.

"What are you doing out here?"

"Laundry day. And you?"

"Same."

★   ★   ★

EVERYONE SUFFERED FROM a stubborn case of The Thule Big Eye, a sleepless condition of the Arctic and a close relative of The Thule Shuffle. You just lay there, with your eyes wide open, and with sudden insight for its name. Medication had no effect at all, unless you consider drinking yourself into a stupor a medical treatment.

"It's the dry Arctic climate," said one of the base hospital doctors.

"Naw, it's the cycling twenty-four-hour days and nights," said another.

Actually, they were baffled, but they did agree there was no cure, and they toasted to our good health.

So, as a home remedy we went to the movies. . .and got drunk, we went to the service club. . .and got drunk, we went to the gym. . .and got drunk. Pretty soon we stopped all this moving around and just got drunk.

I spent my days in the television station, preparing newscasts, editing film and working in the control room. On Saturday night, the station remained on the air until dawn. The show was named in honor of The Thule Big Eye. I was the latest in a long line of volunteers to run the station throughout the night.

It was sort of comforting being in the station all alone. Just me and the film racks. All of the hour-long programs from the previous week were repeated through the night. These were the regular network shows of that time, like *Mission Impossible*, but with all commercials deleted. They were put on film and shipped out in weekly batches from the States, arriving each Monday by air. It included movies, kids programs, news shows and the regular network programs.

I had some latitude during The Big Eye to rummage through the station's own film library. They had the *Richard Diamond* series and the entire *Twilight Zone* collection neatly filed away in the back storage cabinets.

One Saturday evening, I arrived at the station and heard someone in the control room laughing. It was Sergeant Jack Of The Long Forgotten Last Name. He wiped tears from his eyes as he sat in front of the console watching the last reel of the Saturday Night Movie, a western. His finger was poised over the start button of a tape cartridge. I watched for a while, but didn't see anything funny.

"What are you laughing at?"

He pointed at the screen.

"Watch."

I watched for a while. Nothing seemed to be happening.

"I don't see anything."

"Wait."

The scene eventually shifted to a shoot out in the dusty streets. Sergeant Jack hit the cartridge button. The sound of machine guns and exploding artillery shells went out over the air with the western. Jack cracked up again.

"The thing is. . .," Jack paused momentarily to catch his breath, "nobody notices. I've been doing this for a month and no one ever calls."

"You've been here too long, Jack."

"Ten minutes here is too long, unless you like playing in the snow. . .year round. It's a simple pleasure that suits my simple mind."

After his shift was over, and Jack had left, I rocketed up the stairs to the radio studios and recorded a cartridge of sound effects. . .cannons, planes, trains, explosions, anything and everything. He wasn't the only simpleton around here. Pretty soon I was leaning on the console with my finger on the cartridge button and tears streaming down my face.

It really wasn't much of a challenge to go unnoticed on The Big Eye, most of the audience was just getting back from taking their Thule Big Eye Medication at the clubs. Except for Jack. . .he called me.

"Stealing my schtick!?"

"I think so. . .unless schtick doesn't mean what I think it means, in which case I might have. . .or I might not have . . .depending on which one leaves me richer."

"Thank you, Senator."

We hassled it out and finally agreed on what schtick meant, and as usual, I found out I had misappropriated something again.

"Hey, then at least be inventive," said Jack.

I thought about it for a moment.

"I could get in a lot of trouble."

"What are they going to do, send you to Thule?" He cracked up at the thought.

I had a whole editing room available. So I edited. I put the intro and outro together on *Richard Diamond Private Detective*, removing the entire show.

Jack called.

"Great! Great! Everyone thinks they passed out and missed the show!"

And so it began. I spent more time in the editing room and Jack spent more time watching television on Saturday nights.

During a campsite scene in *Gunsmoke*, everyone was nervous and alert, they were far from the protection of the town and the fear of marauding Indians lurked in every shadow. Then a sound—a snapped twig on the ridge above them. They all turned with rifles at the ready, looking up at the ridge peak. A tank column quickly rumbles through the campsite jungle. The scene switches back to the *Gunsmoke* campsite, where they are now relaxed, relief on everyone's face. False alarm, they put down their rifles and turn back to the campfire. . .just another one of those pesky tank columns.

"Fantastic!" shouts Jack.

I'm getting bolder with each passing week, taking more liberties. I'm splicing different shows together like a madman. Except for Jack, the phone remains silent.

I've got Rod Serling on *Romper Room* and Perry Mason joined General Westmoreland's news conference.

My piece de resistance, I splice Captain Kangaroo in the middle of *Star Trek*. Green Jeans and Captain Kirk shared the bridge, the cabbage patch comes to the Starship Enterprise.

I was very proud of myself.

Not everyone was as proud of me, or with what was going on at Thule.

The base commander met with his staff.

"Gentlemen, I'm very concerned about the amount of alcohol consumed on this base."

"I'll drink to that. . ."

"We should remember our mission first and foremost."

"What is our mission?"

"It's. . .well, let's see. . .I know we've got one. . .I've got that somewhere. . .it's. . .I believe it's to stop a Russian invasion."

"Really?"

"And what would they be invading, sir?"

"Why, it would be this base!"

There was stunned silence.

"This base? . . ."

"Yes, and what exactly are we prepared to do to stop it? Half the base is lying around drunk, watching The Big Eye."

"Er. . .I'm pretty sure it's the whole base, sir."

"That just goes to prove my point. I think it's starting to get to me, I'm having hallucinations. I thought I saw Captain Kangaroo piloting the Enterprise."

"You may be right about that, sir. I thought I saw Marshall Dillon leading a tank attack."

"It's gotten to me too, I'm having blackout spells. I saw Richard Diamond begin, but suddenly the show was over."

"You too!? . . . I went to the infirmary."

"What'd they say?"

"Said it was the dry climate. . .or the twenty-four-hour nights. They don't know shit. . .if they did, they wouldn't have been sent to Iceland."

"Greenland."

"What's the difference?"

"Iceland is nicer."

"What we need is to get rid of some of these damn runways and build a golf course."

"Hear, hear!"

"Sir, what do you want us to do about the Russians?"

The base commander was pondering. "I'm liking this golf course idea."

At our Monday-morning station staff meeting, the lieutenant addressed us.

"Have we ever shown Captain Kangaroo on The Big Eye?"

We looked at each other with dumbstruck surprise.

"Why, no sir," was the unanimous answer.

"I didn't think so. But someone swears he saw it."

The lieutenant looks right at me.

Gulp.

"Someone just back from the clubs, sir?" I respond.

"Yes. . .the base commander. I don't expect we'll be seeing anything like that again, do you? Unless someone thinks they might like it better in Bumfuck, Egypt."

"We thought this was Bumfuck, Egypt, sir," we replied.

★   ★   ★

ONE MORNING I was shaken awake by the barracks sergeant.

"You have a phone call at the MARS station."

"What? . . . What'd I do now? Get me a lawyer."

"What are you talking about? You have a phone call at the MARS station."

"I have a phone call from Mars?"

"At the MARS station. You can get a ride there."

"I can get a ride there? . . ."

I caught a ride from the motor pool to the MARS radio station on the outskirts of the base. I sat in a small room with an operator seated next to me. He handed me the phone receiver.

"This isn't a telephone."

"Well, it ain't an ear of corn either, so what are you telling me?"

"It's a radiophone. There is no direct phone line to the States from here, but we can patch you through the MARS radio network. You have a call. . .from your mother."

"You guys weren't kidding when you said I had a phone call from Mars."

"You have to say over when you want to stop talking and want the other party to answer. . .okay? There's another radio operator handling the other end of the conversation, and it's the only way we know when to key to send."

"All right. . .whatever that means. Hello. . ."

"Say over."

"Hello. . . over."

"*When you want your son to answer you have to say over, Mrs. Allingham. . .remember?*"

"Who is that?"

"*It's the radio operator Ma'am. For your call to Greenland.*"

"I don't want a radio, I'm trying to call my son."

"*I know, Ma'am. This is the only way to call Greenland, there are no direct phone lines.*"

"Then why am I on the phone?"

"I hope you realize that we're all in for a bit of fun here," I said to my operator. "Hello. . .over," I repeated into the mouth-piece.

"They can't hear you," said my operator. "We have to wait for them to say over before you can talk again."

"You're going to have a long wait. . ."

"Mrs. Allingham. . .say hello, then over."

"What are you talking about? I want to talk to my son. . ."

"I know, but we have to start somewhere. . ."

"I don't know what you mean. . .hello? . . ."

"Say over."

"Oh, all right. . .over."

"You can talk now, but remember to say over when you're done," said my operator.

"Mom. . .what's going on? Why are you calling me? Over."

The line clicked over to their side. I heard my mother's voice. "Over?"

"Don't keep saying over, Mrs. Allingham."

"But you told me to say over. . ."

The line went back to me.

"I don't think she meant over."

The line clicked back to her.

"Why does everyone keep saying over?"

The line clicked back to me.

"Wait, Mom, listen for a second, I know that may be hard for you, but try. Can you hear what I'm saying. . . over."

Silence.

"They're waiting for you. . ."

"Who's waiting for me?"

"Your son. . ."

"Was that my son? Can I talk to him?"

"If you say over."

"We'll. . .can't you just do that for me? Can't you tell when I'm done?"

"Are you done?"

"No, I'm waiting to talk to my son."

"He's on the line."

"Then why do I keep talking to you?"

"Hello, Thule. Maybe you can help straighten this out. . .over."

"Nobody can straighten his out," I said. "Just let her say whatever she wants to say. We're only supposed to listen any-way. If we actually give her the power to say when she's over, we'll be here all night. Tell her I can't talk, I can just listen. That'll make her day. . . over."

"Sounds good to me. Mrs. Allingham. . .are you still there?"

"Yes, I am. Was that my son talking?"

"Yes, it was."

"He sounded so far away, like he was coming out of the radio."

"We've just lost their transmission, but they are still receiving, so he can hear what you're saying, so go ahead. . ."

"Son? . . . Over."

"You don't have to say over anymore."

"What? I thought you just said I had to say over after every sentence."

"Not after every. . .never mind. . .just say whatever you want to say."

"George. . .Marcella is getting married. . .over. . .and they said this would be the quickest way to get a message to you. . .over. . . although I don't know why I have to say over . . .over. . .oh, I think I just said two overs. . .over. . .oh, I did it again. . .over. . .is that going to cause a problem. . .over. . .this is so confusing. . .over. . ."

I'll just jump in here and paraphrase for everyone, no sense in all of us having to listen to this. Yes, Marcella was graduating midyear and getting married at the same time. It was an emergency, they just didn't want to miss an opportunity for a New England winter wedding. We do all our main family activities in January.

I flew home on leave. Everyone else was taking advantage of the free space-available flights on SAS and going to Copenhagen with their bags chock full of penicillin, but I was going to New Haven in January.

★   ★   ★

So, WHAT DO you think of your sister's wedding?" asked Mom.

"I'd rather have the clap in Copenhagen," I muttered.

"What?"

"It looks like a Name That Relative convention."

"Don't embarrass me."

"It's a little late to start worrying about that, and what chance do you think you have?"

"None, but try anyway. Show some restraint, and some respect for your sister, she's starting out on her own path now." I didn't know if there was sadness in her voice or relief.

"Do they know where they're going to live?"

"They're staying in Connecticut. Marcella wants to try and get her license again, and Virginia still has that ban. . ."

"Well, for once, it's a good thing I'm in Thule. I don't think they can arrest me up there."

"Oh, I think you're safe. They'll be arresting her husband from now on."

"You know, you set back the MARS radiophone operation twenty years."

"What on earth are you talking about?"

"I don't think earth had anything to do with it."

"*Over.*"

One of the bridesmaids came up to me while I was hiding from my relatives under the open bar.

"Hello, remember me?"

"Who said that? How'd you find me down here? You do look familiar."

"You came up last summer. . .and picked up your sister from school."

"Brenda. . .is that you? Brenda, did I ever tell you I was sorry about what happened out in the car?"

"Oh, I don't remember very much about that night."

"Well, in that case, nothing happened out in the car."

"I was pretty drunk. . .all I recall is my nose hurting in the morning. You didn't take advantage of me, did you?"

"No, and I'm sorry about that too. . .I was too drunk myself and passed out."

"Well, maybe you'll do better tonight."

"I don't think so. From the look of things, I'm going to be drunk again, and disinherited by two entire extended families in one evening."

There were many family volunteers to drive me back for my return flight out of the country.

★ ★ ★

I LEFT THULE exactly one year to the day after I had arrived. The only observable difference was that I had been nicely preserved. . . pickled in alcohol, frozen, and hadn't slept in a year. Eventually, I was discharged at the McQuire Air Force Base Processing Center.

"Form a line!"

These were the first and very last words I heard in the air force. I had become so good at forming a line, that I could do it all by myself. The military is serious about the quality of their formed lines, and the United States has some of the best lines of any military in the world. The end of the Soviet threat doesn't mean an easing off of line development. We all know that the Soviets have tucked away some secret line technology they can spring on us at anytime. We can't afford a line gap.

Now, a well-formed line should start from within and wind outward, and always intersect with other lines. This will effectively prevent anyone from finding the end of a line, and channels anyone in the right line into the wrong line. The military faces a day-to-day battle with the banks when it comes to lines, and it takes constant research and new techniques to maintain their lead. However, in my opinion, banks are strictly amateurish bunglers, and at least ten years behind.

Lines should also be tightly packed. Sergeants constantly tend these lines like trained sheep dogs, to make sure the ranks are nice and tight and no light shines through. It's one of the primary duties of being a sergeant, and one can build a nice little career on this alone. Once you're in one of these lines it's possible to fall asleep and just be carried along. However, that would be a fatal mistake. With all the twists and turns, you'd wake up on an airplane with orders stuffed in your shirt sending you to Bumfuck, Egypt. I know all about that, having recently returned from Bumfuck, Egypt.

The out-processing center was built during World War II, and it was a tired old building. The floors were no longer level, and the wind whipped through the ill-fitting window sills creating a nice indoor breeze, unfortunately this was January. The wood beams creaked and snapped with every step. The sound of the typewriters ricocheted off the walls, sounding like firecrackers. This may have been the desired effect, you never know with the military.

I moved slowly along in the glare of naked light bulbs until, at last, I stood in front of a bored military clerk.

"Name?"

"Allingham. . .George. George Allingham."

I was never sure how they wanted to hear it, first name last, last name first, first name first, last name last, so I just covered all the bases.

"What's it gonna be. . .Allingham George or George Allingham?"

And mostly doesn't work at all.

The clerk never looked up as he ran his finger down a list next to his typewriter.

"Serial number?"

"11566059 or 176-42-6638."

"Are you trying to be difficult?"

"Is it my fault you guys switched to social security numbers in the middle of my enlistment? Put the first one with Allingham George and the second with George Allingham. That way, at least somebody will get discharged today."

"Take this and move to the out-process line."

"I thought this was the out-process line."

"Are you trying to be funny?"

"No, believe me, I'm well aware of the service's No Humor Rule."

He held out a form without looking up. I took the paper from his hand. This triggered some kind of automatic mechanism, for he started over again.

"Name?"

I looked around for the out-processing line. And so it went. I was discharged without ever looking anyone in the eye.

Well, say good-bye to lines forever. Just let me out of here so I can go and get my license renewed at motor vehicle.

MAMMY YOKUM NEVER SMOKED POT

ON JANUARY 10, 1970, I was discharged from the service and had my first real encounter with marijuana on the very same day. A scant few hours after saying good-bye to the air force, I was home.

"Did you wipe your feet before you came upstairs? I just finished cleaning this whole house. And don't you dare sit on any good furniture with those pants."

This is my mother's standard "Welcome home" greeting.

"What's wrong with these pants, they're clean?"

This is my standard "Glad to be home" response.

"They're filthy. Go back downstairs and take them off. And don't swear."

This is my mom's standard "Would you like me to make you something to eat?" reply.

"I didn't swear. . ."

This is my standard "sure, thanks" answer.

"One day you'll have to answer to God for all your swearing."

"I swear. . .I didn't swear."

"You are so sacrilegious. One day you'll have to answer to God for being so sacrilegious."

According to my mother, the line at the pearly gates is going to be backed up, right up to the discharge center at McQuire, while I answer to God.

"You're that sacrilegious boy, with the filthy pants, aren't you?"

"Who are you going to believe, me or her?"

Behind me, the killers, the rapists, the robbers, the thieves, and congressmen will be waiting while my filthy pants get a real going over.

I retreated to my room downstairs, but didn't change my pants. These were as good as my pants ever get, but I wasn't going to tell her that, I was already in enough trouble with Heaven's Executive Branch. . .or would that be their Judicial Branch? I've tried to imagine what my mom's Heaven would be like, obviously there are no filthy pants. By all accounts, it seems everyone knows what everyone else is thinking. I don't know about you, but that would be Hell. By comparison, Earth would be Heaven. . .and wouldn't that be a kick in the ass.

I was forced to spend a goodly amount of time that afternoon sitting on the good furniture in filthy pants. It wasn't that I was trying to annoy her, I just didn't know where we kept the bad furniture.

If your mother is anything like mine, then she also knows "everybody" and "all the boys." During dinner I get to hear how everybody is dressing, and believe me everybody is not dressing like I am. Just ask all the boys.

"Everybody's wearing such nice clothes. I wish you would start wearing something decent." I also have morally decrepit clothing, sort of a matched set with filthy pants. "You used to dress so nicely. And your hair. . .all the boys look so stylish. . .and look at you."

"You don't like the way my hair looks?"

"No I don't, especially when it makes you look like this."

"Look like what?"

"Like I don't know."

Boy, have I been here before. . .you just don't even know where to start to chip away at this. "Mom, just for my own curiosity, do you see anything wrong, at all, with what you just said?"

"No."

She was unshakable.

"Well, I think if you check with all the boys, you'll find that your 'looking like I don't know' is a very shaky position. If you don't believe me, you can just ask everybody. . .or anybody."

"You are so disrespectful."

Of this she was positive. There would be no "being disrespectful like I don't know" about this.

"You look great in a crew cut," joined in my father.

My father thinks everyone looks great in a crew cut, even my sister. I'm more surprised he called it a crew cut, usually it's a "butch."

"You look great in a butch."

That's more like it.

I have a theory that Earth is actually what the Catholic Church calls purgatory, we're all here to be punished for our past and present sins. You'll find that I have a lot of other theories equally as absurd. My mom proceeded to try and prove my theory correct as she continued my torture while following me to my room.

"You used to look so nice, and dress so nice. . ."

Her voice trailed off as she went into my bedroom closet and turned on the light.

"When I think of all the money you spent on these beautiful clothes. . ."

My mother began a full-blown closet lament. This could last for hours. I silently closed the door to my room and crept upstairs.

". . .all those beautiful clothes, when I think of all the money. . ." Her voice got louder as she came upstairs behind me.

"Mom, are you going to follow me around this whole house finding things you don't like about me?"

"I think so, there are just so many things. . ."

"Does this make you happy?"

"I've never been happy."

"Well, you might've been, if you had stayed in my closet where I left you."

"George, I want to ask you a question. . .and I want you to answer me."

I can tell you right now that religion is going to get mixed up in here somewhere. It's always bad business when she starts out with "I want to ask you a question," especially if the "and I want you to answer me" amendment is attached. It means she's looking for a real answer, and I emphasize "real answer," because often mothers are not looking for a real answer. The truth can sometimes just cause everyone a lot of unnecessary indigestion and confusion. If your mother doesn't preface a question with "I want to ask you a question," then you're free to answer with practically anything. . .without any repercussions, and it's all perfectly legal. It will stand up in any Parental Court in the land. It's as ironclad as "looking like I don't know." And she can legally ignore your answer, if it suits her purpose to do so. Mothers are forever asking their daughters if they are still virgins and they never start out with "I want to ask you a question. . ." So the daughters routinely lie, and everyone's happy.

"Sit down."

My mother motioned to the kitchen table and sat across from me.

"I just left here," I said.

"Please."

Well, not only has she asked for a real answer, but we are going straight into the home version of Jeopardy. We sat at the Family Interrogation and Binding Arbitration Table. This is about the highest level of serious business that can be achieved in the home.

"Okay, what is it?"

"Are you still a virgin. . .oops. . .sorry. . .wrong list. Church. . .," she started.

"A Christian-era building of worship?"

"Your answer must be in the form of a question."

That gets me every time.

"Why would you ask me this?"

"I haven't asked you anything yet. . ."

"I know where you're going. . ."

"George, I know you're old enough to make your own decisions. . ."

"Really? When did this happen?"

". . .but some things are very important to a mother."

"Well, I see at least you're still ignoring me."

"Do you go to church?"

Backed into the proverbial corner.

"Church? . . ." replied Vinnie.

"Are you still a Catholic?"

"Figuratively or literally?"

"What would be the difference?"

"I don't know, but I'm hoping I can qualify for one of them."

Real answers and religion. . .how much worse can it get? I fully realized she had invoked the preemptive "I want to ask you a question" declaration, but you have to ask yourself if a truthful answer would really do anyone any good at all. Do you think she really wants to know the truth?

"Yes, I am still a catholic, with a small 'c'."

So, I bent the real answer rule with a semitruth. . .unless someone wished to dispute my qualifications for small 'c' catholic. I might have lost in Parental Court, but you don't need to be Einstein to know what's best here, and besides, I didn't want to be branded a heretic. . .she was already calling me a heathen.

"I know you're lying."

"I can't even be a small 'c' catholic? How do you know I'm lying?"

"I can tell from just looking at you."

An amazing turnaround from "looking like I don't know."

"I really can't see the purpose of any of this, Mom."

"I pray for you every Sunday."

"Well, I guess I should thank you for that."

"You should talk to a priest."

I slumped in defeat in my kitchen interrogation chair.

"Does this mean you've already got one here?"

"One day you'll need the church. . .and you'll be sorry you didn't listen to me."

I committed a breach of family interrogation etiquette and left the kitchen before the inquisition was officially declared over. I escaped once again to my room. This time she didn't follow.

THAT EVENING, I was reunited with my friend Tim. We were stopped in front of a secluded home, well back from the main road. We sat in my car, watching the house like thieves in the night. It was quiet and I couldn't see any lights on.

"Hmmm. Looks like my kind of place, a dark house on a dark street. You know, my mother just finished telling me that there would be a time when I would need the church. I think it's here."

Tim got out of the car and walked around the side of the house to a patio in the back. There was a cellar door to one side. He knocked, but didn't wait for an answer. Tim opened the door and walked inside.

It was a small room with a dim light in the corner barely casting a shadow. There were maybe six or so people sitting on the floor, and the air was filled with a distinctive smell. I had never been around marijuana before, but I was fairly sure this was it.

I say that I had never been around marijuana, but that's not quite true. I had a blind date with a nervous girl years before, in '68, right before I left for Thule. Sitting there, in a bar in Georgetown, she fidgeted in her chair and constantly looked around, like she was on the run. . .or had the runs. After an hour of watching this I started nervously looking around myself.

"Who are we looking for?" I asked.

"You know, I'm really not very comfortable," she said.

"Who would be, after erasing half your butt from swiveling around in a wood chair all night. . .and me with an Irish ass."

"It's true. I don't fit in well."

"You're not going to tell me you're out on supervised leave, are you?"

"I don't think so."

"I'd feel better if you were a little more positive about that."

"I'm not sure what you're talking about."

"Well, don't look at me, because I don't know what I'm talking about either."

"What's your name again, I seem to have forgotten it?"

"I'm not surprised. Actually it's better if you don't know it."

"Why?"

"There are probably a lot of legal reasons, but not being a lawyer I don't know what they are. . .I just don't feel like having any surprises pulled on me in court."

"I think we're back to where I don't know what you're talking about. . ."

"Have you noticed that the best sounding names are one or two syllables, and are both first names? Like Jesse James, James Dean, Carey Grant. . ."

"What's this have to do with your name?" She was really spinning around in that chair now. "Don't you want me to know your name?"

"Is George one or two syllables? It doesn't matter, because it lasts longer than three-syllable names anyway. . ."

"So, your name is George?"

". . .you get trapped in elongation, and if you've ever been elongated. . .well, enough said. . ."

"What time is it? . . ."

". . .it's a long road to that last syllable, if there really is a last syllable. Georgy is actually a lot quicker, but please, don't I have enough problems being identified with Porgy already?"

"Stop! I'll do anything if you'll just stop. All she asked was your name," pleaded Tim. "You're the one that's out on supervised leave."

"This is just polite conversation, Tim."

"No it's not. . .conversation means someone else gets a chance to talk."

"If it's such a problem, then go ahead and change it. . .I change my name all the time. I think you should be Chamlers."

"Tonight?"

"Yes."

"Okay."

"I think you both need help," said Tim.

"And I'll be Felicia," said Felicia.

"Am I still Chamlers?"

"Do you want to know why I'm nervous?"

"Go ahead. But I'm not giving up Chamlers."

"I have a problem with public restrooms," said Felicia.

I didn't say anything. "I'm sorry, did I hear that right?"

"I'm self-conscious about going to the bathroom in public."

"Maybe you should try closing the door."

"No, that's not what I mean."

"Well, it's what I mean. Remember the johns in basic training? . . ."

"Is this more of your polite dinner conversation?" asked Tim.

". . .doors? Christ there weren't even any walls, just a line of naked commodes. What was that all about? Just imagine if you were in that bathroom, Felicia."

"Can we stick to my problem?"

"If you're going to insist on it. . .so what exactly are you self-conscious about?"

"About going to the bathroom."

"Why?"

"It bothers me that everyone knows what I'm doing in there."

"Does this have anything to do with why you never see a woman heading off to the can with a magazine under her arm?" I asked.

"You're not going to be of any help, are you. . ."

"Probably not. . .but you might want to think about taking a magazine with you. Listen, everyone has to go to the bathroom, and considering the alternative, we'd all appreciate your using it. Besides, you might have gone in there just to fix your hair, or put on some lipstick. . .or whatever else you women do in there that requires going in flocks. I assume there is a reason why you all leave together to use the john. How would we know what you were going to do in there, unless you had a magazine tucked under your arm? The only people I know who actually use a public bathroom do it strictly on the condition that their skin doesn't actually touch anything. I think you're imagining all this. Besides, a quarter of the people in here are so drunk they're peeing in their pants, so they have a lot more on their mind then where you're off to. . .and probably admire the hell out of you for actually making it to the john."

Well, she pondered this for a minute, then placed her hands in her lap, stood up, and marched off to the can.

"Do you want a magazine?" I called after her.

"I think you've had a breakthrough there, Doctor," said Tim.

"Remind me later to talk to you about this blind date."

"Will that be more of your polite dinner conversation, or will I get to say something? I don't know what you're complaining about, you seem made for each other, Chamlers."

Later in the car Felicia wanted to reward me for helping her and asked, "Do you smoke?"

Now I had been smoking cigarettes all night, and I thought it was pretty strange that she was asking, but you know Felicia. I prepared myself for a new name and reached into my pocket and pulled out my cigarettes. "Yes, would you like one?"

"No," she said. Then she asked again, "Do you smoke?"

I love a good mystery. . .usually. I touched my shirt pocket lightly.

"Yes."

"No," she said.

A tick began to develop in my left eye. "Listen, I was a lot better with the public bathroom thing. I'm missing something here."

"Do you smoke pot?"

Pot! Felicia smokes pot! Well. . .I guess that's not much of a surprise. What a dilemma. What to do! Should I lie? I don't know how to smoke pot. . .although I'm sure it's not all that complicated. I could end up looking like an asshole, which is something I'm not totally unfamiliar with, but that doesn't mean I volunteer for it.

"No, I've never smoked pot."

"Want to?"

Cornered. "No." And I ran for my life.

And that was the end of that. So you see I wasn't entirely inexperienced with marijuana. I had sat next to marijuana.

★ ★ ★

DANDO, ARE YOU in a trance? Snap out of it and follow me," beckoned Tim.

I walked carefully through the darkened room. There was a girl sitting cross-legged, smoking a pipe, and there was another. . .and another.

"*Good lord. . .a room full of Mammy Yokums,*" I thought to myself.

The girl coughed and choked and waved frantically in the air.

Tim took the pipe from her and stirred the bowl with a match and lit the pipe again. He handed it to me.

"Inhale and hold it as long as you can."

It was hot and harsh, and I had to fight back coughing. My eyes were watering, and my throat was burning. Just as I started to recover, the pipe arrived again. This time I suppressed my coughing by blasting short snorts out of my nose. Now my nose was draining and my eyes were watering. This continued for about ten minutes, until Tim put the pipe down.

"Well?" he asked.

"Do you have a towel?"

"How do you feel?"

"My nasal passages have never been clearer."

"Feel anything else?"

"I don't feel anything. . ."

"You will."

I waited and waited, but I didn't. There was a lot of giggling and hushed talking going on. I was really hoping something would happen. It had been a lot of work emptying my sinus passages onto the front of my shirt. I thought I deserved to feel something. I sat there waiting the whole night, but I was only able to psychosomatically induce my legs to fall asleep. I was sure that wasn't the desired effect. Even that, I may have faked.

★   ★   ★

THE NEXT MORNING I stopped by Tim's apartment to say good-bye before my triumphant return to college. The stairwell was littered with trash, and two bicycles that were chained to a cement column blocked the stairway to his apartment. I climbed over and knocked on the door. No one answered. I climbed back over the bikes and went around to the back of the building. Tim had a ground-floor apartment with sliding glass doors that faced a common garage area. I pulled on the handle and the door slid open. I yelled inside, but there was still no answer.

It was a typical Tim apartment. . .the Oklahoma tornado look. A scattering of newspapers, dishes, clothes, assorted unrecognizable crap, and some real crap had been strewn about the living room.

The coffee table was covered with dirty glasses, beer cans, some designer underwear, something that may have been alive at one time, and a stack of album jackets without any albums inside. Scattered on the floor was a matching set of records without jackets.

I took a beer and left a note.

Tim,
Stopped by to say good-bye. Felt something biting me. Start-
ing to feel numb. Rescued your beer from suffering a similar
fate. You can thank me later.

Dando

P.S. The penicillin in the refrigerator is ready.

CAPTAIN NEMO RETURNS

I RETURNED TO A university in the middle of a social upheaval. It was a different place from what I had known only four short years earlier. I adapted, moved in with Mike From New York, another ex-GI, got myself a job as a waiter, grew my hair, accessorized at the army-navy store, and began the semester as a fully integrated pensioner on the GI Bill.

I streamed along the sidewalks with the rest of the students, cut across the courtyards on paths worn down over the years, and from all appearances it looked like I had never left. I skirted someone handing out pamphlets in front of the social science building, then sidestepped a handbill as I entered the main hallway. This was an occupational hazard of college life in 1970.

The corridor was filled with people, some standing and others sitting with either their legs stretched out on the floor or cross-legged Indian style. The hallway was buzzing with the sounds of campus radical chic.

SDS leaflets!

Weatherman Times!

I dodged another pamphlet on the stairway to the second floor, shimmied along the wall to avoid a leaflet in the hallway, crawled on my belly to evade a petition, vaulted over an ultimatum, parried an appeal, and wound up in my classroom.

I was about halfway down the course-required reading list when I realized I was in the wrong class. They were expecting work.

Across from me was another hapless soul going down the same list. We looked at each other. . .

"Add and Drop," we said.

Add and Drop. . .it sounds like some kind of Clay People calisthenics drill, but it is actually a swap meet and commodities exchange all rolled into one. For those who know how to play, it's the Holy Grail of course scheduling. For those who don't. . .it's still the Holy Grail of course scheduling, for if you're here, then almost anything they've got is better than what you've got.

The centrally located student union ballroom held all the action. It looked, smelled, and sounded like the trading pit of the stock exchange. A long row of tables traversed the entire room. Behind each sat the solemn faces of temporary help with boxes of computer cards sitting in front of them. Placard signs rose above each table, Sociology . . .Psychology. . .Humanities. . .and so on down the row. One box of computer cards on the table contained red-bordered cards with large black box letters. . .ADD. A second box with blue borders was labeled. . .DROP. The din of speculative trading was frenzied. There were occasional screams of delight when someone hit a course selection jackpot. Here one could end up with a hotel on Boardwalk.

I slowly wandered through the crowd and kept my ears open, for valuable information was always in the air for anyone ready to listen. I kept myself inconspicuous. I nonchalantly read the school paper as I moved among the traders. I quickly scribbled down any prospective tips that sounded good, and picked up any of these Add Cards that were available. I could barter them later. I sold short on some, and went long on others.

"I've got a two o'clock Criminology. . ."

"Is that a Denfield Criminology?"

"No, it's with Dr. Perkins."

The only "Doctor" you want to see on a course schedule is the one giving the infirmary physicals.

"I'll trade a ten o'clock Psychology 101 and a nine o'clock Modern Novel for any Sociology at eleven."

"Deal. What do you have at one o'clock?"

After a couple of days of trading, I owned the B&O Railroad and had fashioned an interesting group of courses. They fit rather nicely into a midmorning schedule. Unfortunately, this rather eclectic group didn't satisfy any of the university requirements for graduation. They did, however, satisfy the U.S. government requirements to receive cash under the GI Bill. There are higher priorities.

I walked out of the student union, and crossed the campus. I walked up the hill near the cemetery to the dormitory complex known as The Towers. The central courtyard was alive with darting Frisbees and beautiful girls, their long hair and beautiful bodies outlined by the afternoon sun, their long legs and heaving breasts. . .

"Hey look out!"

Clang!

. . .And I walked right into a light pole. The courtyard went silent, the sky dimmed, the world went black, except for the shooting lights.

"Is he all right?"

"Anybody know him?"

"I think he's the new owner of the B&O Railroad."

I was terribly out of practice with Sidewalk Moaning.

I staggered through the back door of the dormitory where I was a waiter. The lounge was packed tightly with bodies pressed up against the locked doors of the dining room, waiting for lunch. Then the lock turned, the dining room door swung open, and like a drain plug being pulled, the vacuum sucked the bodies through the doorway.

I sat there eating my lunch amidst the chaos of grilled cheese missiles passing overhead. My roommate, Mike From New York, walked into the dining room.

He came over and sat down.

"Balls. This is where I'm a waiter?"

The rain of food had started to let up, and the sun could be seen through the juice-stained windows.

"Balls," he said again.

"What's the problem?"

"I must have been crazy to have listened to you."

"That's possible. I know I never listen to me."

Mike pulled out his course schedule and looked it over. "Balls."

He peered up at me. "How'd you get that dent on your forehead?"

"What forehead?"

"Never mind. Take a look at this." He handed me his course schedule. "How'd I ever get a schedule like that. . .eight o'clock across the board."

"Why don't you go into the kitchen and grab a grilled cheese, you'll feel better."

"You think I'll feel better by seeing the kitchen? Besides, I can just reach up and pull one out of the air. What do you think of my schedule?"

"Well, let's see. Hmmmmm. I don't recommend keeping this one."

"What'd you mean?"

"This is simply a university prospectus with the included proposed schedule. . .one you shall reject. Get yourself a double grilled cheese, and come with me."

"Where to?"

"You need to see the Add and Drop Concierge."

So we hopped on a couple of bikes and headed for the ballroom.

The university, in the spirit of the peace, love, dove, and tie dye of the infamous hippie era, bought a thousand bicycles in the school colors and branded with the official school crest. These were for general use. Just pick one out of any campus bike stand and ride it wherever, and leave it there for someone else. It was soon obvious that a lot of the "wherevers" weren't located on the campus, for within a few weeks it would have been easier to find a meteorite. I have seen these bikes in the Grand Teton National Park in Wyoming, and I even saw a peddler riding one on the island of Saint Marten.

Next year I'm hoping the school will buy some campus cars.

★   ★   ★

Our ongoing springtime search for a campus bicycle ended with the Cambodian invasion.

Strike! Strike! Strike!

I'm still unclear on how a student strike actually did anything constructive, and in the end it proved to not do anything at all. . .except to splatter a lot of badly painted raised fists on everything. . .buildings, banners, shirts, pants, jockey shorts, and faces. The paint companies were the only ones to make out on this deal. The only real effect I could see was failing your classes.

"I joined the strike to protest the war."

"Really? And did it have an impact?"

"It sure did! I flunked out of school."

"Well, good for you."

"Then I had to join the service so my dad wouldn't kill me."

"Not the results you expected, I would say."

"They made me an AP. . ."

I continued practicing my Sidewalk Moaning, and went to class. After all, Uncle Sam was paying me, and protesting against him seemed downright ungrateful. Then the university policy came out on striking classes. If you were passing the course and you boycotted class, you would get the credits, but no grade. So, I was wrong again, something constructive did come out of the strike. It didn't take long to realize you could keep the good grades and strike the others. I became an enthusiastic striker that very day, along with several thousand other instant radicals.

"Ah, if we could only have a strike every year," we said.

"If only. . ."

"Too much to hope for, old boy."

"There must be several other wars somewhere in the world that could use a good old-fashioned class boycott."

"One would think so."

"I believe it's our moral duty to find each and every one, and give them our full support."

"Hear. Hear."

"This is even better than the free bicycle program."

"Well. . .maybe. . ."

"I never got a free bicycle."

"Guys. . .those bicycles were just to use, you're not supposed to keep them."

"Really?"

And while we were sitting there, selectively striking our classes, four of us discussed our moral convictions of joining the march on Washington.

"I understand that in D.C. the women outnumber the men seven to one."

"What are we waiting for?" said Mike From New York.

We left that very moment. It was almost midnight, and we packed nothing but ourselves into my car and drove off for D.C.

We arrived at dawn near the campus of the University of Maryland, and Tim met us on the sidewalk outside of his apartment complex. He managed to find us a room with some empty beds.

"I need some sleep before I do anything." I lay down and was lulled to sleep by an intellectual debate among my friends on the merits of coming to D.C. . .and staying in Rooms By Tim.

"Man, this bed stinks," someone said.

"What do you mean?" Another voice.

"What'd do you mean, 'What do you mean?'"

"What do you mean by it stinks?"

"What do you think I mean?"

I fell asleep to the great figuratively or literally stinking bed debate.

★   ★   ★

Hey, wake up. We're ready to go."

The room had gotten stuffy and hot. "What time is it?"

"Almost noon."

Tim stood in the doorway. "We can park in Georgetown and walk downtown."

I stood up and took a deep breath and a stretch. "That's a long walk."

"It's the only place where we're going to find any parking."

It was warm outside, and the sun was bright.

"Where are we? On the Equator? What's the temperature? How hot is it out here?" asked Mike.

"It's in the eighties."

"Eighties!?"

I agreed with Mike, it felt a lot hotter than that. We parked on a side alley in Georgetown and walked down to M Street. The sidewalks were crowded as we moved toward the government district. The closer we came, the more the crowd of people turned into a crush of people. A flatbed truck was blowing its horn as it turned onto M Street. It was full of people waving and yelling, "Come on! Join us! Get on!"

"Great, a ride!" And I started to reach up toward the eagerly outstretched hands. Tim stopped me.

"I don't think you want to go with them."

"Why not?"

"Take a closer look."

So I did.

"So they're wearing helmets, so what. . .some of them even look good in them. I, personally, never did. I think fashion is a personal thing."

"They're Weathermen."

"A truck full of weathermen. . .in helmets. . .how absurd."

"SDS-style Weathermen."

"Ah. . .the going-to-jail-style Weathermen." I pulled my hand back. "I'll keep that. I hope you guys brought along some get-out-of-jail-free cards."

The truck moved down the street. Occasionally someone would be pulled onto the back. In the distance I could see city buses parked bumper to bumper, barricading different buildings. Behind these barricades the police and the army moved about. The human mass continued to move slowly along the sidewalk. Eventually we arrived on the grounds of the ellipse behind the White House. It was hard to make heads or tails out of what was going on. You could hear several different voices over power horns and PA systems, but nothing was very intelligible.

"We should have brought something to drink," someone said.

I looked around for a water fountain. "Come on, let's scout around, maybe we can find some water."

"The hell with water. . .let's find the women."

We made our way to Constitution Avenue, and there, parked bumper to bumper, was everything from Mr. Softie to the Good Humor man.

"Ah. . .capitalism."

"Thank God."

"Well, this is quite the picture. . .us, the White House, helmeted Weathermen. . .and Mr. Softie."

"Don't you have any moral convictions?"

There's always one in every crowd.

"Oh, good Lord, no. In fact, for the last ten years my only principle has been make the team. . .get laid, past that, well there's nothing past that. Truthfully, the make the team part was never as important."

"You mean, that's the only reason you're doing this?"

"No, I mean, that's the only reason I've ever done anything."

"Aaarrrgggggghhhh. . ."

"What are you two talking about?" asked Mike.

"Your roommate is morally bankrupt."

"Well, that's probably true, although I don't see why that has a bearing on anything."

"What about you? Do you have any moral convictions. . .a reason to be here?"

"Sure. . .get laid."

"Aaarrrgggggghhh. . ."

"What? . . ." I was incredulous that Mike wasn't required to make the team. "You didn't have to wear medieval armor suits or stand in the summer sun while someone threw leather-covered balls at you and your only protection was a piece of phallic lumber?"

"I don't think so. I'm sure I would have recalled any phallic lumber."

"Hey, there goes UCONN."

Snaking through the crowd was a group of people carrying a large hand-scrawled banner that said:

UNIV OF CONN SDS - CHAINED TO THE CAPITOL DOOR

Ah, yes. . .UCONN SDS. After the Kent State shootings, several hundred people had shown up at one of their weekly campus meetings. I left right after they came up with the idea to chain themselves to the college president's door. They were soon back down to their customary fifteen members. . .eight weird-looking guys and seven Girls Who Liked To Say Fuck. And now, they were holding a long chain aloft and imploring people to join them as they walked through the crowd.

"Gentlemen, this is the crown jewel of dumb-ass SDS ideas."

"Think they'd care for a Mr. Softie before they left?"

"I count ten, looks like they lost five more with this idea."

★   ★   ★

THE SPRING SEMESTER was a complete success. . .Uncle Sam paid me, although I never did get a bike. I went home for the summer to my parents' townhouse condominium.

When I arrived, my mother was standing in front of her house with a toilet seat in her hand.

"Ah. . .home." I parked and got out. "Mom, I'm home. If I knew you'd be out here, I would have brought along my own toilet seat."

"What? What are you talking about? I'm trying to get someone to fix this."

"So, you stand in the street and wait for a passing handyman while holding onto your toilet seat?"

"Yes. I don't have time to explain, just stay off the. . ."

"Yeah, yeah. . .I know. . .filthy pants and all."   •

Condominium life.

I entered the house and caught my reflection in the hall mirror, and stopped for a moment to check it out. My hair was matted slightly from the heat. The length was just starting to flow over my collar, and a natural part had appeared just slightly off center. The curious thing is, when I work up a sweat my hair looks great. It gets full and slightly wavy. This is usually when my mother tells me I've got my father's hair. . .I wonder how he does it? Once it's washed, the effect is gone. I've tried lots of different techniques to get the look without the sweat, but nothing seems to work. So I've resorted to doing some quick laps before picking up a date. I may stink, but my hair is perfect.

"George. . .I want to ask you a question. . ."

"Already!? . . . I've just walked in the front door. I haven't even unpacked all my filthy pants. I'm not ready for any real questions. . .or the family arbitration table. I've been to church. I've been to confession. I think pure thoughts all day. I hope that takes care of everything."

"Are you eating your vegetables?"

Vegetables. My God, I had forgotten all about my vegetables!

"Mom, you worry about the strangest things. . .and you seem to have an inexhaustible supply. My vegetables? Isn't it a little late to be asking about vegetables? Didn't we have this discussion when I was like six or seven? I believe it was in place of the sex talk, for which, by the way, I'm still waiting."

It may even have started out to be the sex talk, but Mom would naturally gravitate away from anything to do with sex. Based on my mother, it's a wonder that the Polish Catholic population has propagated at all. This is a race that obviously has never heard of make the team. . .get laid.

"No, we never did," she said.

"You mean I didn't even get the vegetable talk? Boy, I have lived a deprived childhood."

"You need your vegetables, are you eating them at school?"

"I eat them. . .if I'm sure they're really my vegetables. You know how people are about sneaking their vegetables onto your plate, and trying to make you think they're your vegetables."

"Is this one of your tricks. . .like the salad in your socks?"

"I don't care what anybody says, that sock idea was a good one."

"You have to eat vegetables. . .you know that."

"Yeah, so I've been told. . .mostly by you."

"It will give a healthy glow to your skin."

"I don't know if I'm looking for glowing skin."

"Everyone wants a healthy glow to their skin."

"Well, why didn't you say it was 'everyone' in the first place. You could have saved us all a lot of time and trouble."

"Everyone" is a close cousin to "everybody."

"Now you better listen to me, you know I'm right. Did you make your Easter Duty?"

"One inquisition at a time, please. I'm still working on 'knowing that you're right.' How can I be expected to jump from vegetables to Easter Duty just like that? . . ."

I snapped my fingers.

". . .It's impossible to make a shift like that without a seat belt. And wasn't Easter some time ago?"

"Is that a guess? Quit stalling and answer my question."

"Can you repeat it for me?"

"Did you make your Easter Duty?"

I thought it over. "Can you define Easter Duty?"

"Let's see Easter Duty. . .hmmm. . .oh, stop trying to distract me, did you or didn't you?"

"Yes, I did."

"Are you sure?"

"I thought I was."

"Well, think it over again."

I was willing to think it over again, and I was willing to lie all over again.

"Yes."

"George, you know you must go to church sometimes."

"Will you define sometimes for me?"

"Easter is very important. Do you know what Easter represents?"

"What. . .a quiz too? I hope this is a rhetorical question."

"You know you have go to church, don't you?"

"Now this one is rhetorical, right?"

"You need a haircut, you look like one of those hippie people."

"Hippie people? . . ."

"You should have it shaped, like all the boys. . ."

I picked up the yellow pages and began looking through the motel listings.

"Everyone has such lovely styled hair. . ."

"Hmmmm. So 'everyone' and 'all the boys' are in this together. . ."

I began making my own sandwich.

"That's too much mayonnaise, all that grease is bad for you."

"It's amazing you're not in some kind of sensory tilt mode right now. What are you going to say to me tomorrow? If I eat some vegetables, will you leave me alone?"

"No. You don't have any lettuce on that sandwich."

"How do you know? Have you been peeking in my sandwich?"

I poured a glass of milk and tried to retreat to my room, but I was bombarded the whole way.

"Your clothes are awful, where did you learn to dress like that?"

"I thought you taught me how to dress."

"Oh no, I didn't teach you to dress like that."

"This isn't going to end with my dressing 'like I don't know' again, is it? Are you sure you didn't teach me how to dress?"

"What? Me? I should say not!"

"You should say yes, I hate to think I had to learn everything in the backseat of a '59 Chevy."

I stuck the sandwich in my mouth.

"I trust all the good furniture has been removed from my room."

"You never had any good furniture in your room."

"Tell me about it. Remember the desk? Oh my God! It's still here! I warn you right now. . .I plan on wearing filthy pants."

"Don't be funny."

"All right, but I may be funny tomorrow."

Home has a certain consistency to it, kind of a thick molasses feel. . .once in, it's tough to get out.

★   ★   ★

THESE ARE THE times that try men's souls and these are the signs. . .No Left Turn. Somewhere in the dark past of the city of Washington, the left turn vanished. Why this happened has also been lost to history. Whatever the reason, it has been banned from the streets of D.C. In a city where it takes an hour to get across the street or across the town, you can't turn left. Well, not entirely. A little one-foot-square white sign hangs next to the traffic lights at the intersections and written on each one is. . .

> NO LEFT TURN
> Except
> 4:30 P.M. - 6:00 P.M. Mon-Fri
> 7:00 A.M. - 8:00 A.M. Sat-Sun
> Open till 10:00 Thurs
> No Turns on Holidays

I especially like the exception days and hours. That's so everyone can pile up behind one another at each intersection, trying to read the one-inch fuzzy print. Since it's practically impossible to drive through a town turning only to the right, everyone drives around it on the beltway. So should you.

My sister came down for a quick visit, to see her old high school friends and to show everyone her new Connecticut driver's license.

"My God, you did it!" they said. "What's left of the car?"

"Did your husband get arrested?" I asked.

"Very funny."

"Who's being funny?" we genuinely asked.

"Very funny," she said again.

"Who's being funny?" we genuinely asked again.

I went into the city with my sister and a friend of hers named Ruth. We managed to find the bar without needing to turn left. Ruth had red hair and was slightly chunky. She said very little the whole night.

Sitting in the bar on a hardwood seat, I balanced on the two butt bones of my Irish ass. Early in my life I wasn't aware this meant having no ass at all. I don't think anyone had an ass early in life. Then we grew up, and my friends all discovered they had one, and then began to remind me that I had seemed to have forgotten mine somewhere along the line. I wonder how people in Ireland feel about this? Do you think they know? Are suspenders an Irish invention?

My sister thought about it a lot. For a girl, not having an ass is a major disappointment. It wasn't her only one. She didn't have any tits either.

Suddenly I felt a hand on the inside of my thigh. I was reasonably sure it wasn't my sister's.

I immediately focused in on the real problem. . .getting Ruth alone. Since I had driven them both into the city, I was reasonably sure my sister expected to be driven out again.

On the drive back, Ruth sat in the middle and kept her hand pressed against the inside of my thigh. I couldn't think of a better place for it either, but having my sister along was keeping me from fully enjoying the moment, if you know what I mean. Ruth didn't seem to care about Marcella being there, but I was bothered by it. How would you like being felt up while your family looked on? Maybe in some homes it's okay, but Mama didn't raise us that way. When it came to sex, she didn't raise us at all.

I bravely carried on with my conversation in various alternating voice pitches.

Then from nowhere my sister spoke.

"Don't worry Ruth, he'll fuck you."

I guess we can say that Marcy was drunk.

"Isn't that right, Geoooooorrrrrge?"

Good and drunk.

What the hell was I supposed to say?

"Yes."

Yes was the right answer. We parked at her apartment, and went up in the elevator. . .Ruth, my sister, and me. How do I get into these situations? I didn't have any idea about what I was going to do, and could only wonder what Marcy thought she was going to do. What was Ruth going to do? You could see the fluffy cartoon caption balloons floating over each of our heads, the three of us all thinking along the same lines, all hoping for something miraculous to happen. I was silent. I believe miracles require silence.

It was Marcy who finally came up with a solution. With a couple of yawns, she stretched out on the couch with her back to us, and immediately began some improbable deep sleep rhythmic breathing. Who was going to buy this?

"I think she's asleep," said Ruth.

I spoke too soon.

"Wait until she starts to snore," I said.

"She snores?"

"She will tonight."

THE SECRET LIFE OF CLOSETS

THE SUMMER RAINS OF Washington consist of late afternoon thunderstorms. The rain comes down so hard the drops vaporize as they crash against the concrete, raising a heavy mist that manages to rise into the air even as the rains pour down and pound the street. The gutters fill almost immediately, overflow the sidewalks, and carry the day's litter down to the storm drains. All the while the thunder booms overheard and lighting flashes continually, sending everyone into the shelter of the closest doorway. They huddle there like refugees, peering out through the dense mist and curtains of rain at the other doorways, and the other groups of refugees. The city traffic comes to a halt as the cars pull over, their wipers no longer able to keep up, and seeing any car ahead becomes impossible as the world disappears into a grayish murk. Twenty minutes later it's all over and a calm returns. The air is fresh for a few precious moments, then the streets dry and the heat returns. Ten minutes later there's no sign it ever happened, and you wonder if you just dreamed it all, that it was just a hallucination brought on by the shimmering summer heat.

I called and made a date with Ruth. I wanted to see how this works without my sister along. The phone line crackled with every flash of thunder. I then whiled away the time practicing my withering sneer in front of the mirror, trying to perfect it. It's something I picked up from my brother. He had a withering sneer, which he used effectively for years. I have only been effective at practicing it for years. He would narrow his eyes and deepen his voice to a gravely doomsday pitch.

"Be gone!"

His victims cowered and shrunk away from his sight. He had hoped they would begin to slowly smolder and then melt before him. But a withering sneer is not a death ray sneer, and for my brother this meant the results were not nearly as satisfying.

"There is no God," he would say.

He felt this way because he had tried to sell his soul to the devil for a working death ray sneer, with no luck. Isn't that the way things always work out. . .the people who want to sell their soul to the devil can't get the time of day from him.

"Be gone!" I said to myself in the mirror.

"George!" yelled my mother.

"What!?"

"What are you doing down there?"

"What!? . . ."

"What!? . . ."

"What!? . . ."

"What!? . . ."

It was Vinnie Barbarino's dream conversation.

"I'm getting ready for a date."

She was down the stairs and standing next to me before the word "date" had passed my lips.

"Really?"

"How'd you do that? Did you take the underwear transporter?"

When my mother hears the word "date," something comes over her. She can't resist prying questions asked with an uncharacteristic sweetness, and she no longer even sounds like my mom. Questions which Vinnie never answers.

"Who are you going out with?" asked Loretta Young.

"What?"

"Where did you meet her?"

"Who?"

"Where are you taking her?"

"When?"

My mother has a never-ending supply of questions, and this often goes on right to my car door.

"Be gone!" I said to her.

"What's wrong with your face? I hope you don't look like this when you're out with people. I would be mortified! I don't know where you kids pick these things up. I honestly give up."

Mothers, apparently, give up dishonestly for a while, so they can finally and honestly give up.

"Be gone!"

"Is that the only thing you can say?"

I got in the car and looked at myself in the mirror. "Be gone," I said to my reflection. . .and I drove away.

★   ★   ★

I TOOK RUTH to a German bar close to my house. My proficiency with the language made it the natural choice. We sat there drinking and talking as the hurdy-gurdy polkas blared away, and the lederhosen barmaids delivered steins of beer, and brought me the mail and menus. Ruth was harboring a deep-seated suspicion that her body was the only reason I wanted to go out with her. I, of course, was prepared to say whatever it took to have her body. . .with or without a deep-seated suspicion.

"Do you only go out with me for my body?"

"No, I go out with you for sex."

"You only go out with me for sex?"

"And what's wrong with sex? Let's not discount how important it can be, I know I certainly never do. Try to imagine what life would be like without sex. . .I know my mother imagines that all the time, and do you really want to be like my mother?"

"What? . . ."

"Exactly."

Well, I don't know if this helped my cause, but it did manage to baffle her, and left her slowly shaking her head for a while. I felt this was a good sign.

"Do you only go out with me for my body?" she asked again.

"Oh, no you don't, you're not going to start this again, like we were stuck in some kind of time warp. . .I say push those Olympic torch levers and get the umbrella disk spinning so we can get on with our lives. I hope this now answers all your questions."

From the look on her face, it didn't appear to. As the night wore on and the number of empty steins began to rise, the suspicions stopped and the hand resting on my leg began.

"I'm getting drunk," she said.

Success.

"This is good," I said.

"What?"

"I said we should go."

Ruth got up from the table, listing slightly to one side. I held on to her and listed to the other side for balance. Otherwise, I would have had to carry her. Did I mention that Ruth was slightly chunky? Carrying her was out. So, we did the spastic tennis walk out of the bar. The people were stunned—who would have thought that Quasimodo had a girlfriend? We just missed the beer stein display as we careened by the tables to the visible relief of the manager.

"Helfen Sie mir bitte mit meinem Gepack," I called out.

"Nein!" he said while protecting his display.

There is never a baggage porter around when you need one.

The night air was cold, and had a sobering effect. Ruth was leaning out the car window.

"I feel sick. . .," she said.

Sobering may have been a mistake. I picked up the speed, and pulled into the parking space in front of my house.

"Why are we here?"

"I think we need to get you inside."

"Afraid I'm going to barf in your car?"

"Like you wouldn't be, if you were in my spot. . ."

"Well, you're honest. . ."

"I wouldn't count on that too much."

The house was dark. Ruth stumbled out of the car and leaned on me as I opened the front door. She steadied herself for a moment, and then slumped against the wall.

"Ssshh. . .my parents are asleep upstairs."

"Then what are we doing here?"

"They're three floors up."

"There's no one three floors up at my apartment."

"Your apartment is miles away."

"And you would like me conscious?"

"Yes. Although that's more or less a loose guideline, and I've never been much for guidelines. . .or much else that has to do with camping."

"I never know what you're talking about."

"Count yourself lucky."

I guidelined her into my room and closed the door.

"I can't see a damn thing in here," she said. "Turn on the light before I trip over something."

"Ssshh." I turned the light on.

"Aaarrrggghhhh! What's that brown thing in the corner?"

"It's a desk. Sit over here."

"Where? There aren't any chairs."

"Sit on the bed."

"I thought you said we came in here to sober up."

"I don't recall saying anything like that. What I said was I think we need to get you inside, and I'm sticking with that story."

I turned off the light and leaned her back onto the bed. She suddenly pushed me away. "What's that?"

"What?"

"Ssssh, listen. There's someone at your door. Is it Marcella?" There was someone murmuring at my door.

"Oh God. . .it's my mother, can't you recognize her murmuring? No one else murmurs like that."

"Why is she murmuring at your door?"

"I don't know."

"Maybe she'll leave."

"You don't know my mother. . .quick. . .get into the closet."

"What! . . ."

"The closet. . .get into the closet."

"What'd do you mean get into the closet? I'm not. . ."

"You have to get into the closet!"

I pushed her out of bed and she fell to the floor with a thump.

"George? . . ." called my mother.

"Great, now look what you've started. . .she's started talking. Ruth, you have to get into the closet."

Ruth stood up. "Now, I'm mad. . ."

"Just give me a minute. . ." I closed the closet door.

"You're locking me in here!?"

"I am not locking you in. . .I'm just going to close the door a little. . ."

"George what's going on in there?"

"Nothing. Just putting something in the closet." I opened my door, but blocked my mother from coming in.

"What are you doing in your closet at this time of night?"

"Sorry to trespass in your territory. Why are you suddenly talking at this time of night?"

"Why was you door locked?"

"Why are you down here checking my door?"

"Why didn't you answer me?"

"Why were you murmuring?"

"Why am I still in the closet?" came a third voice.

"Why do I hear someone else's voice?"

"Why is water clear?"

"Why are you being evasive?"

"Why can't I meet your mother?" came the third voice again.

"Why are you blocking the door?"

"Why don't dogs need toilet paper?"

And so it went for a while, trading questions, and no one giving any useful answers. After a while it got hard to keep coming up with new questions. Not for my mother mind you, but I was nearly exhausted after trying to get her to explain electricity.

She finally gave in, and went back to bed. There would be no closet lamenting for her tonight. I don't usually outlast my mother, but she failed to realize that having a naked woman in my closet could make me pretty stubborn. If you think any of this had any lasting impact on Ruth's amorous leanings, then you don't know Ruth.

"Will there always be someone from your family around?" she asked.

"Yes."

[LATER IN A DIFFERENT CLOSET]

My father, The Colonel, had returned from Germany with a console hi-fi and a car. Most everyone who was ever assigned to Germany came back with either a hi-fi or a camera or a Mercedes. We never seemed to be able to get the right brand of anything. We came back with the DKW. Our hi-fi wasn't a Grundig either, it was a Lowe Opta, or something like that.

This seemed to bother the hell out of my brother. He was entering into his right wing stage and everything was bothering him. I only became aware of this when he informed me that Walter Cronkite was a Communist. This was news to me, but my brother seemed genuinely convinced of it. He was pissed because instead of bringing back a Mercedes and a Grundig we brought back a DKW and a Lowe Opta. I, on the other hand, was pretty impressed by the stereo. It certainly beat the hell out of my Decca record player, but I didn't let on to my brother. I was sure he would just tell me Walter Cronkite owned a Lowe Opta. So, when he ranted I just gave a slow knowing nod, which seemed to satisfy him.

The Lowe Opta crapped out a few years later, as Communist stereos tend to do, and its carcass was pushed into a neglected corner of the utility room. Here it languished until I dismantled this mammoth piece of furniture. I took out the speakers and made enclosures, pulled the receiver, junked the turntable, and cut up the cabinet.

The speakers sounded pretty good in their new enclosures. Why am I telling you this? Well, one day I was sitting on a couch in front of a plywood table at Tim's apartment, and I realized the legs of the table were the two Lowe Opta speakers I had given him. They were facing the floor, which I imagine inhibited their sound projection somewhat, but they were doing a helluva job of holding up the tabletop.

It was my fault I guess, I gave them to him. His eternal pauper plight got to me, and in a weak moment I told him to take them. Stupid me, I thought he knew they were speakers.

"Tim, obviously I neglected to tell you what these wooden things holding up your table are traditionally used for."

"Christ, leave it to you to find them," replied Tim as he struck a match and lit a marijuana cigarette he was holding in his hand.

"Well, it wasn't that hard. They were either the speakers or a couple of columns from the Parthenon. So, you do know what they are?"

"It's only temporary, I'm going to put them in my room."

I heard the apartment door open.

"Tim?" A girl's voice called down the hallway. It was Gerry, a cute Chinese girl Tim had been going out with for the past year. I hadn't seen her since the Mammy Yokum Incident. She was a criminology major, and was hoping to join the FBI when she graduated. Nice kid, but I didn't know about that FBI thing. She came down the hallway and her face lit up as she recognized me.

"George!"

"Gerry. Are you still going out with Tim? I thought you had better sense than that."

"Hey!" Another voice boomed down the hallway. "Who left the front door open?"

Tim glanced at Gerry. "Did you shut the door?"

Gerry seemed surprised. "The door?"

"Yeah, the thing you go through to get in and out."

"In and out?"

"Gerry, listen. . .," I said. "I have some experience with this particular defense, and take it from me, it doesn't really work."

"Then you're not doing it right," she whispered to me.

"Never mind," said Tim.

"See."

Women. When will I learn. . .nookie changes everything.

"Who is that yelling?" I asked.

"My roommate," said Tim. "He doesn't want anyone smoking in here." Tim glanced around. "Take this joint into the closet."

"I'm not going into the closet. I don't even like being in your room," said Gerry.

Well, what goes round comes round, now it was my turn to be shoved into a closet. Tim closed the door behind us and went to talk to his roommate.

"What do you think of the closet?" asked Gerry, her arm sweeping around to show the interior.

"Not bad. I've been getting more involved with closets lately, you know. Do you think that's a sign of the times?"

"Possibly, although I can't be certain."

"Are you still majoring in criminology?"

"Yes."

"Still want to be in the FBI?"

"Yes, I'm interning there this year."

"Drug enforcement?" I asked as I passed her the joint.

Tim opened the door.

"Tim. . .glad you could join us," said Gerry as she moved over to make room. "We were just discussing closets and the FBI. . ."

"Why?"

"Well, it seemed appropriate until you showed up. What's your roommate doing?"

"He's getting ready to leave."

"George. . .George. . .George." Gerry tugged at my sleeve. "What are you doing down here?"

"Down here meaning down here in D.C., or down here in the bottom of this closet?"

"Don't confuse me."

I lit a cigarette. "It's summer, I live here, well. . .not actually in this closet. . ."

The door opened and there stood Tim's roommate. He didn't look like he was there to join us. He stared down at me.

"What are you doing in the closet?" he asked.

"I don't know, I thought we were hiding from you."

"Tim can I talk to you out here?" Tim got up and closed the door behind him. Gerry and I were once again left in the dark.

"Well Gerry, back into the darkness. Have you ever seen my impression of Ray Charles."

"No."

"You're in the middle of it."

"Wow. . .is this performance art?"

"Do you think we'll ever get out of here?"

"Who knows. . ." replied Gerry.

★   ★   ★

WE WERE EVENTUALLY paroled from Tim's closet. The next day, just before dinner, I went upstairs and wandered aimlessly around the living room, not knowing where to sit. Which was the bad furniture? How are you supposed to tell? The kitchen chairs were safe, even for filthy pants.

"You should go to a hair stylist and have your head shaped."

Not safe enough. "Not again. . ."

To this day I don't have any idea of what having your head shaped means. I know it sounds like it's something, but when you really think about it, it surely can't be.

"*I'd like my head shaped, please.*"

"*Certainly, sir. We've been waiting years for someone to come in and ask for this, please thank your mother.*"

"Mom, there isn't any such thing as head shaping."

"Of course there is, all the boys get their heads shaped."

"Ah, why didn't you tell me all the boys were doing it?"

"I've tried, but you don't listen. Everybody has their heads shaped. You need to have something done." She reached over and touched my hair. "It should be cut, and this part moved. You look old fashioned with your hair parted in the middle like that."

Her fingers were flying all over my head, whipping parts from one side to the other. My plate was being showered with dandruff flakes like they were a condiment.

"Christ parted his hair in the middle, or is that what you mean by old fashioned?"

"You leave Christ out of this. He didn't have the advantages of a hair stylist. . ."

"Really?"

". . .otherwise he would have had his head shaped."

"Oh, Lord, please help me."

"You're such a sacrilegious boy."

"So, we were a head shaping away from the last supper looking quite amusing. . .thirteen head-shaped apostles. . .or was it twelve. . .or is that a jury? Do you think the Pope will go along with this?"

"So. . .you never did make your Easter Duty, did you?"

"What? . . ."

"Thirteen apostles. . ."

"Eve, leave him alone." The Colonel speaks.

"But I was just telling him how nice. . ." And she started in again, only this time she was telling me through my father. He would have been better off to have kept out of it, because I excused myself and left the two of them to discuss my hair.

THE SUMMER OF '70 was now in full swing, and I was ready to get a summer job, and looking for a good head shaping. Where '69 was the summer of Woodstock, the summer of '70 was the summer of the Woodstock Movie. This was as close as the ten or so million people who claimed to have gone to Woodstock actually were. They saw the movie so many times that they truly believed they were there, and that the weather and crowds weren't nearly as bad or hard to endure as you might have thought. Yeah, I was able to handle three hours on a cushioned theater seat myself. I saw it a lot that summer, the theater was one of the few places that allowed filthy pants on the good furniture. Like those millions who frequented the movies, I saw it enough times to believe I was actually there as well—and gleefully pointed out myself to anyone who would listen.

"It doesn't look like you."

"Nobody looks like themselves from the back."

"Oh."

"And besides, I was shorter then."

"Oh."

"And had blonde hair."

"Oh."

BEFORE YOU CAN look for a summer job, you must get up and out of bed, one of my weak points.

"George! Get up! Breakfast is on the table!"

I have looked around the house to find out where my mother might put breakfast other than on the table, but I've never found anything.

"I'm up."

I got up and found my breakfast on the table, just as she said "When was the last time you went to confession?"

A left, a right, and an out of left field to the body. I'm down, sprawled on the canvas, down for the count.

"Stop it! You're driving me crazy. Tell me, Mom, will there be any letup at all? This is starting to feel like ten days of rain."

"This is important to me."

"What isn't? Is this more important that Easter Duty?"

"Well. . .it is related."

If you really want to test someone's faith, don't ask them about the last time they went to church, ask them about confession. You can go to church and daydream through the whole thing. I've done it for years, but not in the confessional. You have to say something in there.

I've never been comfortable with this whole owning up to your sins deal that the Catholic Church has worked out with God. I think of sins as personal, and designed to be taken to the grave. This way they can't get loose and hurt anyone. Confession has never been a catharsis for me. I take no comfort in facing a priest who wants to know all about my sins. . .in detail. . .and, like the IRS, want's to see all the receipts. I don't think this is natural, and it's been taken as a sign of a serious flaw in my faith. Although I don't know how any one flaw could stand out from so many others.

I really think that the priests just like to have a few laughs to cut through the claustrophobia of being stuck in that box for hours at a stretch. You can't tell me they don't swap a good confessional story during the sacrificial wine happy hour at the rectory. . .

"You should have heard the story I got today. . ."

There should be a conveniently posted confessional chart. Look up your sin, feel contrite, move to the penance column, multiply that times the number of occurrences, minus any papal exemptions or points you've earned. It's simple, clean, and would really clear up a lot of the congestion around the confessional booth. I've never gotten much support for this idea, but I still think it's a good one.

It wasn't long before I began to give stock sins for a stock penance. All small 'c' catholics do it.

"Bless me Father for I have sinned, my last confession was two months ago (another lie). . .I lied twice, make that thrice. . .disobeyed my mother. . .and took the Lord's name in vain once."

This seems to be the standard for the continental United States. It's the "took the Lord's name in vain" that really sells it.

"That will be three Our Fathers and three Hail Marys, my son."

When I was younger, the whole family went together. There I was, sixteen years old, and the priest was buying it. If this was all I had really done, then I should have been canonized on the spot. As I finished and exited the confessional, I could hear my father from the opposing side.

". . .*I lied twice, make that thrice. . .disobeyed my mother. . .*"

"I didn't raise you to become a heathen, you know," interjected my mother.

"No, I wouldn't expect you would. So, exactly what did you raise me to become?"

"You're getting too big for your britches young man."

Imagine finding out you're still wearing britches, and in the confessional, no less. Knowing the Catholic Church, that's probably a sin too. . .everything else is.

LAWN BOY

THE SUMMER JOB SEARCH was going slower than I had anticipated. Two weeks into it and I hadn't found anything. Something will turn up, hopefully. The summer of '70 was also the Summer Of Concerts By Groups From The Woodstock Movie. Everyone was required to go. We had tickets, but this was mere formality, since the summer of '70 was also the Summer Of *Free* Concerts By Groups From The Woodstock Movie. That depended, of course, on who you talked to. . .talk to me, I had bought tickets. The problem was, you didn't know they were free until you got there. The Woodstock generation had unilaterally declared that all music belonged to the people and was free. . .this came as a surprise to the concert promoters. They were also somewhat dismayed by the news.

I had bought tickets with Tim, my first mistake. Well, it wasn't my first mistake. If anyone is keeping track, and the confessional booth priests surely are, it was my 127th mistake of the new decade. I had closed out the sixties at 2,412. So, was on schedule to set a new record.

I still hadn't learned not to depend on Tim. But then again, I don't think our conversation had really decided anything.

Me: "I'll come over early that day."

Tim: "Whatever."

Me: "What time should we leave?"

Tim: "Whenever."

Me: "Thank you."

I drove over to his latest apartment. Tim was now renting a room in a fraternity house at the University of Maryland. He could stay there for the summer, but had to be out by the start of the fall semester. No problem, Tim rarely stayed in real apartments more than a month or two. Gerry was already there.

"Where is he?" I asked.

"I don't know. I'm looking for a clue. . ."

"I see. . .will this count as part of your interning with the FBI?"

We waited for him in his room.

Tim dumped everything into a pile on his floor until his drawers were empty and the pile on the floor was full. Then he dipped into the heap as needed, until it began heaving and throbbing. This was his own home version of the nitrogen cycle, and it provided a fertile base for the unique and unidentifiable herbage growing on his floor. Finally, Gerry washed it all and put it back in the drawers so Tim could begin the whole process again.

"My god," Tim would think. "It really does work, it not only gets clothes clean, but it puts them back into the drawers as well!"

"He might be running around naked, his nitrogen cycle pile looks full," I observed.

"Oh, he's added to his pile since you last saw it."

We sat in his room like the farmer couple from the American Gothic painting, minus the pitchfork. The pitchfork would've come in handy. We sat there until, at long last, Tim showed up. . .and he wasn't naked.

When we arrived at the music pavilion we found out that this concert had just been added to the Woodstock Free Summer Concert Performance Series. The fences were down, the gates were down, the guards were gone and so was the money we paid for the tickets. Thousands streamed over the downed fences.

We stood on the concrete walkway that circled behind the pavilion, amidst an ocean of people, with the girls sitting on our shoulders. My view was the back of someone's head.

This wasn't quite what I had expected for the evening. My shoulders sank from the weight, each quarter hour I was a quarter inch shorter. My date rested her arms on my head, until I protested that my head was sinking into my shoulders, which were now up past my ears. I could no longer hear the concert. By the time it was over, I was a stubby little deaf man. We sat in silence on the hood of the car and watched the crowd thin out. We were too tired to move.

I was content to be silent on the ride home, just driving along and feeling the cool night breeze blow through the car. I waited for my shoulders to rise back up so I wouldn't have to look through the steering wheel anymore, and would hope-

fully get to see over the top of it. Gerry and I were the only
ones awake. Up ahead there was an exit sign for Cheverly, and
the faint glow of city lights appeared over the tree line.

"Is that Cheverly?" I wondered aloud.

"I don't know," answered Gerry. "I only recognize
Volkswagens."

The FBI is in a lot of trouble.

★ ★ ★

I FINALLY GOT a summer job at a golf course in Washington, D.C.,
at Ft. McNair. It was a small army post tucked into the southwest corner of the city. Everything was on a miniature scale.
This mini-post had a nine-hole par-three golf course fitted
around the War College and snaked its way through the mini-
housing area, finishing at the mini-motor pool. The mini-clubhouse was located next to the mini-swimming pool, where some
of the summer coeds would sun, while our mini-grounds crew
maxi-lusted after them under the maxi-hot summer sun. The work-
day on a golf course began at the maxi-early hour of 6 A.M.

I hadn't considered this drawback when I eagerly accepted
working at the Ft McNair Mini-Golf Club. Drawbacks have a
nasty habit of becoming clear just moments after you can no
longer do a damn thing about them. The drawback became
clear when I stepped off that bus in San Antonio and came
face to face with that drill sergeant. It became clear when I
leapt to body surf that wave at Ocean City and the bottom was
sucked out leaving me suspended in midair with a bare ocean
floor beneath me. I can tell you now that the actual time suspended in midair does not last as long as Wile E. Coyote would
lead you to believe. I immediately plummeted to the ocean
floor, followed closely by the wave crashing on top of me, and
grinding me along the bottom in nature's version of a Cuisnart.
"*Hey. . .some trick, Big Kahoona.*"I applied first aid from the Acme
Medical Kit, but I took far longer to heal than Wile E. ever did.

I knew it that morning at 6 A.M. as I sat there on the edge
of my bed and it was just as dark outside as when I had climbed
into bed the night before. Someone must have changed the
time. . .this must be some perverted type of Daylight Savings Time.

"Did we just go on No Daylight At All Time?"

I struggled out the door, dragging along a body that was
still asleep.

"Hey, if I have to be up. . .you have to be up too."

No response.

My first week on the golf course was spent raking sand traps, filling the water barrels, and changing the water in the ball washers. I had limited exposure to golf, and was relieved when I found out that a ball washer referred to golf balls.

I was heading back to the mini-clubhouse when Jim drove up with two new summer hires in the back of a mini-truck. Jim was the only permanent employee. He was the entire Fort McNair grounds crew, and therefore, the mini-emperor of all he surveyed.

"When you finish, get the apron mower and do four, five, and six."

"I'm almost done. . ."

"Better look at seven too."

"Okay, I'll. . ."

"This is Butch and Tom."

"Hello, nice to met. . ." Jim gunned the engine and drove off, the mini-truck belched a dense cloud of exhaust smoke that obscured everything. . .it was a DKW mini-truck.

". . .where'd everybody go?"

The apron mower. . .hmmm. . .I was being given a field promotion. I had been admiring the apron mower for a couple of days, and I'll admit it, with some envy. It was big, loud and nasty. The three sets of cutting heads scared the hell out of the birds, little kids and me. Jim was the only one I had seen driving it. He quickly cut around the sand traps and the green apron, raised the three cutting heads and roared off for the next green.

I arrived back at the equipment shed and spent some time looking the brute over. I wanted to make sure I didn't do anything stupid, like knocking down the shed wall. I sat in the seat and pulled out the choke and hit the starter. The engine sputtered and then caught. I played with the levers. I had the cutting heads dancing and banging against the floor, one on each side and one directly below the seat.

"And now for the big test."

I pushed the lever into first gear and slowly exited the equipment shed. All the walls were left standing. I drove slowly, taking the long way around to the fourth green. On Ft. McNair, the long way added about ten yards. I exaggerated each turn, getting used to the feel of the machine. The number four green was dead ahead. Butch and Tom were raking the sand traps. Somewhere within the dark recesses of my mind, something emerged, something evil that had been waiting for just this moment. I was powerless to stop it, and now it took over. I was no longer at the controls. . .Captain Cool had invaded my body. He was now at the wheel. I was just along for the ride.

The Captain zoomed around the apron with levers flying and grass clippings shooting off the blades like a hydroplane's rooster tail. Up the high side of the green, and down around the sand traps at a breakneck pace. Butch and Tom just stood and watched with a mixture of awe and respect. It was obvious that Captain Cool knew what he was doing.

Up ahead was the narrow and dangerous apron channel. A section where the green apron rose to a small mound, then dropped suddenly to the sand trap. The Captain lined up the machine so the two side blades would cut each side of the mound while the middle would trim the top, a risky maneuver that only the most experienced would dare try. He slammed the machine into low gear and started slowly up the mound. The engine shuddered and protested as it approached the crown. It was then that things began to go terribly wrong.

The mower teetered for a moment, and then began an agonizing sideways slide, slipping slowly down the incline, heading for the sand trap. The Captain bravely applied more power and steered away from the edge. The wheels dug into the apron, throwing chunks of turf into the air, but the slide continued and gained momentum rapidly. He was going to tip over.

"Oh. . .shit!"

The Captain abandoned the mower, jumping clear of it. The machine slid into the trap, staying upright.

I sat where I landed and watched the blades send sand flying as it excavated its own grave. I wondered if it were going to dig deep enough to sink from view. Mercifully, the sand became too much of a strain and the engine stalled.

Butch and Tom stood there, stunned. I looked around for The Captain. He was nowhere to be found.

Jim was not sympathetic.

$$\star \quad \star \quad \star$$

After Captain Cool had abandoned me and the apron mower at the bunker coffin on the fourth green, Jim relieved me of any driving chores with equipment that had steering wheels.

"We'll keep you on mowers with handles and one blade," he said.

I was sent to the lawn mower Gulag for rehabilitation. I was given a Sunday-in-the-suburbs model to cut the grass around the clubhouse and along the tree line, where it was too tight to use any of their real mowers.

I was humiliated and hid, unsuccessfully, whenever I heard an equipment cart coming, so that none of the other summer hires could taunt me.

"Hey, Lawn Boy!" Tom would yell.

"That's Lawn Man to you, Bub."

"Bub!? What. . .are we on *My Three Sons?* Hell, you can call yourself Lawn King for all I care."

"What'd ya want?"

"I just wanted to tell you they extracted the apron mower from the sand trap. They checked the serial number on the engine and it was one of those lost over the Bermuda Triangle. Ha ha."

As long as you were Lawn Boy, you had to endure this kind of treatment with a smile.

"Fuck you."

A fuck you kind of smile.

After a few days of doing a bang-up job of cutting the clubhouse grass, Jim came out and looked over my work.

"Not bad."

"Not bad? These grass blades cower whenever I come near. Not bad indeed."

He squatted down to his knees and ran his hand over the fresh cut grass. He seemed genuinely interested in doing this. I wasn't sure there was anything you could learn from stroking grass blades. I had a sneaking suspicion he was doing it just for sport, getting a kick out of the thought that I believed he was really doing something down there. But Lawn Boy knew better than to open his mouth.

He looked up and narrowed his eyes. "Know what this means?"

I narrowed mine. "No I don't."

"Bring the mower and meet me back at the shed." He climbed back into the equipment cart.

"Any chance of finding out what this means before I bring the mower back?" I asked.

"No."

"I just hope I won't be looking back at this as a high point of my golf course maintenance career? . . ."

He turned the key in the ignition.

"I mean, I would like this to be a step up from mowing the clubhouse lawn. . ."

He put the cart in gear.

"I don't mind mowing the clubhouse lawn, it's certainly better than being the ball washer, if you know what I mean. . ."

He drove off.

". . .if you know what I mean."

He was out of sight.

I arrived back at the equipment shed, pushing my mower along like Ward Cleaver, just as Tom was leaving.

"Hey! Lawn King!"

"Fuck you."

Jim was bent over a strange-looking machine. It was just about the same size as a regular lawnmower, but it looked nothing like any I had ever seen.

"I'm going to try you out on the greens mower. You might do all right—it doesn't have a steering wheel. Ha, ha."

Lawn King kept his mouth shut. The mower had a large perforated cylinder behind a set of cutting blades—it looked sort of like a miniature steamroller. Hell, on this post, it may have been a steamroller. The blade was like that of an old style push mower, but much smaller. Jim pushed the machine out of the shed and checked it over carefully. Then we walked together with the mower to the first green. Jim pushed a kickstand type of lever down and pulled the mower up onto it, lifting the wheels off the ground. He flipped two clips on each axle and pulled the wheels off. Then he pushed forward and the mower came off the kickstand and rested on the roller.

"Now watch what I do," he said to me.

He started at the top of the green and mowed across, then swung the mower around and cut the grass coming back.

"Very intricate. . .," I said to myself. "Let's see if I have grasped the concept. . .first you mow one way, and then the other. Hmmmmmm."

The roller propelled the mower, and also pressed the grass down just behind the cutting blades, leaving a grain in the green. He continued until the entire green was cut, and as he reached the bottom on his last pass, he cut around the perimeter, then stopped the engine.

"You cut back and forth, then once around the outside. Next time you cut the green, start somewhere else, so the grass don't get used to growing one way."

We went to another green and Jim removed the wheels once again. He stepped aside and motioned for me to take the mower. It sat there idling, and I gripped the handles.

"Line it up and push this lever," said Jim.

I nodded and pushed the mower into gear. Off we went, across the green, and I struggled to keep it going in a straight line. It felt very heavy. I was nearly at the end of my first pass, the edge of the green was getting close and I got ready to swing the mower around. I pushed against the handle, but the mower kept going forward.

"Oh, shit! . . ."

I tugged on the mower handle, but the blades were already into the taller grass just off the green. I pulled back with everything I had, but the roller gripped the ground and dragged me along. Together we cut across the apron and went down an embankment, cutting all the way.

"Take it out of gear! Take it out of gear!" Jim screamed.

What a good idea! I lifted the gear lever and the machine stopped. I turned around to see what damage I had done. There was a bald strip from where I stood that lead all the way back to a wavy lane through the green.

Lawn King had struck again.

"Tougher than it looks, heh boy? You got to raise up 'dem blades before you try and turn. Now start the engine and come on back."

"You want me to do it again?"

"It grows back, boy. We'll tell 'em it's a cart path. Ha ha. Now come on back."

I dragged the mower back up to the green, started the engine, lined myself up, and pushed it in gear. Again I struggled to keep the mower in a straight line. At the edge of the green I raised up 'dem blades and swung the mower. But the blades weren't raised high enough and again we went into the apron. I yanked the lever out of gear.

I was able to limit the damage to just the edge.

"Better," said Jim.

Better? I looked back at my second pass. Not quite as wavy, and at least there wasn't another new cart path this time.

"I blame this all on the hours," I said. "Too early to be steam roller mowing."

"What'd you say, boy?"

"I said, you start work early around here."

"Six o'clock," said Jim.

"Yes, I know. . ."

"So, you want to talk or mow?"

"Hell, I didn't even know we were talking."

"What?"

"Mow. . .I'll mow of course. I mean who wouldn't want to mow on a fine morning like. . ."

"Well, start mowing."

When I had finished the last pass, I attempted the perimeter cut. Although I didn't go into the deeper grass, my outline of the green was distinctly different from its real contours. The overall effect from the wavy paths across the green, and its squiggly outline, made you want to reach for the horizontal and vertical control knobs. A lot of golfers cleaned their eyeglasses that day.

"Done. What'd you think?"

Tom drove by us in the equipment cart.

"Hey Lawn King, what's that? Etch a sketch? Ha ha."

"Heh, heh. Etch a sketch," said Jim.

I waited for Jim's real assessment, not willing to accept Etch a sketch. He walked around the green slowly, looking it over. Then he walked back up the fairway for a longer perspective.

"Well?" I said.

"Working on a golf course isn't really your cup of tea, is it, son?"

Well something good had come out of it—I had been promoted to son.

"I can't really say. . .I've never liked tea."

HOW TO PLAY GOLF

BUTCH WAS LIVING ON the wrong coast, with his California beach boy looks he should have been surfing off Laguna Beach, if there is such a beach. I know nothing about California, so I may have just placed Butch surfing off some shark-infested cliffs in Peru.

"Hey Gringo, wach you dooing here anyway?"

"I don't know. One minute I'm working on a mini-golf course in D.C., the next minute I'm standing here with you guys, holding this surfboard."

"Was youse ze ball washer?" they asked hopefully.

Butch wasn't the brightest kid you ever met, but then, who is? He got everything he was told twisted around, which drove Jim crazy. He'd water the traps and rake the greens, wanted to know why there were no balls in the ball washers, and when told to change the cup, he went out with a stack of fresh Dixie cups.

"Working on a golf course isn't really your cup of tea, is it, son?"

That Jim really liked tea. But as much as Butch drove Jim crazy, he made me laugh, and I appreciate a good laugh, so I kept telling him he was doing a great job, and wasn't appreciated nearly enough.

"They should promote you."

"I don't think that's much of an endorsement seeing as how it's coming from you. . .Lawn King."

He was brighter than I suspected.

Butch had flunked out of college and had no idea what he was going to do once the summer was over and these jobs were gone.

Since Butch had sandy blonde hair, he was required to be a golfer. His choice was either surf or golf, and since this wasn't

Laguna Beach, it had to be golf. We sat around talking about our idea for our own golf tournament. It had started out innocent enough, with just a name. . .The Duffers Invitational.

"How's this tournament going to work?" I had asked.

"You've seen golfers, right?"

"Well, I've seen my father and his friends. . .the Jackie Gleason Golfing Brigade."

"I think you've got the basic idea."

"It shall be an official PGA tournament, a humbling stop on the tour for all the professionals," said Butch.

"Right," Tom and I said. "What's a PGA?"

We committed it to paper, and then committed ourselves. . .

Lawn King presents—The Duffer Invitational. The tournament trademark image is a golfer in iridescent yellow pants with an overhanging belly and a golf shirt with a martini patch on the pocket. The basics: first, it will be held on a typical public golf course, where a fairway is just a concept and hardly ever a reality, and a flag stick is the only requirement for creating a green. Carts will be used, since carts can be their own source of public golf course amusement.

Your equipment: True duffers have great clubs and lot's of them. This is one of the major pleasures of the game and one of the few things connected with golf that duffers do well. They buy frequently, and delight in showing off their latest find. You will need a Tremendous Bag to carry the load. The rule on maximum number of clubs has been changed to a minimum number of clubs for this tournament. You are required to carry at least thirty. You will need a Big Car for your Big Bag. All good duffers have Big Cars for their Big Bags. You will wear orange plaid pants, a salmon-colored shirt with the crest of a prestigious golf course where you have never been, and a hat from your car trunk. All duffers wear hats that look like they found them abandoned in the golf cart.

Some preliminaries: There will be no ball spotters. Each foursome will have three tour members and one professional duffer who can never follow the flight of his or anyone else's shot. Actually being able to follow the flight of the ball is grounds for immediate disqualification. Also, there are no caddies allowed, unless they are there for the sole purpose of mixing the martinis. . .we are not totally without compassion. All-duffer foursomes will also be mixing martinis, as

*well as mixing into the tournament to bring the course popu-
lation up to weekend standards. This is somewhere just below the population of downtown Tokyo. There will be some
minor inconveniences encountered for course maintenance
activities. Finally, be alert, balls will be flying into your foursome from various angles at various times throughout the
match, with or without someone yelling "Four." This may,
on occasion, be followed by a club. . .*

"So, you don't watch golf?" asked Butch as he wrote.

"Watching people walking around an open-air park, and
studying class clippings that they throw up in the air? The only
thing worse I can think of is actually being there, and peering
through those periscopy things." *Captain Nemo here. We've landed.
All the native women are fat, and the men are wearing hot air balloons for pants.* "I mostly think of golf as a pretty decent fat camp
idea for retirees."

"Golf's a sport. . ."

"No! . . ." I was shocked. "Who told you this? I'll bet it was
some fat guy in yellow pants."

"It's in the sports pages."

"So are Ping-Pong and archery. Actually, what you're looking at in the paper is the lawn games section of the sports
pages. It's only in there so people like my father will actually buy a paper, otherwise those reporters would have to get
real jobs instead of flying around the country writing about
bowling. . .and golf."

"Hey Boss, there's a Jarts tournament in Malibu we have to cover!"

"It takes some endurance," said Butch sincerely.

"Which part. . .riding in the carts or stirring the martini?
You're not going to seriously argue that golfers are athletes,
are you?"

"Well, I wouldn't go that far."

"You know, golfers would sure look a lot different if they
had to run to each shot carrying the golf bag. Distance and
time, that should be the game. I think a lot of golf's popularity
comes from being a larger version of croquet. There's just a
lot more space between the wickets, and you get to drive to
your ball. . .with a martini, of course."

"So, you think golf is some kind of moving outdoor bar."

"I know my father certainly does. A lot of those holes just
seem to get in his way of bellying up to the bar, and believe me,
he's got the belly for it. I personally think adopting croquet's
rule of bashing your opponent's ball if you manage to hit it,

would be a great idea. A new kind of club would be needed, of course, which should delight everyone."

"So, you don't watch golf?"

"How'd we get back here again? Okay, I have watched golf, mostly when my father comes in and changes the channel. I think real sports just annoy him. I would prefer watching the Florida Shuffleboard League. . .which is almost like golf, but a lot more fun."

"Mr. Sands is due up, but we're going to have a substitution, Jim."

"I think that's an illegal substitution, Frank."

"No. . .no. . .the rules state if the player is DOA at the line, then a substitution is allowed, and look at this. . .Matilda Jenkins is coming out of retirement to replace Mr. Sands. . .ooohhh. . .look out. . .too bad. . ."

"Looks like there's a twenty-minute medical time-out on the field, Jim."

"So we'll take a break here at the Prudential Medicare Supplement Tourney while they set up the oxygen tent. . ."

"And we'll get some dinner. . ."

"And a martini. . ."

"And a nap. . ."

"So, you think golf is like bowling."

"Whoa. . .I never said that. Bowling is a true American art form. You have to admire a game that has cocktail waitresses built right into the playing field. I believe that's a rule. I don't believe there's any other game where you're expected to order a drink while you play. Bowling *is* a drinking game. . .like Buzz. Ahhhh. . .it makes you glad to be an American."

"What the hell is Buzz?"

"Buzz is like bowling. . .except without the balls and all those pins, and you don't have to go to an alley."

"How do you play?"

"Well, let's get some water, and I'll show you."

After finishing our Buzz game and returning to the course, I saw Butch and Tom taking a twenty-minute medical time-out, and speeding back to the clubhouse in a cart.

"George, you idiot! . . ."

"Heh. . .heh. . .heh." Lawn King strikes back. Unlike Germany, this time it was my fault.

★   ★   ★

A HARD RAIN started shortly after lunch, and the golfers abandoned the course. John, the mini-club manager, would let us

play during the time between the rain letting up and the golfers returning. We used abandoned clubs stored in the back of
the equipment shed. We had our own special rules, and you
could only take one club.

Butch had an unfair advantage. He knew something about
the game and said things like "mulligan" (who I had thought
was one of the Dead End Kids), and "provisional" and "cud-
gel" and a lot of other shit, which meant Tom and I had no
idea whether Butch was jerking us around or not. We were
forced to penalize him.

"For what?" he said.

"First, for using these fake golf expressions from old Dead
End Kids movies. Second, for owning your own set of clubs.
Third, for actually having played a whole round on a course
without a windmill protecting the open whale's mouth, and
finally, for having sandy blond hair, which we all know is the
real secret of being a good golfer."

"I agree," said Tom.

"What's my penalty?"

Tom and I huddled privately.

"You must play left-handed."

"Come on. . .there aren't any left-handed clubs. This isn't
fair. This is ridiculous."

"Yes," we agreed. "It isn't fair and it is ridiculous, that's
exactly the point. I don't know why you think that will change
anything." We ignored his appeal; however, we did manage to
dig up a left-handed club. Tom and I thought we were being
pretty generous for letting him use it.

I placed my ball on the tee.

"All right. . .straight down the pike. . .two hundred yards.
And I hope 'pike' is a legitimate golfing term. I want to do this
right."

"You can't hit a ball two hundred yards," answered Butch.

"You mean I've got the wrong club?"

"You can't hit a ball two hundred yards," Butch repeated.

"All right, smart-ass, how do I hit a ball two hundred yards?"

"For you? Drive the cart down there two hundred yards
and put down a ball."

"I think you can see now why we penalized you. Hmmm." I
rummaged through the bag. "Where are the keys to the cart? If
this ball doesn't go two hundred yards, I'm gonna try that cart
thing you suggested, since you said it was okay and all. Is there
a golf term for that?"

"Yeah. . .cheating."

"Well, finally a golfing concept I'm familiar with."

I held my club over the ball with my best overhand mallet grip and whacked away. The ball went straight up and came down ten feet in front of me.

"Hmmm. . .I seem to be a little short of the two-hundred-yard mark. Get me the cart keys."

"I think your club face was open, you cut the ball slightly thin," said Butch.

"See. . .there you go again. . .with those golf expressions."

"Not enough club," said Tom.

"And now you've got Tom doing it."

I readied myself again and blasted a powerful shot into the side of a parked Chevy. The ball ricocheted into the rough on the left side.

"Ahhh. . .I guess my club face must have closed up and gone home."

"You're going to have to call any combination shots from now on," said Tom.

"Oh sure, after you see I'm good at it, then you want to penalize me."

"Hey, you penalized me!" protested Butch.

"That's different, we like to penalize you."

Butch stepped up and still managed to hit the ball down the middle with his left-handed club.

"What a pisser," Tom and I said. "We obviously gave him a club face that stays open late."

Tom left himself about two hundred yards short. The wiser move would be to play his ten-pound divot and gain ten yards. Our rules allowed playing divots. . .player's choice.

My third shot carried the green. . .and the building behind it. I smacked my ball off the foundation, which I had to duck on the rebound. Luckily it hit a tree and caromed to a spot that gave me a clear shot.

"Did you call that!?" screamed Tom.

"Take it easy on the buildings!" yelled Butch.

"Hey, it's called the War College isn't it?"

Behind me, Tom was reinstalling a massive piece of sod. Butch was waiting nearby. I picked up my ball and threw it at the green. This was allowed under the rules if you ever found yourself with your opponents facing away from you. It landed on the front side and rolled into a sand trap.

"Cheaters never prosper!"

It's possible that I may have taken that rule from my own personal rulebook.

"Whoever told you that!?" I answered back.

Tom hooked his ball into the street, but sliced his divot barely over Butch's head, and a chunk came to rest on the bill of Butch's cap.

"I'm playing that divot, I believe our rules allow that," said Tom.

I proceeded to the trap and watched Butch arc his shot onto the green. Tom launched his ball over the hole, back to about where I had been standing. I planted my feet in the trap as Butch walked by.

"Wait a minute," he said.

I reared back the club, and let fly. It was amazing there was any sand left in that trap judging by the amount I sprayed on Butch. It was more amazing that moving all that earth failed to move the ball, but it did create a nice little sand dune by the green.

"Jesus Christ! Wait a minute," Butch yelled.

"Was my club face open for business on that one?"

I planted and swung again. No sand this time, just the club flying out of my hand and landing on the green.   •

"If that goes in the hole it counts."

"Let me out of here!" Butch turned and walked off the green while I retrieved my club and put my ball down next to the hole. I hustled back to the trap and blasted out some more sand before he had time to turn around.

"What a shot! Just incredible!"

"Bullshit!"

"Hey. . .are you saying I'm lying?"

"Is the Pope Catholic?"

"Well, let me see. . .hmmmm. . .is the Pope a Catholic? That would be with a capital 'C', wouldn't it?"

I mulled that over while lying on the green and using my club like a pool cue. I shot the ball into the cup.

"I can't wait to hear this, how many strokes?" asked Butch.

"What? We're supposed to count 'em? I think you better tell Tom."

John pulled up alongside the green just in time for Tom's ball to go bouncing over his electric cart.

"You'll have to postpone the rest of your game, gentlemen. People are starting to come back in."

Then he was off again. I looked at Butch.

"Did you hear that? He called me gentlemen. He's not the mini-club manager for nothing."

"By the way," yelled John from his departing cart. "We're thinking of having your tournament here."

JUPITER EYELIDS

ONE DAY, IN THE middle of the mini-golf-course summer, the entire Ft. McNair post closed early for a government inventory. This included the mini-golf course. You may find it surprising that the government actually does an inventory, considering the number of ten-thousand-dollar toilet seats that frequently go missing. All I can say is, my mother sure didn't have one. Closing the course was fine with me, for it was already getting hot, and the sweat was beginning to flow.

"You look like shit," said Tom.

"Thank you. . .kind of you to notice."

During this first half of the summer, it had come out that I had never felt the effects of marijuana. Both Tom and Butch assured me that having your legs fall asleep wasn't it.

"You didn't see anybody else toppling over on wobbly legs did you?"

"They might have, they were already on the floor."

"That's because they probably passed out."

"Yeah," agreed Butch. "Now that's what you're looking for."

"Really?"

"Sure," said Tom. "We'll show you."

After the course closed, we drove to my house where Butch and Tom promised I would pass out.

"Is this good? Do I want to do this?" I asked.

"Sure, everyone does."

"We've passed out at some of the best places in town," boasted Butch.

Tom handed a pipe to Butch. "Try not to drop it."

Butch lit the pipe and passed it to me. Even after their glowing endorsement, I still thought getting stoned was all a state of mind, and it was the ritual that was really important.

So I inhaled deeply as Butch held a match over the bowl, and happily proceeded to snort out my nose and cough and gag repeatedly with tears continually flowing from my eyes, as all of these things seemed to be important. Well, this went on for a while. . .then things began to change. There was a painful grin firmly attached to my face. It was impossible to stop, because I tried and tried. It was starting to hurt, but it was hardened in place.

"What do you do about this?" I pointed to my face.

"Oh, there's not much you can do about that. It's part of it too, although it's not as much fun as passing out," said Tom.

"Then I'm stuck like this."

"Could be, but try to look normal," said Butch.

"Like this? . . ."

"What is that. . .your Alfred E. Neuman look normal?", I said.

Could it be that I had turned into Alfred E. Neuman?

"Do I really look like Alfred E. Neuman?"

"Well, not as good looking, of course."

This was ludicrous. I was ludicrous, they were ludicrous, everything was ludicrous, the word ludicrous was ludicrous, and we got a good laugh out of it. Too good a laugh, for I couldn't stop. My face was firmly in grin paralysis, and I couldn't stop laughing.

I tried composing myself with a short walk around the living room. A dust-laden midmorning sunbeam barely penetrated the room through the half-open blinds. We all walked around the room in an aimless sort of fashion, seeking to calm ourselves, but somehow we managed to jam ourselves into one corner and collide into one another. I don't know why I found this so funny, but I shook with gales of laughter, although you'd have to take my word for it because it was all soundless.

My mouth was open as I shook, but no sound was coming out. I couldn't catch my breath, and I gasped for air. This produced a sound reminiscent of a harbor seal. Butch and Tom were startled by it at first, but that soon changed to concern and offers of help.

"Would you like a fish?"

"How about a beachball?"

How about some oxygen? I sure could use some, but you'll have to find another route because it sure isn't going in through my mouth. If I couldn't have some air, then the least I could do was get away from these two. So I pushed away from them and slowly shuffled around the room by myself, with my head down, concentrating. I began to relax and breathe. Oh, how good that dusty indoor air felt. I had done such a good job of concentrating on breathing that I had forgotten completely about Butch and Tom, who in their deep concern had fallen into step behind me, mimicking my shuffle and my head-down amble about the room. We had been in tandem roaming about the living room the whole time, a human train. We looked like an opening scene from *The Monkees*. . .minus the leopard skin tights. I had lost track of them and raised my head to look around. Where'd they go?

Tom began to make steam engine noises behind me. Then Butch joined him. . .

"Wooo Wooooooo. . ."

Butch tugged on the cord to his steam whistle. All that careful preparation. . .shot to hell. I started to sound like a seal again.

"Calm yourself, Lawn King," said Tom. "And Butch, quit playing Grab Ass back there."

"I'm not playing Grab Ass, I thought we were doing the opening to *The Monkees*."

You may think baseball is the national pastime, but based on the number of times I've been accused of playing, it's Grab Ass, and I'm not even sure how you play it. I usually find out I'm in the middle of a game when someone else points it out. So, I don't even know how you start one of these games. The years of playing Horsing Around has taught me that.

It was then that a shift was felt in the gravity field of Earth. I was sitting in the living room, dying of a parched throat and I wanted to go to the kitchen. I could only move my finger like some paralysis victim signaling that they were still alive just as the lid of the coffin is closed on them. The weight of my body sank me into my father's Command Post Chair. I was pressed into it, and fit perfectly for the first time. Gravity continued to increase, and moved up the planetary scale until we reached Jupiter. I had no alternative but to slide off the chair, crawl past Butch and Tom, and slither into the kitchen for a drink. I ducked under the refrigerator door as it opened, which isn't hard when you're gravity squashed to the floor.

I reached into the refrigerator, took out a quart bottle of Coke, and crawled back around the door as it closed. I slithered back into the living room, one hand wrapped around the bottle.

"Don't go anywhere," I said. "I'm going to need your help getting downstairs. I'm afraid that without it, the only thing left for me to do is to Von Hamie down them." A definite GerCrashen.

My gravity-squashed words never reached them.

The effort of crawling across the surface of Jupiter was extremely tiring and I came to a stop in the middle of the living room floor. I didn't have the energy to climb back into the chair. I lay there looking at the bottle of Coke in my hand. . .I was going to die of thirst while only a foot away from the bottle. I couldn't lift my head off the rug for a drink and just stared at the ocean of Coke. . .so close, but it might as well have been on the other side of Jupiter. There didn't seem to be any way I was going to get it to my mouth.

"What are you doing?" Butch's voice broke through my concentration.

"I'm trying to get this bottle to my mouth without raising my head."

"Really? Are you in a contest?"

"No. I just can't lift my head."

I finally angled my head upward while tilting the bottle over. I opened my mouth and caught the bottle as it came down. I lay there, space docked with the Coke bottle. It was cold and flowed down my throat. From rags to riches. . .from dying of thirst to drowning in a Coke bottle. How was I going to get out of this? I was going to have to drink the whole thing. I thrust my tongue into the opening to stop the flow and to buy some time to solve the problem.

"That's interesting, whatever you're doing," said Tom.

"Veehll, Ie donn noo whaph Ie shud du?"

"And you've invented a whole new language."

I tilted the bottle back up and uncorked my tongue.

Tom stood up. "Come on Butch, we're going."

"Wait! Help me get to my room. Don't leave me here like this! I'm on the good rug in my filthy pants!"

They picked me up and helped me to my bed. "Oh no . . .my eyes. . .I've got Jupiter eyelids," I said.

"Today you are a man," said Tom.

"You lucky devil. . .you'll pass out soon," encouraged Butch.

ENLARGED BREASTS AND STINKING FEET

Aren't you going to take those beautiful clothes in your closet?"

Mom hovered like an alien ship as I filled each suitcase. If there is one thing worse than closet murmuring, it's hovering.

"What beautiful clothes?"

"Don't play dumb. . ."

"I thought you decided I wasn't just playing."

". . .you know what clothes I'm talking about, the ones hanging in your closet. You didn't pack them."

"How do you know I didn't pack them?"

"I looked."

"How unfair of you to actually look when you could have just taken my word."

"You forget, I have experience with your word."

"They're really out of style, Mom."

"Oh no they're not. I see all the boys wearing them."

My God, all the boys were here again, and this time they were actually in my closet.

"Damn crowded in there. Mom, I think we have parallel worlds going on here. I'm in one, and you're in another with everybody, because in my world I haven't seen a single shaped head. Those clothes have been in my closet for the last four years, and now they seem to have left my world and somehow have gotten into your world where all the boys have started to wear them. Dad lives in another world where everybody sports a butch, and every public building is a bar. I don't think we should mix any of these worlds together, it would be too risky. You wouldn't want Dad's world getting into your world, would you?"

"You're not taking the clothes. . ."

"I believe that's what I just said."

★　　★　　★

COLLEGE ROOMMATE DYNAMICS are a mixture of choice and whimsy, often the results boil down to plucking an index card off the student union roommate bulletin board, calling the number, and unless the room is located in a swamp accessible only by canoe, you lay your money down.

Mike and I did this exact thing just before we left for the summer. . .plucked a card and laid our money down. That's how we got Ray. Ray was the Head Roommate and a graduate assistant. He held the title of Head Roommate because he also held the lease. Ray was a large, dinosaur boned, grubby kind of character, not someone you would picture as a graduate assistant. He liked to hang around in a ratty brown robe that made him look kind of like a slow moving Mound Creature that had escaped from a laboratory in a science fiction B-movie, that is if he bothered to move at all, which wasn't all that often. It wasn't long before we began calling him Roboton.

When I arrived at the apartment, no one was there. There was a note pinned to the door saying Roboton was at his part-time job down at the corner Texaco station, and to stop by to get the key. So I got back in the car and schlepped over there. I spent a fitful night's sleep on the lumpy living room couch.

I hadn't expected to sleep on a lumpy couch, but it was my only choice. I surmised this after standing in my doorway and staring at a totally empty bedroom.

"What's wrong with this picture?"

It wasn't Ozzie Nelson's bedroom, that's for sure—he would have had a bed in it.

"Now boys," he would have said. "You're going to need a bed. Ricky, sing a song about a bed."

"Ozzie, Is that you?"

"Yes, Harriet."

"The Reverend stopped by while you were out and mentioned that you've never been to work. . .ever. Do you have a job?"

"Why, let me think. No. . .I can't seem to recall any job. I know David has a job, and we let him have that pretty, little wife. . . remember. . .and Ricky. . ."

"I'm Rick now, Dad."

". . .he's a. . .well, I'm not sure if he has a job either."

"How can we afford this house if you don't have a job?"

"Well. . .now. . .now. . .that's a good question, Harriet."

Ozzie stepped off the set and found the producer. "How the fuck can I live in this house if I don't have a job!? Do I have to do every

*Goddamned thing around here! Christ, next thing you know we'll be
doing a show about our foreclosure! Let's have Ricky sing a song about
that! . . ."*

"Hello Foreclosure. . .good-bye house. . .sweet. . ."

"Not now Ricky."

"I'm Rick now, Dad."

"Just be thankful that no one named you Ozzie," said Harriet.

"Amen to that, Mom."

"Maybe you sell Amway or something, Dad."

"Shut up, David."

"I'm Dave now, Dad."

*"Why is everyone changing their name!? And why can't we tell
the viewers what I am!? What is it. . .a fucking secret!?"*

*"Well, we don't know what you are either. . .you've never told
us," said Chamlers, the producer.*

"I'm. . .I'm. . .what the hell am I!?"

Well, I knew what I was. . .I was a man without a bed, and
one sure would have come in handy. I discovered I had neglected to bring mine along. After one night on the couch,
and a morning attempting to uncrook all the crooked body
parts, I no longer thought a bed would simply be handy; I
thought it would be a lifesaver.

That morning I drove into the worst section of Hartford,
to the drive-through Salvation Army store, and bought a mattress at GI-Bill prices. I had it bent in half over my head as I
opened the door to the apartment, the weight pushing my head
down into my shoulders. I could only see out to the sides, and
angled myself around the corners as I walked carefully to the
bedroom. I stooped to get it through the bedroom doorway,
and then heaved it off my head and onto the floor. My head
popped back into place from my shoulders.

"Ah. . .sweet relief."

"Arrrggghhhh. . .balls!"

It was Mike. It was good to hear "balls" again. I had missed
it over the summer. It was all-purpose and remarkably adapt-
able to any situation.

"Mike! Glad to see you. . .well. . .part of you."

He had been standing just inside the bedroom, watching
my mattress and me as I moved through the doorway. Now he
was lying under it. All I could see was part of his leg protruding
from underneath. There was a large black steamer trunk, the
kind you only see used by the passengers on the *Titanic*, sitting
in the corner.

"Here, let me help get that off your face."

I flipped the mattress off him. He seemed rather small lying there on the floor with his dark hair and bold, black mustache. There was something about him that always reminded me of a barbershop quartet.

In the corner was a real bed, and there was a real desk by the closet. I pushed my mattress against the wall.

"Wow. . .has the Nelson family been here?"

"What? . . ."

Mike had enjoyed being a waiter with me so much that he had decided to join me in getting the apartment. The man was a complete fool, which is understandable since he was also an ex-army grunt from upstate New York. He always made sure you understood he was from New York State, and not New York City. New York City enjoys an unparalleled reputation as the world's preeminent source of assholes. And it's not just your run-of-the-mill asshole mind you, but the extraordinary asshole that only The City That Never Sleeps can produce, which just shows you what all that lack of sleep does for them. However, since no one really appreciates an asshole, the effort is kind of lost on the public in general. One of the most cutting remarks I have ever heard was from my brother, who referred to one of his in-law cousins as "the ultimate schmuck from the Big Apple." I think that's about enough on assholes.

Mike's hometown was further from New York City than this campus, and therefore he considered all of us somewhat suspect. We had gone around about all of this last year while waitering. . .

"Where are you from?" he had asked.

I gave him my service brat short-form version, including the freshman nametag incident. He was leery about the whole thing. . .

"Everyone has a hometown," he muttered.

"I do. . .it's Bristol. . .I've just never lived there, but it is my hometown. My father told me so and he wouldn't steer me wrong. I'm a proud Connecticutian."

"And you talk about New York. . .," Mike muttered to himself.

"It's true," said Danny, "he's from my hometown."

Yep, Danny is from Bristol too. He quickly straightened me out about the Bristol Stomp. It didn't originate in the Connecticut town at all. I found this news distressing. After all, Bristol was my hometown. For years I had claimed the Bristol Stomp as my own, a piece of my Connecticutian heritage. Now

I find out I've spent years with misplaced heritage. I had been memorizing our family's permanent home address ever since my father had told me we were from Connecticut, and we would need to know it.

"This is your permanent home address," he said. "Whenever you are asked, you will write this down." He pointed out the state on the U.S. map. "This is where it is."

We kids were in high school, and it was time for my father to pass the information along to his descendants.

"I thought we were from Ireland," I said. "At least that's what the '55 Buick hood ornament hanging in the hallway says."

"You are a Connecticutian," he corrected.

"A Connecticutian?"

"Yes."

All through the world, at all military housing areas, the maps were laid out on kitchen tables and similar conversations were taking place with all the children entering high school.

"*You are a Wisconsinonian.*"

"A Wisconsinonian?"

"*Yes.*"

I looked at the address my father had written down. I was from Bristol, Connecticutian.

"You will be going to college in Connecticut, for it is your home."

And then I met Danny while waitering, and what luck, he was from my old hometown. Danny and I spent endless minutes talking about all our old hangouts in the hometown where I'd never lived, and all our old childhood friends I'd never met. It's good having someone from the old hometown at school with you.

The three of us had talked about getting an apartment together, Mike, Danny, and me. But Danny had already joined another bulletin-board-index-card group.

I dropped my mattress on the floor in the corner and began settling into the college roommate life. . .Mike, Ray, and me.

"Where's the rest of it?" asked Mike.

"You're kidding, right?"

"No. . .usually a bed comes with a head board, railings, mattress, and a box spring."

"Who the hell are you. . .Better Bedding?"

★   ★   ★

A FEW WEEKS into the semester, Mike and I ventured over to see Danny, but it was not something we liked to do. It was a long drive through a lot of back roads where I continually thought I was lost, and I knew by the time I found my way out I would somehow be in Montana. I didn't want to be in Montana.

"Quick, we have to leave," said Danny.

"We just came in, and I risked ending up in Montana to get here."

"Believe me, you'd rather be in Montana."

"Nobody would rather be in Montana."

"You don't want to stay here. . .there's a war going on."

"Over what?"

"The refrigerator. . .it's been partitioned, and now it's spilling over to the apartment. Some salami has gone missing."

"Be grateful, if you had Ray as a roommate, the refrigerator would have gone missing," said Mike.

"So. . .have a meeting and straighten it out," I said.

"It's too late, all diplomatic relations have broken off."

Mike and I had already gone through the labeled food stage, but it was much simpler for us. . .if Roboton found it, he ate it. . .that was it. It didn't matter who bought it. Luckily, Mike and I rarely had any money, so our refrigerator section was a subdivision of the butter tray. When we did manage to buy something, we ate it. . .immediately. The only label in our refrigerator was the large sticker on the milk that read Microbiology Experiment—Warning: Side effects include breast enlargement and foot odor.

"It's not much of a deterrent, since he already has both," I had told Mike.

"I think he's been giving it to his girlfriend to drink."

"What for? Do you think he's hoping her feet will start to stink?"

"I think I've had enough of this conversation," said Mike.

★   ★   ★

DANNY LOST THE Refrigerator Wars, and we took in the little refugee. He packed up all his labeled food and joined us.

"Is this milk safe to drink?" he asked.

"You can ignore the label. . .but it might be a good idea to get yourself a training bra."

My old hometown buddy was now one of us.

No matter what anyone might tell you, college classes are not fun, even when they sound like they might be. That's the way the colleges want it. They claim it has something to do with institutional credibility, or some nonsense like that. The truth is the professors are still teachers at heart, and fun is not a concept they are familiar with. They worry that they won't be taken seriously. And if they're not taken seriously, then they would just look stupid wearing those gowns and the hats with the boards on top of them. It's all very confusing, but just remember this. . .even if the class sounds like it might be fun, don't be taken in. . .be afraid.

"I think I may have found something the administration has let slip through their bony little fingers. . .The Modern Novel." I still wanted to believe.

"Let me see."

"It's right here." I showed Danny the course catalogue.

"Wow, how'd this happen?"

"I don't know, but we better jump on it before they find out."

We both still wanted to believe. We signed up.

It was a disaster—and it sounded so good on paper. It was soon obvious that the university's definition of modern and the definition with which you and I are so familiar, are about a century apart. I thought it meant, roughly, something written in my lifetime. This would qualify, from the university's standpoint, as an ultramodern novel, maybe even as a super-duper ultramodern novel. Nope, we were talking about books written to be placed in the seat pouches of Conestoga Wagonlines along with Ben Franklin's *Farmers Almanac* for some light reading on the trek across the Continental Divide. I wish they'd tell you these things before you sign anything.

That first week, we slugged it through page one of James Joyce's *Portrait of An Artist As a Young Man.* "Young" would be relative, because he would have been approaching a hundred years old based on its publication date. We fought and clawed and toiled and struggled down to the end of the page. It was too much, the class lay exhausted, sprawled across their desks, waiting for oxygen. We were in deep trouble. I raised my hand.

"Yes?"

"This first page is actually gibberish."

A gasp came out of the professor.

"Why would you think that!?"

"What is this moo cow stuff? How can anyone spend a week on just the first page?"

"Obviously I have failed in getting the point across, this first page is key to the entire novel. I have no other choice than to start over."

The class collectively passed out.

Danny closed the book and in a lowered voice spoke across the aisle to me. "I would like to be the beneficiary of your life insurance policy."

"I don't have one."

"Too bad, because it would have been easy money considering the mood you've just put the class in."

I pointed at Janice Literaryoski in the first row.

"She's not upset, she looks happy to start again."

"She would be, she's a Modern Novel major. Look at her, she even dresses like she's ready to follow along behind a Conestoga wagon. I was talking to her the other day. . .," continued Dan.

"Why? Are you looking for nineteenth century sex?"

"I'm not particular about the century. . .anyway, she said you have to be familiar with five hundred years of Irish history to really understand this novel."

"Great. Did she happen to say if five minutes of Irish history buys you anything?"

"No. And what five minutes do you know?"

"The potatoes died. . .my grandfather caught a boat. And I think he brought this novel along with him on the voyage."

"That was about five seconds."

"Yeah. . .and I bet those five seconds aren't even in here, and if they are, they're probably on page four hundred, which at our current pace, we'll get to in about eight years."

"Luckily, we'll still be here."

"Do you two have something you would like to share with the class?" the professor asked.

"No sir, the class has made it clear that if I share anything again, I will be dead."

"Very astute of the class."

I was forced to drop The Modern Novel and substitute Criminology, another class that had nothing to do with my major, but at least I had returned to the modern world. I told Danny he could help himself to my Irish history.

"Well then, I guess I'm all set," said Danny. "Especially now that the entire class associates me with you."

Denfield's Criminology class was so popular it was held in one of the largest lecture halls on campus. It wasn't actually a lecture hall at all—it was the Fine Arts Department auditorium.

There were no pull-up desktops—everything stayed on your lap. In trade, we did get a felt seat cushion instead of the laminated, stonewood, Irish butt-bone crusher of a regular classroom seat. Denfield was standing in front of the first row of seats. He was a short, premature-balding man, not at all what I had pictured. He was leaning back against the stage, engrossed in a stack of papers placed on the stage flooring next to him.

I had just sat down when someone dressed in a fatigue jacket walked quickly to the front of the room and grabbed Denfield. He threw him against the stage and spread his legs. He passed his hands along Denfield's clothes and began shouting. . .

"You're under arrest! You have the right to remain silent! Anything you say can and will be used against you in a court of law! You have the right to attorney! If you can't afford! . . ."

And he continued to frisk Denfield as he shouted out his rights. The auditorium became deathly quiet. Some students were frozen in half-standing positions, their coats not completely on or off. Denfield stood still and uttered not a word. After frisking the outside of his clothes, the officer removed Denfield's coat and began to work the material through his hands. He slowly kneaded the edges of the coat collar until, like some kind of magic trick, a marijuana cigarette emerged.

I thought to myself, "*My, what a convenient place to keep it.*" I just sat and watched in silence. This must have been the right thing to do, since we all were doing it.

The officer turned Denfield around and I expected for him to be handcuffed and hauled off to the sound of wailing sirens, but instead they suddenly seemed chummy.

"Class, I want you to meet someone we'll call Jack. He spent several years as an undercover narcotics agent. He's currently an active police officer assisting with university drug enforcement. So, watch what you do or say around him, ha ha. He's going to tell you about some of his experiences, and what was right and wrong with what you just saw, and what you should do if something like this ever happens to you."

Finally, something practical.

Well, of course, I knew it all the time. What a bunch of saps these other people were. How stupid of them to be taken in by something so obviously staged. You have to get up pretty late in the morning to put something over on me.

Okay, so we were all duped. Especially the two dozen or so that had suddenly run to the john like their morning coffee had just kicked in. Denfield and the agent asked if there were any questions we would like to ask.

I raised my hand.

"Yes?"

"Why did you hide that joint in the collar lining? Why not just in his pocket?"

"Good question. I did that deliberately, to show you that we search everywhere. . .socks. . .shoes. . ."

Another group got up and quickly went to the john.

". . .underwear. . ."

Another group.

". . .coat linings. . ."

Another group.

". . .purse linings. . .feminine hygiene products. . ."

Another group.

". . .cigarette packs. . .individual cigarettes. . ."

The last group left the auditorium and went to the john.

I now sat alone in the hall. Denfield and the agent were sharing a joke up in the front of the room.

"Does this mean class is over for the day?" I asked.

"Yikes! Is there somebody still here!?"

"Yes, sir. In the back. I was wondering if this meant the class was dismissed. . .since they've seemed to have pretty much dismissed themselves."

Denfield eyed me for a moment. "Not as long as there is a single student left in the room."

"Did I mention searching body cavities? . . ." Jack continued.

"No, sir. . ."

I remained in my seat.

". . .film canisters? . . ."

"No, sir. . ."

". . .dirty laundry bags? . . ."

I got up and went to the john.

All and all, a helluva lot better than Jimmy Joyce's moo cow.

DOODYVILLE

Mike and Danny were in the same accounting class. Throughout the semester I had been watching Mike's studying technique with a great deal of interest. Although I thought it unusual, I didn't consider it particularly effective. He would mope around the apartment, going from room to room with his head bowed and the book dangling from his hand. Occasionally he stopped and raised the book and said. . .

"Balls."

That's about all that would happen, moping and the occasional, multipurpose. . .

"Balls."

"Hey Mike, what's this all about? You're starting to depress me."

"I don't understand any of this," Mike said.

This wasn't spoken directly to me, of course, for I certainly wouldn't have been able to help him.

"If it's so hopeless, drop the class."

"I can't keep dropping classes, or I'll have dropped out without having really dropped out, if you get what I mean."

"Why are you a business major? Do you have a business somewhere? Change majors, I can take care of all the Necessary Signatures." Necessary Signatures were one of my college specialties, ever since I realized no one ever checked their validity.

"I don't understand any of this. . ."

And so it went until the day Danny brought in the Great Accounting Guru, GAG for short. . .Pete. He was a fellow of the Great Accounting Guru Association. . .GAGA.

"This guy actually gets C's," said a reverent Danny.

The three of them sat around the dinning room table while I stayed in my room sitting on my mattress. The apartment resembled a noisy library that needed a good cleaning as we studied. They weren't using the moping system, although "balls" was still heavily employed. I'm not sure what system they were using, but it entailed a great deal of moaning and groaning, with some occasional whining and crying. All and all, it seemed to be an improvement over the moping system.

Pete would occasionally make phone calls to another GAGA associate to clarify some of the whines and cries. I closed my bedroom door. The groans eventually died down to extended murmuring, as the phone calls became more frequent. I couldn't help myself. I had to peek. I crawled over and cracked the door open an inch or so. Pete didn't bother to dial anymore, he kept the line open and the receiver was tucked under his chin. Danny was slumped onto the table, his face buried in his accounting book. Mike rocked back and forth in his chair, bumping his head against the wall.

"I don't understand any of this. . .," said Mike.

"I don't know what I'm doing anymore," said Pete.

This was inevitable. I'm not sure you can expect that much from someone in an organization that's willing to be referred to as GAGA.

"Who's gone to class the most here?" asked Danny.

Mike rocked forward. "What difference does that make?"

"None. I just wanted to contribute something more than just using my accounting book as a pillow."

"You know, I had a 'C' when I came in here, but I think that's long gone," concluded Pete.

"Balls," said Mike.

I peeked in on them from time to time, and it didn't take long for the total collapse. They had slipped into slaphappy giggles. They were without knowledge and without hope. The only progress I could see was that Danny was rocking his chair back and forth while Mike had slumped to the table with his head buried in his book. Pete was talking into the phone.

"I don't understand any of this. . .," he said.

"Balls," said Mike.

"Balls," said Danny.

Not that I was much better at this studying thing myself. I went back to my sociology notes. . .

"Balls," I said.

★   ★   ★

I SAW THE three of them the next day in the dormitory lounge.

"How'd it go?"

"Well, we won't have to worry about that class anymore," said Mike.

"Wasn't as bad as you thought it was going to be, heh?"

"No. . .we just won't have to worry about it anymore."

They went into lunch, happy to not have to worry about accounting anymore. I sat in the lounge peacefully reading the campus newspaper, when Big John sat down next to me. He was wearing the air force overcoat I had given him last year. John was one of the few people who was as tall as I was, so I was able to look him right in the eye while standing up, a unique and scary experience, and one I don't care to repeat. I was used to looking down on people, so my natural view was one of a lot of parts in people's hair, something I was not only comfortable with, but made me somewhat of an expert on hair part placement.

Since he was close to my size, John was the logical choice to receive my air force horse blanket overcoat. I was never going to wear it, even if the temperature outside dropped to that of liquid oxygen, which in Connecticut was pretty frequent. I'd rather be found a stiffly frozen corpse.

"He's dead, sir."

"Yes, but he looks better than if he was wearing that hideous overcoat."

I only kept it because the air force made us give back all the nice jackets. . .the fatigue and flight jackets. . .and then heaved this coat on the counter and said. . .

"But you can keep this!"

. . .Like they were doing us some kind a big favor. The truth was they didn't like it anymore than we did, and knew a good opportunity to unload it when they saw it. As I was getting ready to leave the previous spring, I saw my own opportunity to unload it. I heaved the monster over my shoulder, went to John's room, and gave it to him.

"Hey, thanks!"

John liked it, and it liked John.

The coat was still just as hideous as I remembered it, but John didn't think so, he wore it all the time. He took it off and threw it over the back of the dormitory lounge couch, then smoothed it out.

John and I had become friendly while waitering. He had a sly sense of humor that wasn't apparent at first, but which I began to appreciate more as the year went along.

I leaned over and opened the campus newspaper for him to see.

"Look at this. Howdy Doody is coming. You would think that at college we would be getting something a little more appropriate, someone famous in academic circles, like Chesty Morgan, and we get Howdy Doody."

"Is Buffalo Bob coming too?"

"And I can see now that it was the right choice. . ."

"So you're not going?"

"Are you crazy? And miss Howdy Doody?"

"I heard that Mike's dropping out today."

"Where'd you hear that?"

"From you."

"Then it's probably true, although I'm not sure you can trust anything I say. . .but you didn't hear that from me."

"Hear what from you?"

"That Howdy Doody's coming."

"What about Mike?"

"Well, after today, all that remains for Mike to do is to drop his last class." A thought crossed my mind and I decided to catch it before it departed. Too often I have been left with just the caboose of a thought. "If you drop all your courses, have you dropped out? Or is there still something special you have to do? I don't mean in the philosophical sense of dropped out, but in the real sense of not having any courses left, but still enrolled, although I don't know what you would still be enrolled in. . ."

"Can we go back to Howdy Doody?. . ." interjected John.

". . .are you still a student? If you get my meaning."

"I have no idea what you're talking about."

Danny walked into the lounge and sat down next to me.

"Look at this. Howdy Doody is coming," I said.

"Have you seen Mike?"

"Don't ask," said John.

"Why are you wearing that hat? It makes you look like Goofy." Danny was wearing a golfing hat from the trunk of his car.

"You think my hat looks goofy?"

"No, it makes you look like Goofy. . .the dog."

"Goofy's a dog? I never knew what Goofy was. . ."

"What did you think Goofy was?"

"I never really thought about it. I just accepted them all as. . .Disney critters."

"Disney critters?"

"Yeah, like having a mouse as big as a duck that's wearing a crotchless navy suit. You have to just accept that. . .or else you'd have to shoot any mouse that was as big as a duck."

"Or a duck as big as a dog."

"Or a mouse as big as a duck as big as a dog," finished Danny.

"What about that big Disney critter who smoked cigars, and chased Mickey around?" I asked.

"The one that looked like a grubby Jackie Gleason? I thought he was a meat packer or something."

"A meat packer. . ."

"Yeah. I knew that Pluto was a dog, because he barked. He's the only one who barked. That's probably why I didn't think anyone else was a dog, nobody barked but Pluto. . .so why can Goofy talk and not Pluto. . . or why doesn't Goofy bark?"

"You're right, Danny. . .and all the ducks talk, sort of. And so can all the mice. . .even the chipmunks can talk. . .," said John, who was much better at figuring this out than the drop-ping-all-your-classes question. "So what's the story with Pluto? Jesus, if I were him, I'd be really pissed."

"You might be pissed, but you'd only be able to bark to somebody about it," I said.

"Well, it's Disney, I'm sure they all understand barking. I guess Pluto must have really pissed off Walt," said Danny.

"Goddamn it, Walt! I've had enough of this shit! I get a speaking role next time or I walk!"

"Now, Pluto, what would it be like if everybody talked?"

"Everybody does. . .but me."

"No, remember the bumble bee at the beach with Donald, he didn't talk."

"I mean of the regular cast, don't try to confuse me. Look at this script. . .here. . .look at my lines. . .woof. . .woof. . .woof. . .and howl."

"But everybody loves you."

"Fuck you, Walt."

Mike had walked up behind us without our noticing him.

"What is this. . .Disney 101? What were you talking about before Disney? . . ."

"Howdy Doody," we said.

". . .and look, I'm not even surprised."

★ ★ ★

IT WAS THE toughest ticket in town. Who would have thought it would turn out like this? From that innocent notice in the campus paper to the hordes that had to be turned away. I never watched Howdy Doody very much, but from the look of that auditorium I must have been the only one in America who hadn't. . .can that be true?

You know, a mob with a dress theme is a pretty ugly sight. On either side of the auditorium entrance were a bunch of clowns, literal clowns, not the usual campus variety I knew so well. They came complete with red bulb noses and were handing out lollipops. They could have been part of the show, although I couldn't be sure since there were also hundreds of other people dressed as clowns—only they weren't giving away lollipops. There were also plenty of Howdy Doodys and Buffalo Bobs. It was pretty scary, an army of Clarabells, Buffalo Bobs, and Howdy Doodys running around loose in a confined space. A Stephen King kind of setting. . .*Strung Up In Doodyville.*

I want to convey the feel of this scene to you, but I fear I will fall far short of the actual atmosphere and its surreal impact. The auditorium had receded, it was lost in the background blackness, ceasing to exist, and Doodyville had emerged. I stood in the doorway and stared.

"Take this and go inside," said the clown. A lollipop was pressed into my hand. "Go on. . ."

The impact of this scene had paralyzed me, I wasn't moving. "Shoo, Shoo." The clown brushed me away with a sweep of the hand.

It was difficult to see anything in the auditorium. The stage and seats were completely obscured by floating balloons and raining streamers. I was overwhelmed, and risked being shooed along once more. It was very bright, brighter than I had ever seen this auditorium. It was. . .sunny. I know that sounds horrible and it is, and I really didn't want to say it. I know you're probably puking in your lap, I know I just puked in mine, but it's the truth, and it's also a sad commentary that it is better than anything else I could come up with.

I managed to push aside enough of the streamer downpour to shuffle along and find a seat. Paper airplanes began to appear, slowly at first, but soon whole squadrons were flying. I was minding my own business, preoccupied with the effort of unburying myself of the streamer debris, when the entire section across the aisle rose as one and attacked us. It was unwarranted and without any warning. Hundreds of paper airplanes and balloons were unleashed on our unsuspecting section. I was so startled by the suddenness and treachery of this attack that I lost my grip on my lollipop. You can forgive most things, but not a lost lollipop. . .not in Doodyville. Every section began hoarding planes and balloons, and the whole auditorium turned into a heaving mass of rising-and-pummeling adjacent sections. Oh, the lollipops that were lost that night. . .

When the time came, I rose with my section to defend our honor, our borders. . .our women. Then we cowered under the return barrage.

"Captain Nemo here. . .reload the balloon tubes. . .and send over the Doodyville women."

If you have ever seen Doodyville women, then you know that Captain Nemo should keep his mouth shut.

It was war in Doodyville.

Through this din of raining streamers, balloon attacks, and paper airplane warfare, someone on stage was trying to get the attention of the crowd. It was hopeless, and he too was beaten back by a balloon barrage.

"Please! Please!" he shouted.

But his words went unheard and unheeded. It became clear that everything was out of control and this mayhem could possibly go on forever, but someone with a clearer head knew exactly what to do. The houselights dimmed and strategically placed television monitors came to life with an old black-and-white Howdy Doody show.

The auditorium became silent, people were standing frozen in place, balloons still in their hands, their arms cocked with an airplane ready to launch.

They knew what they saw. It was a wooden God.

As the show ended and the last fuzzy image faded from the screen, the auditorium lights came up slowly, and the stage curtains were raised, revealing a Howdy Doody set on stage and an emcee standing there.

"And now. . ."

That was as far as he got, from out of the wings walked Buffalo Bob. Pandemonium broke out. A deafening roar rose from the crowd. Buffalo Bob just stood there, helplessly holding the microphone in his hand. The thunder continued. . .and continued. People were ripping at their clothes, prostrating themselves on the floor, tears rolling down their faces. The noise reached such heights that it became soundless, turning into an indistinct rumble where you could no longer make out anything. I felt a burning flush flow from my head and spread through my body. I wanted to hurl myself onto the human pyre and worship at the altar of Howdy Doody.

Buffalo Bob stood there amazed, unashamed gratitude beamed from his face. It fueled the crowd even more. He stood there with the microphone gripped in his hand with absolutely no chance that he was ever going to be able to say one word.

I slumped to my chair, overcome with emotion. A grayness was clouding over my eyes. That was the last thing I remember.

TUB DANCING

RAY HAD THE SMALL bedroom all to himself, and he lived there like a hermit. We rarely saw him, except for the occasional smudge of his brown robe disappearing around a corner. Being such a large man, his brown robe was capable of blotting out the sun. So, when he came out of his room and headed for the bathroom, it was like an eclipse. It was both a rarity and a blotting out of the sun. It stopped all of us in our tracks, which you should do whenever cast into total darkness. A few minutes later the sun returned and the shower came on.

"You know, I forget that he lives here," said Mike.

Ray had inspired me.

"I'm getting an idea. . ."

"Well, don't hurt yourself."

"Too late. . .follow me."

"Hey, do I look like I'm still in the army?"

"Let's not go into how you look, it's too late to do anything about it anyway. . .especially that mustache. Just follow me."

"What's wrong with my mustache?"

We went out into the hallway.

"Do you ever get the urge to sing when you go by a barber shop?"

"One thing I do know, I will not discuss any of my *urges* with you."

"And I thank you for that."

Each apartment had a small wooden access panel located close to the floor. Behind this small opening was the access crawl space to the bathroom plumbing for each apartment.

"Here we go."

I removed the panel and exposed a set of pipes with two shut-off valves.

"This controls the water."

I turned one of the handles.

"Aiiieeeeee!..." Ray's voice came booming through the wall.

"Apparently the hot water." I turned the hot water back on, hesitated a moment.

"Then this would have to be the cold water. . ."

"Aiiieeeeee!..."

"Wait a second, you ran through that too fast." Mike reached down. "You said this one was the hot water. . ." He turned the handle.

"Yeeooowwww! Goddamn it!" There was some fancy tub footwork going on in the bathroom.

". . .and this one is the cold water."

"Aiiieeeeee. . . Son of a bitch!"

"Exactly. You may be from New York, but I think you have grasped the basic concept here. And now once more to reinforce this knowledge."

"Aiiieeeeee!"

Mike and I are on the floor, snorting and crying, trying to stifle our laughter, and playing with the valves.

"This is sort of like an Indian rain dance. . .if Ray does it right, he gets hot water. . ."

"Yeeooowwww!..."

". . .or cold."

"Aiiieeeeee!..."

Ray is yelling and screaming, dancing around the tub, and frantically adjusting the shower's handles. We were choking with laughter. I grabbed both valves.

"The grand finale. . .no water." I shut off both valves.

"I guess that would be really screwing up the rain dance," said Mike through gales of laughter.

"*WHAT THE FUCK IS GOING ON WITH THIS GODDAMNED SHOWER!*" Ray's voice boomed through the wall. Ray was spinning the handles on and off. I went back into the apartment and knocked on the bathroom door.

"What's going on in there?"

"The fucking shower is screwed up. Now there's no goddamned water!" Ray's fist hit the shower wall. The hot water came on.

"Aiiieeeeee!..."

Then just the cold.

"Yeeooowwww! . . ."

Ray was starting to breathe hard. He was having quite a workout in there.

"Should I call someone?"

★   ★   ★

IT WAS GETTING harder for Mike to concentrate on studying as the semester drew closer to the end and he had less and less to do. He was down to his last course by this time.

"What do you think about Vietnam?" he asked.

These are the kinds of questions a roommate with only one course asks.

"Would this be for a vacation? . . ."

What was this all about? I knew he had been in Vietnam. I had been in Thule. It was the first time I could think of a place where the Thule travel brochure would have been true. . .*NICER THAN VIETNAM*. . .at least our forecast didn't call for gunfire, light to medium.

"You make no sense at all," said Mike.

"That's why I'm going to college. What was that question again?"

"What do you think about Vietnam?"

"I don't think about it. I've never been there."

"I was there." What could I say? I figured this was a statement and didn't require an answer. "I was just curious about what you thought."

"What would you like to discuss? Going off to war? Whether we were right or wrong? What'd you want to know?"

"I don't know what I want to know."

"I have to warn you. You're starting to sound like my mother."

Mike turned his chair around from his desk and faced me. I countered by putting my book down and leaning back against the wall.

"You don't have to answer if you don't want to. I'm just making conversation. I don't think I'm going to be around here next semester, not with my grades. . .that is, if I get any grades. I think you still have to be registered in a class to get grades. Is it possible to complete a semester of college and have no grades at all?"

"You're on the vanguard of that one, Mike. They won't flunk you out though, not in midyear, they'll wait until the end. . .money changes everything. You could stick around."

"Naw. . .I'll finish out this semester, and then that's it," answered Mike.

"Well, I'll be sorry to see you go, Mike."

"What you mean to say is you'll be sorry to start the refrigerator wars all over again with someone new."

"I can't argue with that," I replied, looking inscrutably intelligent. "My breasts are as large as I want them to be, but that doesn't mean I'm not getting sentimental over you leaving. Our bonds go deep. We invented tub dancing together. Who taught me how to say Balls? I don't know what to tell you about school, but I'm sure your mother will. . .she's probably already gotten wind of every word that's been spoken here, and has been sitting bolt upright in her bed ever since you said you were going to leave."

"Let's change the subject. Let's talk about Vietnam," said Mike.

"You don't want to talk about Vietnam. You just don't want to think about school. . .or your mother. . .the poor woman."

"Now, I know what I like about you. . .nothing."

"Well, it is my best quality."

"You drive me crazy."

"Well, then you would have a reason to leave school. Your mother probably wouldn't even object. The poor woman."

"Quit calling her the poor woman."

"Imagine having her son leave school, and be crazy to boot. . .the poor woman. You really want to know what I think about Vietnam?"

"Oh, so now you want to tell me about Vietnam."

"I never said I wanted to tell you about Vietnam, this was your idea. . ."

"Shut up and tell me."

"Do you have deep feelings about it?"

"Why?"

"Because I try not to talk to anyone about anything they might have deep feelings about. . .a general rule. I subscribe to the 'It's better to keep your mouth shut and let them think you're cool than to open it and prove you're not' philosophy."

"Never heard of it."

"Well, I'm not surprised, considering what I've heard you say."

"Is this your 'Be Mysterious. . .If You Can't Be Cool Theory?'" asked Mike.

"Yes, it is. . .and it's a damn good one."

"It's you who's crazy. Your mother probably doesn't even know it. . .the poor women."

"Is this your lame attempt to turn the tables on me?"

"Yes," said Mike.

"Nicely done. Still want to know what I think about Vietnam?"

"Go ahead."

"Okay." I sat up to give my pronouncement. "I once saw an interview with Grace Slick and Paul Kantner of Jefferson Airplane. They were talking about how brushing your teeth was an establishment plot, and that they had stopped because of it. That's my opinion about Vietnam."

"Why am I not surprised? That's your answer?"

"I think I've made myself perfectly clear."

"In your world I suppose that's true. Well, I guess I should have expected this, and to think I actually asked for it."

"Let me ask you. Do you think you can run a war when your side thinks that toothbrushes are a government plot? I think not. I say get out, and get out quick, while you still have your teeth."

Mike's eye's widened with astonishment.

"So, you're serious."

"Well, you did ask. Do you think Paul and Gracie still have their own teeth?"

"Let's ask Ray. . ."

"Owww. . .yeow. . .fucking shower!"

★   ★   ★

THE NEXT MORNING I sat on the couch reading our next-door neighbor's newspaper, not that he knew I was reading his paper. A quick morning dash down the hallway in my underwear and it was mine. All my morning dashes were attired in underwear. I returned the paper later, carefully folded. Outside the cold north winds were swirling through the parking lot. . .winter was here. It was a sad sight.

The doorbell rang. I answered the door. It was a brunette. . .a girl brunette. . .and she was standing at our door.

I stared and began asking myself questions. . .none of which were "Do you think you would like to come in?" Why would a woman be knocking on our door? Why would a good-looking woman be knocking on our door? These are separate questions, although related. Why am I standing here in my underwear? Why would I answer the door in my underwear? Is this a dream? Well, if it's not, it will be soon. Time for plan two, pretend there's nothing wrong.

"Hi," she said.

"Hello."

"I'm Nancy. . .I live downstairs. I thought I'd come up and say hello."

"And what a good thought that was. . .come in."

"Well, you don't really look ready for visitors."

"Nonsense. . .come on in. I'll change into some good underwear and be right out. Sit anywhere you like. . .you're in luck, we have no good furniture."

Danny said nothing.

"This is Danny, my roommate."

Danny said nothing.

"Danny, meet our neighbor. . .Nancy."

"Hello," said Danny.

Nancy said hello and stepped into the living room. I slipped into the bedroom and put on some clothes. When I came back she was sitting on the couch.

"You have a nice living room."

"Is this polite conversation or do you really think so?"

"Well. . ."

"Danny and I have worked hard on it. Isn't that right, Danny?"

"Hello," said Danny.

"If I'm not mistaken," I continued, "isn't this a duplicate of yours?"

"I don't know, it looks different somehow."

"Don't you have a fake fireplace with a crumpled roll of aluminum foil rotating in it?"

"Well, yes. . ."

"Yes, indeed. . .an architectural triumph if there ever was one. The rest of the decor is ours, of course."

The Salvation Army semi-overstuffed chair with the bottomless seat, and a couch with mismatched cushions.

I think she was starting to regret coming here. She looked uncomfortable, but then it was impossible to look comfortable in our furniture.

"Try and relax. We're actually seminormal," I said. This didn't seem to help much. "Well, you wouldn't be the first person to get nervous in here, at least you haven't run and jumped off the balcony, others have, but then it's early yet."

And the conversation stopped there and stalled. And thus began the obligatory awkward period of silence. I've gone through the awkward period of silence many times before, so I know that every conversation is required to have one. I sat there enjoying ours, waiting to see who would crack first. I would have looked to Danny for some help, but I was sure he would just say hello again.

It was only a short time before everyone's palms began to sweat, but I was the one with words beginning to form in my mouth. I tried to hold them back, but they were out before my hands could reach up and clamp my mouth shut.

"What's your majorummpphhh?"

This woke Danny up, because his eyes rolled back, his head rotated completely around, and he fell over backwards.

"Psychology. What's yours?"

"Mmuuphhuurgg. . ."

It was too late now, so I took my hands off my mouth and answered.

"I'm between majors right now." Danny struggled back into his seat. Nancy quickly got to her feet. I quickly guarded the door to the balcony. "Please, I only have a few more insufferable things left to say."

She went to the front door.

"I have to get going."

"Well, it was nice meeting you."

"Yes," she said. "You're both very unusual."

"Is that good?"

"Good-bye," she said.

"Good-bye," I said.

"Hello," said Danny.

CARY GRANT

WE SAID OUR GOOD-BYES to Mike just before semester break. I wanted him to stay, but he left right after discovering he was no longer enrolled in any classes. He dropped out without having to officially drop out, saving everyone a lot of paperwork. I went home for the break.

"Did you wipe your feet before you came upstairs? I just finished cleaning this whole house. And don't you dare sit on any good furniture with those pants."

In short order, mostly thanks to Mom, I found myself out of the house and on my way to go out drinking with Tim. I had been going to bars in D.C. ever since high school, when I would sneak in behind my brother and his friends. The drinking age in D.C. was eighteen, surrounded by states where it was twenty-one. Some bars were noticeably more lax in checking IDs than others, they also had noticeably more patrons. . .and visits from the police. I would follow along behind my brother and his friends, where by the time they finished checking their IDs, they usually just waved me through. If they stopped me, I would suddenly be shocked that I wasn't in line for a museum tour.

"This isn't the mint?"

We would be forced to turn around and find a different bar. And for the next group in line. . .

"This isn't the Smithsonian?"

You have no idea how many people were out looking for late-night museums on a Saturday night in D.C.

By this time my brother wasn't nearly as adverse to my tagging along as he used to be, and didn't even mind the occasional about-face at the door of a bar/museum. Older Brother Poundings had dropped off considerably, and we were just going through the motions. He would half-heartedly pound, and

I would half-heartedly yelp. The satisfaction level was down on all sides. Soon, we gave it up completely. I even stopped tormenting my sister, and since she had become the cause of some visits to the Commonwealth of Virginia court system herself, I no longer even had to dodge her. In fact, she had taken to skulking into the house looking over her shoulder, while I paraded boldly through the front door.

Once I had made it into a bar with my brother, I'd sit quietly and maintain an older, dignified look in case any bouncer became suspicious of my peach-fuzz face. I would attentively listen to my brother and his friends tell their stories, just happy to be there. We'd all end up standing in line at Eddie Leonard's All Night Sandwich Shop after the bars had closed. It was the pimps, the prostitutes, and then us. We were all there to order some sandwiches with extra grease. Extra grease was one of Eddie's specialties. It always amused Eddie to have some white kids in the line.

"Now, how youse figure youse gonna get out of here alive?"

And now that I was old enough to drink in the surrounding states, we still came back to the D.C. bars like lemmings. However, we stopped going to Eddie's sandwich shop when we started to realize that Eddie really wasn't amused at all, and we could no longer figure out how to get out of there alive.

I picked up Tim at his new apartment.

"Well, I see you've settled in. Have Wheel Barrel and Pitch Fork Review been here yet?"

"Very funny."

"I thought so."

I cleared a spot to sit on the couch, if it truly was a couch. It was shaped like one, but since it was entirely covered in Tim Debris, it may have only been a trash pile fashioned to appear like a couch. I pushed on the seat area to make sure it wasn't something that could hurt me.

"Your apartments are really a kind of an achievement, in some peculiar way. I suppose you should be congratulated, or at least cited by some health agency. . .although I doubt you could get any of them to come in here."

"Please, shut up. You're starting to give me a headache."

"I'm starting to give myself a headache." I sat on the seat cushion and began to disappear from view. "Help! Quicksand! Get a tree branch or something, before I sink!" Luckily, there were a few lying around, and Tim handed me one. "No, you have to hold onto the other end and help pull me out!"

He pulled and I pulled, popping me out of the couch.

"Whew. Tim, we have to get out of here before someone gets hurt. Maybe Ramar can lead us out."

"Where to?"

"I thought we'd barhop in the city, hop right along to Georgetown."

"My, what an original idea," said Tim.

"I'm glad you like it. I spent most of the day working on it, with some encouragement from Mom, of course."

"Yeah? What'd she suggest?"

"Did you wipe your feet before you came upstairs? I just finished cleaning this whole house. And don't you dare sit on any good furniture with those pants."

"Same thing she suggested to me the last time I was there."

"It's the same suggestion she's had for the last twenty years."

We went to the 1789. We liked to call it the 1789, but that was actually the name of an upscale restaurant upstairs, which we had never been in. The bar in the cellar was really named The Tombs.

"I haven't been here in years."

"That's one of the reasons why I picked it. . ."

"Not since the summer of '67. . ."

". . .that's right. . .it was the summer of '67, which I believe is when you last had money. . ."

". . .and the girl who wanted to know if you smoked. . ."

". . .whom, if you'll recall, you fixed me up with."

"Who could forget her. . .or your polite dinner conversation."

"Well, Tim. . .I'd just like to say that you're the closest thing I've had to a date in months."

"That makes me very comfortable, knowing that."

"This is the bar Karen dumped you in, right?"

"Is that why we're here. . .so you can torture me?"

"Mostly. Actually that just came to mind while I was sitting here. Usually I don't have anything come to mind, as you well know, which is too bad for you."

Karen was one of Tim's former girlfriends, and she dumped him in this bar just before he could get the first bite of a giant bar burger up to his mouth. Since we were both in the air force at the time, Tim officially received the Brown Helmet citation at a squadron awards ceremony. Lieutenant Corker and a coterie of Perry Como officers presided.

Tim didn't take it well—he had bought an engagement ring and everything. His mistake was letting her see his apartment. *"Help! Get a tree branch or something, before I sink!"* The Brown Helmet citation followed shortly.

"Look at the bright side, at least you've been decorated," I had told him. "The only citation I ever got is for blowing the shit out of the army's target hinges in Texas. . .and we didn't even get a ceremony."

I felt the real tragedy here was the loss of a giant bar burger.

"I think Karen still bothers you, or else you'd be eating a giant bar burger and not the barmix nuts. . ."

And how exactly did Rice Chex cereal ever get confused with bar nuts?

"Aren't we a little young to be reminiscing?"

"Nope. I believe everything said in a bar is reminiscing. . ."

"You remember putting on Ronnie's wig and going into the food store?" Tim asked.

"I thought you just said that we were too young for reminiscing."

"That was then, this is now."

"Are you using one of my confusion tactics?"

"Possibly. So, do you remember it?"

"Are you using one of my turning the tables tactics?"

"I believe so."

"This is so sad. . .and so cheap. . .and actually pretty good. . .you've learned well. And who was this girl again? . . ."

"Ronnie."

"I think you're confused. . .Ron is a guy's name. I don't know what kind of shameful affair you're trying to start here. . ."

"Are you using one of your confusion tactics?"

"I thought I was. All right. What's so special about Ronnie? I knew her all of six months, and she was your neighbor. . ."

"So what if she was my neighbor? What's that got to do with anything?"

"I don't know, it sure sounded like it had something to do with anything. . .until you challenged it. Actually Tim, I'll tell you a little secret. . .remember the girl who lived with Ronnie and her husband?"

"Sure. . .Susan."

"Well, one time I came in their apartment just in time to see the two of them jumping off the bed."

"So?"

"They were naked."

"Get out. . ."

"It's the truth. . .and I couldn't have been more shocked unless it had been Karen jumping off the bed. Things weren't all bad. . .I did get to see them naked."

"And you never said anything. . ."

"Well, I was hoping someday to be naked with them."

A waitress came by with a fresh pitcher of beer.

"I'm shit faced." Tim slid his chair away from the table and weaved his way to the jukebox. He weaved his way back and sat back down.

"You think I'm fucking my life up, don't you?"

"Is that the song you just played?"

"It's a question."

"I don't think you're fucking your life up. . .how would I know? Actually, I haven't thought past getting out of this chair and taking a piss, which just goes to show you how little thinking I actually do. . .and how sad is that? I may think you're a fuckup, but that doesn't mean I think your whole life is fucked up."

"How is that different?"

"I don't know. I was sure there was a difference when I started the sentence. Just take my word for it, there's a difference."

"This conversation is even dumber than your polite conversation on the use of the public facilities."

"Then, that would make it the dumbest bar conversation of all time."

We went around and around for a little while longer on just who was more fucked up, and setting an even lower/higher standard for the dumbest conversation. Later, I went to the jukebox and played, *Just Because I Think You're Fucked Up Doesn't Mean I Think Your Whole Life Is Fucked Up.*

★ ★ ★

A few days later, I returned to school. Cruising down the highway, I tuned the radio to a country radio station that was playing *You Think I'm Fucking My Life Up, Don't You?*

Back on the campus, the dormitory invited all of the waiters to their new semester kick-off shoot. A shoot is what a college mixer is called in New England. I can offer no explanation for it. I met Cathy, and we hit it right off. I base this on the fact that she let me slip my hand into her pants right out on the front lawn that very night. I immediately asked her for a date. I can't think of a better reason to ask someone out.

Danny and I were now sitting in her dorm lounge. Danny was going to the movies with a friend of hers, and we waited, full of anticipation and excitement, for the both of them to come down. And she came down the stairs with long flowing hair. I knew it was dark the other night, but I didn't remember the long hair.

"Is that her?" I asked Danny.

"You mean you don't know? How the hell am I supposed to know?"

"I thought she had short curly hair."

"You may just be confusing things. Tell me. . .what you thought you saw. . .did it resemble Willie Nelson on a bad hair day?"

It looked like her, but then again my concentration has never been very good when my hand is in someone's pants. Make that when my hand is in some girl's pants.

"You are Cathy, right? You look different."

"It's my hair. . .I'm wearing a fall."

"Oh. . ." I love it when they say things they think you understand. When I wear a fall, it is usually down the stairs.

Her girlfriend came down and Danny left for the movies with her.

"Where are we going?" she asked.

"How about The Coffee House?"

"That's fine."

The Coffee House is what they turned the student union ballroom into on the weekends. Gone were the real bands, and now it was a campus coffeehouse with whiny folk singers. . .and no coffee. God it was awful . . .but it was free. I've never understood the allure of music that sounds like they're singing while their pubic hair is caught in their zipper.

The corridor outside was crowded with the rest of the monetarily challenged, grimacing to the cacophony of whines coming from the ballroom. There were no chairs—everyone sat on the floor, Indian style, on the nice soft linoleum tiles. And me—caught once again with my Irish ass.

I was squirming around, shifting the weight from one bony part of my ass to another, making Mr. Coleman's observations look pretty darn good.

"Never sit on a linoleum floor with an Irish ass."

"Excuse me?"

"Just an old Irish expression."

"Do you want to go?" asked Cathy.

"Not if you want to stay, but I will need an entire new ass."

I've always needed an entire new ass.

"Then let's leave."

I didn't ask her where she would like to go, I just drove straight back to the apartment. The hallway was jammed with people. They had overflowed from a party down the hall. The doorway looked familiar, it was the apartment where I picked up my morning paper.

"Would you like to go to their party?" I reluctantly asked.

"Do you?"

"It could be risky."

"Why is that?"

"People have been seen running from that apartment dressed only in their underwear."

"How do you know I don't find that a good reason to go?"

"Then let me quickly add that those same people end up coming here."

I opened my apartment door.

"There are people in here dressed only in their underwear?"

"I'm very hopeful."

The apartment was empty, and we settled down in the living room in front of the roaring aluminum foilplace, slowly progressing to my bedroom, shedding our clothes along the way. The stereo was on softly, her naked body embraced in mine. The night was right, the moment was right, we were right. . .we were right in the middle of someone knocking on the door.

Cathy's body tensed up.

"They'll go away," I said.

The knock came again.

"They'll go away," I said again.

The knock came again and again.

"I'll get rid of them."

I got up, found my pants, opened the door and gave them my friendly neighbor greeting.

"Did you wipe your feet before you came upstairs? I just finished cleaning this whole house. And don't you dare sit on any good furniture with those pants!"

"What? . . ."

The face at the door was sort of familiar, someone I vaguely thought I knew, but not here. . .and certainly not now.

"Well?" I said as I drummed my fingers on the doorway.

"I'm sorry, I'm really sorry. . ."

"You're sorry!? . . ."

". . .but can they use your bathroom?"

"What do I look like. . .Roboton Texaco!?"

Before I could say anything else, two girls pushed past me and rushed into the bathroom. One was crying. The door closed behind them. I poked my head into the bedroom.

"Just one minute, Cathy."

I closed the bedroom door. From the bathroom came hysterical voices.

"He hates me. . ."

"No he doesn't. . ."

"You saw him. He's ignoring me. . ."

More crying.

Once more I've left the normal world where everyone gets to end up naked in front of a nice roaring aluminum foilplace all by themselves, and no one needs keys to the restroom. I have two hysterical women, whom I don't know, in my bathroom, and a naked lady, whom I do know, waiting in my bedroom, and I'm standing alone in the living room. I checked the hallway. The next person to knock on this door will be my sister.

What was it I did in a prior life to end up like this? Have I been repeating these scenes all through time? Have I been in a Roman parlor with Ruthiticus lying on a Roman bed, and Marcellus snoring on the Roman couch? If Houdini couldn't get a message back, then how the hell am I supposed to know what I did wrong. . .or how to change it?

"Answer me that Maharishi Yogi. . .," I said to the bathroom door. "Never mind. . .who wants advice from someone named after a bear in a necktie and wearing Ed Norton's hat."

The sobs continued.

"He doesn't care. . .he just ignores me."

I poked my head into the bedroom.

"Just one more minute, Cathy."

This was starting to sound like a Cary Grant and Katharine Hepburn movie. More sobs from the bathroom.

"He's just trying to make you jealous."

"I can't go back in there. I can never leave this bathroom!"

"Whoa, wait a minute." I tried opening the bathroom door, but it was locked. I poked my head into the bedroom.

"I'll be with you in a minute, Katharine."

I knocked on the bathroom door. "Hello in there. Can you hear me? Can you open the door?"

"Who is that?" asked Girl One.

"I don't know," answered Girl Two.

"Go away, this bathroom is occupied."

"Go use your own bathroom," they said.

"You don't understand, I don't need to use the bathroom. . ."

"He doesn't need to use the bathroom."

"Then why is he knocking on the door?"

I poked my head into the bedroom.

"I'll be with you in a minute, Katharine."

"Why are you knocking on the door?" they asked.

"Because there's a girl in my bedroom and. . ."

"Then why do you want to come in here?"

"I don't want to come in there. . ."

"Then why are you knocking on the door?"

Cathy came out of the bedroom fully dressed. I was stunned.

"Where are you going!?"

"I'm leaving." She opened the apartment door and then turned to me. "Let me just say that having bizarre conversations with yourself while standing in front of a bathroom door is no way to attract a lady."

"Who said I was trying to attract a lady?" I said to her retreating figure.

I slumped to the floor in front of the bathroom door.

"I think something just fell out there," the girls said.

"Hey in there. Do you have room for me?"

"Now he wants to come in. . ."

"I thought he didn't need to use the bathroom."

TITY WHISTLES AND WET WILLIES

WE MET THE REST of the girls from the apartment downstairs. Yes, in spite of my jockey shorts door greeting, we were invited down to their apartment. Indeed, I was sitting at their dinner table. There was no dinner on it, but let's not get too pushy— we were at least in the door.

The sounds of their laughter during nude pillow fights only made us all the more frantic to meet them. Danny claimed that we can't be sure they were actually nude, but he can have his version and I'll have mine. There we all were, sipping tea at the table with the four of them. . .Nancy, Vivian, Melinda, and Dreaded Jan.

"Do you like tea?" they asked.

"I drink it all the time," I answered.

"Cream and sugar?"

"I drink it all the time."

What a pleasant visit it was, and Danny even found something to say besides hello.

"Good-bye," he said as we left.

We began to stop by their apartment after diner for more of their tea. Then we began stopping by just to visit, and for more of their tea. The visits became longer and more frequent. Tea was consumed by the gallon.

One evening, as we sat around their living room talking and sipping tea by the crumpled aluminum foil fireplace, I rolled a magazine into a tube and began to describe Wet Willies in Vivian's ear. She claimed to have never heard of them. Sure.

"You would stick a finger full of spit into someone's ear?" she asked.

"Not me, of course," I said. "But it was legal as long as you said Wet Willie when you did it."

"And if you didn't say it?"

"Then it wouldn't be a Wet Willie, just somebody sticking spit in your ear, and who'd want to do that?"

"Why would anyone do it?"

"It was fashionable."

She broke out laughing again.

"I'm serious," I said.

She broke out laughing again.

"You have to understand that this was tradition. A high school has to have traditions; or else what is it besides a brick building full of kids with nothing to do? I was mostly a victim because I was busy trying to open the end flaps of my ice cream carton before someone stabbed it with a knife."

"What? . . ."

"If you left the lunch line without your ice cream flaps open, it was legal to stab it."

"I think your flaps are open."

"No, my fly is usually open, I'm pretty good about closing my flaps."

We were starting to attract some attention. . .me speaking through the magazine tube into her ear and her laughing. Someone would have thought I actually had something funny to say.

"How about Tity Whistles?"

She broke up in laughter again.

"What. . ."

"Tity Whistles."

"I don't think I want to know what they are. . ."

"Actually Tity Whistles were something limited to guys."

"I don't doubt that. . ."

"Girls just aren't that much fun when it comes to stuff like this. They never seemed very interested, although it certainly wasn't for lack of trying on my part. They weren't much for Wet Willies either."

"I can't imagine why. . ."

"Well, anyway, you'd grab someone's tit and say Tity Whistle. Then if they could whistle you'd let go. But it's pretty hard to whistle while someone is squeezing your tit, let me tell you."

"I bet."

"And you'd win that bet, just try it sometime. . ."

"I don't think I want to. . ."

"Well, suit yourself."

On the way back to the apartment Danny couldn't wait to find out what was being said through the magazine tube.

"What were you two talking about?"

"Nothing."

"She was sure laughing a lot about nothing."

"We were just talking."

I opened the door to the apartment, and Danny was right on my heels.

"Why won't you tell me? . . ."

The noise from downstairs stopped Danny in the middle of his sentence.

"Ssssh! It's another nude pillow fight," I said.

We listened quietly.

"Wet Willie!" yelled one of the girls.

"Aaaiiieee!"

A lot of running feet, the splat of a pillow against a door and then. . .

"Tity Whistle!"

"Stop! Ppffhhhtt. . .I can't. . .ppffhhttt. . .whistle. . .ppffhhttt."

Whomp! Another pillow splat.

"Whistle through that!"

Stopping by the girl's apartment after diner became a regular part of our day. And although I waited patiently for an invitation to the nude pillow fights and the Tity Whistle competitions, none was forthcoming. I felt bad about that. After all, it was I who had given them the game.

★　★　★

THE FOLLOWING SATURDAY evening, we were sitting around the apartment. . .Danny, me, another waiter named Norm, and Norm's girlfriend Kris. In midconversation, Danny started to lose control of himself. He was soundless, just a wide-open mouth and shaking body gave away that he was trapped in the little-known medical phenomenon of Laughter Terminitus. Nobody was paying particular attention until Danny began struggling to catch his breath and blurted out. . .

"I'm dying! . . ."

This medical phenomenon is more widely known.

"I think he's serious," said Norm.

"Well, you'd probably know, you're premed," I concluded.

We gathered around Danny and studied him.

"Diagnosis?" asked Kris.

"Seems to be a straightforward case of Excruciating Laughter," said I.

". . .with oxygen deprivation," added Norm.

"I concur," said Kris.

This did not seem to be helping Danny very much and his condition worsened in spite of our efforts.

"He's getting hysterical," said Norm.

"We must prepare for a Laughectomy."

Danny's eyes widened. He didn't know what a Laughectomy was, and neither did we, but he wasn't about to stay around and wait for us to look it up in *Medical Operations You Can Do At Home*. The best thing for him to do was get away. There was no chance he would be able to get onto his feet, so he rolled over onto his knees and made his dash for freedom.

Unfortunately, the sight of him knee dashing across the living room was ridiculous, and even he knew it. His own laughter caused him to career of course, and he toppled against the coffee table before getting two good knees away. The table flipped up, launching everything through the air, a newspaper, some books, pens, pencils, binders, ashtrays and a small bag of marijuana. The bag landed across the room followed closely by one of the bookstore's larger joke textbooks, which landed dead center on the bag, exploding it like a firepower demonstration hut.

"My God! Call 911!" yelled Norm.

Indeed, it was a Laughectomy gone terribly wrong.

Norm knee dashed past Danny's collapsed body, ignoring him completely, and carefully began to pick up as much as he could, but the marijuana began sinking into the rug right before his eyes. We all pitched in, separating the fibers, trying to coax the rug to return what it had taken, but it was no use.

"I'll never be able to sleep peacefully now, knowing that any cop with a good Hoover has got the goods on us."

The words were barely out of my mouth when Danny (having made a miraculous recovery) came storming into the room wielding an imaginary Excellosuck vacuum cleaner. He cut a path across the carpet.

"Vvvvrrruuummmm!" It was the most coherent word he had spoken in fifteen minutes.

Kris jumped to her feet and began furiously sweeping up just in front of Danny's vacuum with her invisible dustpan.

I became part of the invading police and yelled. . .

"Quick! Seize the woman."

Kris began to furiously eat her dustpan.

Norm looked at his watch. "Hey, let's go out and get something to eat before everything closes."

We stopped vacuuming the rug.

"This idea has a lot of merit."

"Let's eat our way through the kitchen!" beamed Kris.

We considered this for a moment.

"This idea has even more merit."

It was a lot easier than actually leaving the apartment. I wasn't ready to face the struggle of driving anywherehigh on marijuana. It was always a battle just to keep the car going. I've tried this before, with consistently poor results. Every time I would look at the speedometer we would be going about ten miles an hour, which is all right when your college is in the middle of nowhere. . .everyone was going ten miles an hour. I wasn't able to recognize any of the passing countryside. From moment to moment I would have to rebuild where I was by a process of elimination.

"Is this Colorado?" No. . .I would decide.

"Is this Argentina?" Maybe. . .I would decide.

"It looks like Europe." Eventually I would get around to Connecticut and recognize where I was and relax. But suddenly I would be jolted by the realization that I wasn't sure where I was anymore, and I would start all over again.

"Is this Brussels?"

You had to hope you hadn't passed where you wanted to go while you were trying to figure out where you were. The campus was full of people driving around baffled and shouting to each other at the intersections. . .

"Is this Costa Rica?"

We stayed, and began eating our way through the kitchen.

First to be devoured were the English muffins, soaked in butter, spread with parmesan cheese, and top browned in the toaster oven. I personally had fifty of these. I held back because I didn't want anyone to think I was a pig. Then it was peanut butter on Ritz crackers, peanut butter on toast, peanut butter on chocolate chip cookies, peanut butter on a spoon, and then without a spoon.

We began to realize how little our refrigerator had to offer, forcing us to be inventive. My personal favorite was the cheese and pimento olives sandwich. You deal with what you've got. Our belts were loosened, our stomachs stuck out. We hopped around to force some settling, and still we wanted more to eat.

"There's nothing left in this kitchen," pronounced Danny.

"Are you sure?" Norm's head was buried in an empty cupboard and his voice echoed through the cabinet caverns. "What's this?" Norm had found a box of Bisquick biscuits. From the sound of the thud as the box was placed on the counter, this was the original box of Bisquick, and would be worth a fortune today on the collectibles market.

"We can't be this desperate," I said.

"I think we can handle making these, the ingredients are water and a stove," answered Norm.

"I stand corrected."

I got a bowl, opened the Bisquick and turned the box over. Nothing came out. I smacked the bottom and the pain of the impact shot back up my hand and through my arm.

"We're going to need big kitchen tools. . .hammers and things."

After pounding on the box with various heavy-duty kitchen implements, jagged brown chunks clunked into the bowl. We added water.

A sort of batter began to foam.

"How do we know when it's ready?"

"When it starts to look like something they served at Woodstock."

Norm kept stirring. "I think they call this a slurry."

We spooned what was passing for dough onto a pan and baked it. In a few minutes out popped these miniature versions of the Austrian Alps, complete with craggy mountain peaks. We all smacked our lips in anticipation.

The outer crust was hard and brittle, but cracked open once your jaw applied enough pressure to turn coal into a diamond. Inside was something that resembled Silly Putty, but not nearly as appetizing.

I removed it from my mouth.

"Tastes like a foot bath."

"It's not as good," said Kris.

"We should have gone out and risked ending up in Austria."

THE OLYMPIC BUNK BED HOP

We HAD BEEN INSPIRED by the gymnastic performances on television. . .and not just by the women's outfits, which I'm all for, by the way. Not wanting to be left out of the competition, we held our own Olympic floor events in our bedroom. The apartment wasn't really suitable for the more traditional contests, so we came up with our own Olympic apartment gymnastic event. . .the bunk bed hop.

From across the room we took the three steps from the track and field triple jump, combined it with a gymnastic leap, and a one-hundred-eighty-degree midair turn, finally landing in a sitting position on the top railing of Danny's bunk bed. This was the first successful combination of track and field and gymnastics, as far as I know. We hold the copyright.

We were starting to get pretty good at it, and I was thinking of skipping the Olympics completely to turn professional, as soon as I found a professional Bunk Bed Hop League, when, on a particularly fine leaping spin where I stuck a perfect landing. . . CRRAAACCCKKK!

"Whoooa! . . ."

I quickly leapt off the top bunk with a particularly fine leaping evacuation spin. The officials called a halt to the competition.

We carefully looked over the whole bed, running our hands slowly over the wood rails, feeling for any cracks. We looked underneath, nothing seemed wrong.

"Oh, but you know something's broken. That crack wasn't you breaking the sound barrier," said Danny.

"And it wasn't me breaking wind, either. You'll have to get in it."

"Are you crazy?"

"Well, you're going to have to, sooner or later."

"I choose later."

"Come on, you have to do it now."

"Why?"

"Because you won't rest until you know whether you'll fall through, you'll get all anxious until you almost explode and have to run in here anyway and jump on the bed. So why not just get it over with right now."

"I'm not feeling anxious. . ."

"Well, okay, suit yourself, but I'm not the one who has to sleep in it. Remember, I'm down here on the floor with my good-old pancake mattress. But if it will make you feel any better, I'll do some testing too, right after you. . ."

"Oh, well thank you, how generous of you. Now I feel a whole lot better."

". . .no. . .it's logical. I weigh more than you. If you can lie in it without ending up in the bottom bunk as a pile of rubble. . ."

"You amaze me with the way you can make this sound like it's the right thing to do."

". . .then we can take the next step. . .we'll get Ray."

"Gee. . .why don't we just put your car in it."

"Well, if you want to, but I don't see any difference."

Talking to himself, Danny climbed gingerly into the top bunk. Nothing happened. He lay there a few moments then slowly rolled over.

Nothing happened.

He rocked back and forth.

Nothing happened.

He began to jump up and down.

Nothing happened.

The doorbell rang. Danny escalated to doing somersaults, back flips, belly flops, and an inward two and a half with a full twist. I left to answer the door.

"What's going on up here?"

It was Nancy, and I wasn't even in my underwear.

"What are you doing coming up here when I'm not in my underwear? Didn't we have an agreement? Well, it's too late now. . .come on in. We're in the middle of testing the bunk bed."

"Why?"

"For the Olympics!"

CRASH!

From the bedroom came a mournful cry. I looked at Nancy.

"We're at a momentary halt in the competition."

Danny was buried under slats, mattresses, and pillows.

"Danny! Where are you?"

"Aarrrgghhhhuuuuppphhh. . ."

At least that's what it sounded like.

"Danny, I can hear you! I just can't understand you! What are you trying to say?"

Thrashing arms pushed aside some of the wreckage, and Danny emerged with feathers in his hair and a dazed look in his eye.

"I said, it's your turn to climb into the top bunk. . ."

"What top bunk?"

All that was left were the spires.

"I don't care. Get up there."

"Look. . .we have a guest." I shoved Nancy in front of me. "She's here to. . .to. . .why are you here Nancy?"

"You've made a medieval bed," she said. "A castle bed."

★   ★   ★

I DRANK MORE tea during that first month of visiting the girls downstairs than I had in my entire life, and I don't even like the stuff. Just shows what you're willing to put up with when invited down to share tea with young quivering breasts. We would have come down to have a cup of sauerkraut juice. Oh, what a game of Tity Whistle we could have had. They weren't willing to set foot in our apartment until we cleaned our bathroom.

"Is there something wrong with our bathroom?"

They collectively shivered at the thought of our bathroom. Pretty soon we were all shivering over the thought of our bathroom. But Dan and I hosed the place down and they relented. Except Jan, she never went anywhere. She always had a suspicious look in her eye whenever we were around, like she was going to have to count the silverware again.

"I don't think Jan likes us," I said.

"Sure she does. Jan just doesn't know you."

You had to sympathize with Jan if you were going to be fair, and although I'm usually against fairness on principle, I could see her point. The girls meet us, and a few gallons of tea later, they're grabbing her tits and asking her to whistle. All she ever said to me was No. I decided to have a little chat with her, straighten everything out. I could be a pretty persuasive guy, you know, look what I did for Felicia.

I'll just knock on her door and open up a dialogue.

"Hello Jan, are the girls home?"

"No."

"Well, tonight's the night, Jan. They're actually coming to our apartment. Are you coming?"

"No."

"Well, if you change your mind, just come on up, it might be fun. Shall I add you to the guest list?"

"No."

Oh, how persuasive I was being, and how she was opening up to me. I think I'll sign myself up as a psychology major.

"Do you ever dress up in black garters?"

"No."

She slammed the door closed.

"Would you like to?"

"No."

"Do you care that you just smashed my face with the door?"

"No."

So the rest of the girls came to our apartment bearing my favorite gift. . .food.

We sat on my mattress on the floor, which I had pulled out from the wall and had moved in front of the stereo. I called this "sprucing up the place." Danny's semirepaired bunk bed was against the back wall and the ladder now came down to the edge of my mattress. As I lay there, looking up at the ladder, the room resembled a ship's cabin, especially in the low lighting, and after some mood-altering "going to Austria" stimulants.

"Someone please take these away from me," said Vivian.

She pushed away a box of cookies. My mattress had become a junk food smorgasbord, covered in crackers, cheese, and cookies.

Five minutes later.

"Why do I still have these?" Vivian again pushed away the box of cookies, although by this time they were mostly a box of air.

"How do you keep finding these? I just took them away from you."

I took the box away from Vivian again and handed it to Melinda.

"Now just keep your hands to yourself."

Vivian was now full. Whenever she talked, a fine cookie crumb mist would spray out of her mouth.

"Maybe you should jump up and down a few times."

She tried, but the Jupiter Gravity got her, and she never made it to her feet.

Five Minutes later.

"Someone take these away from me," said Melinda, her words sprayed a fine mist of cookie crumbs.

"How'd you do that, this box was empty. . .are you some kind of magician?"

Vivian had begun listening to the music with her head bowed. Nancy was quietly watching her. Then Nancy spoke.

"Where's that note going? Follow that note. . .where is it?"

Vivian held up her hand and slowly brought it down as the notes descended the scale, then raised it back up as the notes went up. The music ended and her arm came to a rest.

"It's stopped. . .," said Vivian.

I put on the *William Tell Overture*.

"You'll like this. . .it has lots of notes."

The music started with a gentle pastoral setting.

"It's a meadow, a green meadow," said Nancy.

"I should play Rusty Drooper for you sometime. . .vindicate my youth."

"What? . . ."

"Bambi's meadow," interjected Melinda.

The three of them were now entranced, captivated by the scenes they painted. Dan and I took the opportunity to eat all the cheese and crackers while they were away. The music changed into a sinister mood.

"A stormph's cominph," said Danny, the words barely getting out through his cracker impacted mouth.

I took the opportunity to eat all the cookies while Danny was away. I looked up the ladder and it was clear to me that the ship was in trouble.

All the food was gone, and now, so were we.

"Everybody hold on!"

The music broke into a violent crescendo. The mattress began heaving back and forth. We were being thrown against each other. Danny was knocked off the mattress.

"Save him! He'll be swept away!"

We grabbed him and pulled him back on board. He jumped to his feet.

"We have to take down the sail!"

I was knocked into him, and we both came crashing down on top of the girls, knocking Nancy overboard.

"Save her! She'll be swept away!"

Arms appeared and grabbed Nancy as she bobbed in the heavy seas. Dan tried to get to his feet again, still yelling about the sail, and fell again as the waves tossed the ship around like it was the hardest word to say three times fast in the English language. . .a toyboat. He slid across the deck and into the churning water.

"Danny's gone over! . . ."

I reached for him, but the music hit another crescendo and knocked me into the sea.

"Help! . . ."

Melinda and Vivian were hurled from the ship. The strain of struggling against the currents was exhausting, and I felt myself slipping under when a hand came from nowhere and grabbed onto me.

It was Danny.

"The sail. . .," he said. ". . .we have to get it down."

It was a valiant struggle, but it was no use. Slowly we were all dragged into the boiling sea. Our futile cries were silenced by the howling wind.

The music subsided, and so did the storm.

"We're saved!"

We dragged each other back on the mattress.

"Is everyone all right?" asked Nancy.

Danny finally stood up and took down the sail.

"There. . .Goddamn it!"

Then the top Olympic bunk collapsed into the bottom Olympic bunk as the opening cadence of *The Lone Ranger* filled the room.

"Oh no! . . ."

"They're after us!"

Danny jumped up. "Quick. . .saddle up!"

We ran to our waiting horses. Danny placed his ear to the mattress.

"They're coming."

Frantically we struggled with the horses, trying to calm them enough so we could mount. Vivian was getting hysterical.

"I can see them! I can see them!"

"Slap her!" yelled Nancy.

"I can't slap her," I protested. So I slapped Danny.

"What!? . . ."

"You're getting hysterical!"

We finished saddling up the mattress and headed out for the open range at a full mattress gallop. . .all lined up in a row.

"Hurry! . . ."

The countryside was a blur and tree branches whistled overhead. The mattress heaved under the pressure. I spurred my mount violently, and a tuft of feathers flew into the air. The wind roared past our ears.

"Faster! Faster!"

"This is as fast as these feathers can go!"

I hugged the saddle horn; at least I think it was a saddle horn.

"Hey watch those hands mister!" yelled Melinda.

The music hit the final crescendo and we were all thrown to the ground. The five of us were sprawled around the room. After resting for a moment Nancy sat up and tried to push some of the feathers back into my mattress.

"Sorry about your bed," she said. "Both of them."

CAN YOU DEFINE ZEUGMA?

WAY BACK IN A forgotten corner of the supply room of the information office at Langley Air Force Base was a big old school-house electric clock. The cord was so dry it had become brittle, and had cracked in several places exposing the copper wire beneath the covering. It had been discarded long ago, and had remained undisturbed until I discovered it when I was stationed at Langley. One day I found it while getting some office supplies for the lieutenant.

I put the clock on the lieutenant's desk. He looked at the mounds of dust and dirt that fell off the clock and onto his desk.

"Well, I thought I asked for some paper, but I guess I really needed an old clock and a desk full of dirt."

"Can I have this?"

"I believe this is still U.S. government property, even in this dilapidated state. You should have just taken it, rather than dumping it on my desk."

"Can I have this?"

"You know, I never fully understood the no fraternization policy until you came to the office."

"Can I have this?"

"Please. . .I'm begging, leave me alone. Take the clock."

"Yes, sir."

I took the clock home, cared for it, fed it a new cord and plugged it in the wall. It repaid my kindness by running with flawless precision and accuracy, and we soon formed a strong attachment to each other.

That clock stayed in my room at home and waited patiently for me to return, marking the time until my discharge, when it would be reunited with me. I named her Florence. She now hung on the wall over Danny's semirepaired bunk beds. Like a huge harvest moon sentinel, Florence tirelessly blazed the time for all to see. . .ceaselessly. . .incessantly. . .endlessly.

"Aarrgggggghhhhh!"

Danny could stand it no longer, and I came into the room to find Florence covered with a towel. The moral, I guess, is to never get a big wall clock with a roommate who has nothing to do.

"Well, I can tell by the old towel on the wall that I'd better get started on my paper. . .or take my shower. . .or go to bed. . .or get up for class. I hope I'm getting my point across."

"It was killing me."

"Florence was killing you? That's not like her."

"That's right. . .you named your clock. I just found her a little overzealous in her job."

"My god, a 'Z' word in a sentence. Did you know that there's only about twelve of them and mostly they're 'zither' and 'zeugma' . . .although I quite like 'zounds'. Do you realize there are actually more 'Q' words than 'Z'. Who would have thought it. . .although the 'Z' is a good ending letter for the alphabet, don't you think? Real solid looking. It can be tough to find a good way to end things."

"Arrrgggghhhhh! Help me! I'm trapped in zaniness."

"Hey, pretty good, two 'Z' words. . .now try getting 'zeugma' into a sentence. . .appropriately."

"Can you define zeugma?"

"Zounds! He's done it!"

"Zip it, pal," said Danny.

"You're like a 'Z' word professional. Well, as much as I'm enjoying this, I've got to get my paper done today. It's due tomorrow, so I know that even you can see the urgency and I would appreciate a little quiet."

"Sure. And I'm glad to see that you've precisely managed your time once again."

"Hey, you were the one who covered the clock, bub. And what the hell would be the sense in getting it done before it's due? I've never understood that."

"Most people are not sure how long their research is going to take."

"What research?"

I set the typewriter on my mattress, no longer having Mike's desk in the room required some innovation in logistics. I sat cross-legged in front of the machine. Danny was lying on the bottom bunk with his legs over the side. We no longer trusted the top bunk to hold anything heavier than an apple. I inserted a piece of paper into the carriage and prepared to begin. Just as my fingers danced onto the keys, Danny spoke.

"Do you ever think about the future?"

I now had "slzfjk" written perfectly upon the page. Damn these electric typewriters. I removed the paper and crumpled it.

"Who turned on the aluminum foilplace?" asked Danny.

"That was just me crumpling the first page of my paper."

"Didn't like it, huh. . ."

"No, I didn't. . .thank you." I placed a second piece of paper in the carriage.

"Why are you thanking me?"

"Didn't I just say listen, I'm going to be doing a paper, it's due tomorrow, so I would appreciate a little quiet?"

"Yeah."

"And didn't you say sure?"

"Yeah."

"So, what just happened?"

"I guess it just didn't work out. Sometimes relationships are like that, sometimes things don't go the way you'd like."

"Okay. . .let's try it again. I'll answer your question, then it will be silent while I work on this paper. . .fair enough?"

"Sure."

"Fine. Now, do you want to know about mine, or yours?"

"Mine or yours what?"

"Future."

"Yours."

"Mine?"

"You're giving me a headache," said Danny.

"Well, something, at least, is going right. No, I've never given it much thought," I said.

"Why not?"

"Because I don't want to."

"I like your reasoning, but doesn't it bother you?"

"I don't think so. But then again, I didn't think you'd bother me either. The present. . .obviously, is tough enough, thank you very much. . ."

"There you go, thanking me again."

". . .the future is just going to have to wait, and I suppose it really doesn't have a choice unless you're H.G. Wells. . .that being the nature of things."

"Boy, talking to you is almost as bad as going to class."

"Hey, that's why we're here, right? So we'll have a future. . .at least that's what they told me."

"I really don't know what I'm here for."

"I've had this conversation before. . .it must be something about this room. You're sounding like Mike. And just to head things off, it's because Paul and Gracie stopped brushing their teeth."

"That would have been my next question. . ."

"When I was going through what you're going through, I joined the service. . .thought I'd be the better for it. . .and I'd know just what to do with my life. I found out I was no better at figuring out my life than I am at figuring out math with letters in it. And now look at me. . .I'm in this room with you and a couple of beds from *The Last Days of Pompeii.*"

"I don't know what to do. I can't get interested in school. I try. . .but I keep finding myself still in bed."

"You just need some incentive. A good incentive can get you out of that bed. Now, if I stay in school, then Uncle Sam keeps paying me. In the world of incentives, that just about tops the list. You have to realize that this is really my job. You, on the other hand, are still just a student. I've been there, and I ended up talking to penguins in Greenland."

"I don't mind working, I like to get up and raise a sweat," said Danny.

And this from a man still in bed.

"Well, don't raise it in here. I remind you that people don't say, 'Honey, I'm off to fun.' There's a reason they call it work, and just remember. . .they have big clocks on every wall."

I set the margins on the typewriter. Time to get serious about my paper. Once again my fingers softly landed on the keys in preparation.

"I might join a commune," said Danny.

I now had "eklrif." Damn these electric typewriters.

"Well, I might have guessed this was going to happen," I said as I removed another sheet of paper. "I'm sure somewhere in here it's probably my fault. Aren't you the one who couldn't get along with three roommates in that house? Now you want to live with three hundred?"

"Alternative life style. . ."

"Really? . . . You know, Clarabell lived an alternative lifestyle. But saying it doesn't mean you're ready for it. . .or for Doodyville. I know, I've seen the women in Doodyville. But don't take my word for it, just ask Captain Nemo."

I once again arranged all the reference books I had hauled out of the library in a semicircle, and began my clockwise sweep, pulling selected paragraphs to start building my paper. My hands were poised. I waited for Danny. . .

"And what do you think plagiarizing a paper is going to get you out in the real world?" he asked.

"Right on cue, my boy. . .and plagiarizing is the real world. What do you think everybody's doing in those office buildings? Do you think there's a bunch of Einsteins out there running around the fortieth floor of the Sear's building? There's nothing the real world hates more than a smart-aleck innovator, who's going to put all their jobs in jeopardy. Nope, not me. I'm going to march right in there and tell them straight out. . .I'm a complete fake who's never had an innovative idea in my life, and I pose no threat whatsoever. They'll probably make me president of the company. I'm wasting my time. Fine, go the Greenland. . .it's nicer than Iceland. This is not plagiarizing. . .it's thesis engineering, like building a bridge, and highly respected on any fortieth floor in the country. You think stitching all these paragraph pieces together is easy? I'm a literary architect, and a damn good one."

"Can you major in that?"

"Isn't everyone? Tell me if you plan to continue this, because if you do then I'm going to start using your typing paper."

"Want me to shut up?"

"Yes."

"Is there anything more I can do to help?"

"No."

"So you plan to spend the entire day writing your paper?"

"Unless the girls downstairs invite me down for a nude pillow fight."

★　★　★

DANNY WENT HOME early Saturday morning. I lay in the bunk listening to all the hubbub coming from downstairs. I have always found hubbub a pleasure to listen to. . .as long as it wasn't my hubbub. They had vacuum cleaners going, and the squeaks of clean windows, and the flush of Tidy Bowl and all of the other sounds that never echoed through our apartment. The truth is, girls are much better at this kind of thing than guys. They have higher standards. Well, they at least have standards. Danny and I are still carefully exploring all our options in regards to standards. I lay there and pretended all that cleaning hubbub was coming from here, and that our whole apartment was getting cleaner and cleaner. By the time I got up to answer the knock on our door, our apartment was spotless.

Once again I stood in my underwear staring at Nancy.

"You're just lucky I knew it was you," I said.

"Don't you ever wear anything else when you answer your door?"

"You may find this hard to believe, but I've only answered this door twice in my life in my underwear. . .excluding dreams, of course."

"Of course, but I don't believe you."

". . .and I don't blame you, but I'm sticking with the story nonetheless. You just happen to have good timing."

"I came up to invite you to a party tonight, unless you plan to wear your underwear."

"I'd be happy to come."

"I hope so, everybody else has canceled on us, we're so short of people, we need anybody we can get."

"And thanks for adding that. Maybe they've been to one of your parties before."

"Oh, don't say that. . ."

"I already have. . .and after such a glowing invitation, I'd be delighted to come."

"And not in your underwear?"

"Yes."

"Yes you are, or yes you're not."

"Whichever one means I won't be in my underwear."

"Good. Because we aren't letting anyone in who's wearing their underwear. We can't make an exception just because you're our neighbor."

"I swear I'll not be in my underwear, but I do find it vindicating that you're expecting that others might show up in theirs. If it makes you feel better, I won't wear any at all."

"But there'll be other clothes on, right?"

"If you insist."

"I'm afraid I have to, because we aren't letting anyone in who's naked either."

"Well, I'm certainly sorry to hear that."

★ ★ ★

THIS PARTY WAS tough on everyone. I was forced to lie around and do nothing all day but wait for evening while they cleaned and buzzed around downstairs. Mine was a long and arduous task since I had to do it alone, but I was up to it, and when the darkness fell, so did I. I stumbled and crashed onto their freshly vacuumed rug. They had vacuumed it to the point where the rug nap had become a road hazard.

"My God! This is a very clean rug. . .and so tall. You should place barricades around it, just how much hubbub did you put into it?"

"Look! George is crashing our party!" said Nancy.

She was true to her word; there was no one there.

"I must be early, am I the first one to trip over your rug?"

Vivian came out and gave me a beer.

"No Wet Willies tonight," she said, and went back to the kitchen.

"Boy, this party isn't going to be any fun at all. I suppose Tity Whistles are out of the question?"

Jan walked by and gave me the evil eye. "Cancel that last question." The doorbell rang. "I'll get it!"

A group came in, followed a few minutes later by another, and another. All the people who said they weren't coming had found out they couldn't find anything else to do. I was forced over to the couch as the party grew and filled the living room. I sat on the end and chatted away. There was a constant changeover of couch people, but I held onto my seat. I knew very few of them, and my seat was a comforting oasis.

Eventually people quit coming to sit on the couch. My being stretched out and asleep on it may have had something to do with that, but I still did my job, being there through thick and thin, helping the girls out. You can count on me.

As the hour got late I tried to listen to what Vivian was saying to me, but I kept drifting off.

I was shocked awake.

"Tity whistle!"

"No fair, you said. . ."

"Wet Willie!"

Back to sleep I drifted. I was standing in a parking lot naked. . .I had made the natural progression from underwear dreams. There was a cardboard box on the ground by me. I reached for it, but I fell to the ground. I couldn't get up and tried to crawl, but for some reason I could hardly move. I struggled to push myself forward, but I wasn't getting anywhere. I reached out and grabbed for the box. . .

". . .are you asleep?" asked Vivian.

"Were my eyes closed?"

"Yes."

"Was there deep rhythmic breathing?"

"Yes."

"Then I was either in a coma or asleep, unfortunately for you, it turns out I was asleep."

"I wanted to tell you. . .you could stay here and sleep on the couch if you wanted. . ."

"Thanks for waking me up to tell me that. . .I appreciate it."

That was the last thing anyone said until the knock on the door. The sun had risen and was streaming into the living room and onto me.

"Hold on. . .," I mumbled and rolled back over.

Suddenly, Danny was standing over me.

"Hello! What are you people doing!?"

ROOMS FIVE BUCKS

DANNY HAD HIS FIRST LSD experience at home in Bristol while I
was in a coma on the girls' couch, and he had been up the
entire night. He decided to return to the campus early in the
morning to wake us all up with his incredible idea.

"Let's go to the beach. . .it's a beautiful morning. . .I
watched the sunrise on the way up here. . .we should go to the
ocean. . .I bet it's fantastic. . .we should go now. . .you should
get up. . ."

He was talking without the need for periods in his sentences, a mile a minute. . .no breaks. He stood there with a
toothbrush inexplicably protruding from his mouth, bobbing
madly as he spoke. My head bobbed along sympathetically. The
ocean in early April?

"But it's only April Dan. . ."

"I'm hungry. . .can we eat?" asked Vivian.

"We can do whatever we want!" shouted Danny.

"We can sure get a jump on the beach traffic," said Nancy.

"By two months. . .," I said.

"Yeah. . .see?" Getting a two-month head start seemed like
a good idea to Danny.

Danny drove. We had a huddle to determine if that was
such a good idea. It went something like this. . .

"Do you want to drive?"

"No."

"No."

"No."

"No."

End of huddle.

And so we left for the shore. Danny pointed out all the
Day-Glo pink and incandescent orange flora along the way. I
stopped looking around trying to find this stuff when I realized he was the only one seeing it. I was in the backseat be-

tween Vivian and Melinda, and I decided a nap was a good idea. If we were going to die in a collision with a Day-Glo pink tree, then let Saint Peter wake me up and tell me about it. . .and let's hope I'm not wearing filthy pants.

We made it to the ocean and pulled into the driveway of Danny's parents' cottage. The street was deserted with all the people here at this time of the season. Standing there in the cold ocean wind, I knew why the streets were deserted. . .it was the season of Bumfuck, Egypt.

"What does this place remind you of!?" yelled Danny.

"Greenland. . .with some streets?"

"Nooooo. . ." Danny took off his shoes and his pants.

"Danny, what are you doing!?" screamed Nancy.

"You can't come to the beach without going into the ocean!" Danny stripped down to his shorts.

Nancy turned to me.

"I have never had as many people stand around in their underwear as I have since I met you."

"What!? You're blaming this on me?"

"Yes."

I looked for some shelter from the wind and ducked behind a sand dune. It was crowded. . .Vivian and Melinda were already huddling against the slope as a barrier against the cold.

"Don't go out there, and if you do, don't strip down to your underwear. . .what the hell am I saying? Please, feel free to strip down to your underwear."

"What!?"

"Precisely."

"You're going to die!" screamed Nancy at Danny.

"So, now who's driving back?" we asked each other.

"You're all standing in the middle of Valhalla!" yelled Danny over the roar of the icy wind.

"I thought this was Watch Hill," Vivian said to me.

"I thought it was Thule."

"This is the pot of gold at the end of the rainbow!" continued Danny. "This is the leprechaun showing us where the treasure is hidden! . . ."

"Isn't the pot of gold at the end of the rainbow and the leprechaun's treasure the same thing?" asked Vivian.

"You ask that like you think I might know. I really depend on everyone not asking me any questions."

Danny jumped up and ran for the breaking waves.

"He's going to do it!" screamed Nancy.

He hurdled the first wave then disappeared into the second. His head broke the surface.

"Is that him?"

"Just how many other people do you see out there?" I asked.

"Yes. . .it's him," screamed Nancy.

He ran out of the water and stopped on top of the sand dune we were gathered behind.

"None of you realize where you are!" he cried.

"The pot of gold at the end of the rainbow," said Melinda.

"The leprechaun showing where the treasure is hidden," said Vivian.

"Come on. . .I'm stuck with having to say Valahalallaeiaaa. . .ei. . .ei . . .ooo?" I asked.

Danny threw up his hands in surrender.

"Let's go back to the house," he said.

We went to his cottage and I tried building a blazing fire.

"That's a lousy fire." Even in Danny's current state, the fire looked miserable.

"What do you want from me. . .my role model is rotating aluminum foil?"

So I built a smoldering woodpile that set off all the smoke alarms. We sat around breathing through handkerchiefs. I did accomplish getting everyone's clothes to smell like smoke. This fire was good enough to put everyone to sleep.

By the time we woke up it was getting dark.

"We should go," said Nancy.

I pushed the blanket of soot off me.

"Good idea."

We piled back into the car for the trip back. All was quiet for the first few minutes on the road.

"Look!" said Danny. "I'm still hallucinating, everything is getting dimmer."

"Yes! I can't see either!" I yelled. Wait a minute, why can't I see? I was starting to get worried when the answer came to me.

"It's your headlights, Danny. They're dying."

Sure enough, the headlights were slowly getting dimmer and it was getting harder to see.

"We're not going to make it like this. . .we have to pull over," I said.

We sat on the side of the road with the lights off, the engine idling.

"Well, now what?" asked Melinda.

We had no ideas. It went something like this. . .

"Do you know how to fix a car?"

"No."

"No."

"No."

"No."

End of ideas.

It was just a formality—you could have substituted anything. . .

"Do you know how to fix a mechanical pencil?"

"No."

"No."

"No."

"No."

After figuring out that we couldn't figure it out, we decided we might be able to limp along to the closest house and call for help.

"It's worth a try."

Danny turned the lights back on and they blazed like a newborn sun.

"What happened?"

"Hurrah! They must have heard us, they fixed themselves!"

Back on the road we sailed along for a few miles and then the dimness began to return.

"Arrrgggghhhhh. . .they've unfixed themselves!" cried Dan.

And so it went. . .sit on the side of the road with the lights off, engine idling. . .then blaze along for a few more miles. . .back to the side of the road and on. . .and on. . .and on. After the sixth stop, the *Guinness Book of World Records* was waiting for us.

"*A new world record! The slowest return trip ever from Valahalallaei. . .ei. . .ei. . .ooo!*"

★ ★ ★

A WHILE LATER, Tim called. Danny answered the phone.

"Hello."

"Dando!"

No one in Connecticut knew I was Dando, they thought I was Tripod. So naturally Dan thought he was Dando.

"Yes," Dan said.

Well, they talked for a few minutes before either one realized they hadn't the slightest idea who they were talking to, or what they were talking about—something of a record I suppose.

"This isn't Dando, is it. . ."

"Well, I thought I was, but after listening to you, I surely can't be."

"Do you have a Chamlers. . .or a George there?"

"Oh, you mean Tripod."

"What's going on?" I asked.

"It's for you." Danny handed me the receiver.

"Hello."

"Dando!"

"Well, no wonder this is all screwed up."

"Is this any way to greet someone who's inviting you down to Florida for spring break?"

"Will you be coming?"

"Well, of course I'm coming!"

"Do you have any money?"

"Now, let's not be bitter."

"So. . .what is it then. . .you need a ride to Florida?"

"You should treat me better than you do."

"Why? Are we going steady, because, if we are, I'd like to know. . .so I can quit trying to get a date."

"Maybe we should forget this Florida trip."

"You mean we haven't been going together for even a minute, and already we're breaking up? . . ."

"I think I'd rather talk to your roommate."

"No one wants to talk to you. . .watch this. Dan, that was Tim you were talking to. . .The Tim."

Dan immediately reached into his pocket and held onto his car keys, then he grabbed his wallet with his other hand and held tight.

". . .see? Just like Pavlov's dog."

"Now, how can I see. . .I'm on the phone."

"Well, I'm sure you get the idea. If I come down over break, I'll call you, and we can talk about it."

"I'll reserve a spot for you."

"Use a pencil."

★   ★   ★

I CAME HOME for spring break.

"Did you wipe your feet before you came upstairs? I just finished cleaning this whole house. And don't you dare sit on any good furniture with those pants."

I lounged around on the good furniture just long enough for my mother to try and get me to the hair shaper again.

"No, no!"

"Look, pictures. . .see. . .here's Mark Spitz."

"Aaaiiiieeeee! . . ."

I grabbed the phone cord, pulled the telephone into the closet with me, and immediately called Tim.

"Please come get me! Don't leave me here! I'll give you money."

"Who is this?"

"Tripod."

"Dando!"

★   ★   ★

SOON, WE WERE all motivating on down the road in an old Mercury Vomit, headed due south on Interstate 95. There were four of us. We were all still full of good cheer about the trip. It was early yet. The cheer would be running out very soon. Thirty straight hours in a car doesn't seem like so much, until you actually do it.

By North Carolina I was starting to become unglued.

"You used to be good at curing phobias. . .," said Tim. "Heal yourself."

"I can't. I can only cure others."

"That's unfortunate. You better do something, we still have twenty hours to go."

"If there was only something I could look forward to. . .something that's closer than Florida."

"Well, maybe that will help." Tim pointed to a billboard coming up.

"Can you make it out?"

"Not yet."

"Looks like South of Bordertown. . ." Finally it came into full view.

"South of the Border. . .restaurant. . .discount store. . .amusements . . .miniature golf. . .no tax cigarettes. . .gas. . .lodging. . .open twenty-four hours. . .truckers welcome. . ."

"*South of the Border! Aiiieeee. . .arriba. . .andale. . .you steeeenking gringo. . .soon ve'll be at South of ze Border and my troubbels ve'll be over.*"

Five long hours later and all I'd seen so far was a hundred more signs for South of the Border. How many of those damn things do they have? . . .

"Are these guys part of Burma Shave?"

"What?"

"Nothing."

"*Here's your South of the Border order for a thousand signs.*"

"*I didn't order a thousand. That's supposed to be a hundred!*"

"*Says here a thousand.*"

"*Well, it should be a hundred.*"

"*Probably a computer error. We'll straighten it out.*"

One week later.

"*Here's your order for ten thousand signs.*"

"*That's supposed to be a hundred!*"

"*Says here ten thousand.*"

"*Well, it should be a hundred.*"

"*Probably a computer error. We'll fix it.*"

"*No! Please, no! I'd rather I got fixed. I'll take it just as it is. Just stick 'em along the highway every ten feet for a couple of thousand miles, I guess.*"

"I would if I were you, because this is the largest truck we got. The next shipment will be by rail."

Here it is! By God we're here! I jumped out of the car, ran across the parking lot and into a. . .gift store.

Yes indeed, South of the Border was a giant gift store that smelled and looked like a bus depot. . .though not quite as nice.

"Where's the restaurant?"

The gas pump attendant spit some tobacco juice onto the pavement.

Splat.

"Out back."

We looked in the direction he was pointing.

"It's amazing how many people can mistake a hot dog stand for a restaurant."

"Miniature golf?" asked Tim.

Splat.

"Behind the restaurant."

It was the world's only six-and-a-half-hole miniature golf course. It was the first time I had seen temporary tees or tar runways in miniature golf. It was complete with clubs that used to be plumbing fixtures.

Cigarettes? They had those by the thousands, and cheap. Behind the counter was the gas pump attendant's elderly mother.

"What'll it be?" Splat.

"Marlboro."

"Good choice." Splat. "I prefer chewing tobacco myself."

"And it's quite becoming. . ."

"Did you get one of our burgers? We slaughter our own cows right out back."

"Help."

"Ain't no fresher than that in the whole dang state." Splat.

"Help."

"I think you should git one of these here banners."

"Help."

"Hey Dando! Grab some plumbing fixtures and let's play a round of golf!"

"Pardon me, madam. I must go."

"Sure thing." Splat. "Don't furget we got prizes fur that golf thing."

I grabbed my plumbing fixture and smiled as I backed out the door.

"You got a hole in one on the last hole! Right over those miniature construction barricades and into the temporary cup! Dando! You're a winner."

"What do I get?"

Splat. "A free burger."

"Help."

"I think it's time to get going."

I curled up in the backseat and fell asleep clutching a carton of cigarettes and a South of the Border banner. The ten thousand signs had promised more. . .turned out the signs were worth more than the place. Little did I know this was the high point of the trip.

Morning. I unkinked myself and sat up. A one-lane road stretched out to the horizon. Swamps lined both sides of the highway. Occasionally I would see a pick or some shovels of a chain gang arcing above the ditches. Only the solitary figure of a guard, with a shotgun in his lap, was in full view. It would not be a good idea to get stopped here.

"Where are we?"

"Georgia."

One of Tim's friends was driving, let's call him Jed, and he had found a game to amuse himself. Whenever we were behind a truck he would wave the cars behind us to pass, but only when he saw a car coming from the opposite direction. He seemed to really be enjoying it when they pulled out to pass and then swerved back to avoid a collision. You can imagine how much I was enjoying it.

"Just how many pileups have we left behind us since last night?" I asked.

"What? . . ." he said.

"So, you must be pretty good with a pick and a shovel."

"What? . . ."

I was almost hypnotized by the passing countryside when Jed yelled out. . .

"Your turn to drive!"

He pulled over to the side of the road.

"Time to change drivers, it's your turn," he said again.

I was grateful for the chance to get him out from behind the wheel. It was midmorning and the smell of oranges was in the air.

"We're getting close," I said.

You start smelling oranges when you're still three hundred miles away, and I can't shake the feeling that it's better to still be driving to Florida than actually being in Florida with these guys. Arriving is usually the beginning of most of the problems when you're with Tim. I was chain smoking and driving, enjoying the last moments of peace, and the closer we got, the more nervous I got. Boy, I was sure glad I bought that carton of cigarettes. How many miles to the pack was I getting?

"Exactly where are we going?"

"We're not sure. . .yet," said Tim.

Well, this was really my own fault, first for being on the trip at all, and then for asking stupid questions. South of the Border now seemed like a wondrous place. I wished I was back there, getting myself fitted for a Mexican dunce cap. I thought maybe I should have got a job on their miniature golf course.

Splat.

So, we were cruising into Florida through a lot of fog and confusion. . .on our way to Tim World. The sun was setting over the orange groves when we finally entered the outskirts of Fort Lauderdale. . .Mecca. It was a very pretty scene. First things first, we decided to get a good meal! Then we'd check into that plush motel.

"There's Burger Doodle!"

Oh, the hell with food anyway. We decided to just go on and find our luxurious motel.

"Remember that place that had the line of chairs with the safety rope strung across to keep everyone from sliding off during the night?" Jed said to his buddy. . .let's call him Jethro.

"Yeah, that was real cheap, we saved a bundle there." Jethro turned to Tim with excitement. "They even had a wake-up service, you could pick the time they let your rope drop!"

"Yeah. . .ha..ha..ha."

This is what inbreeding will do. I clung to the hope that this was Clampett clan humor.

For an hour we cruised up and down the street looking only at motels where the room price sign was larger than their name.

"Here it is!"

We had done it. We had found one where the room price was their name. We pulled into Rooms Five Bucks.

The desk clerk was sucking the food out of his teeth with his tongue, snorting out his nose, drinking a beer, and watching television simultaneously. I thought it was a rather impressive display.

"Can I help you boys?"

"We have a reservation."

"How many rooms?"

Jed and Jethro began a slow laugh from down deep, beginning somewhere around the Yucatan and building into quite a cackling duet. The clerk, who was obviously a member of the same Clampett clan, started a sympathetic chuckle of his own. Soon, the three of them were a roarin' and a knee slappin', and then the clerk slammed a key down on the counter.

"Four fifteen."

"Is that the price or the room number?" I asked, trying to join in on the homespun humor.

The clerk glared at me.

"Who are you, boy?"

"He's all right, he's with us," said Jed.

"Okay. . .but you boys keep him away from me, ya' here?" We left the office with the clerk still sucking the food out of his teeth, snorting away, drinking a beer, and watching television.

"I find it interesting that we have a room number of 415 in a motel with only two floors."

"Look, we got you out of trouble once, don't start again," said Jethro.

We made our way up the stairs and found the room. One room, one single bed. . .no bathroom. I left the three of them busily making up the schedule for using the bed while I went searching for a bathroom. . .any bathroom. I was hoping it was in the same building. That turned out to be a feature of Rooms Ten Bucks. Our bathroom was across the parking field. I found it, but I didn't have any change on me, so I couldn't use the john. We would need some dimes. . .and some quarters for the shower. . .one quarter for five minutes, another quarter if you wanted warm water. The collection tank on the roof looked plenty big, so there should be enough water, unless it hasn't rained in a while. I stopped by the motel office to ask about their recent rainfall, and to pick up some motel stationary, but the night clerk was cleaning his .44, and I thought it best not to disturb him.

I think it's wise to not ask for anything from a man with a gun. I went back to the room.

"You're going to need dimes and a couple of quarters for the john in the morning."

"What. . .you need warm water?"

Why am I not surprised?

"You've stayed here before. . ."

The two of them nodded together.

"Hell man, this here's our favorite. We look for 'em wherever we go," said Jethro.

His partner, Jed, nodded in agreement. Tim and J&J had worked out the bed schedule, and were pleased with the results and with themselves.

"You get the bed first," Jed said.

Well, finally, a good decision. Goodnight everyone.

★ ★ ★

AH. . .MORNING ON the beach. The four of us stood on the undisturbed sand, alone with the ocean. Seeing as it was six in the morning, it was no surprise we were alone. The sun was slowly rising on the horizon, and we prepared for our morning ocean bath.

We had started out by trying the motel shower. Armed with a massive number of quarters, I inserted the coins, turned the handles and watched as the water from the collection tank above began to slowly drip out of the showerhead. Then it picked up speed and the showerhead began to rattle. . .then rock under the strain, the pipes groaned with the effort, then a frog came flying out, followed by several other unfamiliar water creatures.

"What the hell is in that tank!?"

We went up on the roof, climbed the ladder to the top of the water tank, and peered into the dark waters below.

"I've seen this before. . .they had this on *Disney*. . . 'The Living Water Tank.'"

"That was 'The Living Desert,'" corrected Tim.

"What's the difference?"

"There would be sand and scorpions flying out of the shower."

So, we now stood four abreast with shampoo and towels in hand, standing on the beach, facing the sun. When the sunlight began to bathe our toes, we ceremoniously marched into the ocean.

We stayed in the water and watched the beach grow with people, slowly at first, then the pace quickened. By the time the beach became tightly packed, we had already been there for four hours. . .four very long hours. Most of my time was spent in the water as a defense against the hot sun turning my Irish skin into Hiroshima. I sat there, a white prune person in an ocean of Coppertone bodies. I began to be used as a beach landmark.

"*We're right over there, just to the right of that white prune person thing.*"

"*The one without an ass?*"

"*Yes, that's the one.*"

Only six more hours until I got to go back to the motel. . .I was enjoying Florida.

"Hey, let's get some lunch," said Tim.

"Are you suggesting I leave this spot on the beach? Do you know what you're asking? Christ, no one will know where they sit."

"What the hell are you talking about?"

"If I leave, these people will be lost, there will be great chaos here, Big Kahoona. The cost in lost beach towels alone would equal Mexico's central treasury."

"And what would that be. . .five towels. . .and a hat?"
"Did you ever see one of their hats? They're like small UFOs."
"Let's get some lunch."
There was an audible groan and a lot of commotion as we got up and left the beach. This was followed by a lot of frantic searching for a new landmark. Everyone tried to pick out something quickly, before that seamless ocean of bronze bodies closed over our spot, and thousands of beach towels would be gone forever.
"Look, I'm sorry, I got hungry!" I said to the crowd.
"Too bad. . .you were perfect," they replied.
It was the first time I had ever been perfect. Someone wrapped a white beach towel around a lounge chair and stood it on end near our spot. They all agreed it was a good likeness. . .especially the ass, and everyone settled back down.
"Let's go to the The Elbow Room," said Tim.
"The Elbow Room. . .like from the movie *Where The Boys Are*? There's really such a place?"
"Sure, come on."
We were off to see Jim Hutton and Paula Prentiss. We left the beach, walked down the boardwalk, and right into. . .this can't be it. There was no parking lot where Jim and Paula cavorted, no fish tank where that guy with the glasses fell in, no lobby, no food. . .no tables, no chairs. What it had was a square bar that barely fit into this shabby boardwalk storefront, with just enough room for the barstools. If Rooms Five Bucks ever had a bar, then this was surely it.
"First it was South of the Border, then Rooms Five Bucks, and now this. . ."
"Now what?"
"Forget it. . ."
We squeezed into a spot leaning against the wall and waited for a stool to open up. Tim had just passed a beer to me when a fight broke out about four elbows down between Sasquatch and Drunk #14. It was threatening to spread to the wall, which wasn't saying much since the wall was only two feet away. It ended quickly. Drunk #14 was rolled out the door and onto the boardwalk where he lay motionless. I was amazed by the way everyone casually stepped over or around his body, without breaking their stride, and then continued to walk along like he was litter. Then he began to stir. Slowly he got to his knees. His head hung low and blood dripped onto the boardwalk. He sat back on his heels and wiped his face on his sleeve. He was up!

Yes, he was on his feet, unsteady, but on his feet neverthe-less. I expected him to slowly disappear down the boardwalk, but instead he glared back into the bar and motioned to Sasquatch to come on out.

Luckily a cop came along, smacked him on the head with his nightstick, cuffed him, and hauled him away. It just wasn't this guy's day. Well, his stool was available and Jethro quickly sat down and began an animated conversation with Sasquatch. There was genuine admiration from Jethro, and I suspected he was inviting him out to dinner.

"How about a Burger Doodle, Big Fellow?"

★ ★ ★

DINNER AT THE Burger Doodle, lunch too. . .and breakfast. We left to get some dinner. Sasquatch stayed, and fed occasionally from a carcass hanging from under his barstool.

We ambled down the boardwalk, stepping over the other bodies littering the sidewalk from all the other Elbow Rooms, and made our way to Burger Doodle. The four of us ordered.

"What are your specials of the day?" I asked.

The Doodletendant narrowed his left eye and cocked his right, an intricate move.

". . .burgers."

"Ah, yes, burgers."

"We do have deep-fat boiled chicken parts pressed to look like a patty. . .the Cockadoodledoo. . .for those of you wishing to test your immune system."

"Isn't that your breakfast immune system special?"

"That's the Doodlesant. . .reconstituted eggs, with imita-tion cheese food melted over pork renderings, served on a Won-der Bread croissant."

"Sounds delicious, but I think I'll have the Maxi Doodle with some Doodletators and a Cola Doodleoda."

"Would you like that Doodlesized. . .only a dime extra."

"Absolutely."

He pulled out a Doodletub and began to fill it. I grabbed my order and took some napkins from the container. All I got was a handful of air. No napkins.

"You need some more Doodlekins out here," I said.

"We're out."

"I know, you need to get some more. . .like from the back storeroom."

"We're out."

Doodlekins were optional at Burger Doodle. Didn't bother Jed and Jethro, this is what sleeves are for. I made do with my Doodlewrappers.

As we went out the door, they were loading the napkin containers with reclaimed Doodlekins from the trash.

We spent the evening hanging out under the streetlights, drinking beer on the curb, listening to the sounds coming from Rooms Ten Bucks. . .the voices. . .the music. . .the laughter. . .the screams. . .the gunfire.

"It don't get no better than this," satisfaction filled Jethro's voice.

"Too bad Rooms Five Bucks can't afford its own gunfire," I observed.

"Sure is," replied Jed. "But, there may be a poooolice car chase, we had one last year about this time."

"Something to look forward to."

"Yup, they crashed right up yonder in the parking field, almost came right up to our room."

"You were on the first floor last year?"

"Nope. Then they spun around and came close to taking out the water tank."

"Frogs splattered everywhere. . .," I conjectured.

"It was right then that we knew that Rooms Five Bucks was the place for us."

"And to think that you're sharing this all with me."

"Like I said, it don't get no better than this."

I sat up in bed with the parking field lights casting the shadows of ambulance attendants picking up the bodies outside, and went back over my first full day of spring break in Florida. This really wasn't what I had in mind. It didn't seem likely to improve. What should I do? I couldn't face another day watching the sun rise on the beach with my back scrubber in hand, waiting with Jed and Jethro for the noontime fights to start on the boardwalk, and finishing the night curbside at Rooms Ten Bucks. . .even though Jed promised that tomorrow we'd sit curbside at Rooms Fifteen Bucks. I got up and packed my bag. Tim woke up.

"What are you doing?"

"That's it for me. You can have my side of the floor. I'm out of here."

"Where are you going?"

"You're driving me to the bus station."

"Now?"

"If I hurry, I can grab a Doodlesant and just get in a round of golf at South of the Border."

Splat.

VICARIOUS COWBOYS

I WAS STANDING IN front of an elevator. It wasn't coming. I went to use the stairs, but all the steps were gone. People were clinging to the walls as they made their way around. It was a gutted shell. Like rockface climbers, they moved slowly along, negotiating the remains of the steps that still managed to cleave to the sides. Below them was the massive wooden cover of a giant cesspool. No one said anything, men in suits and ladies in dresses stuck to the walls like human flies, moving along like it was all perfectly natural. The elevator seemed a better choice.

The elevator bell rang. I ran to catch it. There was no door on the car and it didn't stop at the floor, but continued on by like a moving assembly line. Everyone charged and jumped for it. I caught the car floor and dangled there, holding on for dear life as I looked down into the cavernous abyss of the elevator shaft that was suddenly several times larger than the car itself, and we began to sway around inside like an Olympic bunk bed. The swaying became more violent, but the people held on without saying a word. It was a real improvement over the stairs, and all perfectly normal. I was starting to feel fairly comfortable hanging from the floor, when we were suddenly flying through the caverns doing sharp turns.

I was tossed onto a landing and tumbled across the floor. I ended up at the feet of several people standing there waiting. No one seemed too concerned as the people tumbled on by as they exited the elevators. I got up and dusted myself off. Another elevator without doors went slowly by with everyone inside pulling on a set of ropes, like a dumbwaiter, pulling their way to the next floor.

"I don't know how anyone gets to work in this building."

The elevators disappeared and I was standing at an amusement park boat ride. I was in the front seat watching the people stepping into the boat. It was the captain's seat, and I was the captain. I don't have any idea what I was supposed to do. What are these controls all about? I wonder. A couple of steering levers that looked like they're from a bobsled and a long lever with a lighted knob on top that blinks and belongs on a H.G. Wells' time machine. What the hell was I going to do with them? How do they work?

I tried to sit down, but I was too big to fit in the seat. The controls were out of my reach. Don't they check these things before they just throw someone behind a blinking stick? I thought. Shouldn't I have some kind of a license before I take people out in two feet of water?

We were off, with my legs hanging out over the sides and my hands blindly groping underneath the boat's bonnet swiping at the controls. I kept pushing and pulling the damn levers, with my feet dragging in the water, and nothing happened at all. When I looked up, everything was gone, and I was in a car asking directions at a gas station, and then the car was gone.

"*Say, I was sitting in a car when I stopped here, wasn't I? So why am I sitting on a sawhorse now. . .and why am I in my underwear?*"

"My dreams are killing me."

"Would you rather be at South of the Border?" asked Dan.

"It's a toss up."

"So, aren't you glad to be back here with me?"

"It's still a toss up."

★   ★   ★

BOB JANBECKER LIVED in one of the coolest places around the university. At least that's what I thought back then. Today I wouldn't live there on a bet. It was a tiny one-man cottage, with one and three-quarter rooms. There was a main room with a bed and wood stove, and a small kitchen area with a bathroom so tiny that the sink had to be put in the shower stall.

The cabin was several hundred yards down a long, narrow, dirt road, where a pine tree grove gave way to a small clearing. Three large trees formed a protective ring around the cabin. There it nestled among the branches, obscuring all but the front door. The mailbox was carved from an oak tree, and the name was chiseled in olde-style German letters. . .Hansel.

Well, as much as there should have been a chiseled oak tree mailbox, there wasn't. . .there was no mailbox at all. An oak tree mailbox with chiseled German letters would not have been out of place.

The land sloped away from the cottage and was bordered by a stone wall on one side and the pine grove on the other. Bob was an artist, the only artist I have ever known. He was actually pretty good, if you're willing to take my word for it, but beware—I liked lava lamps. . . secretly still do.

His paintings were everywhere, even in the woodshed behind the cottage. I don't know why you'd have a painting in a woodshed, but being an artist, there was probably a pretty good abstract reason for it. Danny had become particularly enamored with the one in the woodshed, and finally Bob gave it to him.

Bob had decided to invite everyone to an End Of The College Year celebration, and when we arrived we could hear the music drifting down the long road. It looked more like Earth Day At The Olde Artist Colony than a party. A parachute had been draped over the branches of the three big pine trees surrounding the cabin, and a large fire burned underneath. I assumed we were all just waiting for the parachute to ignite and turn the celebration into an End Of The College Year Forest Fire. The women were all wearing granny dresses, and glided across the pine needle forest floor in bare feet, their bodies moving slowly in time to the music. They made every song sound like flute music. It was really horrible.

I sat next to Tom, Nancy's boyfriend, in the open side door of a van that had been parked by the stone wall. Nancy came gliding over.

"This is like a dream," she said.

"Not like any of mine," I replied.

"Oh! Listen to the piano."

She wiggled her fingers in the air, then opened her green eyes wide, and stood up.

"Let's play the piano with our toes!"

Tom and I sat there, watching her.

"Ooooh, you're no fun. Like this. . ." She stood on her toes and danced across the imaginary piano keys. Tom then jumped to his feet and danced across the same piano with Nancy. I decided it was a good time to leave.

They were leaping from one end of the keyboard to the other as I walked over to the fire. I stared into the flames, watching the embers rising up to the parachute, and waiting for a pissed off Smokey the Bear to come storming out of the woods.

"Hey! What the fuck do you think Only You Can Prevent Forest Fires means? Put it out before I come over there and kick me some skinny artist colony ass!"

I began to be aware of someone standing next to me. He was being very still and very quiet. It started to make me nervous. I cautiously glanced over at him. He was a small, heavily bearded man wearing an old corduroy jacket adorned with patches depicting scenes from the old west. The fact the he knew where you could get old west patches made me suspicious, his actually wearing them made me want to make a run for it. I was willing to risk bumping smack into Smokey the Bear.

He slowly looked over at me and spoke.

"I live vicariously through cowboys."

"Ummm. . ."

He lapsed into silence again. A Vicarious Cowboy. . .and he's running loose at Earth Day At The Olde Artist Colony. . .and I get to stand next to him.

"Where's Danny?"

Thank God. It was Tom.

"I don't know, I'll go look for him."

"I didn't mean you had to go find him."

"No, I'd really enjoy it."

"I was only asking. . ."

"No, I should find him."

I left Tom by the fire and walked down toward the stone wall. I could hear a voice behind me.

"I live vicariously through cowboys. . ."

"Ummm. . ."

Where was old piano toes Nancy when you needed her. I should have paid less attention to what was going on behind me and more to what was in front of me, like the stone wall. . .the stone wall I was stumbling over.

"Aiiieeeeee. . ."

It was one clumsy step followed by a lot of flailing arms before the final thud. I came to rest looking into the night sky. I've learned a lot of astronomy exactly this way. Oh look, there's Orion. . .and Ursa Major. . .and some of those Bremerhaven Constellations.

"Are you all right?"

No one believes me when I tell them I'm the picture of grace when I'm all by myself. I can walk along a stretched piano wire, suspended over hot coals, backwards, carrying a couple of suitcases while blindfolded and wearing Clarabell's shoes when I'm all alone. Put me in front of people and I can't get one foot in front of the other without tripping over a dust mite. I'm sure there are lots of people who are uproariously. . .and privately, falling down all over the planet. . .

"Can you hear me? Are you all right?"

"Danny! I was looking for you."

"Is that what you call that."

"Help me up."

"You looked pretty good going over with your arms spinning around like a helicopter. I thought you had a good chance of taking off there for a second. . ."

"I'm glad you found it entertaining."

"You might think about giving up literary engineering for aeronautical engineering."

Tom was coming over on the dead run, leaving the Vicarious Cowboy pointing out some of his patches to the vacant spot where Tom had stood.

"Are you okay," said Tom.

"Yeah, I think so."

"Why didn't you warn me about that cowboy guy?"

"What'd you want me to say. . .Don't talk to Wild Bill here because he's a total loon, and he's deaf as a post so he can't hear a word I'm saying? . . ."

"Yeah."

Tom had brought along a stranger.

"I want you to meet a friend of mine," Tom said. "I've known this guy since I was in grammar school."

"No one knows anybody from grammar school, Tom. Where's Danny, where'd he go?"

"This is my friend Jim."

"Well, thank God you're not wearing any patches, Jim."

Jim began to extend his hand—everything went into slow motion. The hand arced slowly across the open distance toward mine. It was tilting downward slightly, no, it was tilting slightly upwards. What would it be. . .traditional or The Hippie Handshake?

It was the only true gymnastic event of the hippie generation. . .besides the Olympic Bunk Bed Hop. There were midair contortions and corrections, instant judgmental decisions as your hands reached across the empty void toward each other. There were quick glances from the eyes to the hands and back to the eyes, trying to read this correctly—trying to get yourself lined up properly. The hands would stutter step through the air as they began their aerial approach—Yes. . .no. Yes . . .no. Tilt up. . .tilt down.

No one wanted to be caught with the wrong grip in mid-shake, and forced to try adjusting while clasped together, both hands slipping and sliding around, trying to lock into something, anything. It was a pretty miserable sight, and turned the brotherhood statement into a bad version of thumb wrestling. Absolutely no one thought of calling a halt to it and asking. . ."So which is it going to be? . . ."

Our hands collided, and on close inspection we discovered we had achieved no discernible grip of any kind. We settled for that and I left to find Danny again. From the end of the road I could see the fire sending up a column of bright orange cinders into the sky. They spiraled up into the night, their glow casting shadows of women prancing against the pine trees.

"What's going on up there, a hootenanny? . . ." said Danny as he came down the road.

Somewhere in there, Nancy was playing piano with her toes while Tom forced Jim to shake hands with everyone in sight. Poor Jim.

★ ★ ★

THE NEXT MORNING, Danny and I decided to take one last farewell trip to Diana's state park. We drove slowly across the countryside absorbing the solemnity of the moment.

"Hey look! There's Tom and Nancy," said Danny.

"So they've made a full recovery, the both of them."

It was the worst case of piano toes that had been seen around these parts in years. But there they were, romping around the front lawn of Tom's rented house.

"There's Vivian. . .what are they doing standing outside on the lawn at this time in the morning? This looks pretty suspicious to me. I think they spent the night there."

"You don't say," replied Danny.

"Yes I do say, and I think there were sexual things going on there last night."

"You don't say."

"Yes I do say. We're never invited to any of the good stuff, no Tity Whistle parties, no nude pillow fights, just more of that goddamned tea."

We rolled down the windows as we passed, and with great dignity we began to frantically yell and scream, make frenzied waving gestures, loud Ozark Mountain hollers and hoggish snorts.

"Woo hoo!"

"Hey, Nannceeee!"

We had to be quick to get in our whole repertoire before we flashed by the house. Nancy waved back, but Tom never lifted his eyes from the ground. Vivian had a tired look on her face. It could have been a stunned look, our repertoire has had that effect on people, but her expression didn't change as she gazed at us while we sped by.

"Our entire stage production, and hardly even a nod our way," said Danny.

I wiped my nose clean. "Serves 'em right for not inviting us, maybe next time they will."

"Yup, who wouldn't after seeing that?"

We pushed onward to Diana's Park. . .and parked. A light rain began to fall and a fine mist coated everything with a sheen that deepened the natural colors. We passed by the first natural amphitheater for which the park is named, a deep basin of clear water fed by the surrounding high country springs and overlooked by cliffs. We pressed on to the second natural pool, deep in the park. The banks were lined with huge willow trees with their long reedy limbs arching down to the water in green cascades. It was here we chose to spend our last moments, alone with our thoughts, alone with our feelings, alone with no women, alone. . .

"Hellooo! . . ."

"Woo hoo! . . ."

"I think someone's coming," Danny said.

"And they're stealing some of our repertoire."

"Where are you guys?"

It was Vivian, Nancy, and Tom.

Vivian bounced across the rocks, leaving Tom and Nancy following behind her. She arrived flushed and out of breath.

"Hi. . .," she blurted out. "I thought you guys were headed here."

"Vivian!" started Dan. "How are you? We saw you. . ."

"Terrible! It's been a real bad night! I spent the whole time fighting off Tom's friend. I'm dead tired. I couldn't get any sleep. Every time I closed my eyes he would attack me."

I sat there and listened quietly.

"Don't you have anything to say?" she asked.

"Were you naked?" I asked.

"We saw you standing outside. . .," Danny started again.

"Why didn't you guys stop! When I saw your car coming down the road. . .I was so glad to see you. I was never so happy to see that old car. . ."

". . .old car?"

". . .but you went right on by making barnyard noises . . ."

". . .barnyard noises?"

". . .I could have just died," finished Vivian. "So, what are you guys doing?"

"Personally, I'm contaminating the spring water with my feet and pissing off all the fish. I don't know what Danny's doing. . ."

"What'd you mean by barnyard noises? . . ." asked Danny.

"Can we go?" she said.

"What does she mean by barnyard noises? . . ."

"We just got here. . .," I said.

"I need some tea," said Nancy.

"Don't we all," said Tom.

So we left our last pilgrimage to Diana's and went for one last goddamned tea with The Girls.

JAPANESE TRACK SHOE BOUQUET

THE SEMESTER ENDED. I sat on the apartment balcony watching everyone pack their cars and head home for the summer. Right below me, Nancy and Melinda were trying to put everything they had accumulated from the entire school year into cars that had started out overloaded back in September.

"Hummphhh. . .this isn't going to fit."

"Girls! You're going to need a truck to haul all that crap."

I managed to handily get everything into Big Red, my '65 Chevy, with room to spare. On my budget, I actually had less than I started out with. I packed for home while Nancy and Melinda were still trying to fit a hundred pounds of shit into a fifty-pound bag.

"We're going to need a truck to haul all this crap," they said.

"You might think about keeping the lease through the summer, and leaving some of it here," I said.

"But we've graduated. . ."

"Well, then that would be a much longer lease."

"You'll be here next year. . ."

"I'll be here until Uncle Sam runs out of money."

"What if we left some of our stuff in your apartment for a while?"

"You can leave whatever you want, and I would really like it if you left a bed and a desk."

★　★　★

EIGHT HOURS LATER I walked into my house.

"Did you wipe your feet before you came upstairs? I just finished cleaning this whole house. And don't you dare sit on any good furniture with those pants."

In record time I decided to visit my brother at his new apartment. He had wisely decided to move out on his own.

"Did you wipe your feet before you came in? I just finished cleaning this whole apartment. And don't you dare sit on any good furniture with those pants."

I was looking at my future.

I was browsing through his John Birch literary collection and listening to The Doors. Quite the combination. The phone rang and it was Danny. My brother handed me the phone.

"How'd you get this number?" I asked.

"I called your home."

"My home? Who'd you talk to?"

"Your mom."

"So, just why are you calling my mother, anyway?"

"I was calling you."

"A likely story."

"We wanted to come down and see you, can you put us up for a few days?"

"Who are we talking about?"

"Tom. . .Nancy. . .Vivian. . .and me."

"Well, this is all very exciting."

And it was, and they came.

I met them at the front door in my underwear. . .just for old time's sake.

"I suppose this is just the third time. . .," said Nancy.

"I'm doing it just to make you feel right at home."

"Well, it doesn't make me feel at home," said Tom.

"I was doing it for the girls' benefit."

"I would certainly hope so."

Now my parents have always been very accommodating when it came to people visiting. My mother turned into Loretta Young. . .again, and she didn't even chase after everybody with towels to keep their hair from touching the "good furniture." This was really a betrayal, since everyone was expecting to meet the mother I'd told them about. . .my real mother. The Colonel was undisturbed by it all, the only things that really bothered him were pulling his head up on the short game and a martini glass that held less than a quart.

When they arrived, my mother greeted everyone right at the front door, like a receiving line.

"Oh, don't mind my son, it's so nice to have all of you here."

Even Danny, whose hair was almost down to his ass, didn't hear one word about it. I couldn't stand it. If she wasn't going to say anything, then I was. . .

"You should get that hair shaped, Danny."

"What?"

"George has told me so many things about all of you, but he never mentioned what nice-looking kids you are."

"Everyone is still a kid to my mom," I said. "Oh my God, did I just say Everyone! Help! I'm turning into my mother."

"Oh, don't listen to him, come in. . .come in."

She dismissed me with a wave of her hand, and brought them all into the royal household. . .The House of Buick.

At first they milled around the living room, not sure where they could sit. They had all heard about the good furniture.

"Please, sit anywhere and relax," she said.

"But George said. . ."

"Oh, don't listen to him. . ."

I had to sit there and take it with a smile as my mother continued to prove to my friends what a wonderful person she was and how utterly wrong I had been about her. It was a relief when it was finally time to find a bed for everyone, and get to sleep.

"Your mother is really nice."

"Yes, isn't she. . ."

Mom continued in the morning right where she left off by suspending the filthy pants laws and cooking a glorious full-course breakfast and laying it out on the dinning room table that was covered with The Good Tablecloth, the one that's kept around in case the Pope visits.

"So, where are you kids off to today?" She fluttered about the table, filling glasses with orange juice, replenishing the bacon and sausages, serving the eggs, keeping the stacks of English muffins and pancakes high.

"I thought we'd go into town," I said.

"Oh, that's a good idea. Have any of you ever been to Washington?"

There were a few muffled replies from the stuffed mouths at the banquet table that indeed no, they had never seen the Capitol, or seen anything like this breakfast. She beamed. She saw us off from the doorway, wishing us a good day.

"Your mom is a nice lady."

"Yes, isn't she. . ."

So, we kids were off to the city. There are many obstacles in Washington, but none is more formidable than trying to park on the Smithsonian mall. Around and around we went at a slow crawl looking for a spot. As the sun got higher and the temperature rose, the patience plummeted. With each pass the pleas became more urgent, do something they begged, anything, as if I had the power to come up with a parking space. It would have been easier to come up with a Spanish treasure galleon without having one of those maps they sell in Disneyland. A few more passes and we would pass out from heat stroke. Manners were now in short supply.

"Let me out! I can't stand it anymore!"

And that was me.

"Do something!" they yelled.

"One more pass," I said.

"Aaarrrghhh!"

The windows were rolled down, but that was no relief. It just let in the exhaust fumes from the buses, mixed in with the stifling heat of a hot D.C. day. Then it happened. . .a space.

"YEEAAAA!"

They shot out of my car like it was on fire, which was pretty close to the truth. We had done it, found the impossible, and we did it without a single barnyard noise.

"Look. . .there's a UCONN bicycle," said Danny.

We spent the morning wandering around museums, and after lunch we settled under one of the sprawling oak trees that lined the mall. The breeze shook the leaves with a comforting sound. The breeze felt good and I was resting nicely, thank you. It was some time before I heard Danny speak.

"Let's go back inside before the place closes."

"What? . . ."

"I said, let's go back inside before the place closes."

I opened my eyes and looked around. Several of us were gone.

"Where did everybody go?"

"They're out taking a walk."

So Danny and I went back in, past the leaping tiger in the entrance that scared the crap out of Nancy the first time around. She really had her piano toes moving then.

"At least it's not in its underwear," I pointed out as she jumped back.

"Which way?" asked Danny.

"Pick one."

He glanced around then pointed. "This way."

We followed the corridor and ended up back outside.

"Well, we certainly know how to get out of the building."

"Let's try a different one," said Danny.

We crossed over one street and went into the technology museum. Following a narrow corridor, we entered a room that contained models of navy ships, and lots of diving suits. The ship models were large and very intricate.

"You could probably sit on one of these and float along. I wonder what the navy used them for?" I asked myself. "Look back here on the battleship *Missouri* model, they even have a little surrender table set up on the deck. . .what are these for?"

"Check this out," said Dan.

It was a diving scene, recreated in a wall display case. There was a small dingy on the surface, and a woven basket shaped into a long slender funnel descending into the water and flaring out over the head of a person who was walking along the bottom. The caption next to the case ended with. . .THIS WAS NOT SUCCESSFUL.

Shows you what I know, I thought it looked like a good idea.

"I wonder how they found that out?" mused Danny.

"Because, he's probably still wearing it on the bottom of that bay. The world's biggest straw hat."

We wandered all through the museum, providing this sort of sage insight wherever we went.

When we finally went back outside, everyone had miraculously reappeared from their walks.

"Can we go to Arlington cemetery?"

"We'll have to drive."

"Can we park at Arlington cemetery?"

"Maybe."

I opened up my car and slid behind the wheel. Everyone climbed in, but our eyes soon widened, and there were blood-curdling screams as panic filled the car.

"God, something crawled in here and died!"

It was not a good and orderly evacuation. There was a lot of scrambling to get back out, at any cost, at any risk, no matter who got hurt. Luckily I was right next to a door. It was the people in the backseat that suffered the most, and they needed plenty of air once we got them out, and laid them down under the trees.

"What could have caused such an incredible smell?"

"What do you think happened?" asked Tom.

"Could be swamp gas. I've heard it causes flying saucers, it could have caused this," said Danny.

"I don't think this was an Earth odor, it's more like some alien smell. Your car has Alien Smell," said Nancy.

"I know what it is," I said.

"What?" They all asked.

"My Japanese Track Shoes."

"Oh. . ." came a knowing chorus.

Yes, I still had them. . .my infamous Japanese Track Shoes. I kept them even after Nancy, in one of her rare visits to our apartment, and while in the midst of a conversation, had picked them up and taken them out of my room and put them out on the porch. . .the definitive editorial comment if there ever was one.

They were beautiful, but they stunk. I had a hard time convincing people that it was the shoes and not my feet. I still have a hard time convincing people that it's the shoes, but it's true. The smell was as bad as their looks were good. They looked so good in fact, that I was willing to overlook the fact that they smelled so bad. Others, however, weren't quite so accommodating. Flies dropped right out of the sky when they flew over those shoes. They were better than a Shell No-Pest Strip.

I had forgotten about those beautiful shoes being in the car, and baking in the hot sun all day long. . .they were done. . .and so was the car. We abandoned it, and went for a walk around the basin. Near the Jefferson Memorial we sat watching the sun set and the planes drift down the Potomac River as they lined themselves up for a landing at National Airport. It was a perfect evening, a slight breeze with a hint of Japanese Track Shoe, and the fiery glow of the setting sun spreading across the sky.

It was peaceful and comfortable. A time for reflections on once again saying good-bye to people you have grown close to, and to those you may never see again. Service brats are used to doing this. I had been doing it all my life, but it was something new for my college friends, and harder to take. . .especially since they all actually still knew kids from grammar school.

GRADUATION DAY

THE DAY WAS BRIGHT and sunny, and almost warm. And we were bright and sunny, and almost warm, just like you should be for a college graduation. The time had come. . .Uncle Sam had run out of money. It was a day no one, including me, ever thought would happen. You see, I hadn't been a promising student. I know that comes as a surprise.

The weight of the gown surprised me. It tugged against my shoulders, and I feared I looked stupid in the hat.

"You look stupid in that hat."

And this from my mother, who had come all the way from Virginia to the Connecticut countryside just to tell me that. Unfortunately, she was right.

"It's a mortar board, not a hat," said my father.

Well, no wonder I look stupid, I'm wearing a board instead of a hat. The gown appeared to go on forever, a black waterfall that went down and down and stopped just above. . .

"George, are you going to wear those shoes?"

"What!?"

"Don't you have some better shoes to wear?"

"No."

"You mean to say that in this whole apartment those are the only shoes you have?"

"Yes, that's what I would mean, if I had actually said it. But now that you've said it, I don't have to say it."

"I don't believe you."

"Which part?"

"That those are your only shoes."

"Why not?"

"Because no one only has one pair of shoes."

"I am the first."

"I don't believe you."

Well, damn, now what?

"I admit I have more shoes, but I won't tell you where. And believe me, Mom, you don't want me to take off these shoes, not unless you've seen some flies in the kitchen."

She took a few quick glances around, as if she just might be able to spot the toes of a smart pair of wingtips peeking out from under the bed, or perhaps the heels of a pair of shinny black Bostonians blocking the closet door. But all the closet doors were closed and the only thing peeking out from under my bed was a giant dust ball, which quickly scampered for cover when it saw my mother looking around. But the joy of the day prevailed and my mother looked for something else to find fault with, and since there is a never-ending supply of these, I was off the hook on the shoes. I was going to get to wear my Japanese Track Shoes to my college graduation, and my mother was going to let me.

I was the most unlikely of her three kids, or for that matter, any three kids, to get through college, and I think this was one of the reasons that she and The Colonel had come all this way to see my graduation. I was perfectly willing to have my diploma mailed to me, but they scoffed at the idea.

"Diplomas aren't mailed, unless you're graduating off the back of a matchbook cover."

She was well acquainted with matchbook cover schools. She had thought this might be my only chance, so during my senior year of high school, while the other students were leafing through college catalogues, my mother was leaving match book covers in my room.

The thing is, I believed it too, and applied to "Learn shoe repair at home" as well as "Learn to dry clean in your spare time." So, it was just as much of a surprise to me that I was graduating from a school that had an actual catalogue. There I was listed in the program, right under the School of Home Economics, right there among all the Gertrudes and Penelopes.

My father had retired from the army while I was finishing college, and settled permanently outside of Washington, D.C. They picked Washington because they liked the mix of traffic jams and shopping malls. I think another reason he came to my graduation was because he couldn't believe I was graduating from the School of Home Economics.

"I can't believe my son is graduating from the School of Home Economics," my father slowly shook his head as he stared at the program.

My mother wasn't concerned, she was happy to have the chance to straighten out my closet, and go tsk. . .tsk. . .tsk in my kitchen.

"Be happy he's managing to graduate at all," she said. "It cost us a fortune in free dry cleaning."

"There's much truth in what she says," I replied. "You have no idea how many signatures I had to forge."

The School of Home Economics was picked for the very best of reasons—I needed a major that didn't require a language. I'm sure you'll recall the screw job I took at the college language proficiency exams. After an exhaustive search I found something called Consumer Economics buried under a pile of grant applications in my advisor's office.

"I think I can do this," I said.

"You're an English major."

"So."

"That's a BA program. This is a BS."

"BA. . .BS. . .what's the difference?"

"And it's in the School of Home Economics."

"Yeah, so. . ."

"You want to go through life having to say you graduated from the School of Home Economics?"

"I'm going through life now having everyone think that I run away when the boys come out to play and I kiss girls to make them cry."

My adviser signed the papers. A first for me, a real signature. The university balked at accepting Consumer Economics as a major with English as a minor. This is what you get for having a real signature.

"They aren't related."

"So? What does it matter? You think there's a job out there for either of these?"

"Your minor is supposed to have a relationship to your major. It says so right here in our catalogue."

This is what you get for going to a catalogue school.

"I don't see how we can approve this for a BS degree."

"Well, this is a fine time to tell me, my parents are coming all the way up from Virginia to see me graduate, and now you say my minor isn't having a relationship with my major."

"Your advisor approved this?"

"With a real signature and everything."

"We'd like to verify that, but he received a grant this year and is off researching Mediterranean Wines and Cheeses for the Adult College. So, I guess we'll have to take your word for it."

"I think you're the very first to 'have' to take my word."

"Don't rub it in."

My father continued to stare in disbelief at the graduation program until I took a black ink marker and blotted out the word "Home."

"Here you are, Colonel."

His face immediately brightened, and he appeared genuinely satisfied.

"Well, sorry to say son, but now you've gone and done it. No more service brat life for you, no more fooling around. Time to get a real job and get settled into life. . .heh. . .heh. So, how do you feel about that?"

"Don't rub it in. Can I go back around, and get into the line again?"

"I don't think anybody would want that. . .especially the Germans."

"No chance for a rich relative to leave me their money?"

"Which relatives would those be. . .the ones you call by the wrong name, or the group you called douchebag?" said my mother. "If you do manage to start over again, this time, stay off the couch."

"And get your head shaped," finished The Colonel.

"Dad. . .you've been with Mom too long."

"Tell me about it. I haven't sat on a piece of good furniture in twenty years.

"Tell me about it," I said.

"Another martini, my dear?"

EPILOGUE

I HAVE ALWAYS WANTED to have an epilogue ever since I saw my first episode of *The Fugitive*. Other television shows had epilogues, but *The Fugitive* was the first one for me. All epilogues had the same thing in common—they never had much to say. All you saw was David Janssen running to next week's show with the announcer's voice telling you things you already knew.

I always thought a better ending to *The Fugitive* was to find out that he really did it. Let's give Lieutenant Gerard a break, he deserved it after eight years of just missing Doctor Kimble in every single small town in America. Only Hamilton Burger was treated as shabbily, but he didn't have to travel anywhere for it, and he didn't have to hang his head as yet another local police department knew that the lieutenant had missed again.

For those of you who care to know, I ended up marrying one of The Girls who lived in the apartment downstairs. I felt it was important not to have to go very far to find a wife. Never underestimate the power of a Tity Whistle, with some modifications, of course.

She saw me in a different light after that, obviously a very dim light, and soon we were married. We graduated together, both standing there in our matching Japanese Track Shoes. Later in life, while our kids were learning to ride on a pair of UCONN bicycles, she said to me, "You should write some stories about your high school traditions."

"I believe I have, you're holding them."

"My god, that was fast."

"Just like me in bed. Did I ever tell you my cars and sex theory?"

"I'm afraid to ask," said Vivian.

"Well, since you haven't dismissed me entirely yet, here goes."

"Should I sit?"

"If you like."

"All right, go ahead."

"Well, people make the mistake of assuming that sex is pretty much the same for everyone, that is, everyone thinks they know what's normal. . ."

"I'm afraid to ask what you think is normal, but, okay. . .so far."

"I haven't gone anywhere."

"That's probably why we're okay so far."

"To continue. . ."

"Please."

"Actually, sex is like makes of cars. . ."

"Here's where we start to go wrong."

"There are the Nash Ramblers, which would be like the missionary position once a week, because the church said they had to. . ."

"Really, Nash Ramblers have sex?"

"Okay, then Nash Ramblers don't have sex. . .and their church doesn't care. . .sounds like my mother."

"That's better."

"Then we have the Chevrolet family car, that'll be the sex once a week group, ten o'clock, Saturday night, missionary, and no funny business."

"What would be funny business?"

"Any of the things you hate to do."

"So you admit they're funny business?"

"No, for Chevrolet's they're funny business."

"Go on."

"Then we have Cadillacs, they like sex more often, and with a few more trimmings, a little funny business is all right."

"That would be me?"

"We'll see. You can begin to see that the variations in cars are almost as wide ranging as sex or vice versa. I'm unclear about which is the vice and which would be the versa."

"What would be a Nash Metropolitan?"

"I'm stunned you even know about a Metropolitan."

"My father had one."

"That explains a lot."

"What do you mean?"

"Let's go on. We have the semi-sporty cars like Mustangs and Camaros. Sports cars like Corvettes and Jaguars, sport sedans and exotic sports cars, hot cars, street racers, and on and on. . ."

"There can't be that many variations in sex."

"Somehow your saying that doesn't surprise me."

"So, the ultimate might be to have sex in the right car."

"That's what we thought in high school."

"Why is this even in your book?"

"Without it, my epilogue would have been like what Andy said to Amos after walking through the stagefront house Amos had just been suckered into buying. . . 'Nice place, but mighty thin.'"

"I think you're a Nash Metropolitan."

"Thank you."

"And goodnight."

"Buy the book, and make my wife rich."

"Please."

Epilogues have a lot in common with Captain Midnight's secret decoder ring message. . ."Drink more Ovaltine." They were really an excuse to sneak in some more commercials and shameless plugs before ending the show. Here's mine. . .

I still think the title would be good for a movie or television series, and I'm waiting to hear from Hollywood.

★   ★   ★

A FINAL FEW words about what happened to some of the people who had the misfortune to cross my path. . .sort of in chronological order.

Mom passed on and sits permanently on display in the martyr's position on Heaven's good furniture.

The Colonel decided to take the other route after hearing there would be "hell to pay" at their bar.

Marcella moved to California where she has set to work at breaking The Colonel's record for martinis. She has dispensed with the golf, saying it just gets it the way.

Dave is gone now, but he maintained his cauliflower farts until the very end. He could clear any room in less than five minutes, and find himself alone by the horse's ovaries. I'm sure he would appreciate the irony of being remembered for cauliflower farts.

Ted disappeared on the West Coast. He lives in fear of anyone showing up on his doorstep with another Rusty Drooper record. He never fully recovered from being one of the Bandstand Four

Earle fixed his Mercedes, and he never fully recovered from the Olympic Canoe Team. I don't know if he ever became a CEO, but he'll still sell you a pair of jeans behind the Russian War Memorial.

Wherever Margaret is, I'm sure she's glad the girdle era is over.

The last thing I heard Steve say was. . .well thank ya. . .thank ya very much.

Butch is somewhere in the Midwest, hiding out from his parents, and still in debt from the Hummels.

I don't think Bill ever became a congressman. So I guess he settled for white-collar stick-up artist.

The baseball team train compartments never came clean. They are now part of a national museum about the occupation days.

Tim didn't fuck up his life after all, and is a well-known photographer for a nationally distributed newspaper. I still wouldn't sit on his couch if I were you.

Felicia now takes a magazine on every date.

Butch and Tom are both surfers off Laguna Beach, which turned out to be a real place, but not in Peru.

Roboton is a full professor, reason enough to stay away from the University of Connecticut.

Mike disappeared into upstate New York and never goes within two hundred miles of NYC.

Danny left college and continues to cover clocks with towels.

Tom married Nancy and they play piano with their toes at some of the best places in the country.

The Catholic Church, after reviewing transcripts of fourteen years worth of my confessions, has decided to canonize me. . .at least, I think that's what they said. . .the phone connection wasn't very good. . .*over.*

For all the lawyers of Disney, Hanna-Barbera, Ramar, Dead End Kids, Gilligan, Nelson Productions, and UCONN. . .I have no money.

AFTER REVIEWING ALL this, it seems that I have been out and about a lot in my underwear, and probably deserve all those dreams.

I am stumped as to why anyone would care to know anything about an author, even though my wife swears that people do. I contend that it only serves to provide enough clues for the delivery of many subpoenas. If you've read the book, then all you need to know is contained in the old adage, "We have met the enemy, and we are theirs."

I picked the above photograph because I have never looked better. It's hell to hit your peak at eight years old. As you can see, I was totally unafraid to head out into the world with my fly open, not aware that this wasn't considered fashionable. I suppose that I thought no one else did it with quite my flair, which would account for the apparent look of pride on my face. Unfortunately, this stance also set the tone for the life that followed. Conveniently, I have no memory of the day this photo was taken.